Editor
DIANA SCHUTZ

Assistant Editor
BRENDAN WRIGHT

Design & Digital Production
CARY GRAZZINI

Publisher
MIKE RICHARDSON

This volume collects issues 117-123 of the Dark Horse comic book series *Usagi Yojimbo Volume Three*
along with stories from *Dark Horse Maverick 2001* and *MySpace Dark Horse Presents* issue 35.

Visit the Usagi Yojimbo Dojo website
UsagiYojimbo.com

Published by Dark Horse Books
A division of Dark Horse Comics, Inc.
10956 SE Main Street
Milwaukie, Oregon 97222

DarkHorse.com

First edition: July 2012
ISBN 978-1-59582-910-8

Limited hardcover edition: August 2012
ISBN 978-1-59582-909-2

1 3 5 7 9 10 8 6 4 2
Printed by Lake Book Manufacturing, Inc., Melrose Park, IL, U.S.A.

USAGI YOJIMBO™

— TRAITORS OF THE EARTH —

Created, Written, and Illustrated by
STAN SAKAI

Introduction by
WALTER SIMONSON

DARK HORSE BOOKS®

Usagi Yojimbo

The Sound of One Pen Drawing

Stan Sakai's *Usagi Yojimbo* has been my favorite comic book, like . . . forever.

It's the one comic I have read regularly for years. But be warned. I haven't memorized it; I would fail a Usagi Yojimbo trivial pursuit contest. I don't have that much unused memory storage left anyway. But I have read this comic book, since its beginning, for all the right reasons. Regularly, like clockwork, it brings me the unalloyed joy of reading a well-told, well-drawn story, about characters I have come to care about. For me, that's the highest praise I can give any comic book.

In some ways, I am transported back to the comics of my youth when I read the adventures of Usagi. Stan eschews bombast, the use of elaborate panel layouts, black gutters, or artwork extended beyond the edge of the page and trimmed. Any given issue is liable to contain thought balloons and sound effects. He fashions his stories using all the classic tools that comic books have used for years. In other words, Stan fills his comic book, every month, with straightforward storytelling that is by turns lyrical, direct, subtle, engaging, funny, and occasionally tragic. Stan's art, in every sense, is always at the service of his story.

I keep a copy of a quotation taped on the bookshelf to my right in my studio.

It is there to remind me, lest I forget, of the nature of the business in which I am engaged, both as an artist and as a storyteller. It is a quote from C. S. Lewis, from his book *The Great Divorce*:

> "Every poet and musician and artist, but for Grace, is drawn away from love of the thing he tells, to love of the telling till, down in Deep Hell, they cannot be interested in God at all but only in what they say about Him."

I do not work thinking that the Eye of God is looking over my shoulder and prodding me to do His will, or anything else for that matter. I fervently hope He has more important things to worry about. Mostly, I try to keep in mind the old quotation, sometimes erroneously ascribed to the Bible, that "God helps those who help themselves."

For me, the meaning of Lewis's quotation is that I do not want to be caught and seduced by the cleverness of my own storytelling. I want whatever words and pictures I put down on paper to be at the service of my story. I will do things sometimes that are less than straightforward, but always with the thought that I am trying to make my story better.

Stan Sakai's *Usagi Yojimbo* is the complete exemplar of that idea. Stan never wastes a panel; he never throws away a moment or a word balloon, and his stories are fashioned with craft, care, devotion, and a deep respect for history. With every issue, Stan creates a comic that is a story for an audience of every age, in the best sense of that expression. Perhaps that is why these books transport me back to the days of my youth. That was when I read the stories of another writer/artist about whose work I feel the same way: a Mr. Carl Barks, purveyor of duck stories for about a quarter-century.

The biography of the masterless ronin, Usagi Yojimbo, continues. I invite the reader to join me, and accompany Usagi on his marvelous journey.

WALTER SIMONSON
NEW YORK
JANUARY 2012

CONTENTS

Usagi and the Kami of the Pond   7

Cut the Plum   13

Traitors of the Earth   15

What the Little Thief Heard   89

The Hidden Fortress   113

A Place to Stay   137

The Death of Lord Hikiji   161

Story Notes   185

Groo vs. Usagi: Who Would Win?   187

Cover Gallery   188

Author Bio   198

"STAN LEE" WAS THE FIRST NAME I ASSOCIATED
WITH COMIC BOOKS. I NEVER IMAGINED THAT
I WOULD ONE DAY MEET HIM, MUCH LESS WORK
WITH HIM AND REGARD HIM AS A FRIEND.
THIS ONE IS FOR YOU, STAN.
EXCELSIOR!

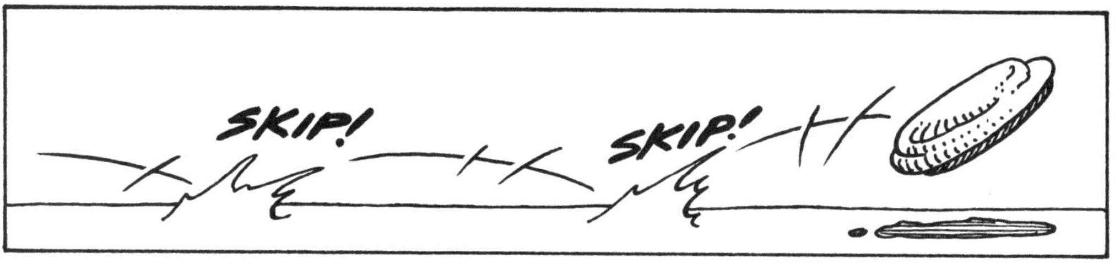
SKIP!
SKIP!

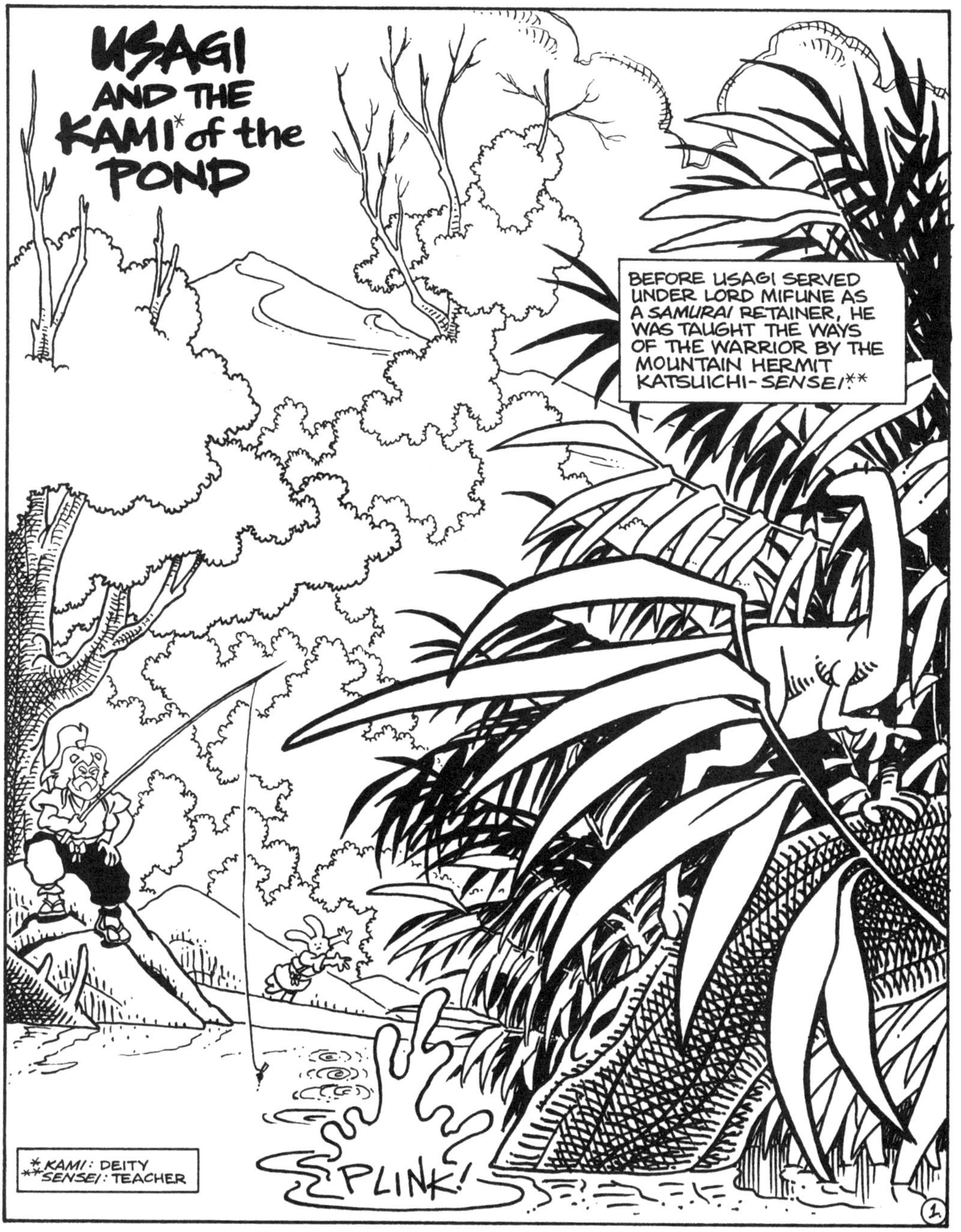
USAGI AND THE KAMI* of the POND
BEFORE USAGI SERVED UNDER LORD MIFUNE AS A SAMURAI RETAINER, HE WAS TAUGHT THE WAYS OF THE WARRIOR BY THE MOUNTAIN HERMIT KATSUICHI-SENSEI.**
*KAMI: DEITY
**SENSEI: TEACHER
PLINK!
1.

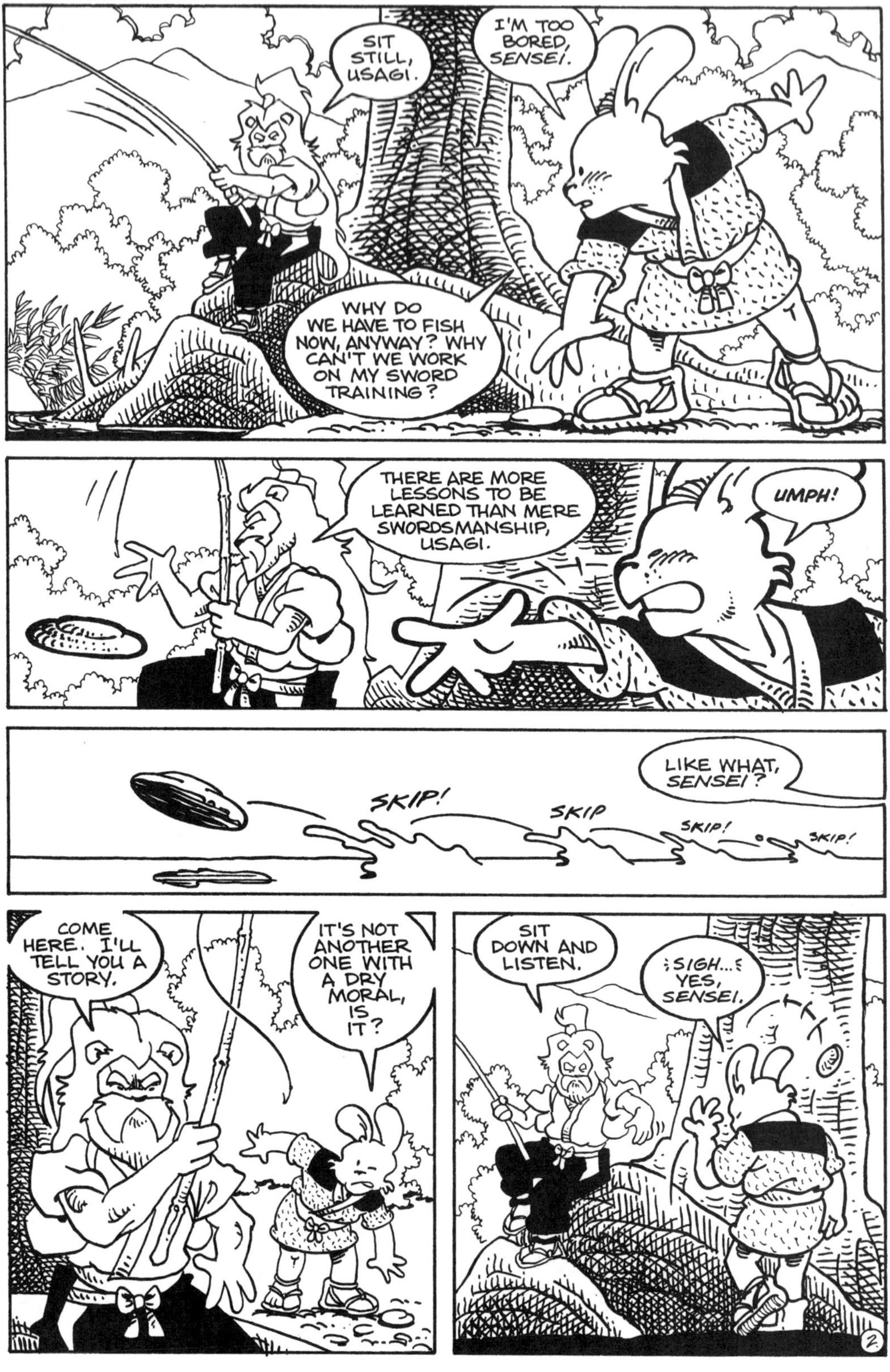
SIT STILL, USAGI.
I'M TOO BORED, SENSEI.
WHY DO WE HAVE TO FISH NOW, ANYWAY? WHY CAN'T WE WORK ON MY SWORD TRAINING?
THERE ARE MORE LESSONS TO BE LEARNED THAN MERE SWORDSMANSHIP, USAGI.
UMPH!
LIKE WHAT, SENSEI?
SKIP!
SKIP
SKIP!
SKIP!
COME HERE. I'LL TELL YOU A STORY.
IT'S NOT ANOTHER ONE WITH A DRY MORAL, IS IT?
SIT DOWN AND LISTEN.
SIGH... YES, SENSEI.
2

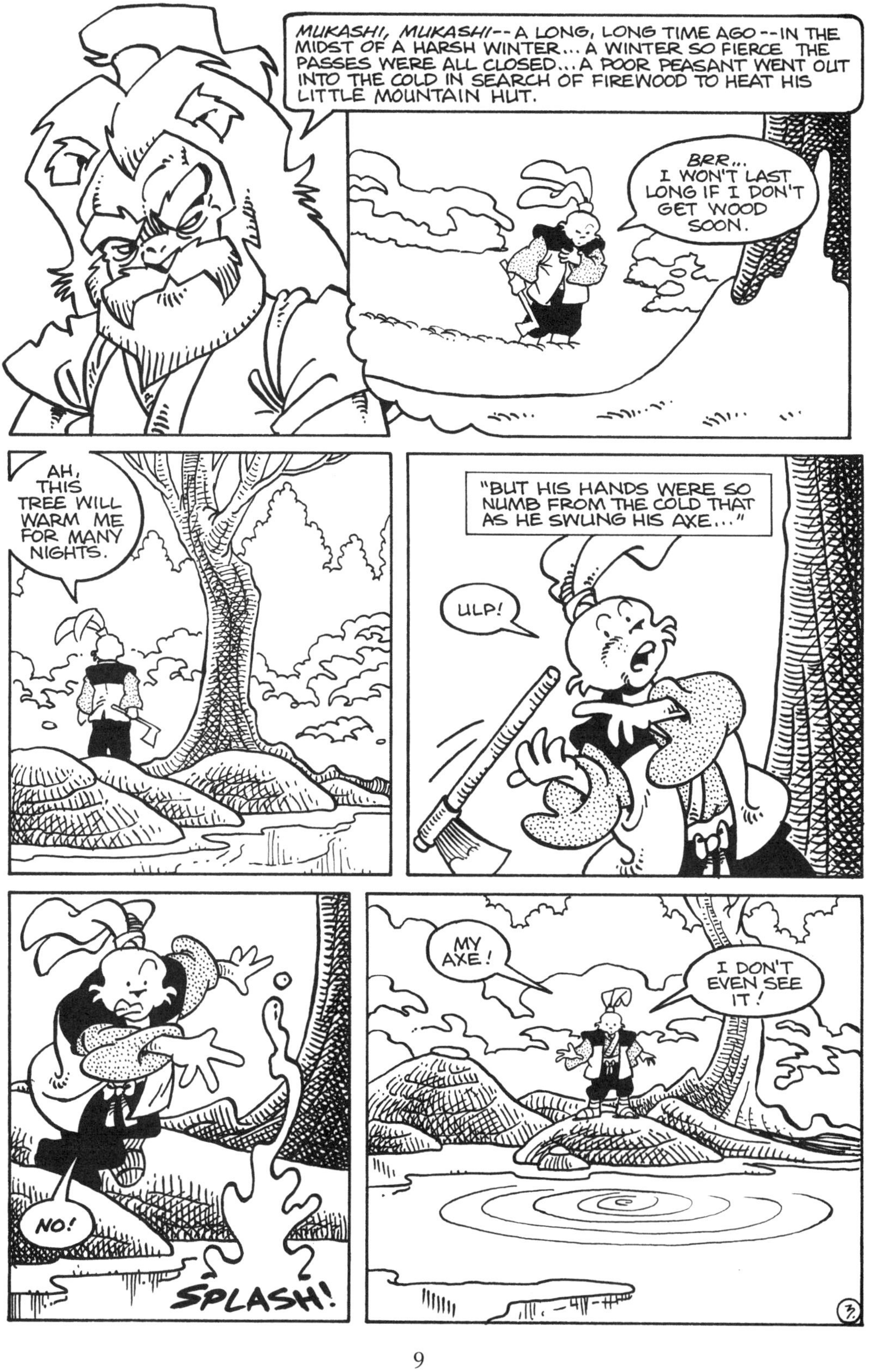
MUKASHI, MUKASHI--A LONG, LONG TIME AGO--IN THE MIDST OF A HARSH WINTER... A WINTER SO FIERCE THE PASSES WERE ALL CLOSED... A POOR PEASANT WENT OUT INTO THE COLD IN SEARCH OF FIREWOOD TO HEAT HIS LITTLE MOUNTAIN HUT.
BRR... I WON'T LAST LONG IF I DON'T GET WOOD SOON.
AH, THIS TREE WILL WARM ME FOR MANY NIGHTS.
"BUT HIS HANDS WERE SO NUMB FROM THE COLD THAT AS HE SWUNG HIS AXE..."
ULP!
NO!
SPLASH!
MY AXE!
I DON'T EVEN SEE IT!
3.

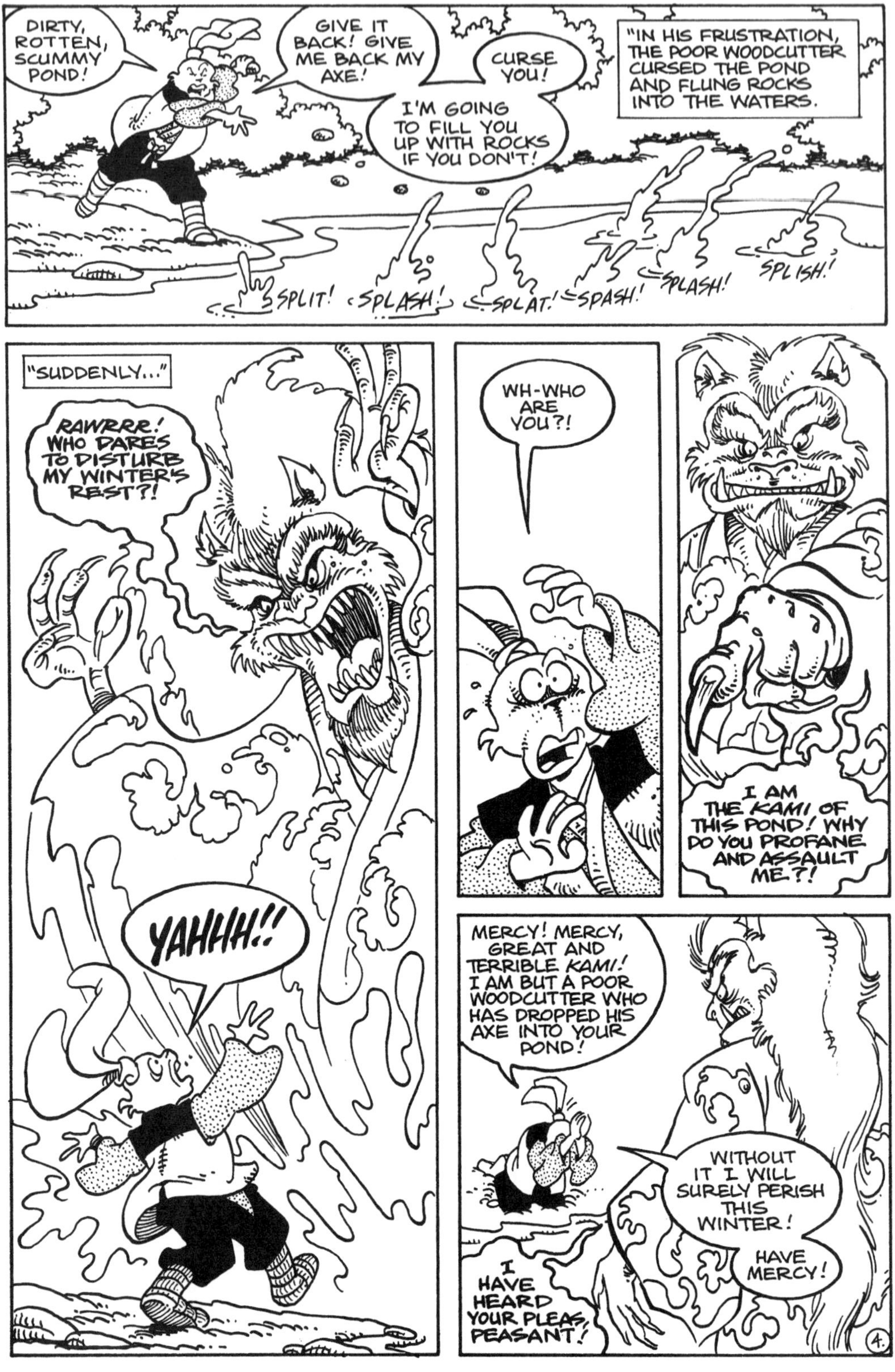
DIRTY, ROTTEN, SCUMMY POND!
GIVE IT BACK! GIVE ME BACK MY AXE!
CURSE YOU!
I'M GOING TO FILL YOU UP WITH ROCKS IF YOU DON'T!
"IN HIS FRUSTRATION, THE POOR WOODCUTTER CURSED THE POND AND FLUNG ROCKS INTO THE WATERS.
SPLIT! SPLASH! SPLAT! SPASH! SPLASH! SPLISH!
"SUDDENLY..."
RAWRRR! WHO DARES TO DISTURB MY WINTER'S REST?!
YAHHH!!
WH-WHO ARE YOU?!
I AM THE KAMI OF THIS POND! WHY DO YOU PROFANE AND ASSAULT ME?!
MERCY! MERCY, GREAT AND TERRIBLE KAMI! I AM BUT A POOR WOODCUTTER WHO HAS DROPPED HIS AXE INTO YOUR POND!
WITHOUT IT I WILL SURELY PERISH THIS WINTER!
HAVE MERCY!
I HAVE HEARD YOUR PLEAS, PEASANT!
4.

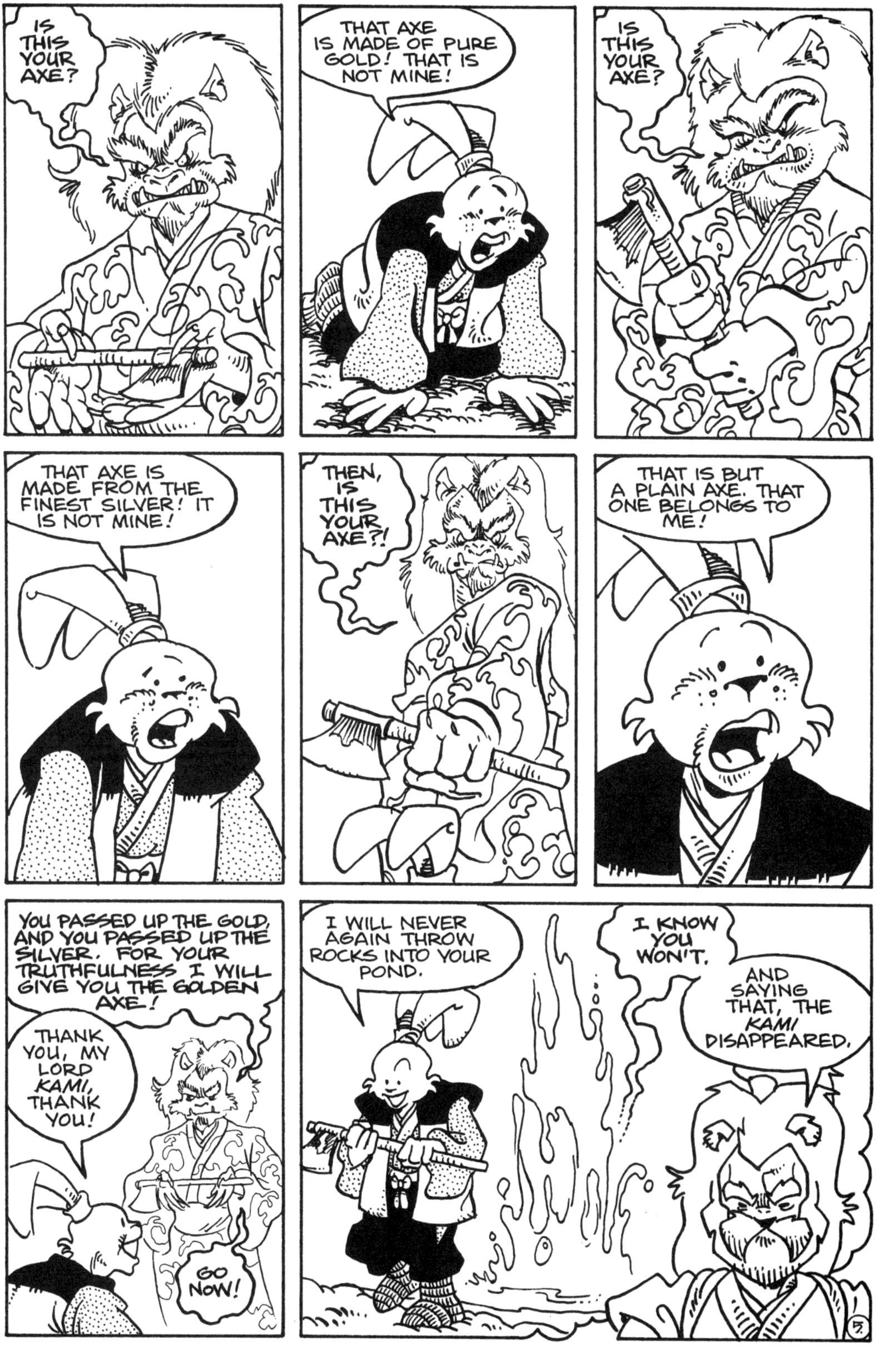
IS THIS YOUR AXE?
THAT AXE IS MADE OF PURE GOLD! THAT IS NOT MINE!
IS THIS YOUR AXE?
THAT AXE IS MADE FROM THE FINEST SILVER! IT IS NOT MINE!
THEN, IS THIS YOUR AXE?!
THAT IS BUT A PLAIN AXE. THAT ONE BELONGS TO ME!
YOU PASSED UP THE GOLD, AND YOU PASSED UP THE SILVER. FOR YOUR TRUTHFULNESS I WILL GIVE YOU THE GOLDEN AXE!
THANK YOU, MY LORD *KAMI*, THANK YOU!
GO NOW!
I WILL NEVER AGAIN THROW ROCKS INTO YOUR POND.
I KNOW YOU WON'T.
AND SAYING THAT, THE *KAMI* DISAPPEARED.

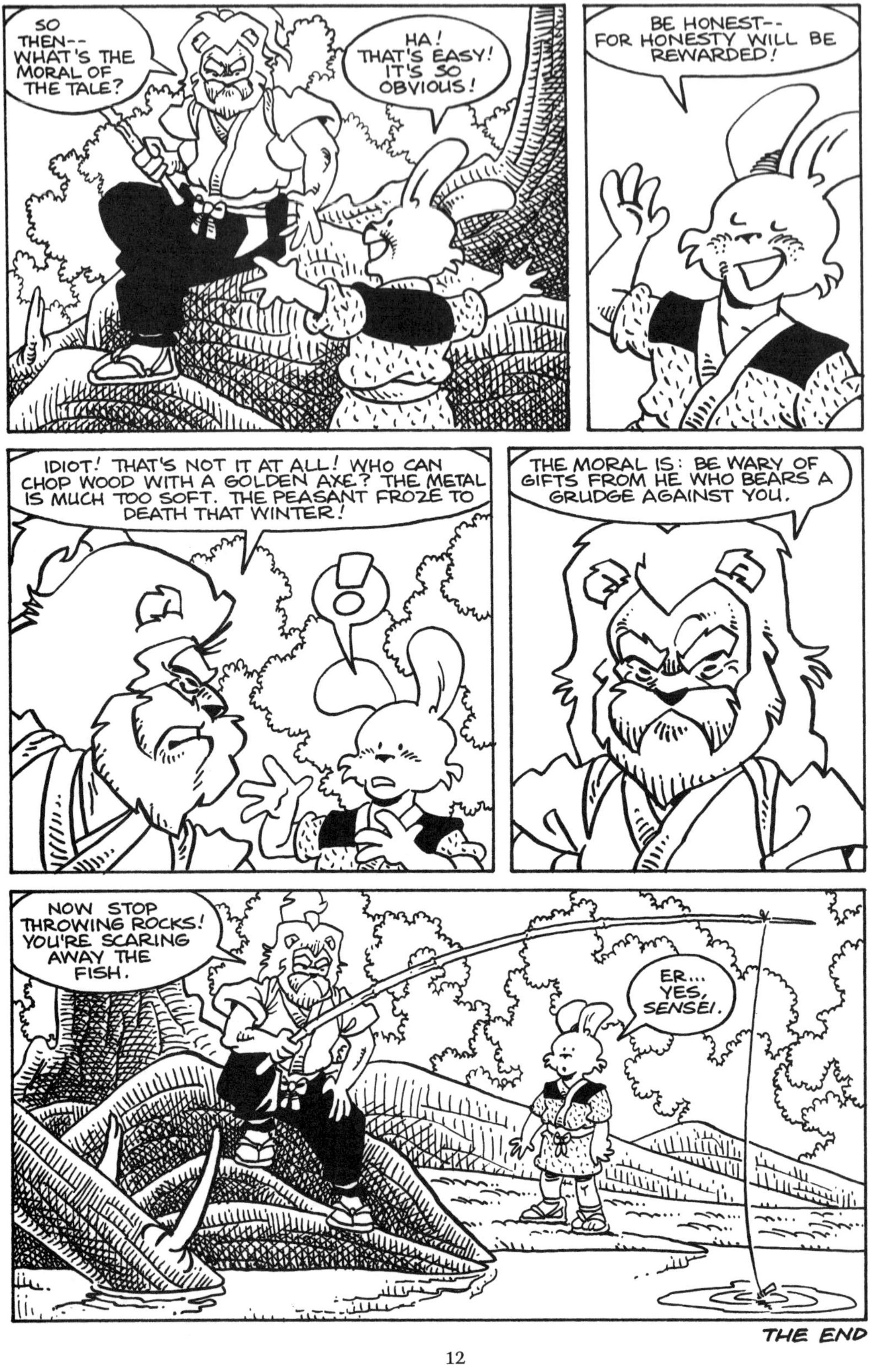
SO THEN-- WHAT'S THE MORAL OF THE TALE?
HA! THAT'S EASY! IT'S SO OBVIOUS!
BE HONEST-- FOR HONESTY WILL BE REWARDED!
IDIOT! THAT'S NOT IT AT ALL! WHO CAN CHOP WOOD WITH A GOLDEN AXE? THE METAL IS MUCH TOO SOFT. THE PEASANT FROZE TO DEATH THAT WINTER!
!
THE MORAL IS: BE WARY OF GIFTS FROM HE WHO BEARS A GRUDGE AGAINST YOU.
NOW STOP THROWING ROCKS! YOU'RE SCARING AWAY THE FISH.
ER... YES, SENSEI.
THE END

CUT the PLUM

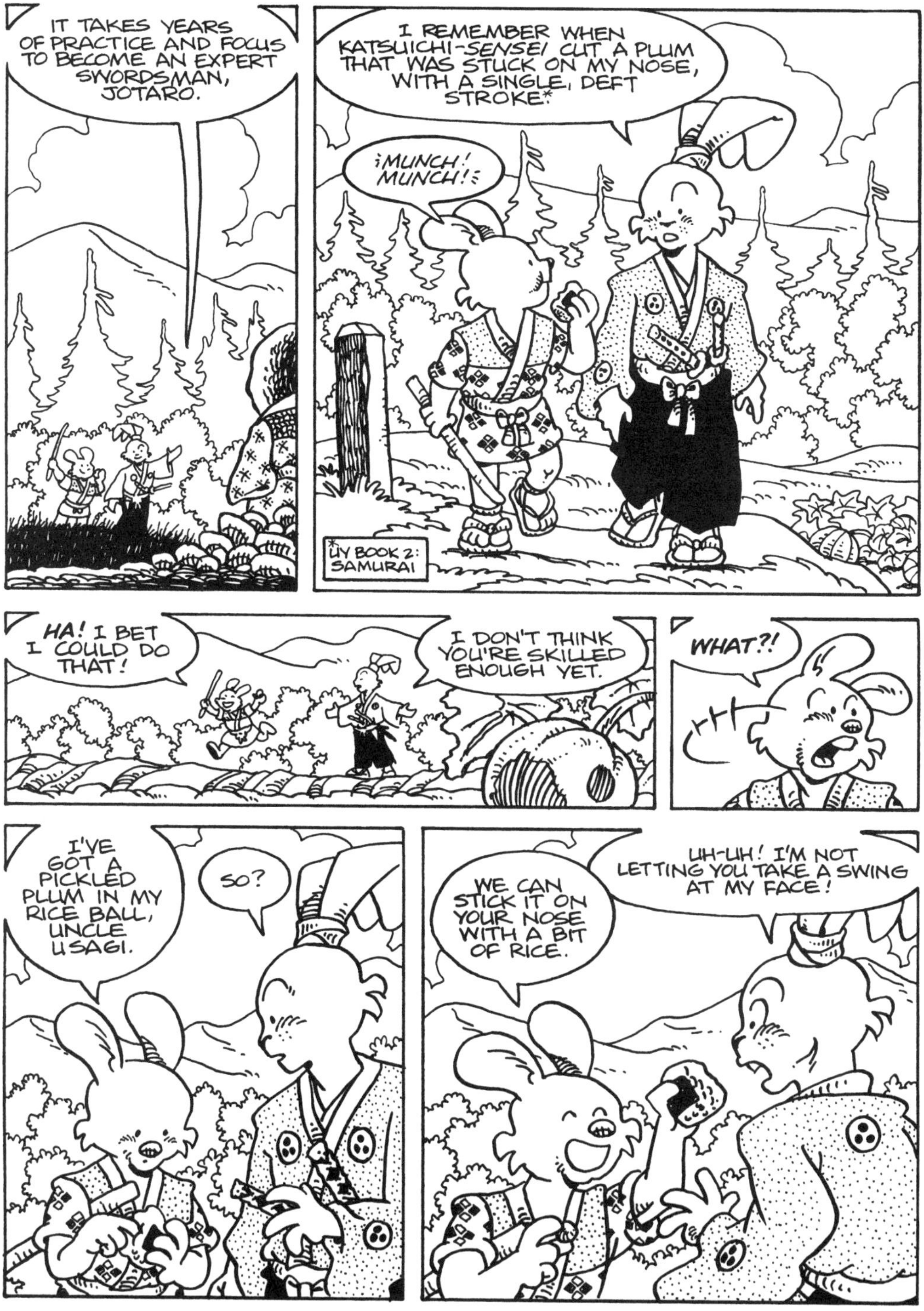

IT TAKES YEARS OF PRACTICE AND FOCUS TO BECOME AN EXPERT SWORDSMAN, JOTARO.
I REMEMBER WHEN KATSUICHI-SENSEI CUT A PLUM THAT WAS STUCK ON MY NOSE, WITH A SINGLE, DEFT STROKE.*
¡MUNCH! MUNCH!¡
*UY BOOK 2: SAMURAI
HA! I BET I COULD DO THAT!
I DON'T THINK YOU'RE SKILLED ENOUGH YET.
WHAT?!
I'VE GOT A PICKLED PLUM IN MY RICE BALL, UNCLE USAGI.
SO?
WE CAN STICK IT ON YOUR NOSE WITH A BIT OF RICE.
UH-UH! I'M NOT LETTING YOU TAKE A SWING AT MY FACE!

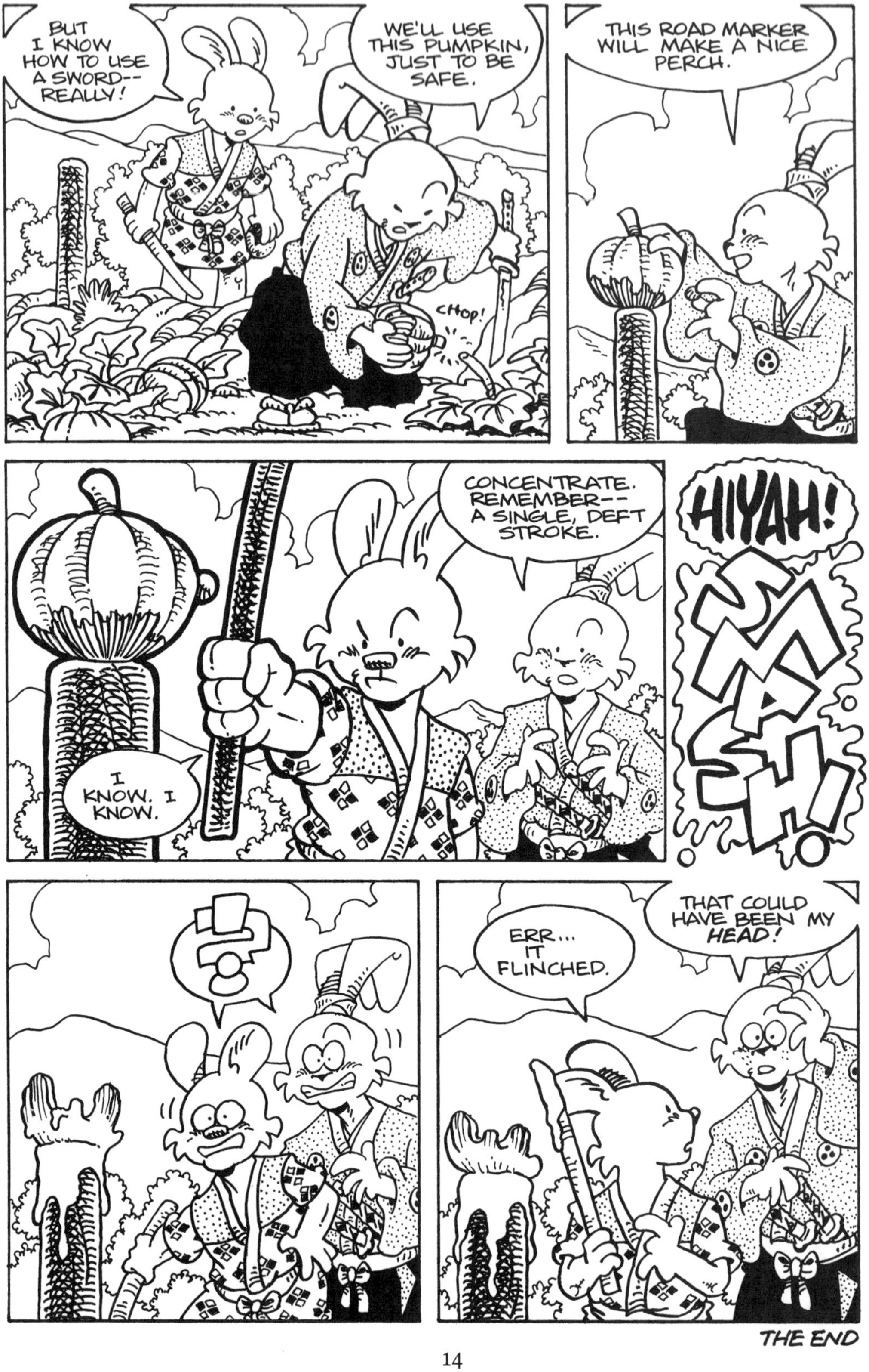
BUT I KNOW HOW TO USE A SWORD-- REALLY!
WE'LL USE THIS PUMPKIN, JUST TO BE SAFE.
CHOP!
THIS ROAD MARKER WILL MAKE A NICE PERCH.
CONCENTRATE. REMEMBER-- A SINGLE, DEFT STROKE.
I KNOW. I KNOW.
HIYAH!
SMASH!
?
ERR... IT FLINCHED.
THAT COULD HAVE BEEN MY HEAD!
THE END

THREE HUNDRED YEARS AGO, THERE WAS AN UPRISING WITHIN THE OTOMO CLAN WHEN LORD HAYASHI TOOK UP ARMS AGAINST HIS LORD MIYAKE.

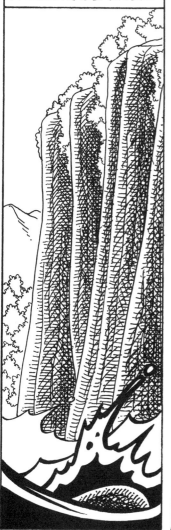

THE FINAL BATTLE WAS FOUGHT NEAR THE BLUFFS ABOVE THE RAGING MAZÉ RIVER.

THE TWO GENERALS POSITIONED THEIR FORCES AT OPPOSITE ENDS OF THE GREAT FIELD...

...LORD MIYAKE TO THE EAST...

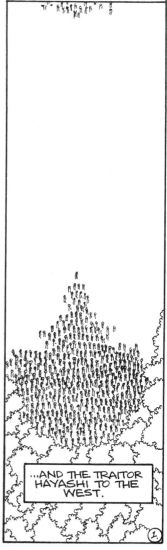

...AND THE TRAITOR HAYASHI TO THE WEST.

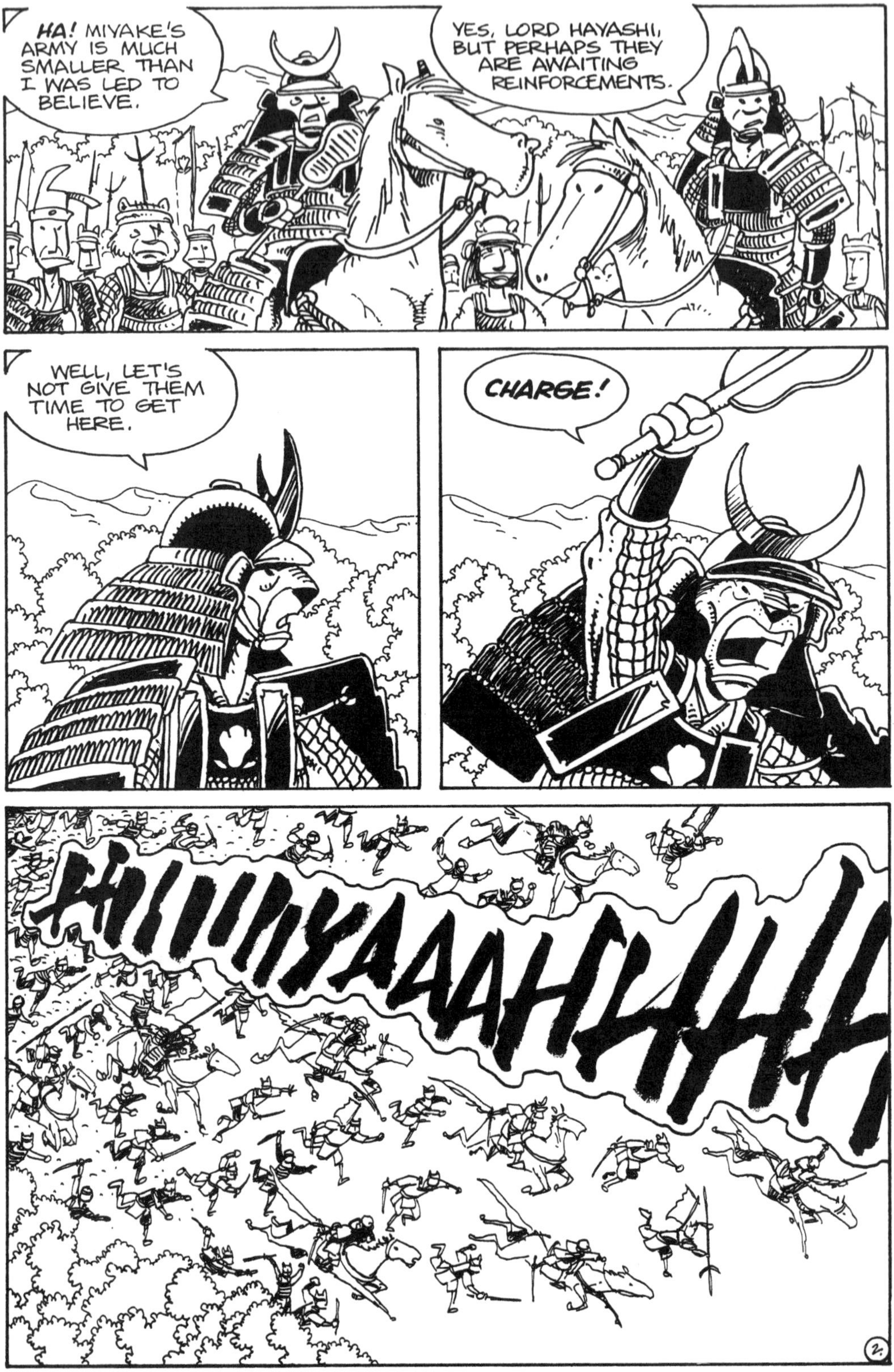
HA! MIYAKE'S ARMY IS MUCH SMALLER THAN I WAS LED TO BELIEVE.
YES, LORD HAYASHI, BUT PERHAPS THEY ARE AWAITING REINFORCEMENTS.
WELL, LET'S NOT GIVE THEM TIME TO GET HERE.
CHARGE!
HIIIIIYAAAAHHHH
2.

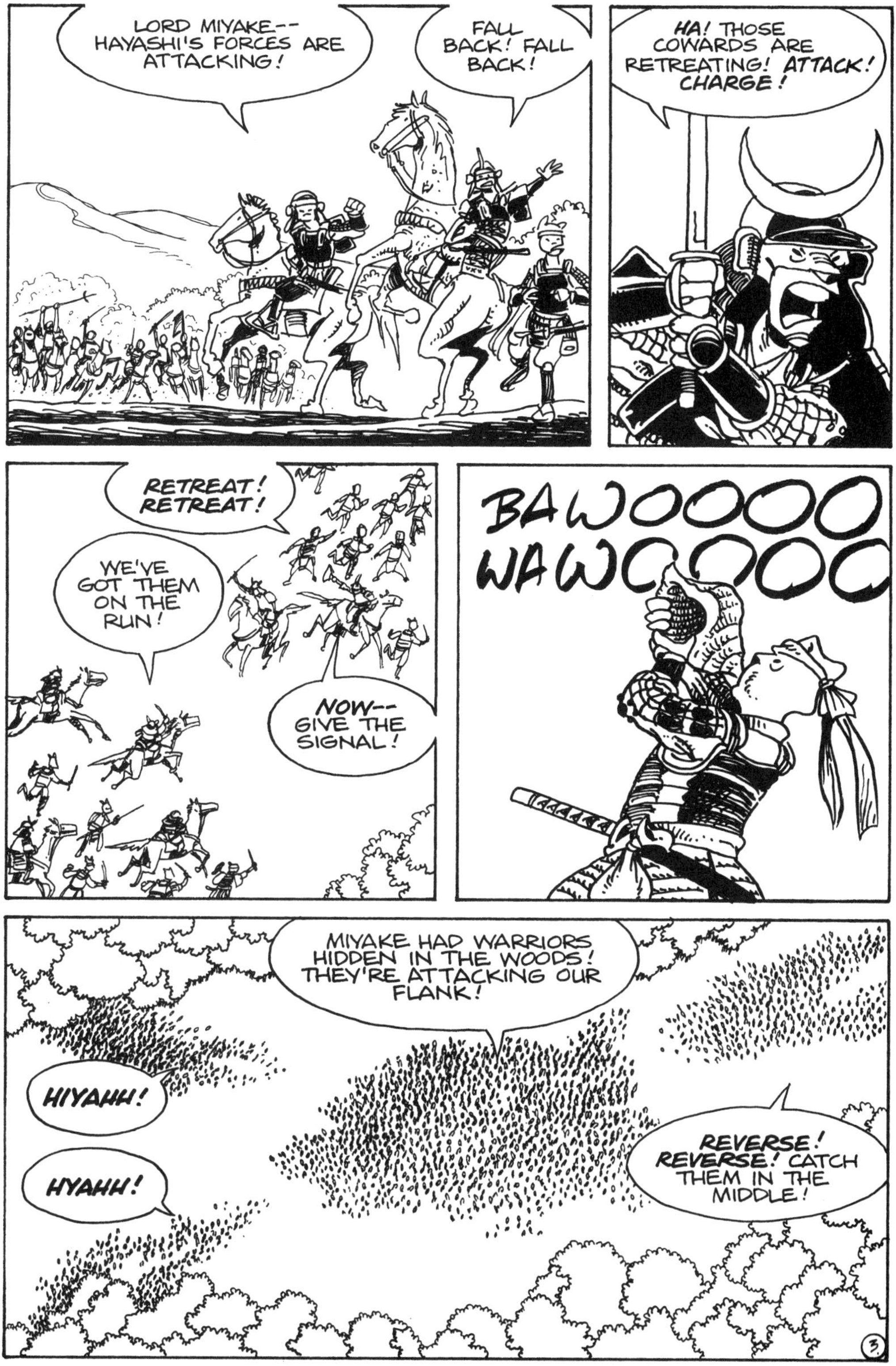
LORD MIYAKE-- HAYASHI'S FORCES ARE ATTACKING!
FALL BACK! FALL BACK!
HA! THOSE COWARDS ARE RETREATING! ATTACK! CHARGE!
RETREAT! RETREAT!
WE'VE GOT THEM ON THE RUN!
NOW-- GIVE THE SIGNAL!
BAWOOOOO WAWOOOOO
MIYAKE HAD WARRIORS HIDDEN IN THE WOODS! THEY'RE ATTACKING OUR FLANK!
HIYAHH!
HYAHH!
REVERSE! REVERSE! CATCH THEM IN THE MIDDLE!
3

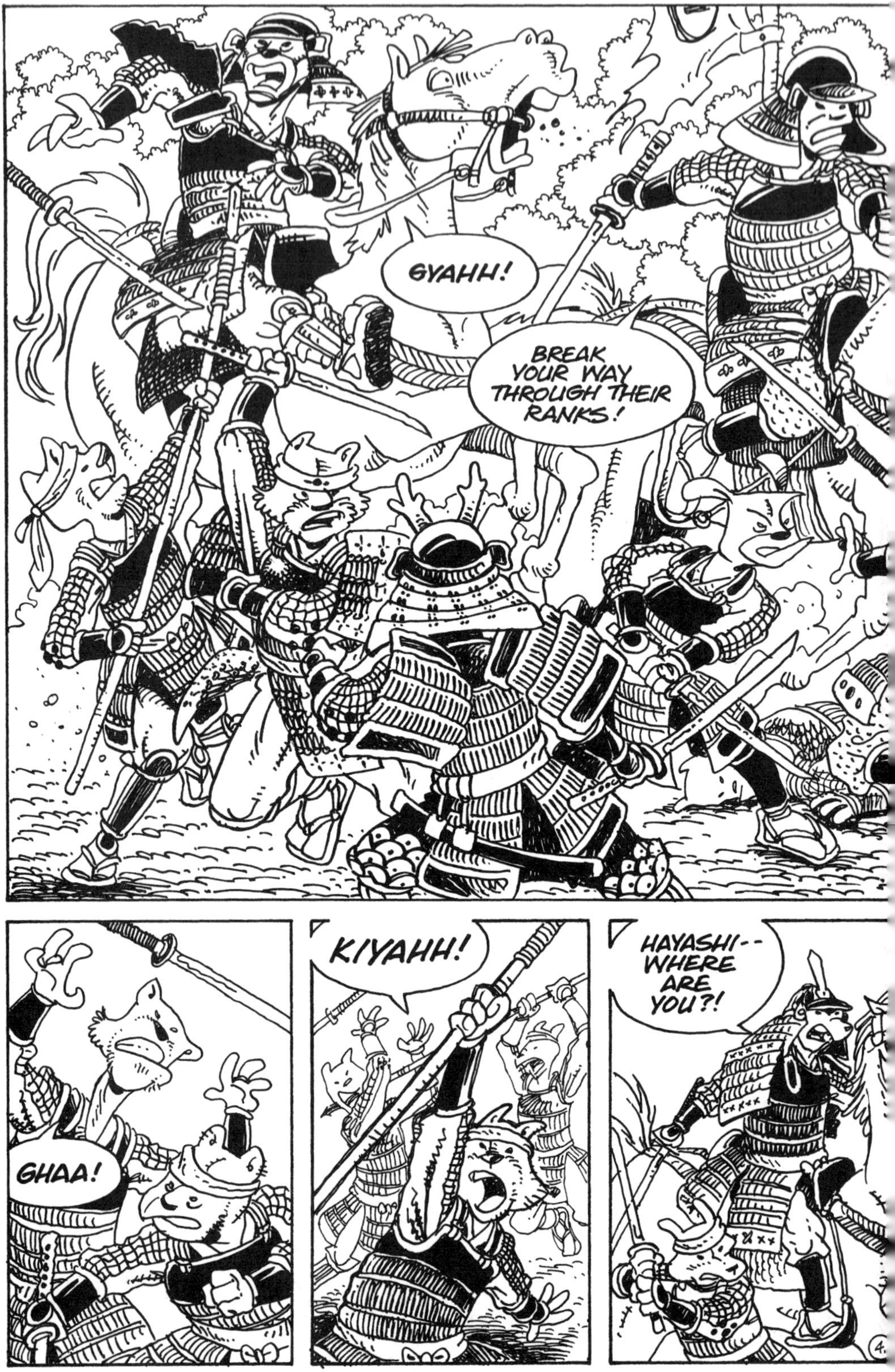
GYAHH!
BREAK YOUR WAY THROUGH THEIR RANKS!
GHAA!
KIYAHH!
HAYASHI--WHERE ARE YOU?!

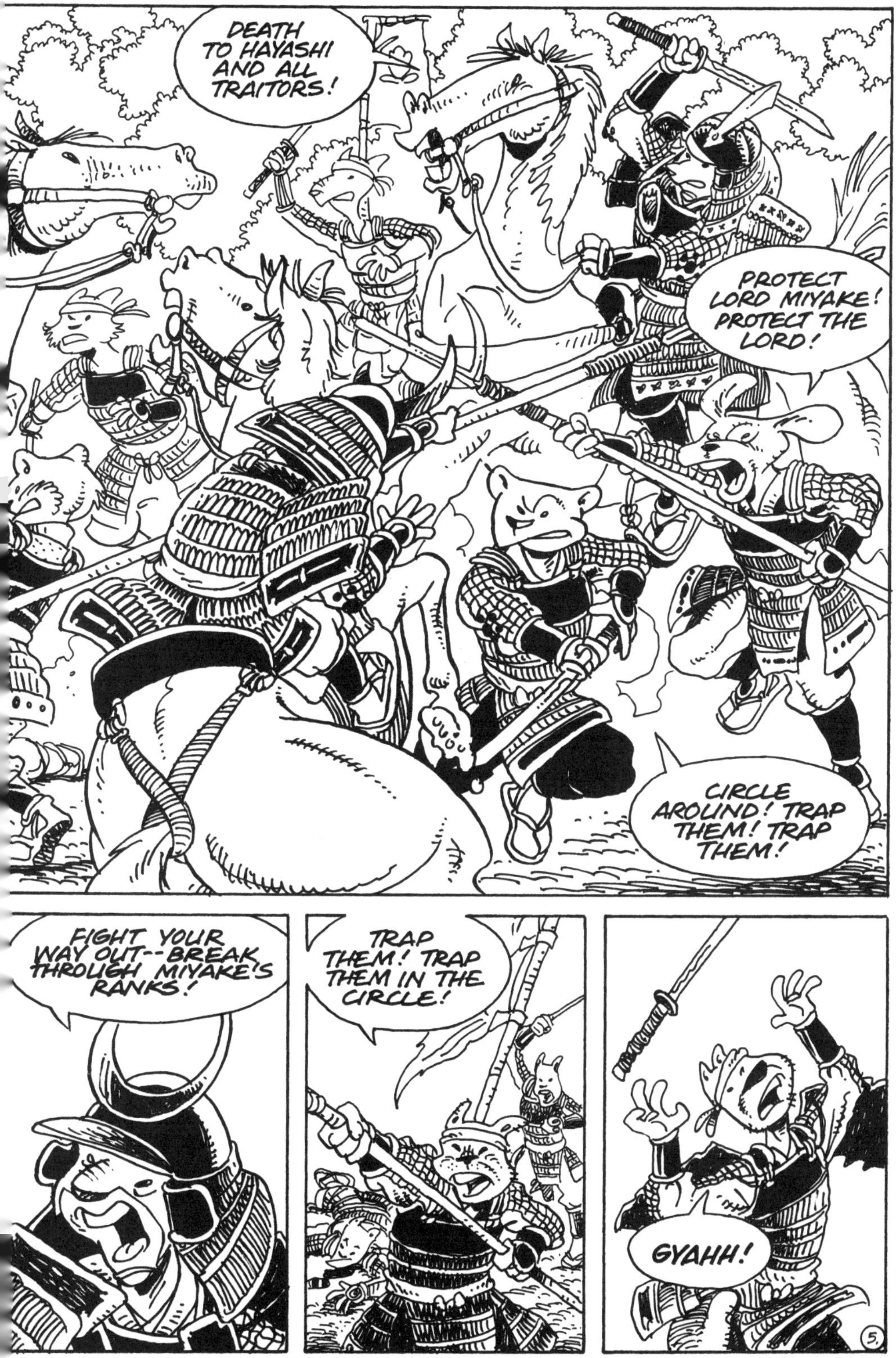
DEATH TO HAYASHI AND ALL TRAITORS!
PROTECT LORD MIYAKE! PROTECT THE LORD!
CIRCLE AROUND! TRAP THEM! TRAP THEM!
FIGHT YOUR WAY OUT--BREAK THROUGH MIYAKE'S RANKS!
TRAP THEM! TRAP THEM IN THE CIRCLE!
GYAHH!
5.

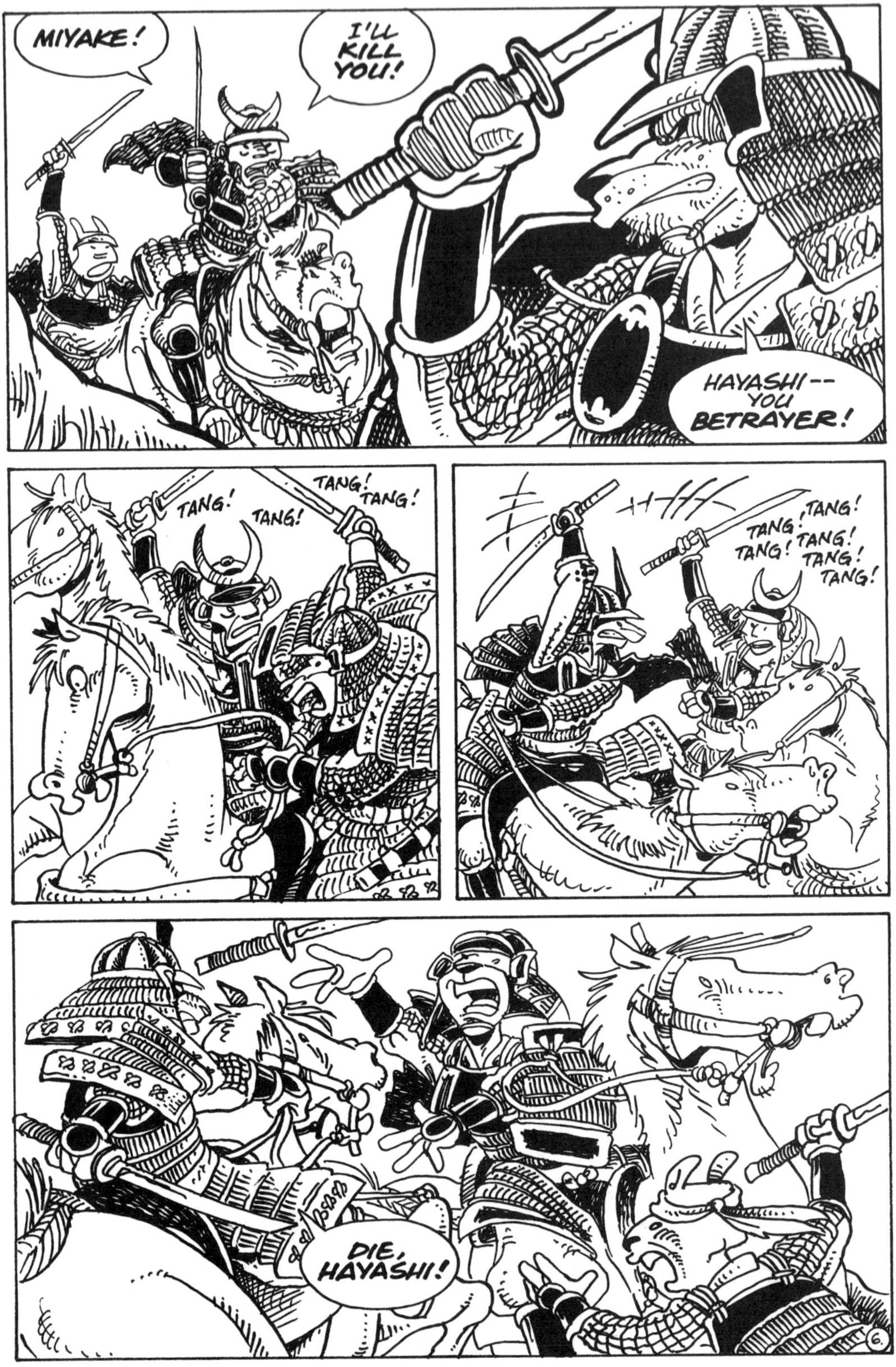
MIYAKE!
I'LL KILL YOU!
HAYASHI-- YOU BETRAYER!
TANG! TANG! TANG! TANG!
TANG! TANG! TANG! TANG! TANG! TANG!
DIE, HAYASHI!
6.

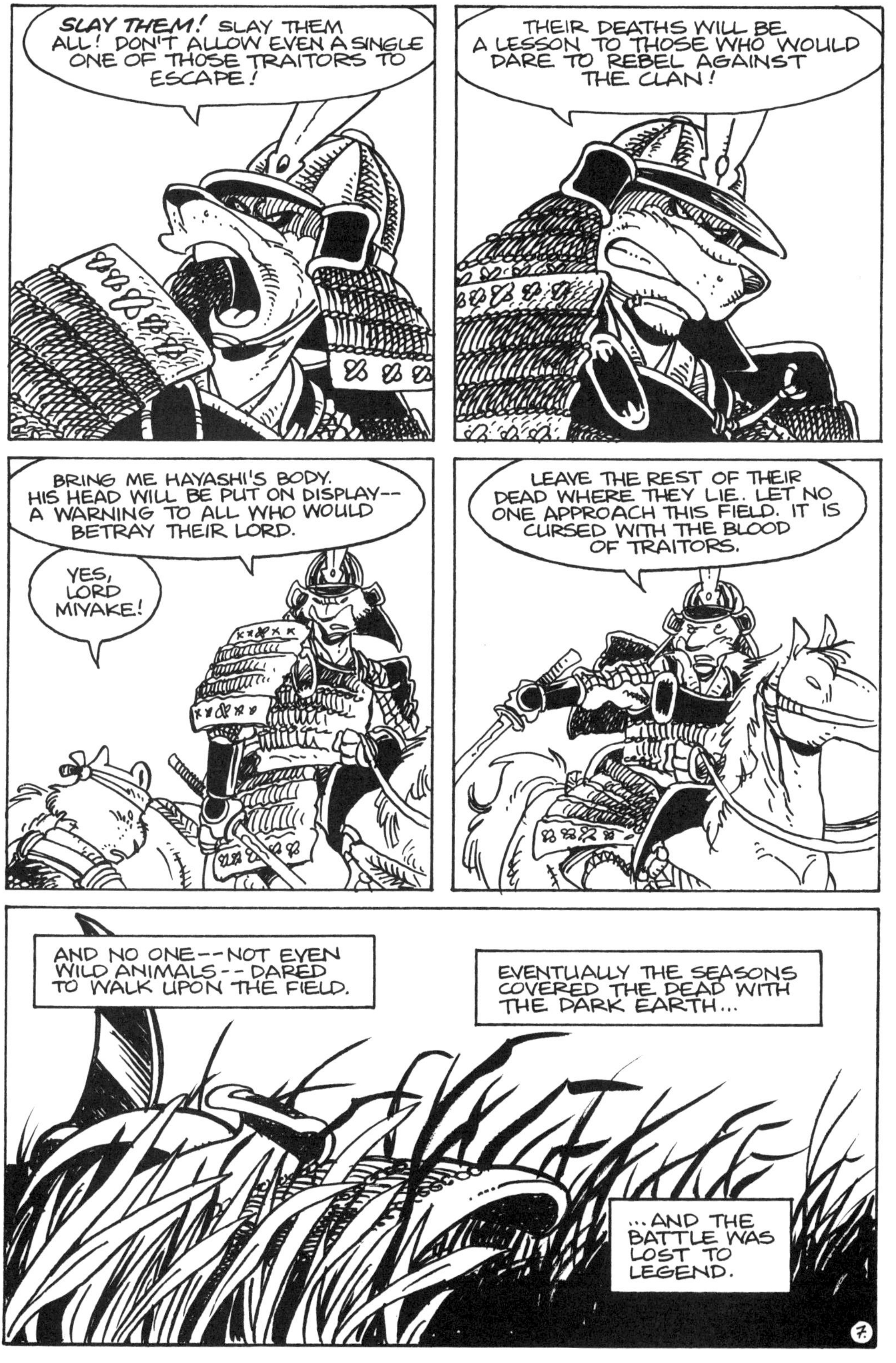
SLAY THEM! SLAY THEM ALL! DON'T ALLOW EVEN A SINGLE ONE OF THOSE TRAITORS TO ESCAPE!
THEIR DEATHS WILL BE A LESSON TO THOSE WHO WOULD DARE TO REBEL AGAINST THE CLAN!
BRING ME HAYASHI'S BODY. HIS HEAD WILL BE PUT ON DISPLAY-- A WARNING TO ALL WHO WOULD BETRAY THEIR LORD.
YES, LORD MIYAKE!
LEAVE THE REST OF THEIR DEAD WHERE THEY LIE. LET NO ONE APPROACH THIS FIELD. IT IS CURSED WITH THE BLOOD OF TRAITORS.
AND NO ONE--NOT EVEN WILD ANIMALS--DARED TO WALK UPON THE FIELD.
EVENTUALLY THE SEASONS COVERED THE DEAD WITH THE DARK EARTH...
...AND THE BATTLE WAS LOST TO LEGEND.
7.

TRAITORS OF THE EARTH PART ONE

...AND OUR TRAGIC HERO RIDES HIS STEED ALONG THE DRAGON'S SPINE....

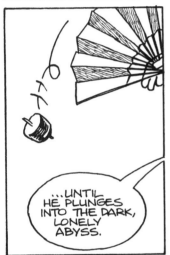

...UNTIL HE PLUNGES INTO THE DARK, LONELY ABYSS.

HA HA! WONDERFUL!

WHAT A SAD STORY!

THANK YOU, THANK YOU.

CLAP! CLAP!

CLAP! CLAP!

CLAP!

CLAP!

CLAP!

FLICK!

PLEASE SHOW YOUR APPRECIATION, IF YOU ENJOYED THE PERFORMANCE.

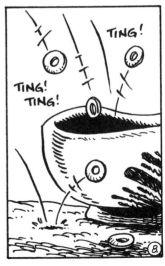

TING!

TING! TING!

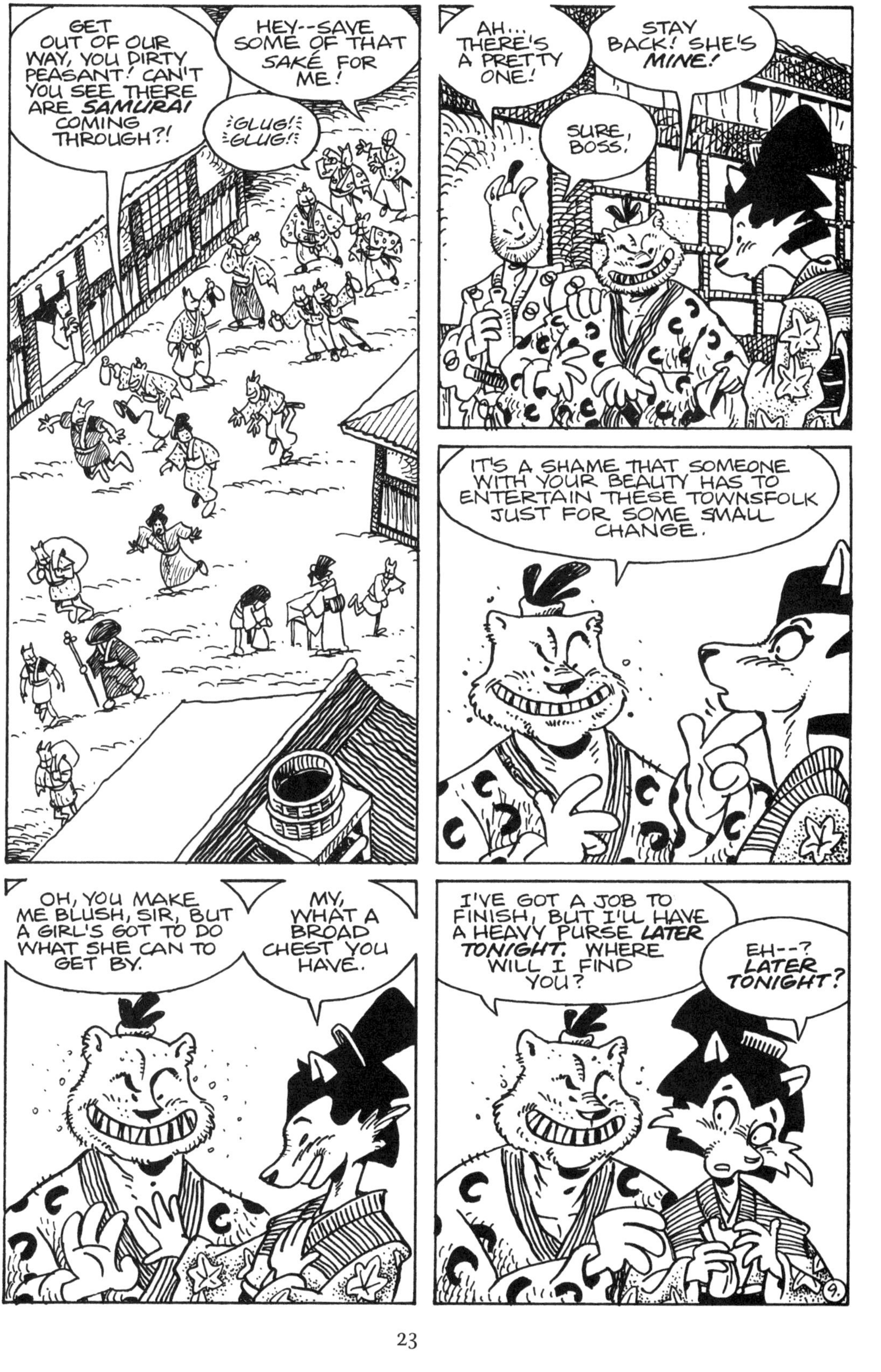
GET OUT OF OUR WAY, YOU DIRTY PEASANT! CAN'T YOU SEE THERE ARE *SAMURAI* COMING THROUGH?!
HEY--SAVE SOME OF THAT *SAKÉ* FOR ME!
GLUG! GLUG!
AH... THERE'S A PRETTY ONE!
STAY BACK! SHE'S *MINE!*
SURE, BOSS.
IT'S A SHAME THAT SOMEONE WITH YOUR BEAUTY HAS TO ENTERTAIN THESE TOWNSFOLK JUST FOR SOME SMALL CHANGE.
OH, YOU MAKE ME BLUSH, SIR, BUT A GIRL'S GOT TO DO WHAT SHE CAN TO GET BY.
MY, WHAT A BROAD CHEST YOU HAVE.
I'VE GOT A JOB TO FINISH, BUT I'LL HAVE A HEAVY PURSE *LATER TONIGHT.* WHERE WILL I FIND YOU?
EH--? *LATER TONIGHT?*
9.

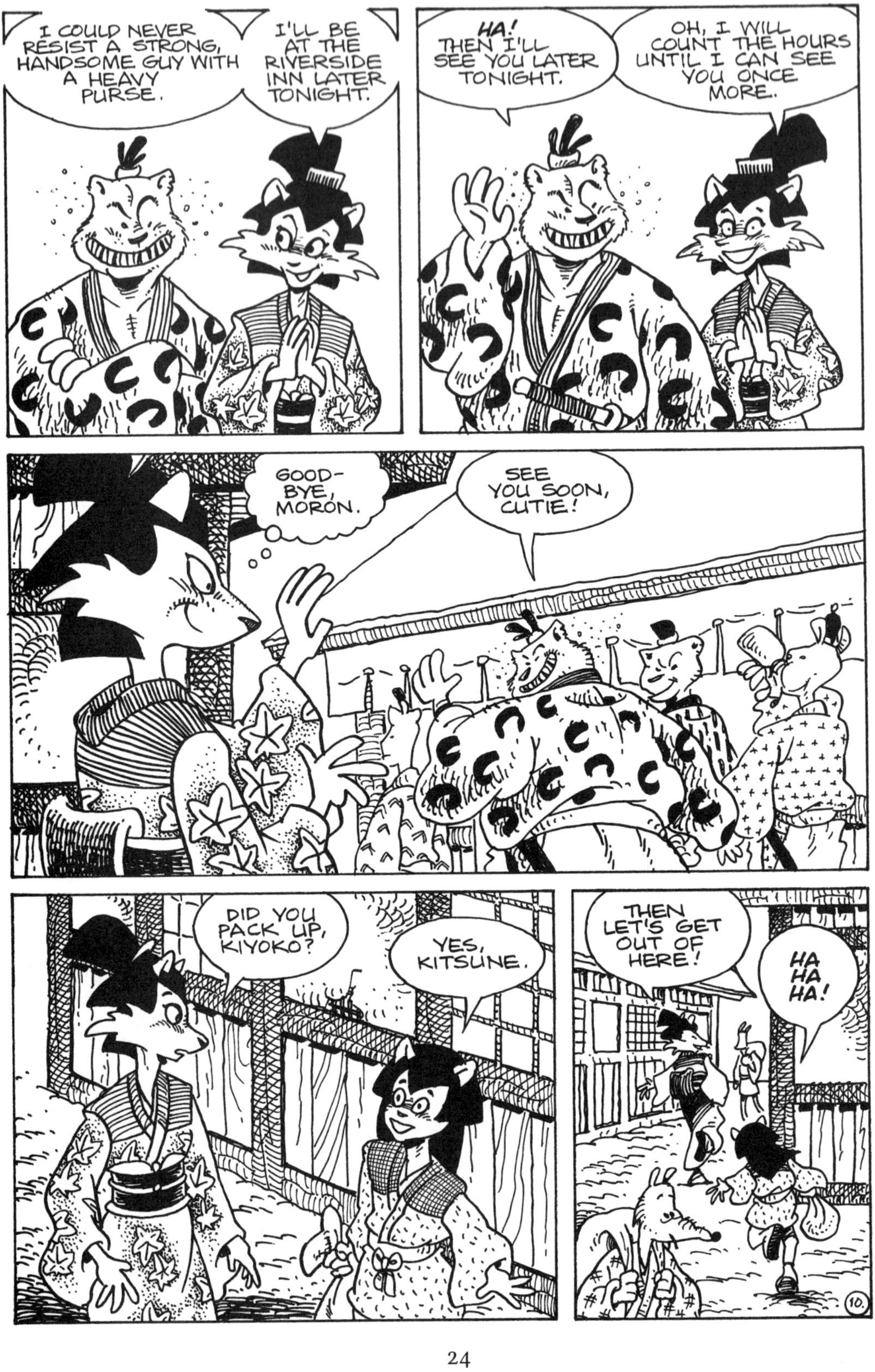
I COULD NEVER RESIST A STRONG, HANDSOME GUY WITH A HEAVY PURSE.
I'LL BE AT THE RIVERSIDE INN LATER TONIGHT.
HA! THEN I'LL SEE YOU LATER TONIGHT.
OH, I WILL COUNT THE HOURS UNTIL I CAN SEE YOU ONCE MORE.
GOOD-BYE, MORON.
SEE YOU SOON, CUTIE!
DID YOU PACK UP, KIYOKO?
YES, KITSUNE.
THEN LET'S GET OUT OF HERE!
HA HA HA!
10.

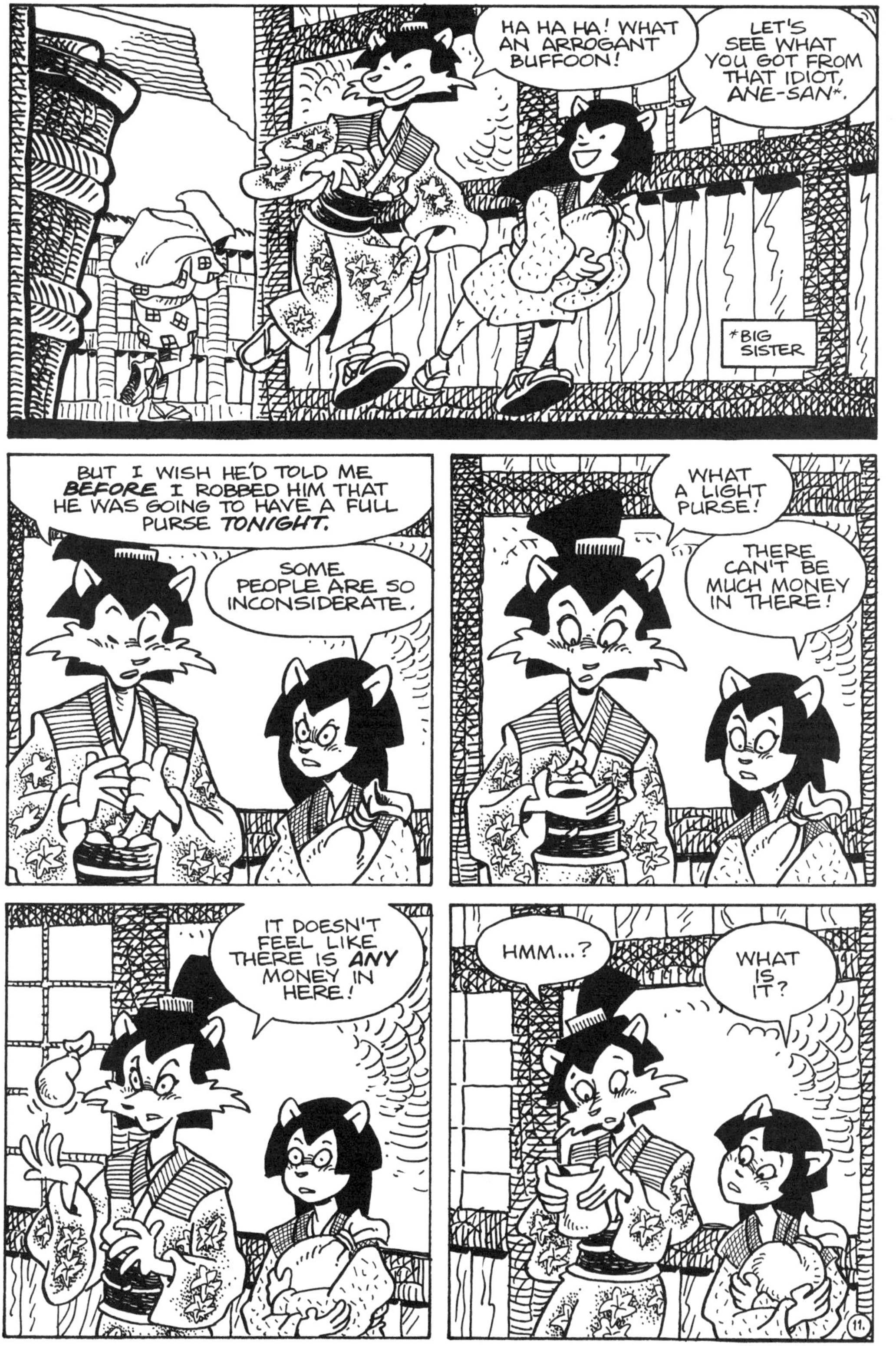
HA HA HA! WHAT AN ARROGANT BUFFOON!
LET'S SEE WHAT YOU GOT FROM THAT IDIOT, ANE-SAN*.
*BIG SISTER
BUT I WISH HE'D TOLD ME BEFORE I ROBBED HIM THAT HE WAS GOING TO HAVE A FULL PURSE TONIGHT.
SOME PEOPLE ARE SO INCONSIDERATE.
WHAT A LIGHT PURSE!
THERE CAN'T BE MUCH MONEY IN THERE!
IT DOESN'T FEEL LIKE THERE IS ANY MONEY IN HERE!
HMM...?
WHAT IS IT?
11.

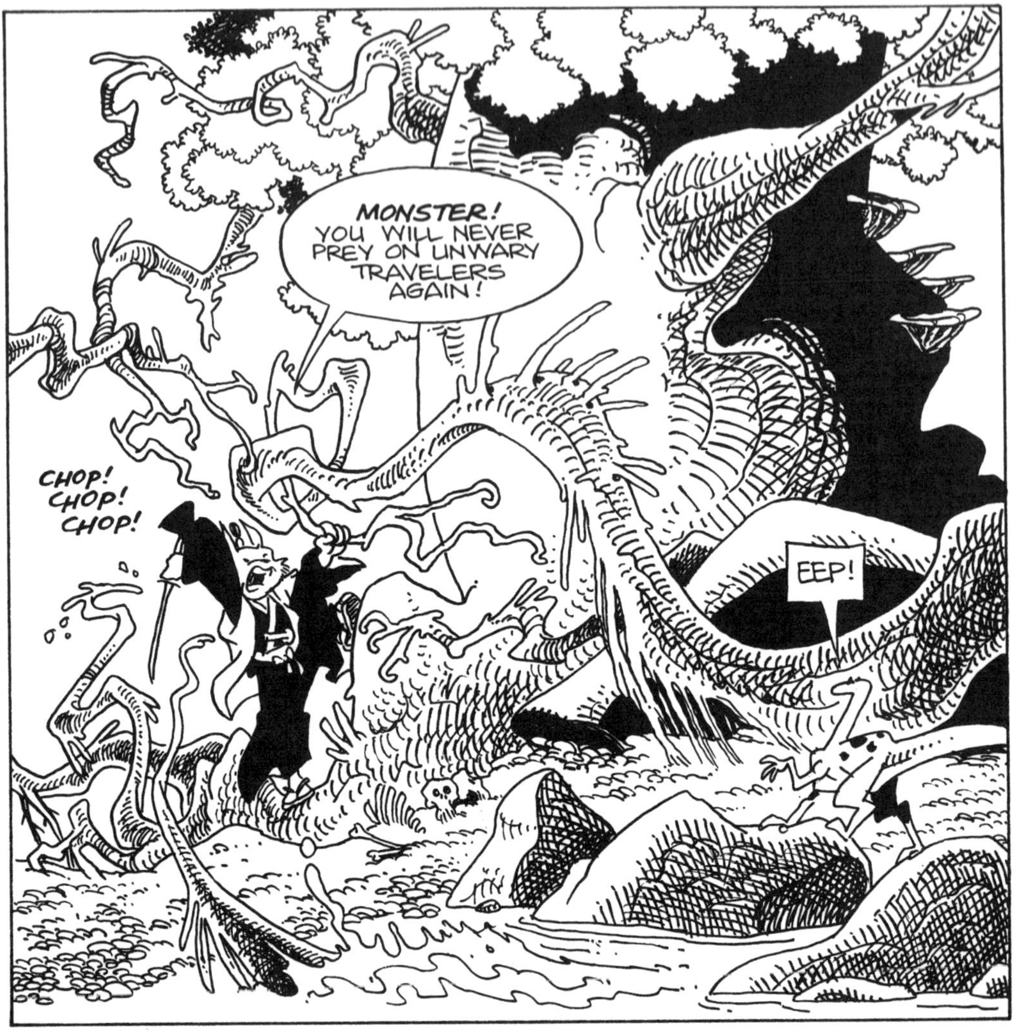
MONSTER! YOU WILL NEVER PREY ON UNWARY TRAVELERS AGAIN!
CHOP! CHOP! CHOP!
EEP!

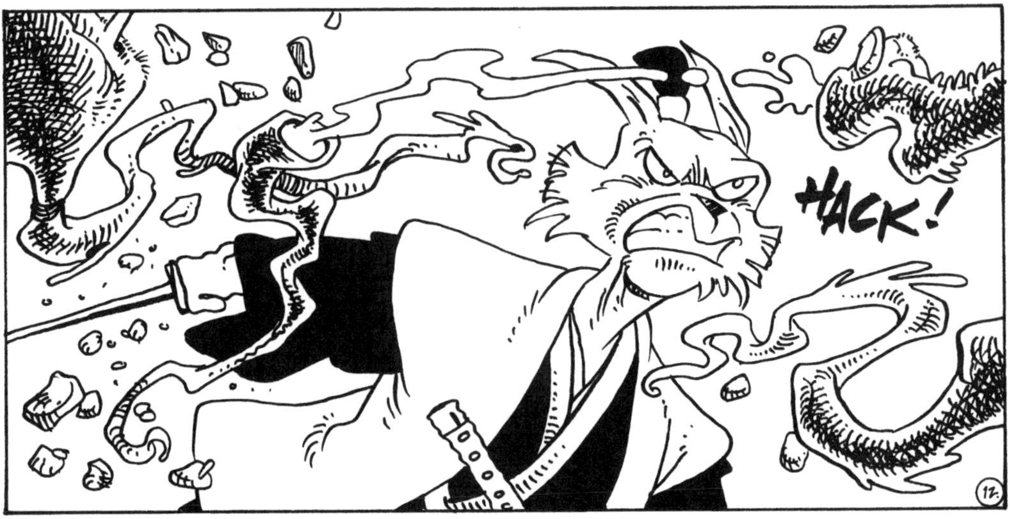
HACK!
12

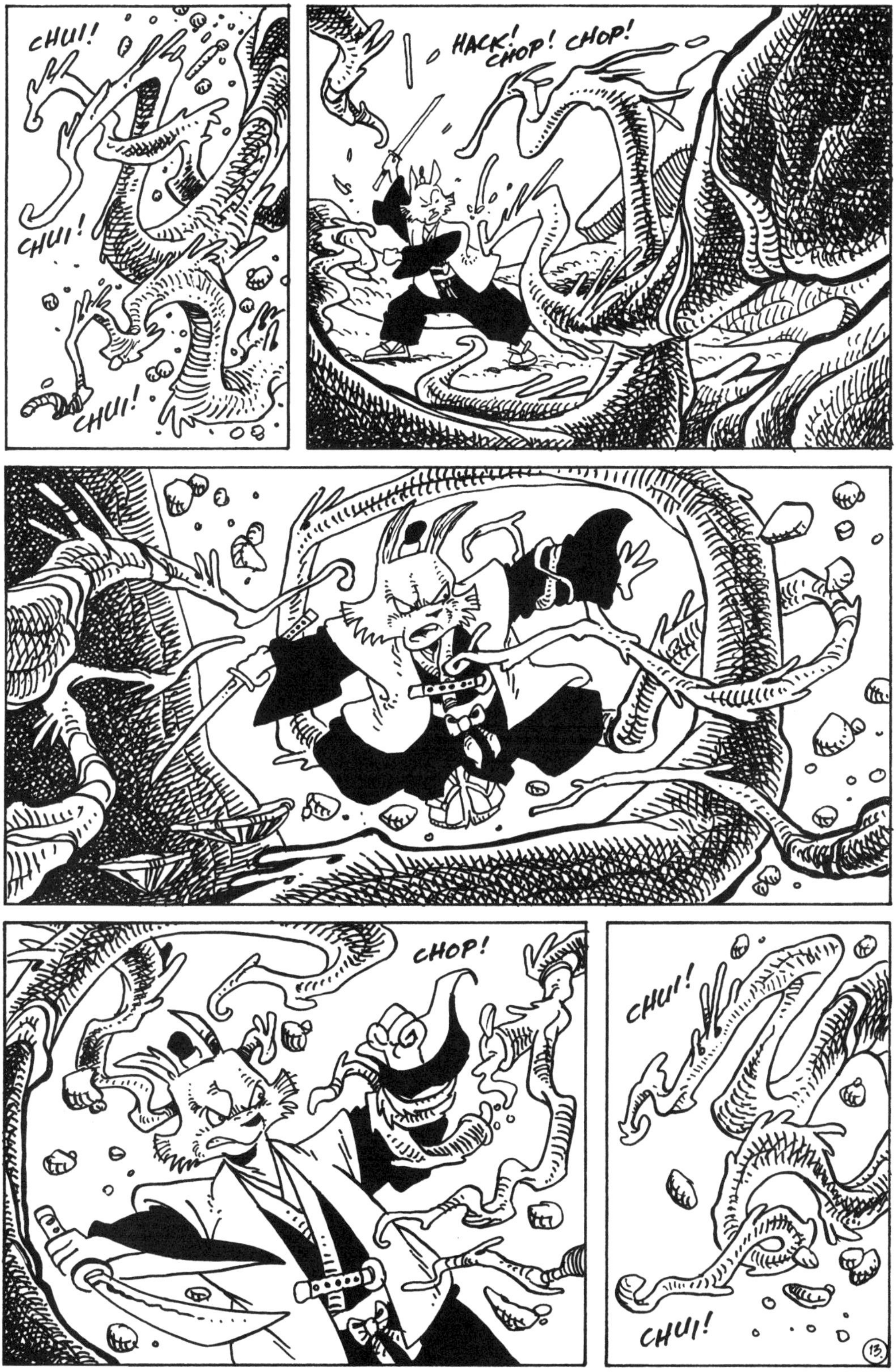
CHUI!
CHUI!
CHUI!
HACK! CHOP! CHOP!
CHOP!
CHUI!
CHUI!
13

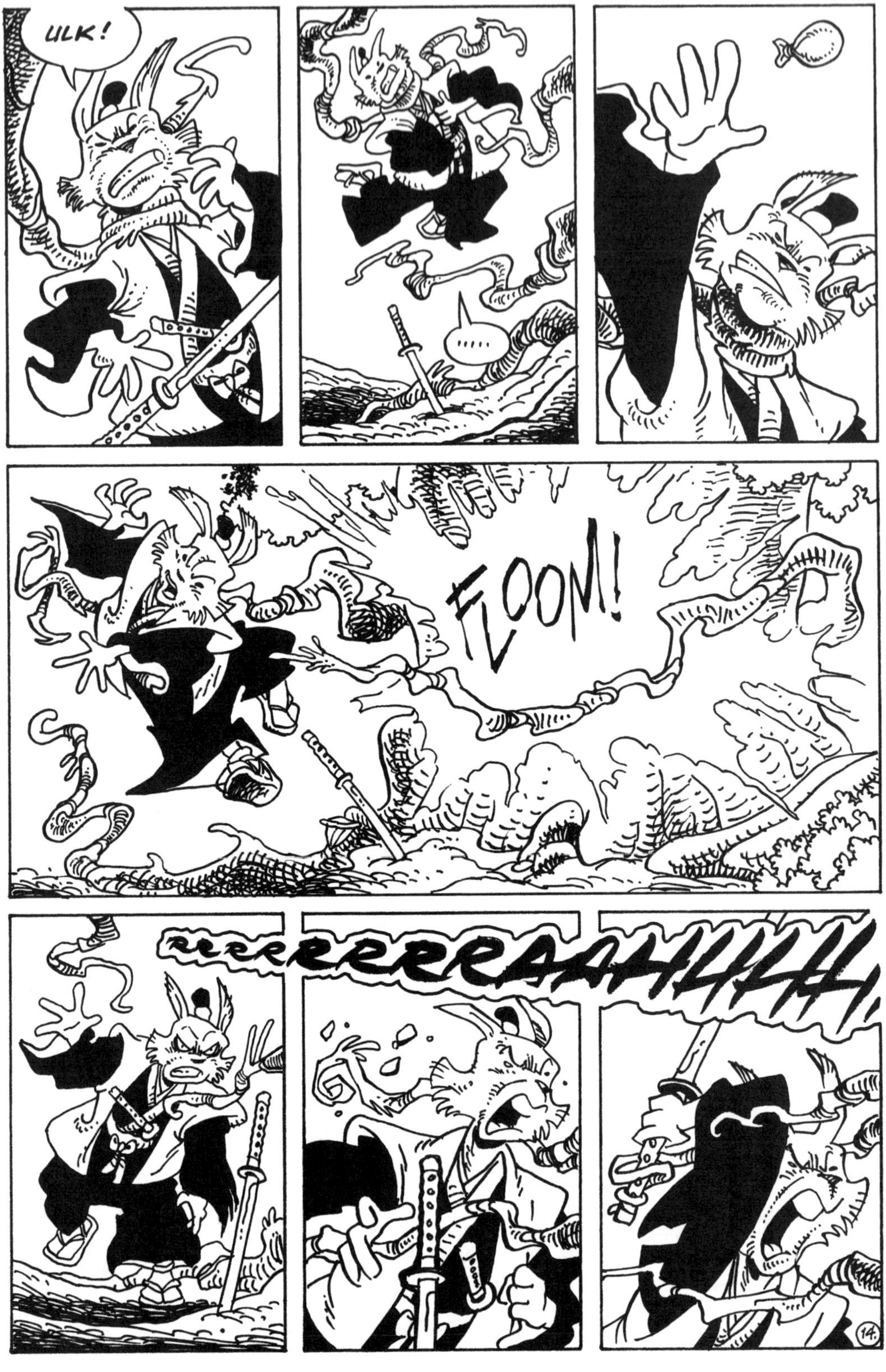
ULK!
.....
FLOOM!
RRRRRRRRRRRAAHHHHH!
14.

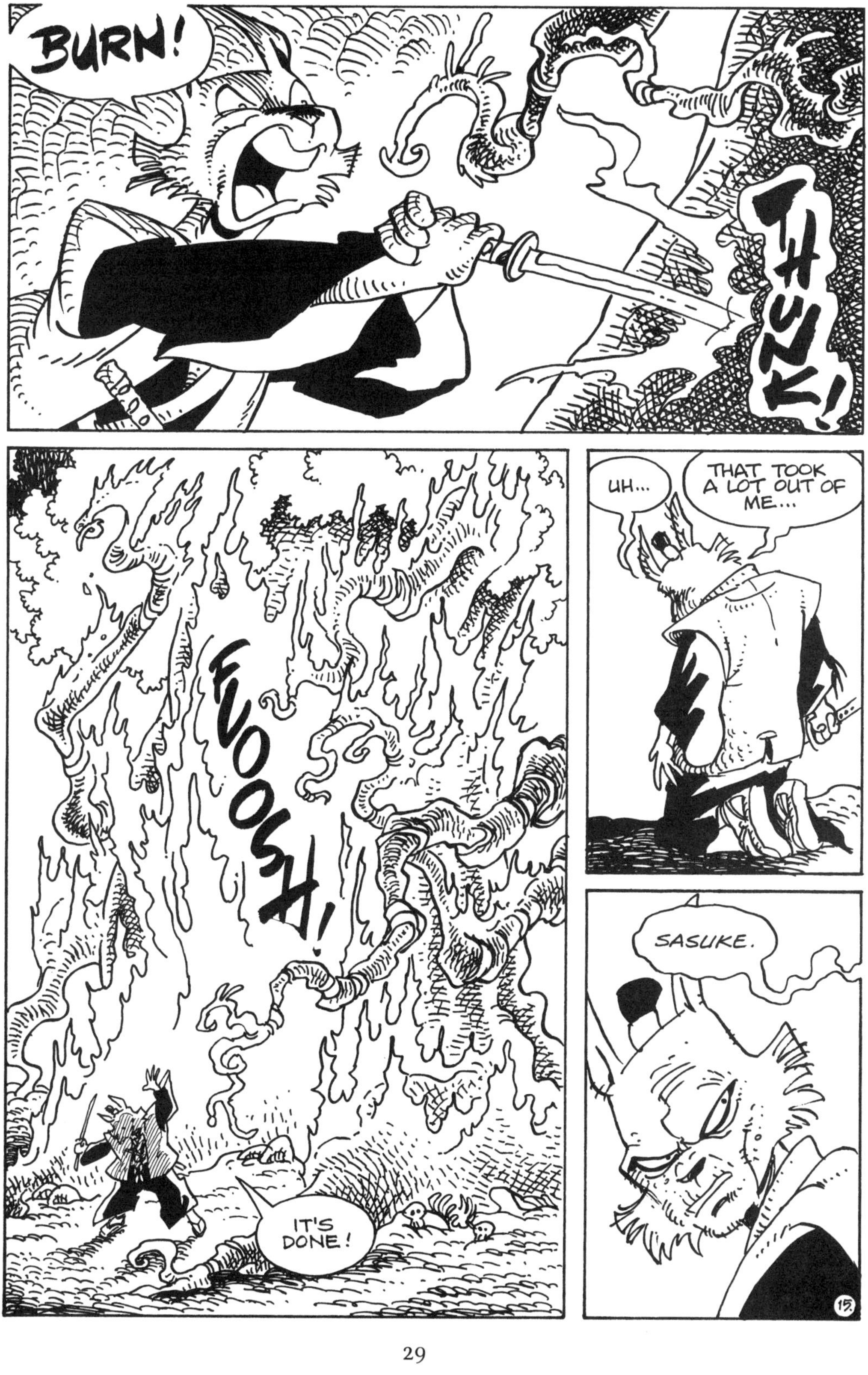

BURN!
THUNK!
FWOOSH!
IT'S DONE!
UH...
THAT TOOK A LOT OUT OF ME...
SASUKE.
15

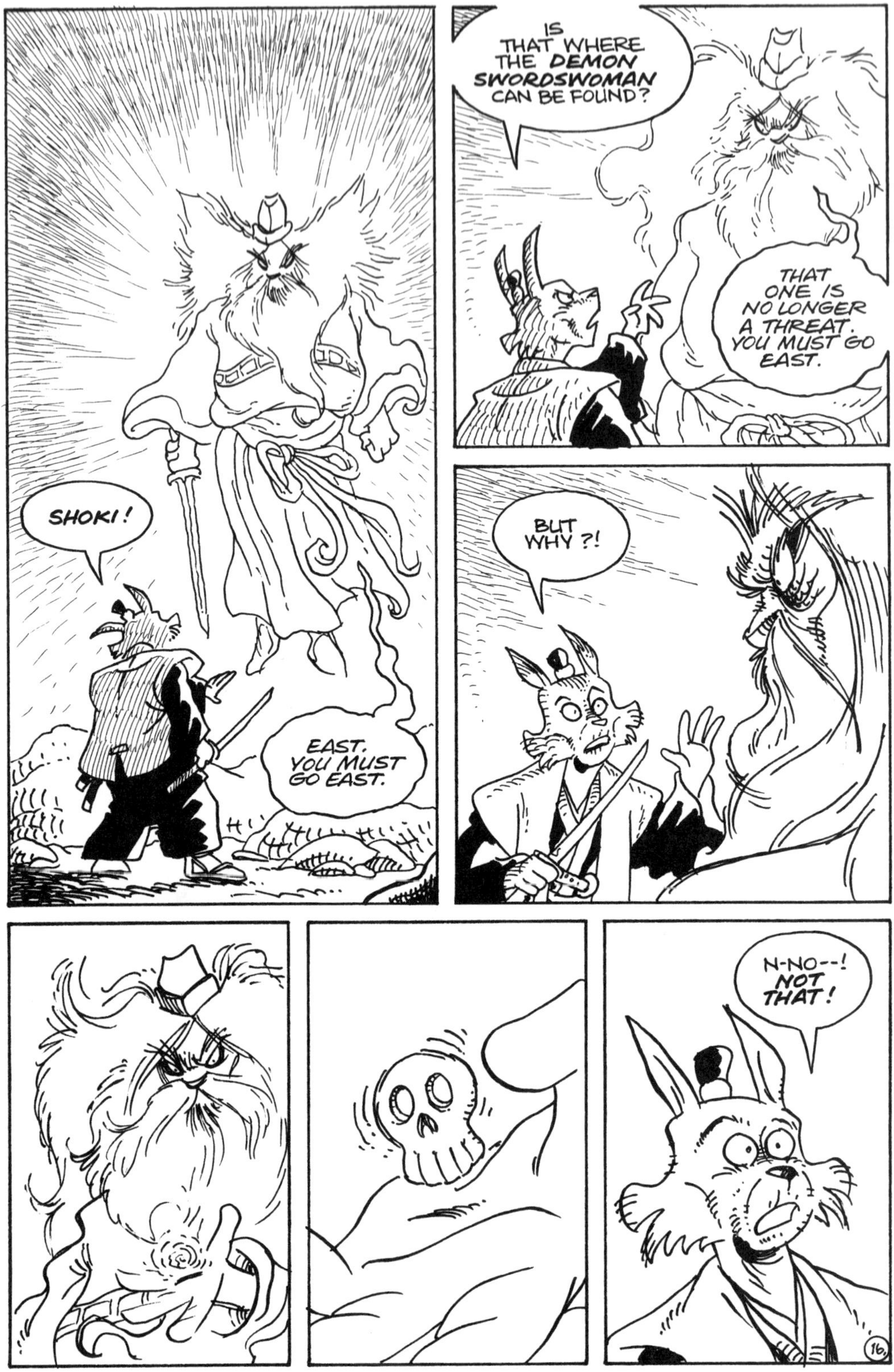
SHOKI!
EAST. YOU MUST GO EAST.
IS THAT WHERE THE **DEMON SWORDSWOMAN** CAN BE FOUND?
THAT ONE IS NO LONGER A THREAT. YOU MUST GO EAST.
BUT WHY?!
N-NO--! **NOT THAT!**
16

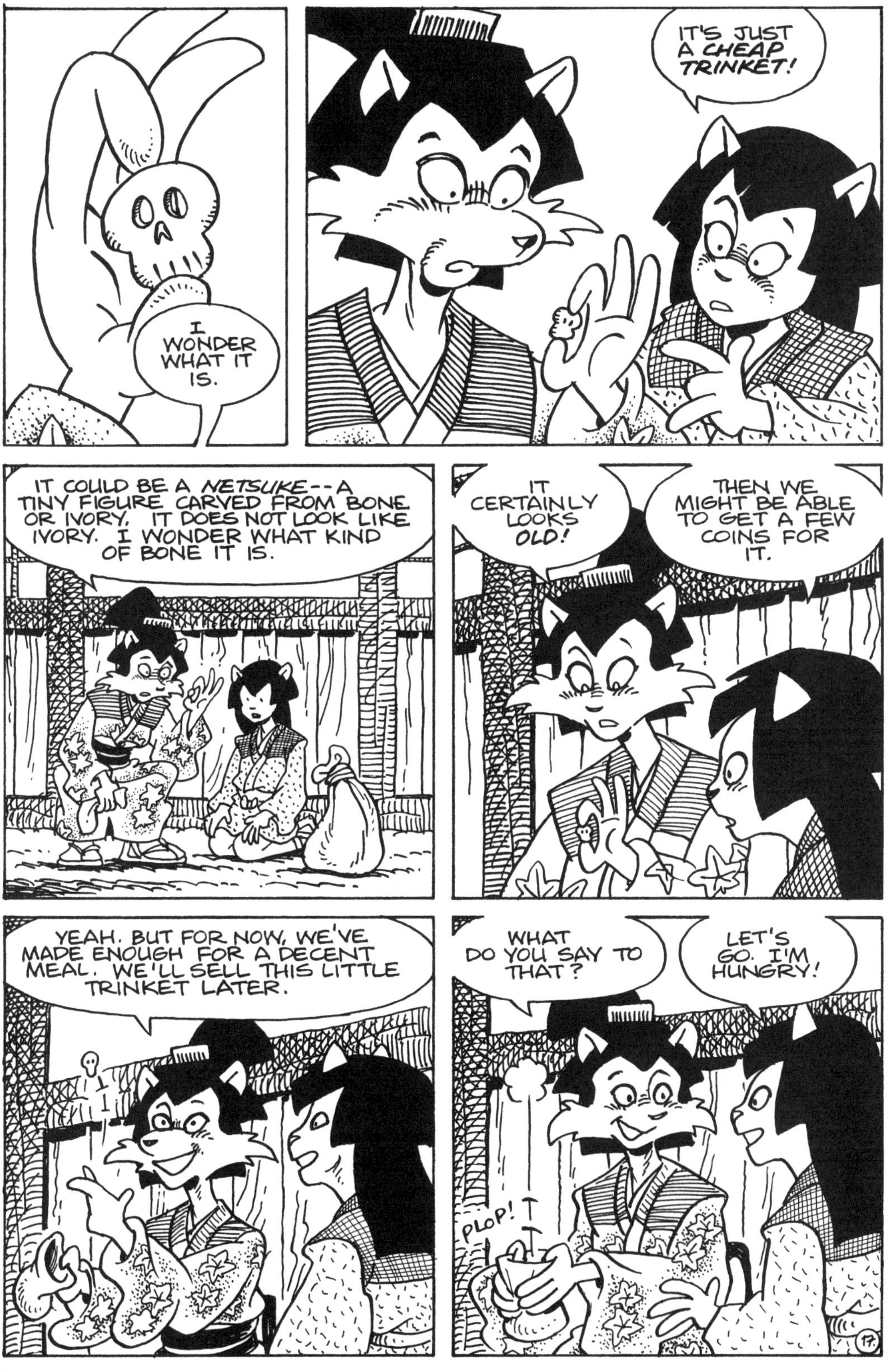
I WONDER WHAT IT IS.
IT'S JUST A *CHEAP TRINKET!*
IT COULD BE A *NETSUKE*--A TINY FIGURE CARVED FROM BONE OR IVORY. IT DOES NOT LOOK LIKE IVORY. I WONDER WHAT KIND OF BONE IT IS.
IT CERTAINLY LOOKS *OLD!*
THEN WE MIGHT BE ABLE TO GET A FEW COINS FOR IT.
YEAH. BUT FOR NOW, WE'VE MADE ENOUGH FOR A DECENT MEAL. WE'LL SELL THIS LITTLE TRINKET LATER.
WHAT DO YOU SAY TO THAT?
LET'S GO. I'M HUNGRY!
PLOP!
17.

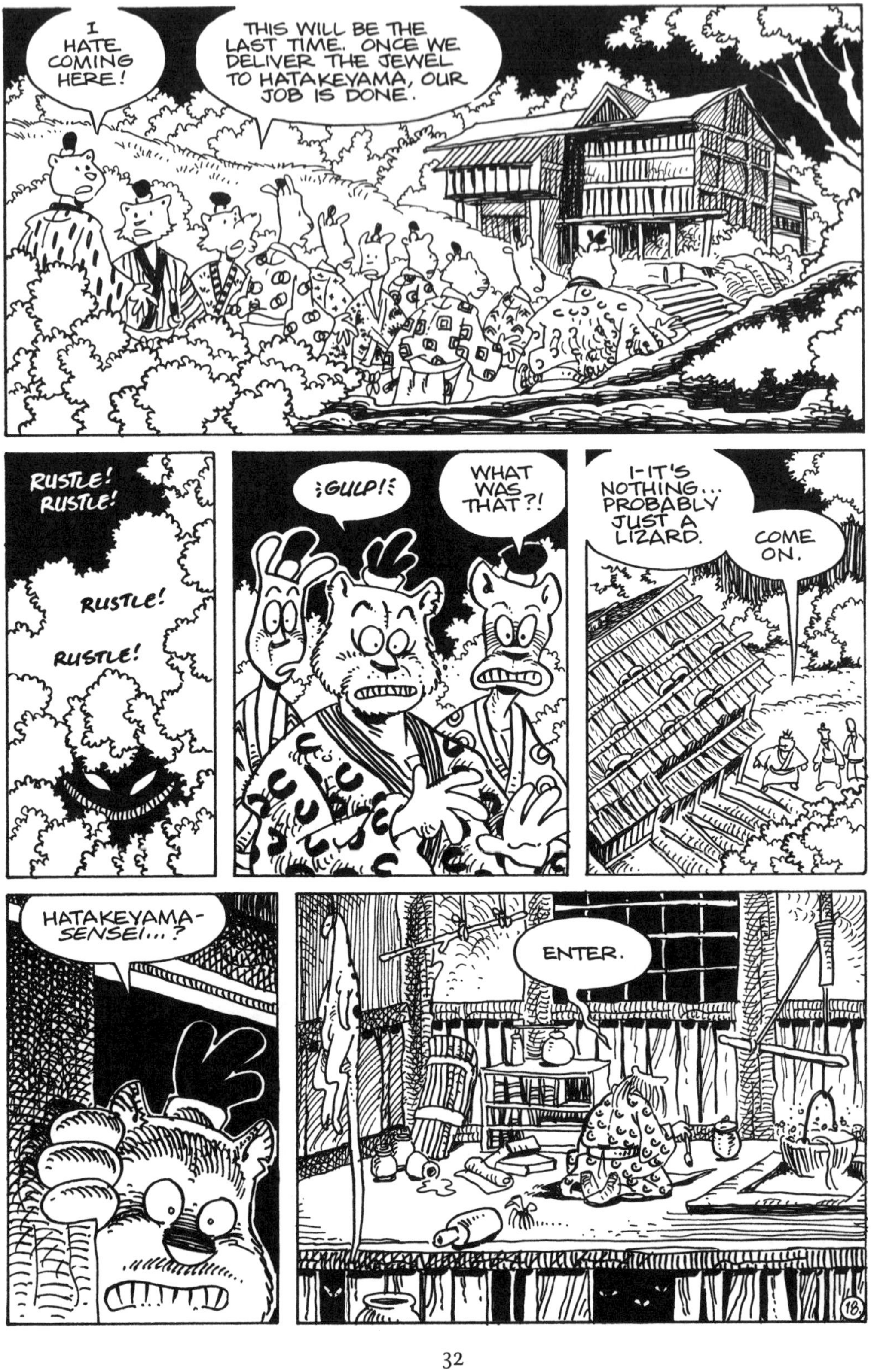

I HATE COMING HERE!
THIS WILL BE THE LAST TIME. ONCE WE DELIVER THE JEWEL TO HATAKEYAMA, OUR JOB IS DONE.
RUSTLE! RUSTLE!
RUSTLE!
RUSTLE!
GULP!
WHAT WAS THAT?!
I-IT'S NOTHING... PROBABLY JUST A LIZARD.
COME ON.
HATAKEYAMA-SENSEI...?
ENTER.
18.

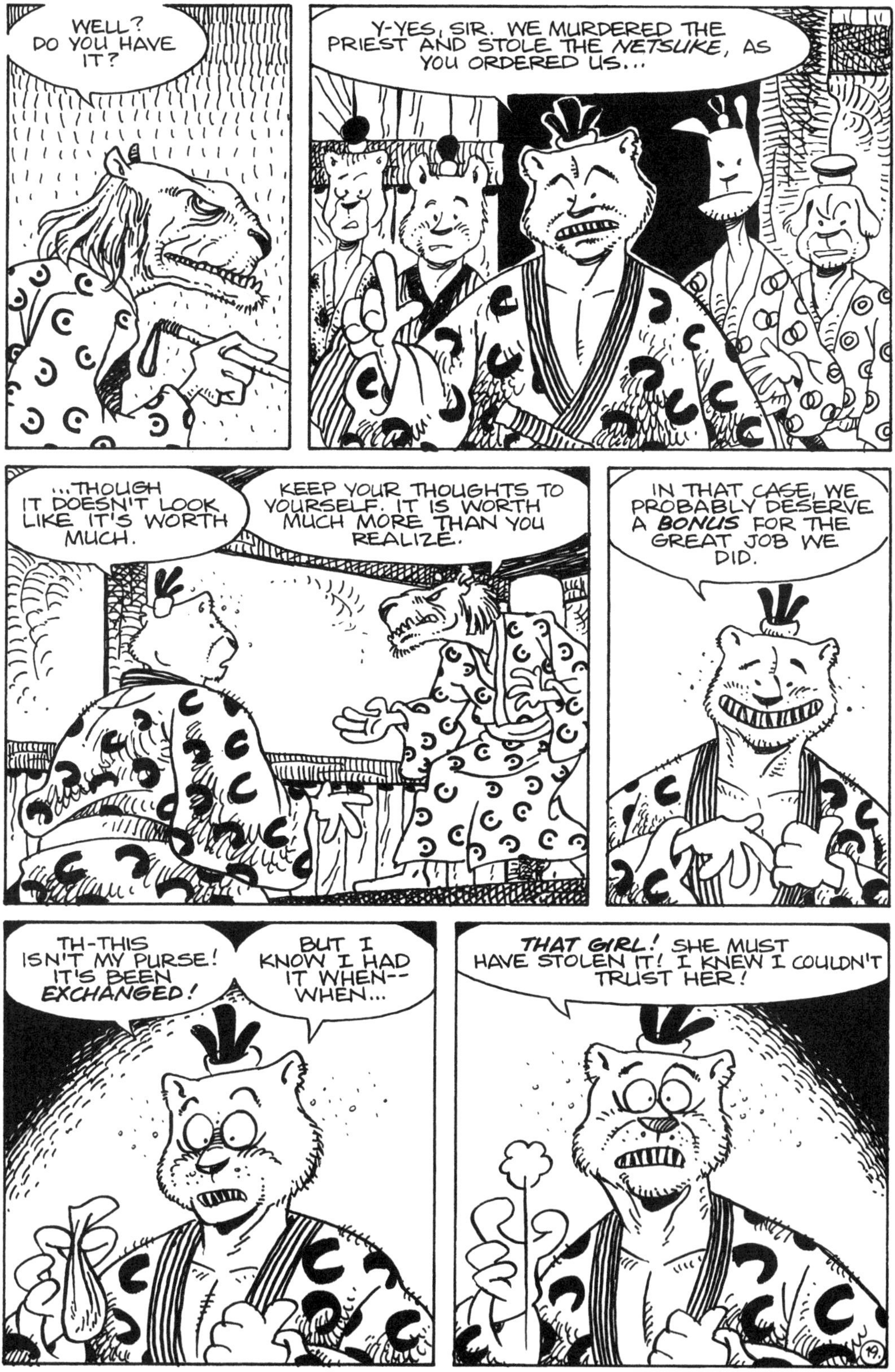
WELL? DO YOU HAVE IT?
Y-YES, SIR. WE MURDERED THE PRIEST AND STOLE THE *NETSUKE*, AS YOU ORDERED US...
...THOUGH IT DOESN'T LOOK LIKE IT'S WORTH MUCH.
KEEP YOUR THOUGHTS TO YOURSELF. IT IS WORTH MUCH MORE THAN YOU REALIZE.
IN THAT CASE, WE PROBABLY DESERVE A **BONUS** FOR THE GREAT JOB WE DID.
TH-THIS ISN'T MY PURSE! IT'S BEEN **EXCHANGED**!
BUT I KNOW I HAD IT WHEN-- WHEN...
THAT GIRL! SHE MUST HAVE STOLEN IT! I KNEW I COULDN'T TRUST HER!
19.

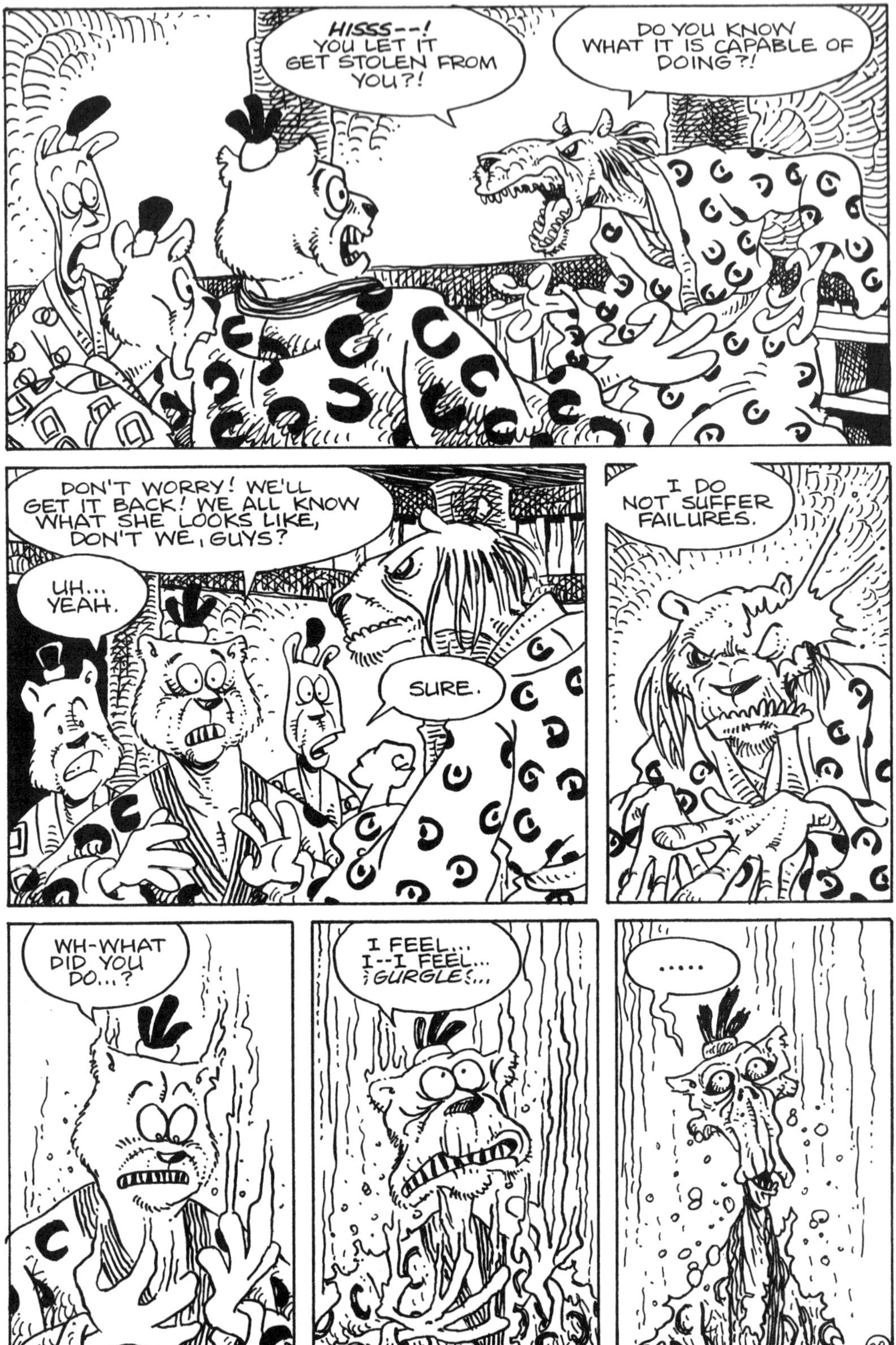
HISSS--! YOU LET IT GET STOLEN FROM YOU?!
DO YOU KNOW WHAT IT IS CAPABLE OF DOING?!
DON'T WORRY! WE'LL GET IT BACK! WE ALL KNOW WHAT SHE LOOKS LIKE, DON'T WE, GUYS?
UH... YEAH.
SURE.
I DO NOT SUFFER FAILURES.
WH-WHAT DID YOU DO...?
I FEEL... I--I FEEL... ¿GURGLE¿...
.....
20.

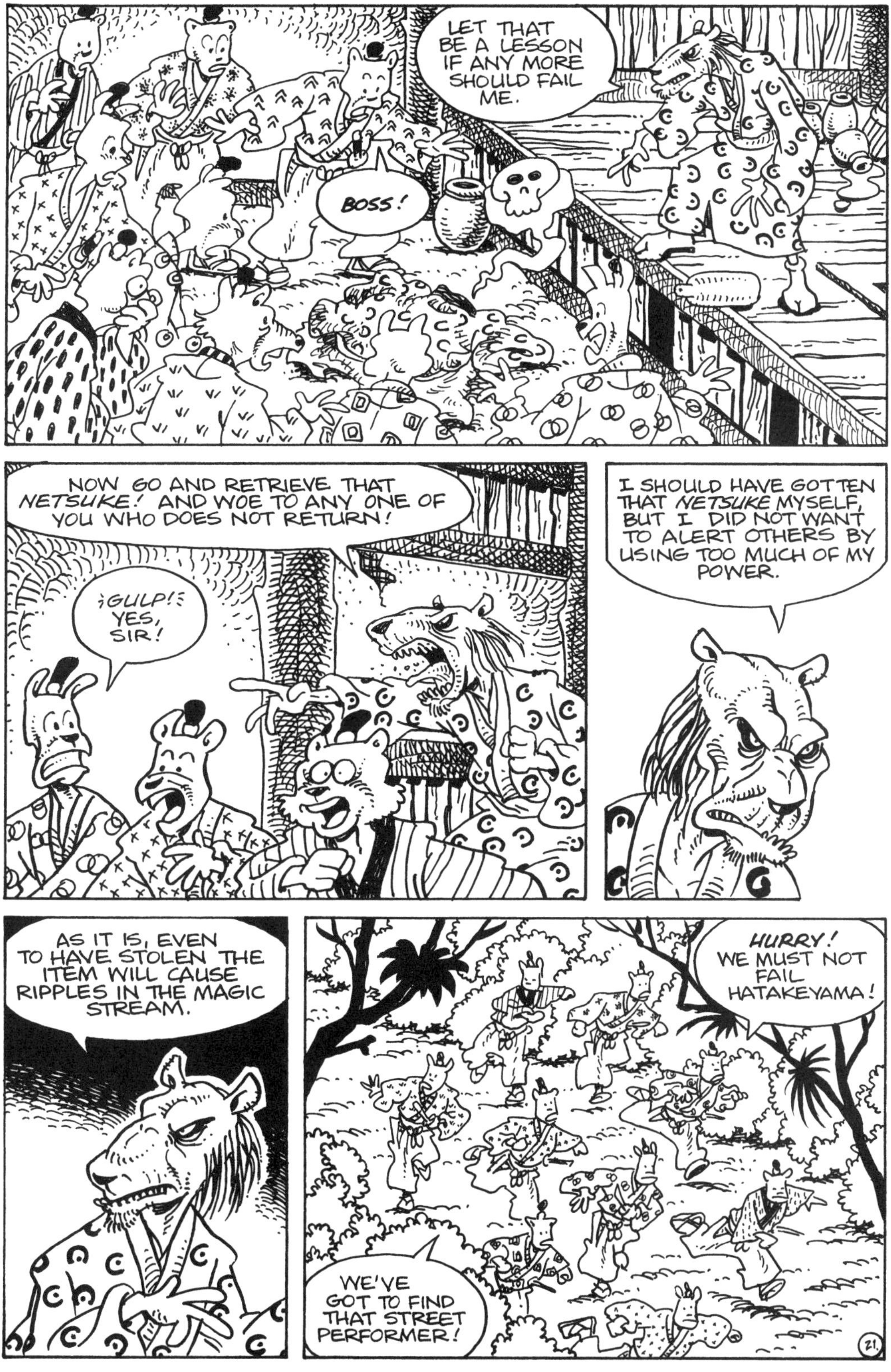
LET THAT BE A LESSON IF ANY MORE SHOULD FAIL ME.
BOSS!
NOW GO AND RETRIEVE THAT NETSUKE! AND WOE TO ANY ONE OF YOU WHO DOES NOT RETURN!
GULP! YES, SIR!
I SHOULD HAVE GOTTEN THAT NETSUKE MYSELF, BUT I DID NOT WANT TO ALERT OTHERS BY USING TOO MUCH OF MY POWER.
AS IT IS, EVEN TO HAVE STOLEN THE ITEM WILL CAUSE RIPPLES IN THE MAGIC STREAM.
HURRY! WE MUST NOT FAIL HATAKEYAMA!
WE'VE GOT TO FIND THAT STREET PERFORMER!
21.

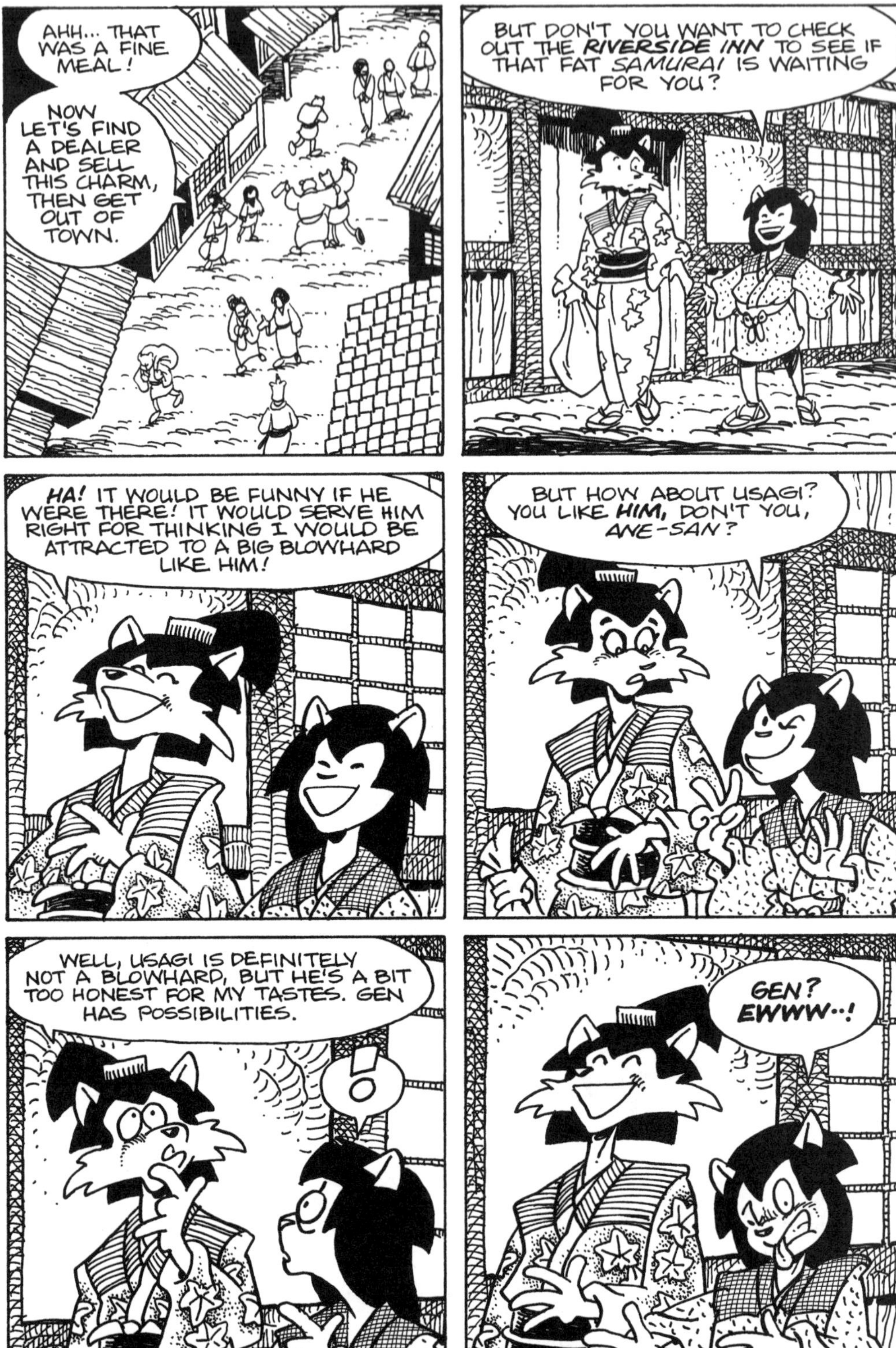
AHH... THAT WAS A FINE MEAL!
NOW LET'S FIND A DEALER AND SELL THIS CHARM, THEN GET OUT OF TOWN.
BUT DON'T YOU WANT TO CHECK OUT THE RIVERSIDE INN TO SEE IF THAT FAT SAMURAI IS WAITING FOR YOU?
HA! IT WOULD BE FUNNY IF HE WERE THERE! IT WOULD SERVE HIM RIGHT FOR THINKING I WOULD BE ATTRACTED TO A BIG BLOWHARD LIKE HIM!
BUT HOW ABOUT USAGI? YOU LIKE HIM, DON'T YOU, ANE-SAN?
WELL, USAGI IS DEFINITELY NOT A BLOWHARD, BUT HE'S A BIT TOO HONEST FOR MY TASTES. GEN HAS POSSIBILITIES.
!
GEN? EWWW..!
22.

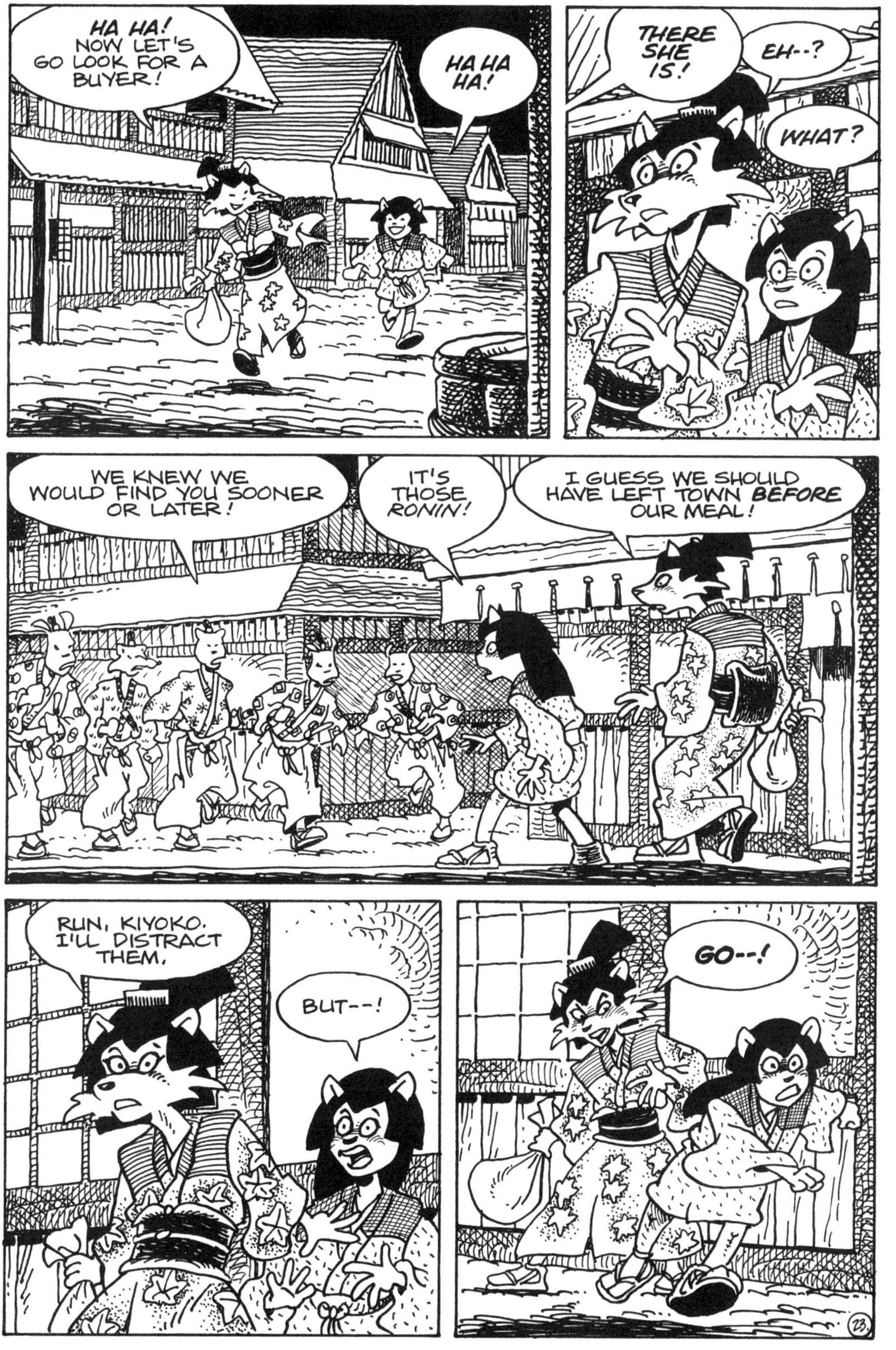
HA HA! NOW LET'S GO LOOK FOR A BUYER!
HA HA HA!
THERE SHE IS!
EH--?
WHAT?
WE KNEW WE WOULD FIND YOU SOONER OR LATER!
IT'S THOSE RONIN!
I GUESS WE SHOULD HAVE LEFT TOWN BEFORE OUR MEAL!
RUN, KIYOKO. I'LL DISTRACT THEM.
BUT--!
GO--!
23

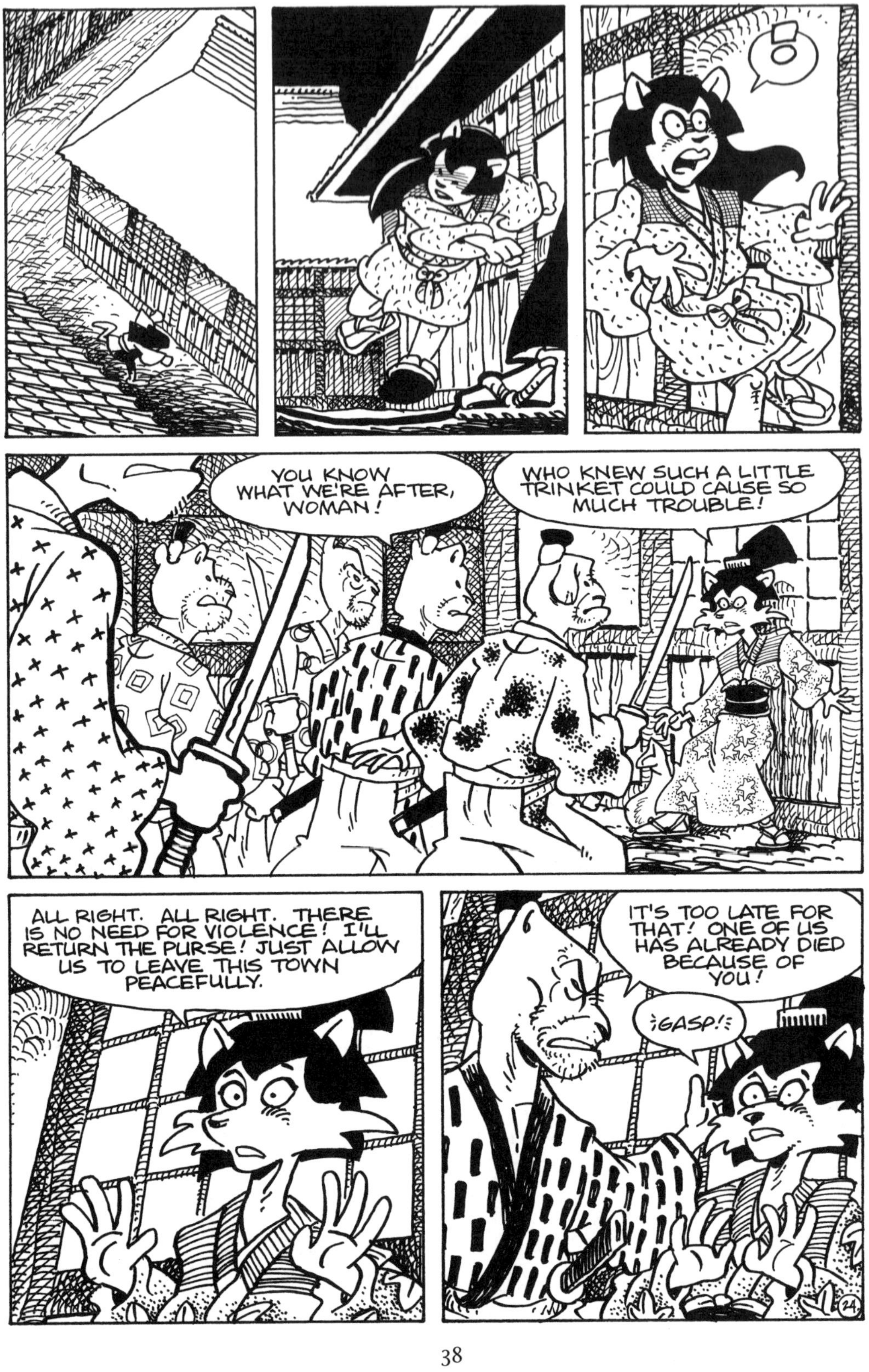
!
YOU KNOW WHAT WE'RE AFTER, WOMAN!
WHO KNEW SUCH A LITTLE TRINKET COULD CAUSE SO MUCH TROUBLE!
ALL RIGHT. ALL RIGHT. THERE IS NO NEED FOR VIOLENCE! I'LL RETURN THE PURSE! JUST ALLOW US TO LEAVE THIS TOWN PEACEFULLY.
IT'S TOO LATE FOR THAT! ONE OF US HAS ALREADY DIED BECAUSE OF YOU!
¡GASP!¡

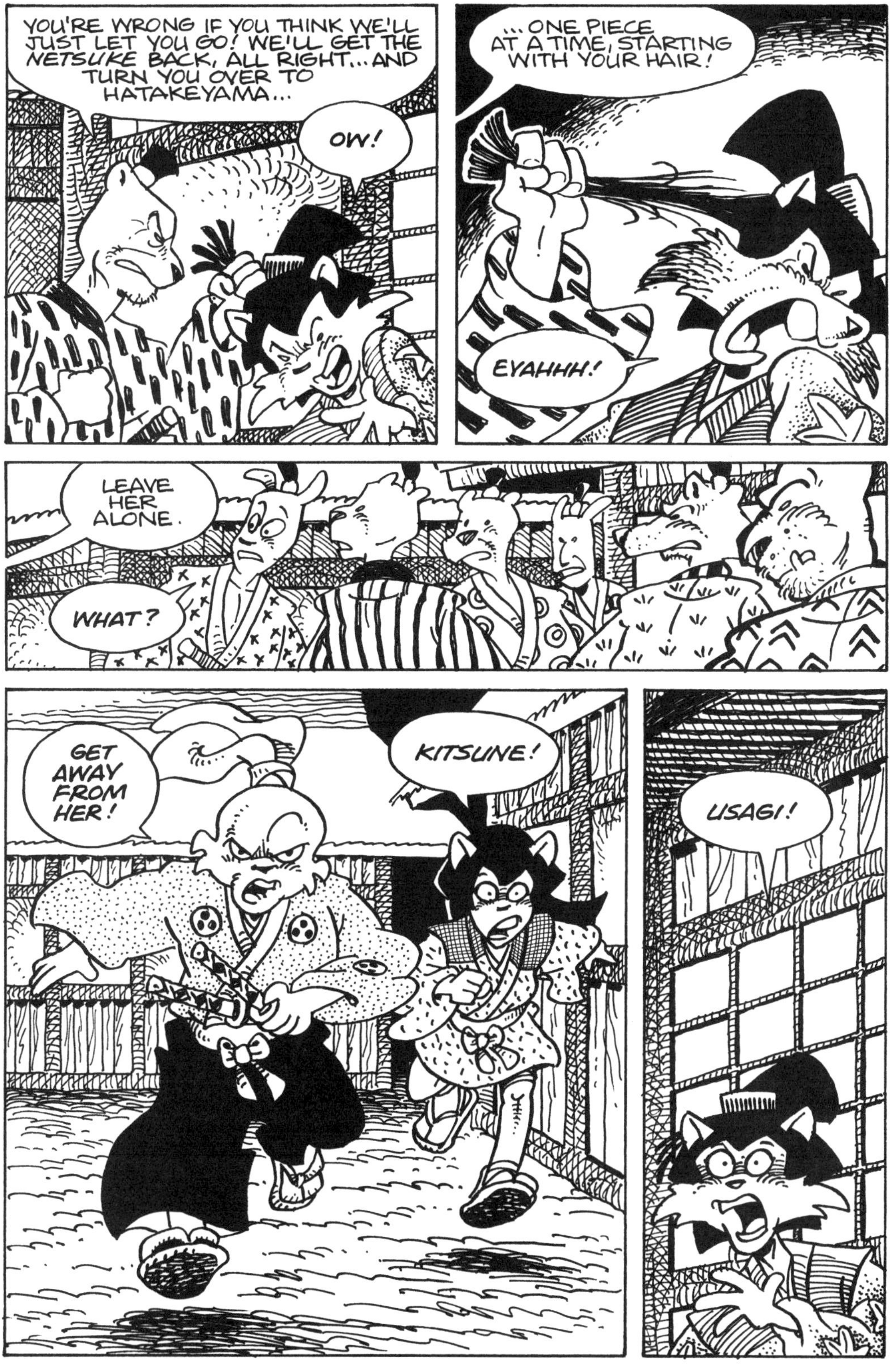
YOU'RE WRONG IF YOU THINK WE'LL JUST LET YOU GO! WE'LL GET THE NETSUKE BACK, ALL RIGHT... AND TURN YOU OVER TO HATAKEYAMA...
OW!
...ONE PIECE AT A TIME, STARTING WITH YOUR HAIR!
EYAHHH!
LEAVE HER ALONE.
WHAT?
GET AWAY FROM HER!
KITSUNE!
USAGI!

TRAITORS OF THE EARTH PART TWO

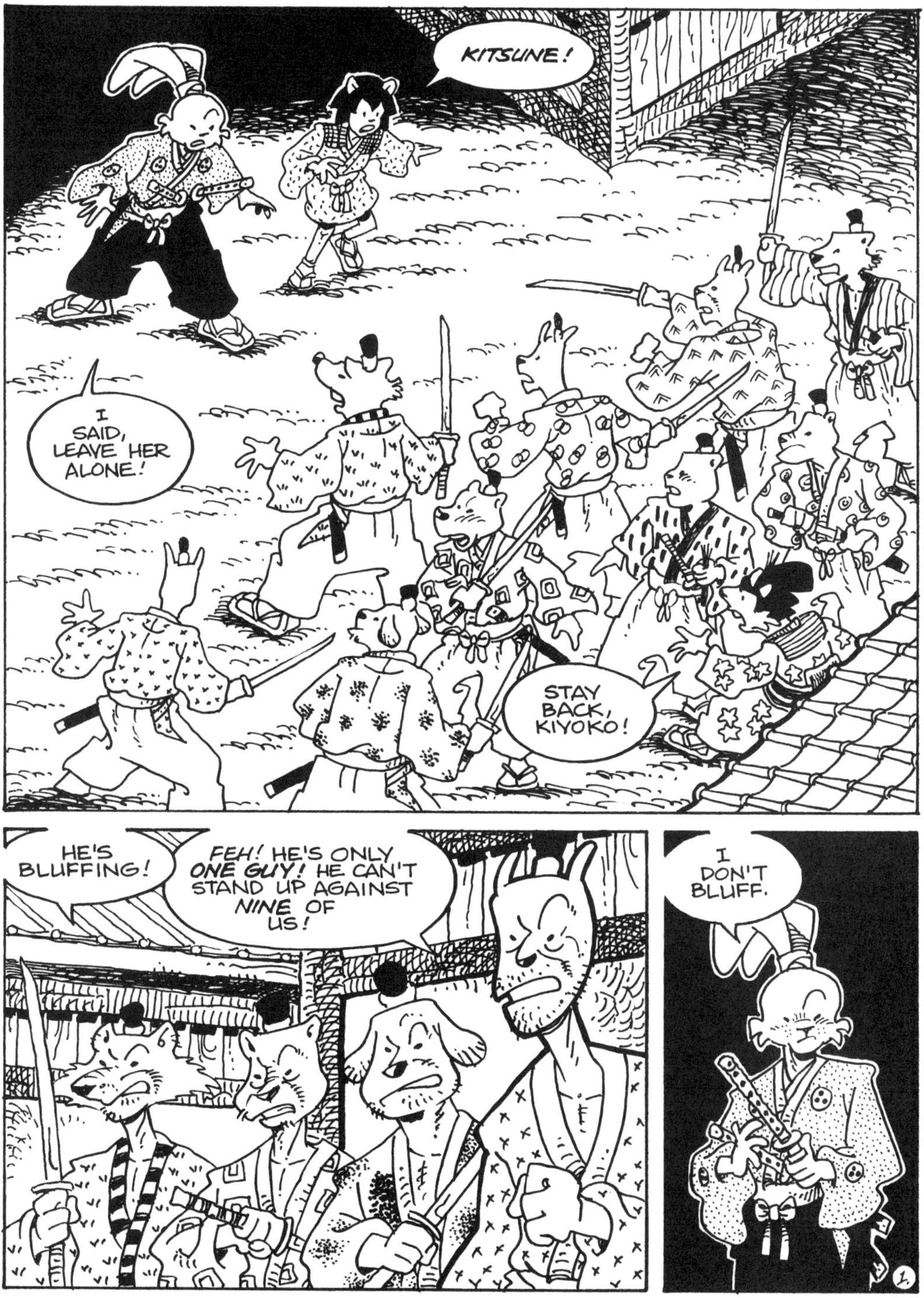
KITSUNE!
I SAID, LEAVE HER ALONE!
STAY BACK, KIYOKO!
HE'S BLUFFING!
FEH! HE'S ONLY ONE GUY! HE CAN'T STAND UP AGAINST NINE OF US!
I DON'T BLUFF.

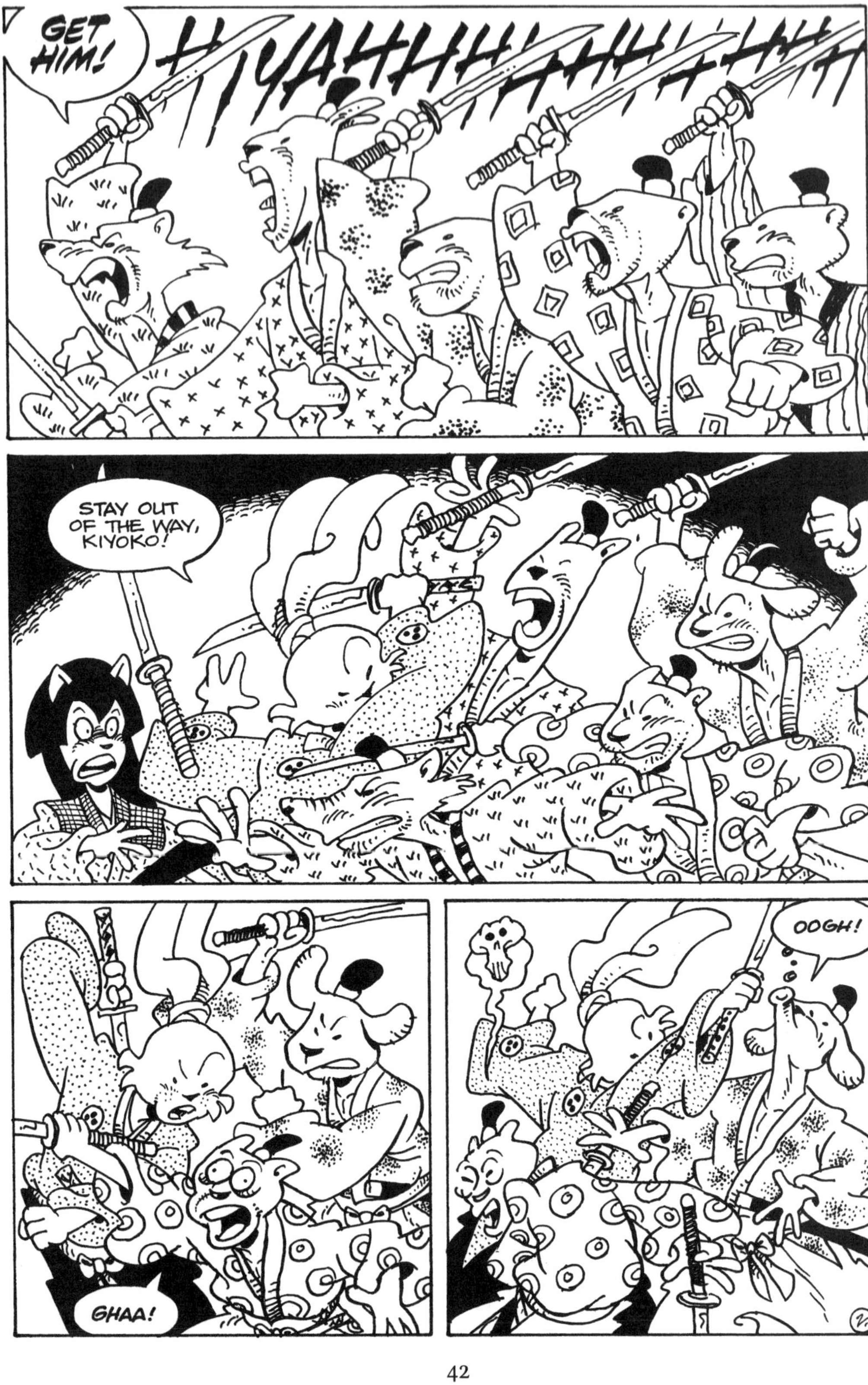

GET HIM!
HIYAHHHHHHHHHHHH
STAY OUT OF THE WAY, KIYOKO!
GHAA!
OOGH!

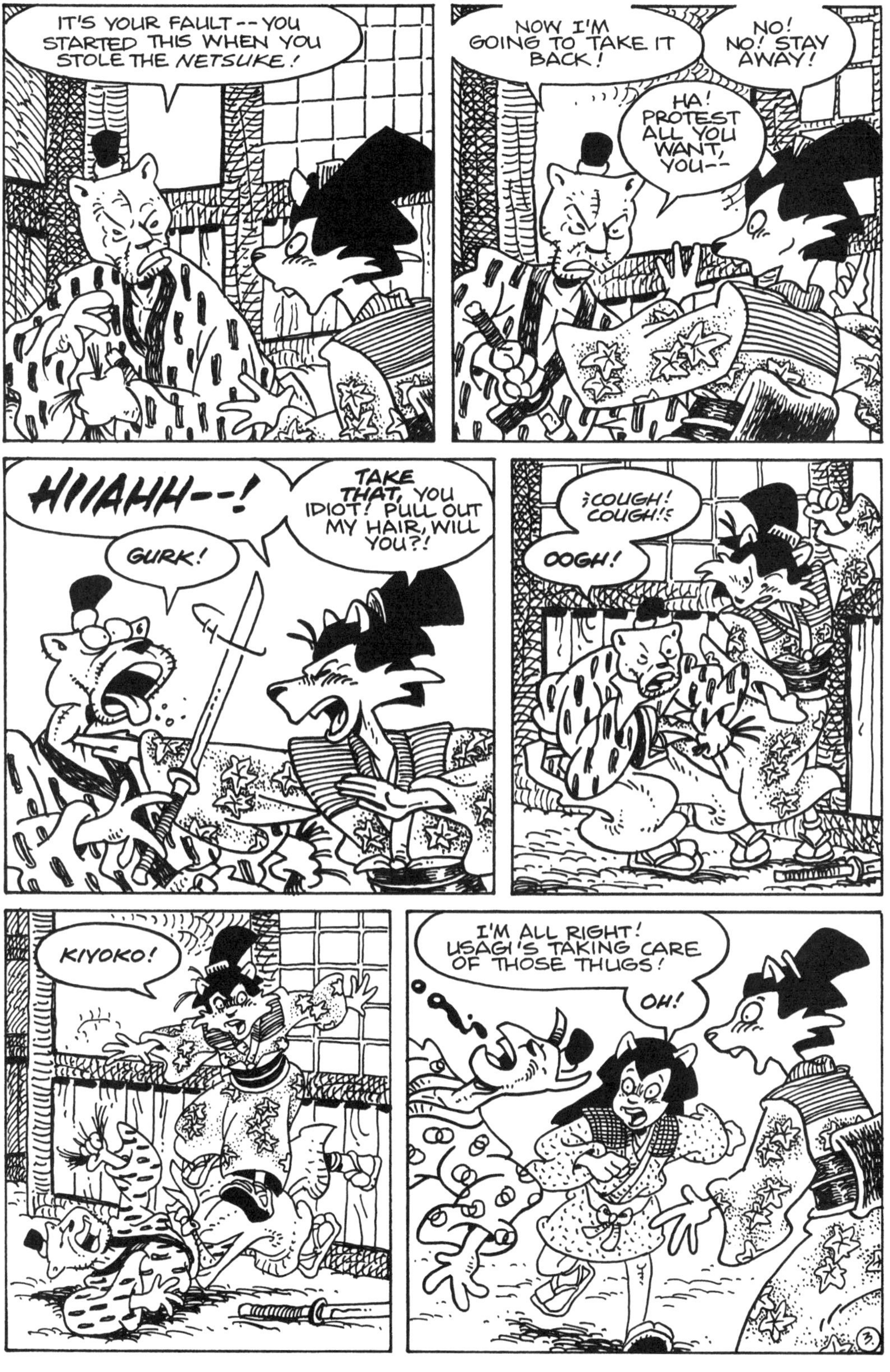
IT'S YOUR FAULT -- YOU STARTED THIS WHEN YOU STOLE THE NETSUKE!
NOW I'M GOING TO TAKE IT BACK!
NO! NO! STAY AWAY!
HA! PROTEST ALL YOU WANT, YOU--
HIIAHH--!
TAKE THAT, YOU IDIOT! PULL OUT MY HAIR, WILL YOU?!
GURK!
COUGH! COUGH!
OOGH!
KIYOKO!
I'M ALL RIGHT! USAGI'S TAKING CARE OF THOSE THUGS!
OH!
3.

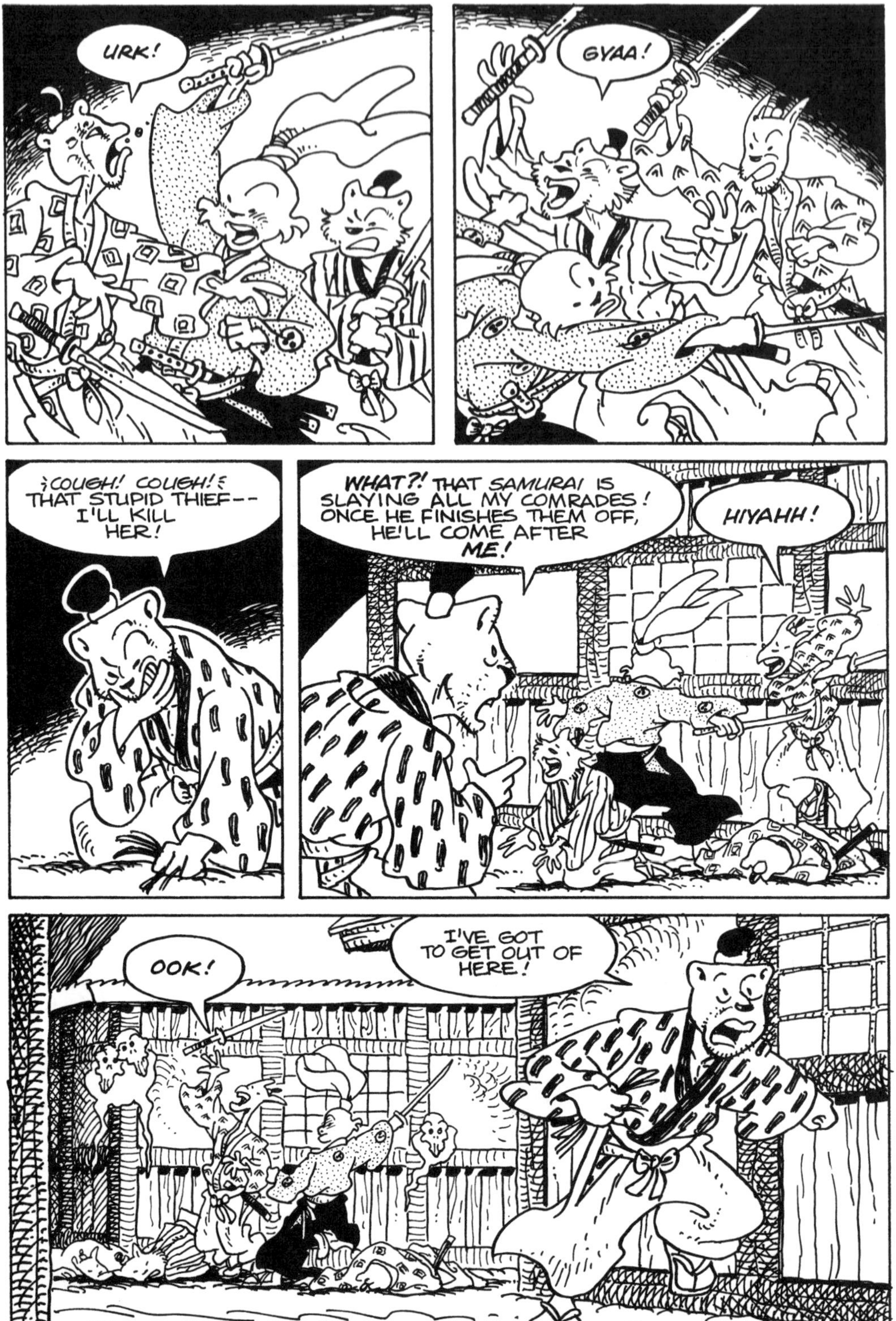
URK!
GYAA!
COUGH! COUGH! THAT STUPID THIEF-- I'LL KILL HER!
WHAT?! THAT SAMURAI IS SLAYING ALL MY COMRADES! ONCE HE FINISHES THEM OFF, HE'LL COME AFTER ME!
HIYAHH!
OOK!
I'VE GOT TO GET OUT OF HERE!
4.

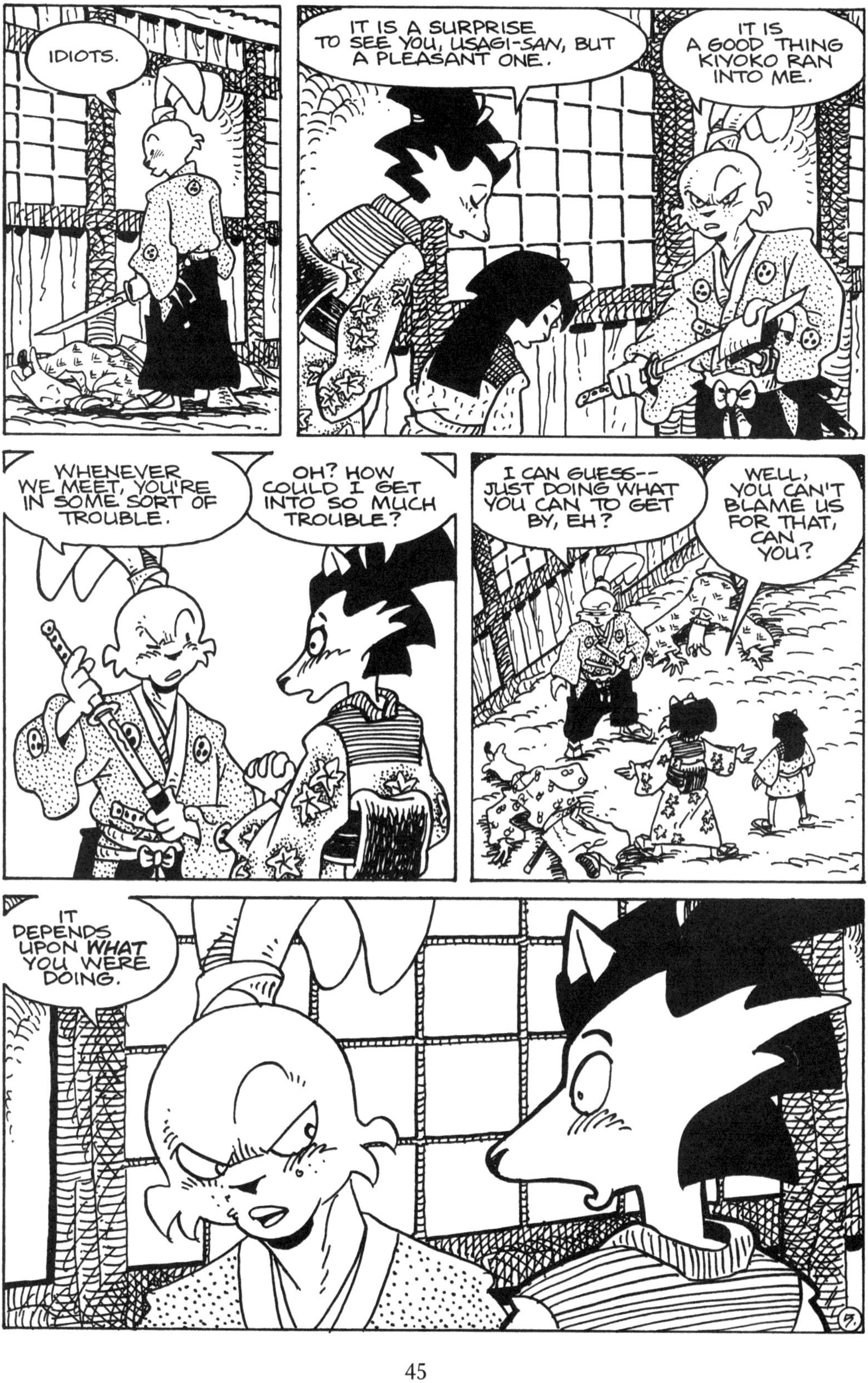
IDIOTS.
IT IS A SURPRISE TO SEE YOU, USAGI-SAN, BUT A PLEASANT ONE.
IT IS A GOOD THING KIYOKO RAN INTO ME.
WHENEVER WE MEET, YOU'RE IN SOME SORT OF TROUBLE.
OH? HOW COULD I GET INTO SO MUCH TROUBLE?
I CAN GUESS-- JUST DOING WHAT YOU CAN TO GET BY, EH?
WELL, YOU CAN'T BLAME US FOR THAT, CAN YOU?
IT DEPENDS UPON **WHAT** YOU WERE DOING.

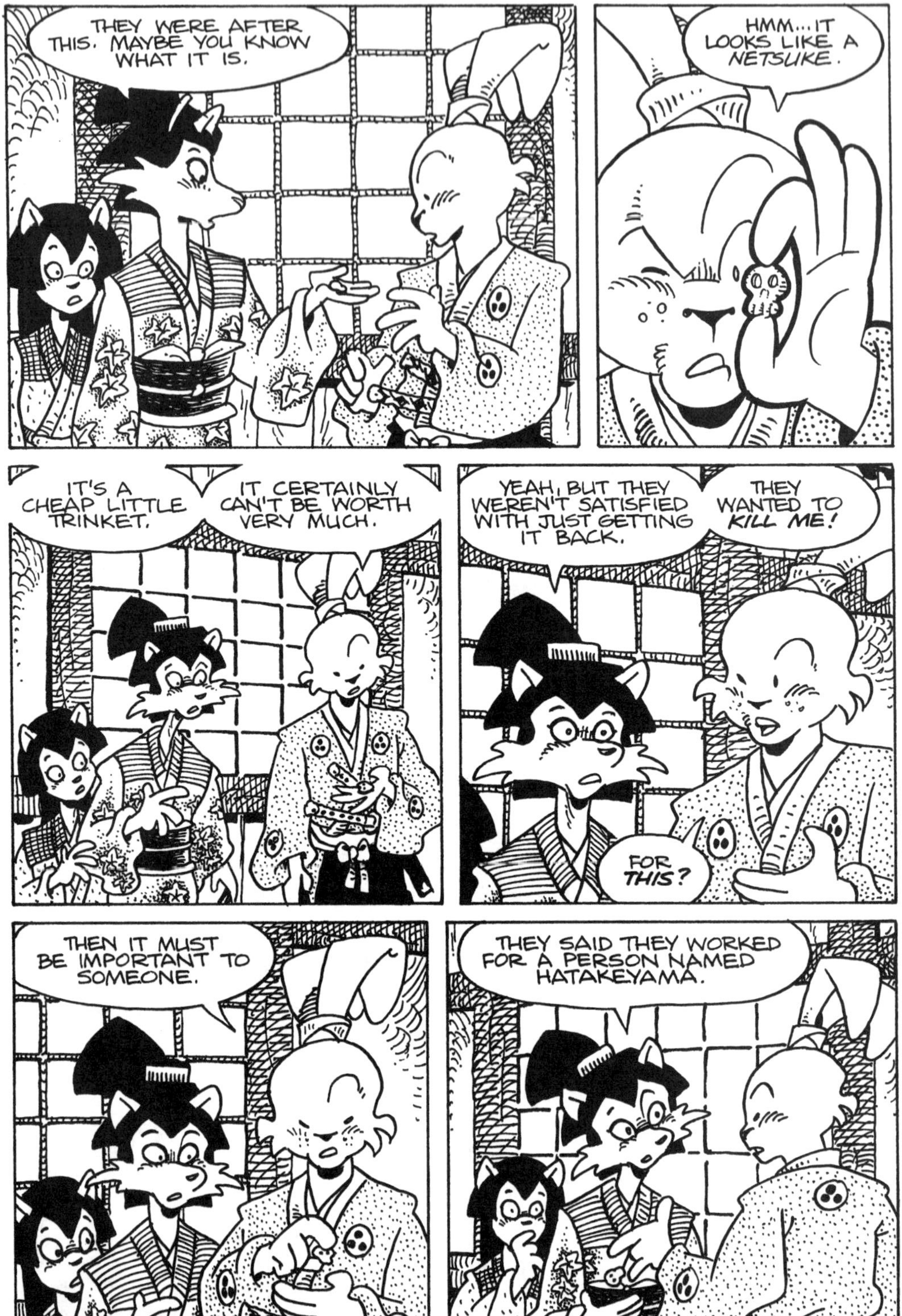
THEY WERE AFTER THIS. MAYBE YOU KNOW WHAT IT IS.
HMM... IT LOOKS LIKE A *NETSUKE*.
IT'S A CHEAP LITTLE TRINKET.
IT CERTAINLY CAN'T BE WORTH VERY MUCH.
YEAH, BUT THEY WEREN'T SATISFIED WITH JUST GETTING IT BACK.
THEY WANTED TO ***KILL ME!***
FOR ***THIS?***
THEN IT MUST BE IMPORTANT TO SOMEONE.
THEY SAID THEY WORKED FOR A PERSON NAMED HATAKEYAMA.
6.

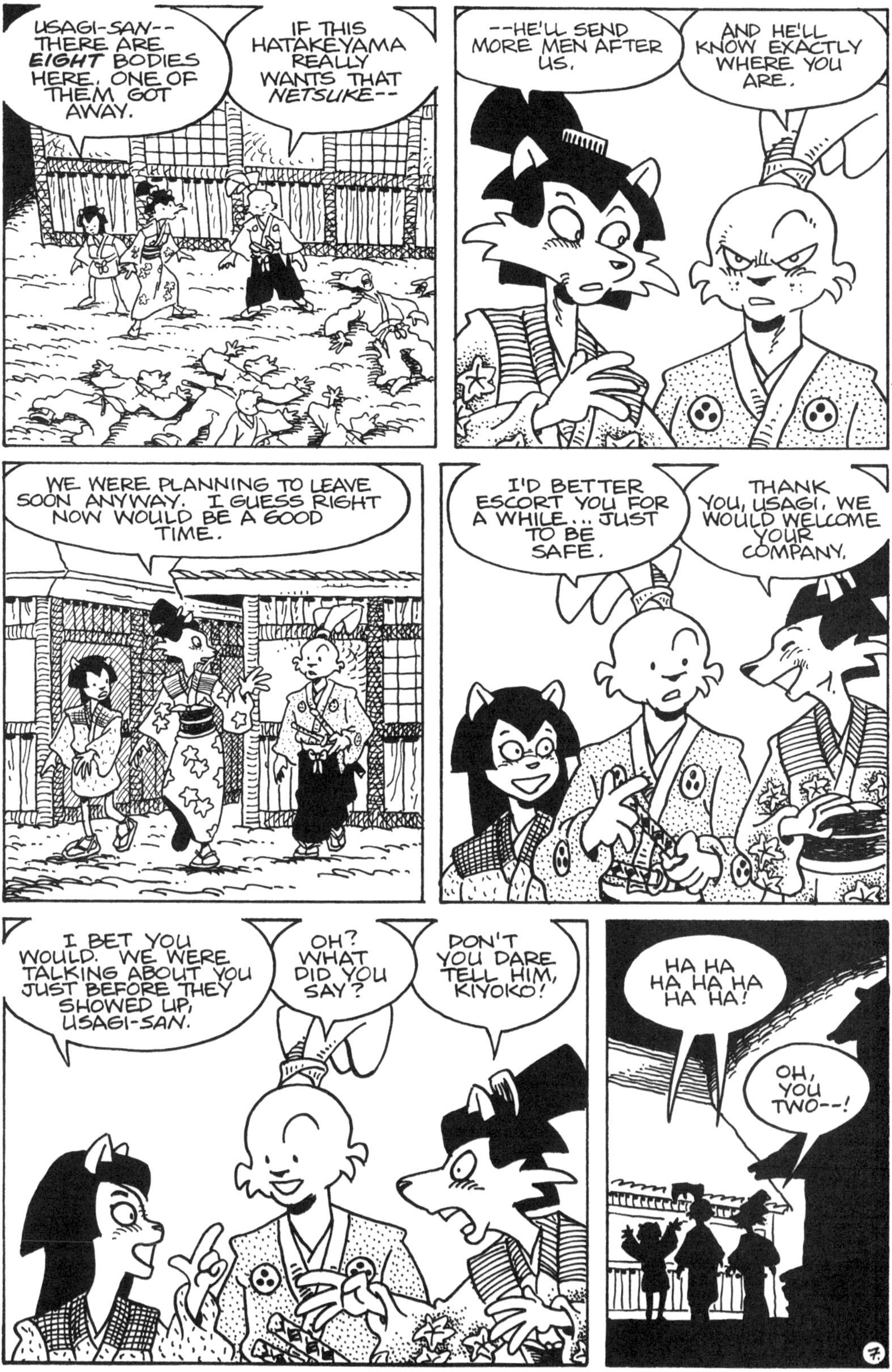
USAGI-SAN--THERE ARE EIGHT BODIES HERE. ONE OF THEM GOT AWAY.
IF THIS HATAKEYAMA REALLY WANTS THAT NETSUKE--
--HE'LL SEND MORE MEN AFTER US.
AND HE'LL KNOW EXACTLY WHERE YOU ARE.
WE WERE PLANNING TO LEAVE SOON ANYWAY. I GUESS RIGHT NOW WOULD BE A GOOD TIME.
I'D BETTER ESCORT YOU FOR A WHILE... JUST TO BE SAFE.
THANK YOU, USAGI. WE WOULD WELCOME YOUR COMPANY.
I BET YOU WOULD. WE WERE TALKING ABOUT YOU JUST BEFORE THEY SHOWED UP, USAGI-SAN.
OH? WHAT DID YOU SAY?
DON'T YOU DARE TELL HIM, KIYOKO!
HA HA HA HA HA HA HA!
OH, YOU TWO--!
7.

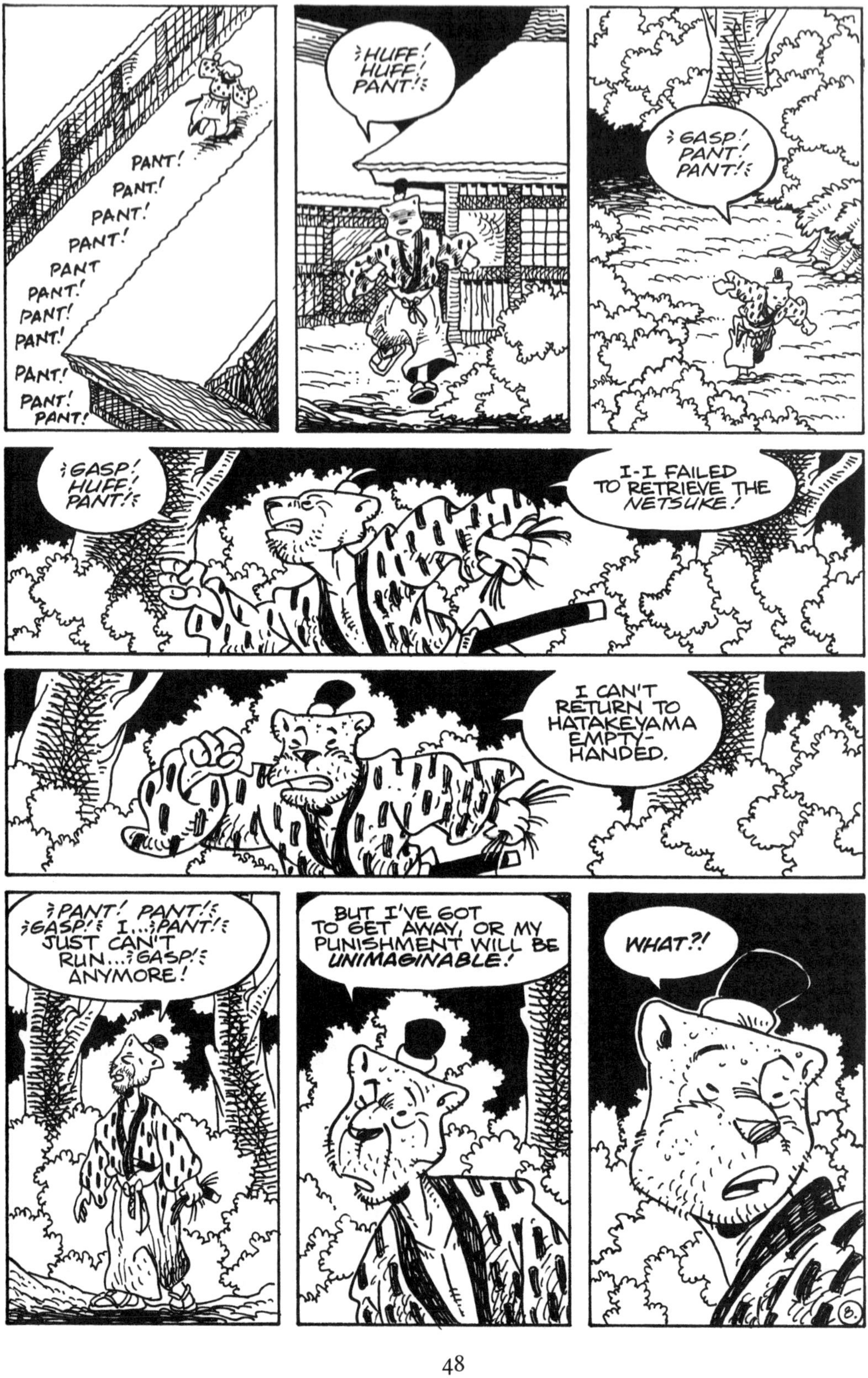

PANT! PANT! PANT! PANT! PANT PANT! PANT! PANT! PANT! PANT! PANT!
HUFF! HUFF! PANT!
GASP! PANT! PANT!
GASP! HUFF! PANT!
I-I FAILED TO RETRIEVE THE NETSUKE!
I CAN'T RETURN TO HATAKEYAMA EMPTY-HANDED.
PANT! PANT! GASP! I... PANT! JUST CAN'T RUN... GASP! ANYMORE!
BUT I'VE GOT TO GET AWAY, OR MY PUNISHMENT WILL BE UNIMAGINABLE!
WHAT?!
8.

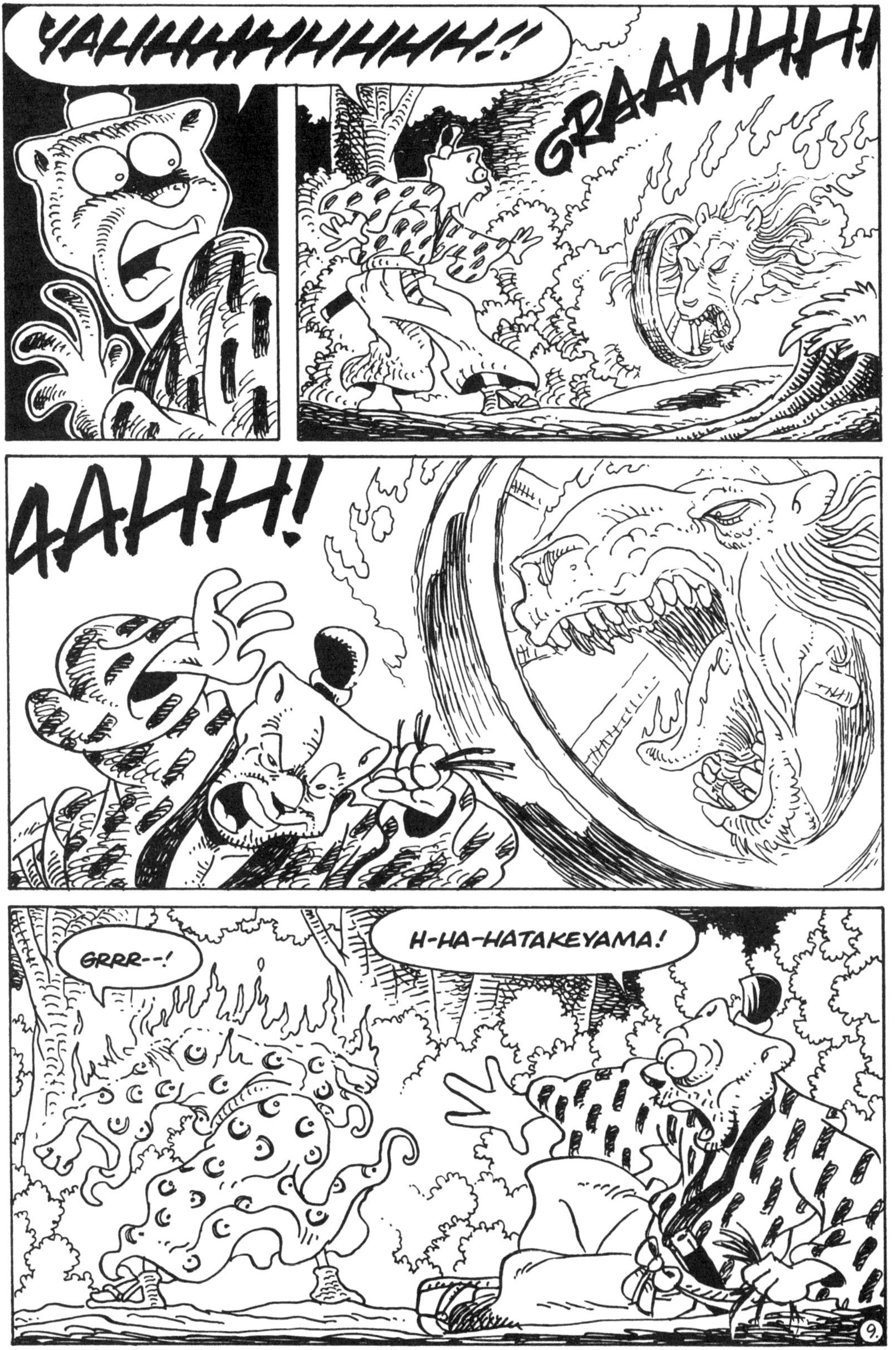
YAIIIIIIIIIIIIIIIH--!!
GRAAHHHH
AAHH!
GRRR--!
H-HA-HATAKEYAMA!
9.

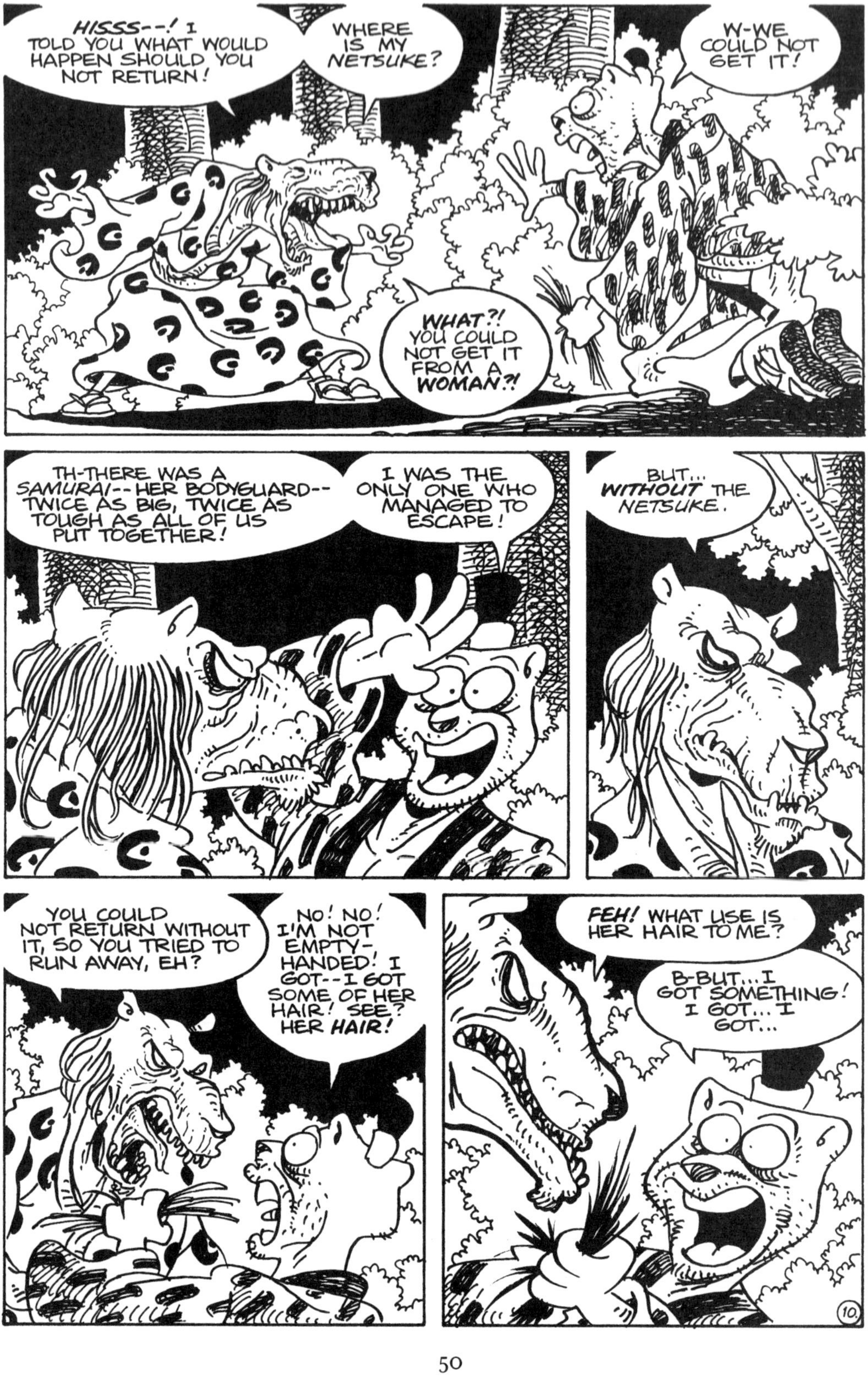
HISSS--! I TOLD YOU WHAT WOULD HAPPEN SHOULD YOU NOT RETURN!
WHERE IS MY NETSUKE?
W-WE COULD NOT GET IT!
WHAT?! YOU COULD NOT GET IT FROM A WOMAN?!
TH-THERE WAS A SAMURAI--HER BODYGUARD--TWICE AS BIG, TWICE AS TOUGH AS ALL OF US PUT TOGETHER!
I WAS THE ONLY ONE WHO MANAGED TO ESCAPE!
BUT... WITHOUT THE NETSUKE.
YOU COULD NOT RETURN WITHOUT IT, SO YOU TRIED TO RUN AWAY, EH?
NO! NO! I'M NOT EMPTY-HANDED! I GOT--I GOT SOME OF HER HAIR! SEE? HER HAIR!
FEH! WHAT USE IS HER HAIR TO ME?
B-BUT... I GOT SOMETHING! I GOT... I GOT...
10

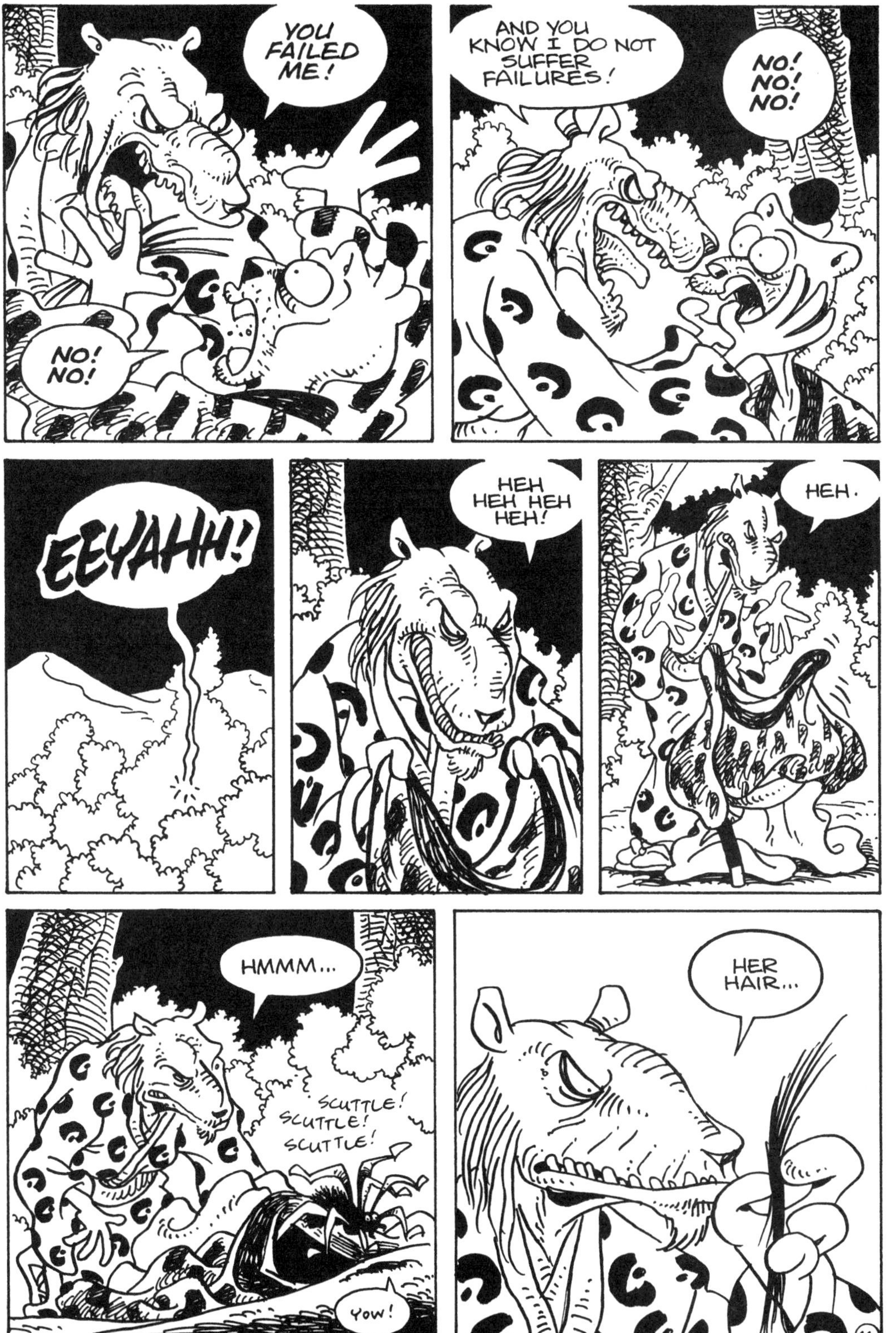
YOU FAILED ME!
NO! NO!
AND YOU KNOW I DO NOT SUFFER FAILURES!
NO! NO! NO!
EEYAHH!
HEH HEH HEH HEH!
HEH.
HMMM...
SCUTTLE! SCUTTLE! SCUTTLE!
YOW!
HER HAIR...
11.

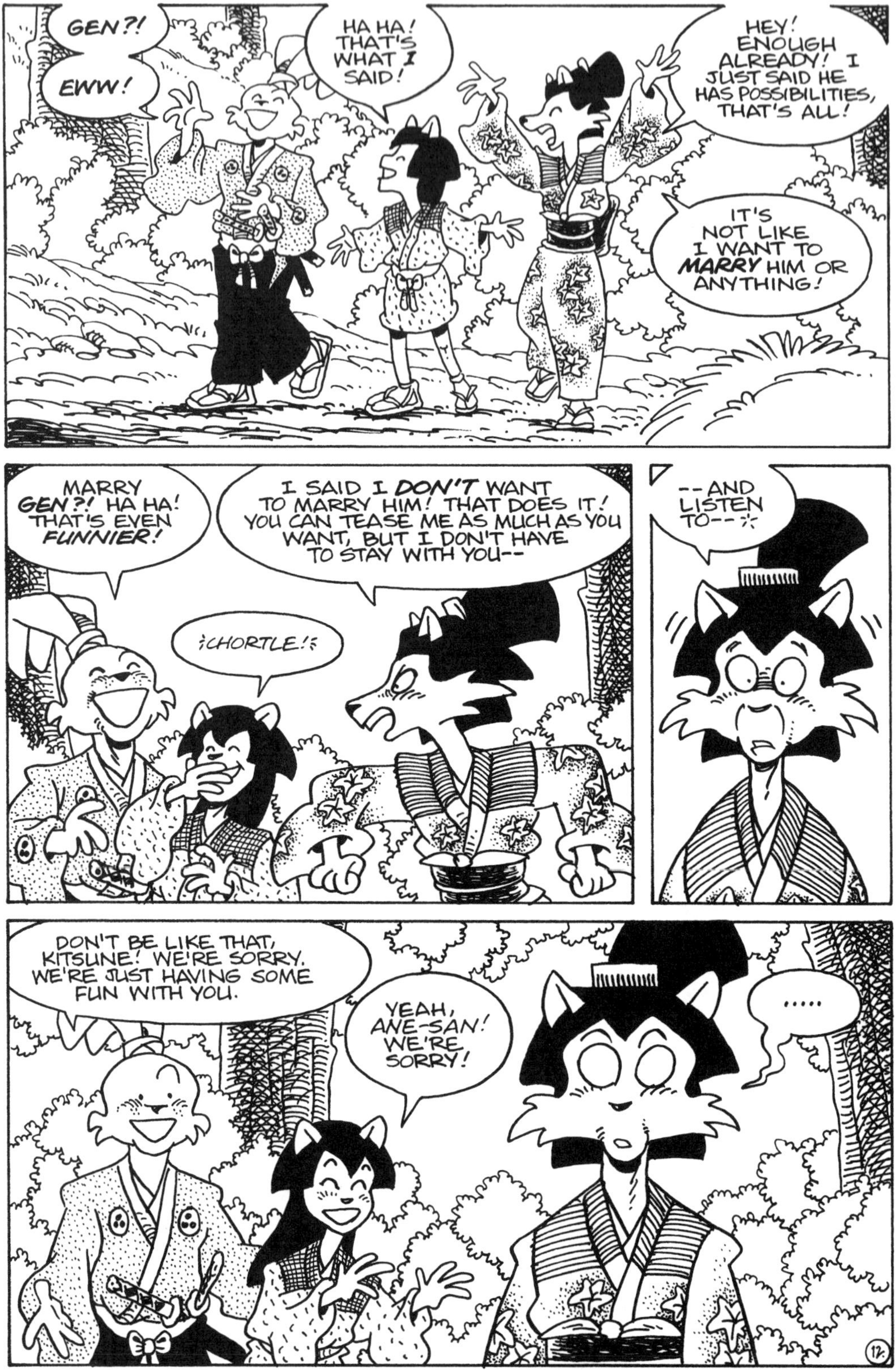
GEN?!
EWW!
HA HA! THAT'S WHAT I SAID!
HEY! ENOUGH ALREADY! I JUST SAID HE HAS POSSIBILITIES, THAT'S ALL!
IT'S NOT LIKE I WANT TO MARRY HIM OR ANYTHING!
MARRY GEN?! HA HA! THAT'S EVEN FUNNIER!
¡CHORTLE!
I SAID I DON'T WANT TO MARRY HIM! THAT DOES IT! YOU CAN TEASE ME AS MUCH AS YOU WANT, BUT I DON'T HAVE TO STAY WITH YOU--
--AND LISTEN TO--
DON'T BE LIKE THAT, KITSUNE! WE'RE SORRY. WE'RE JUST HAVING SOME FUN WITH YOU.
YEAH, ANE-SAN! WE'RE SORRY!
.....
12

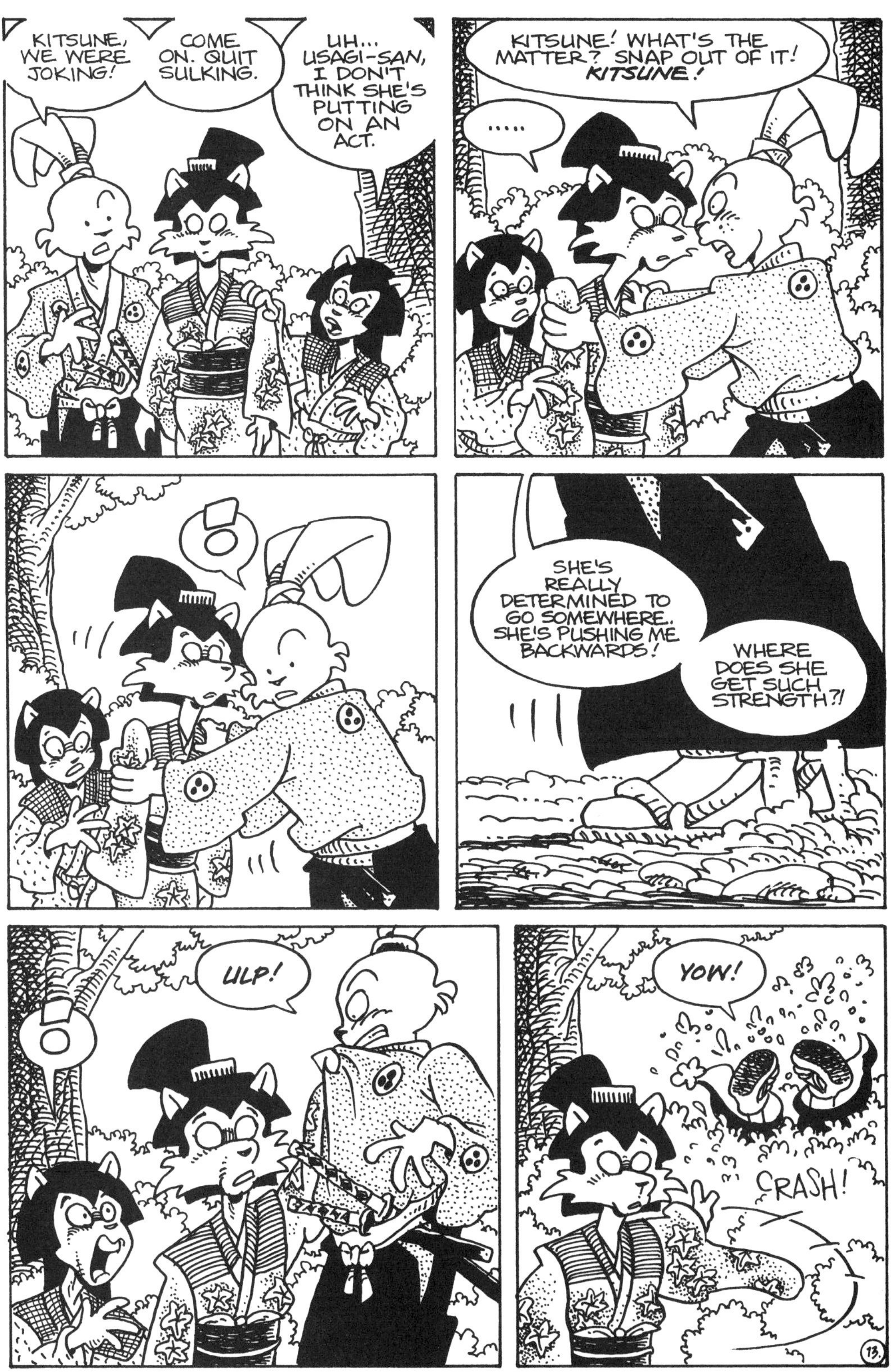
KITSUNE, WE WERE JOKING!
COME ON. QUIT SULKING.
UH... USAGI-SAN, I DON'T THINK SHE'S PUTTING ON AN ACT.
KITSUNE! WHAT'S THE MATTER? SNAP OUT OF IT! KITSUNE!
.....
SHE'S REALLY DETERMINED TO GO SOMEWHERE. SHE'S PUSHING ME BACKWARDS!
WHERE DOES SHE GET SUCH STRENGTH?!
ULP!
YOW!
CRASH!
13.

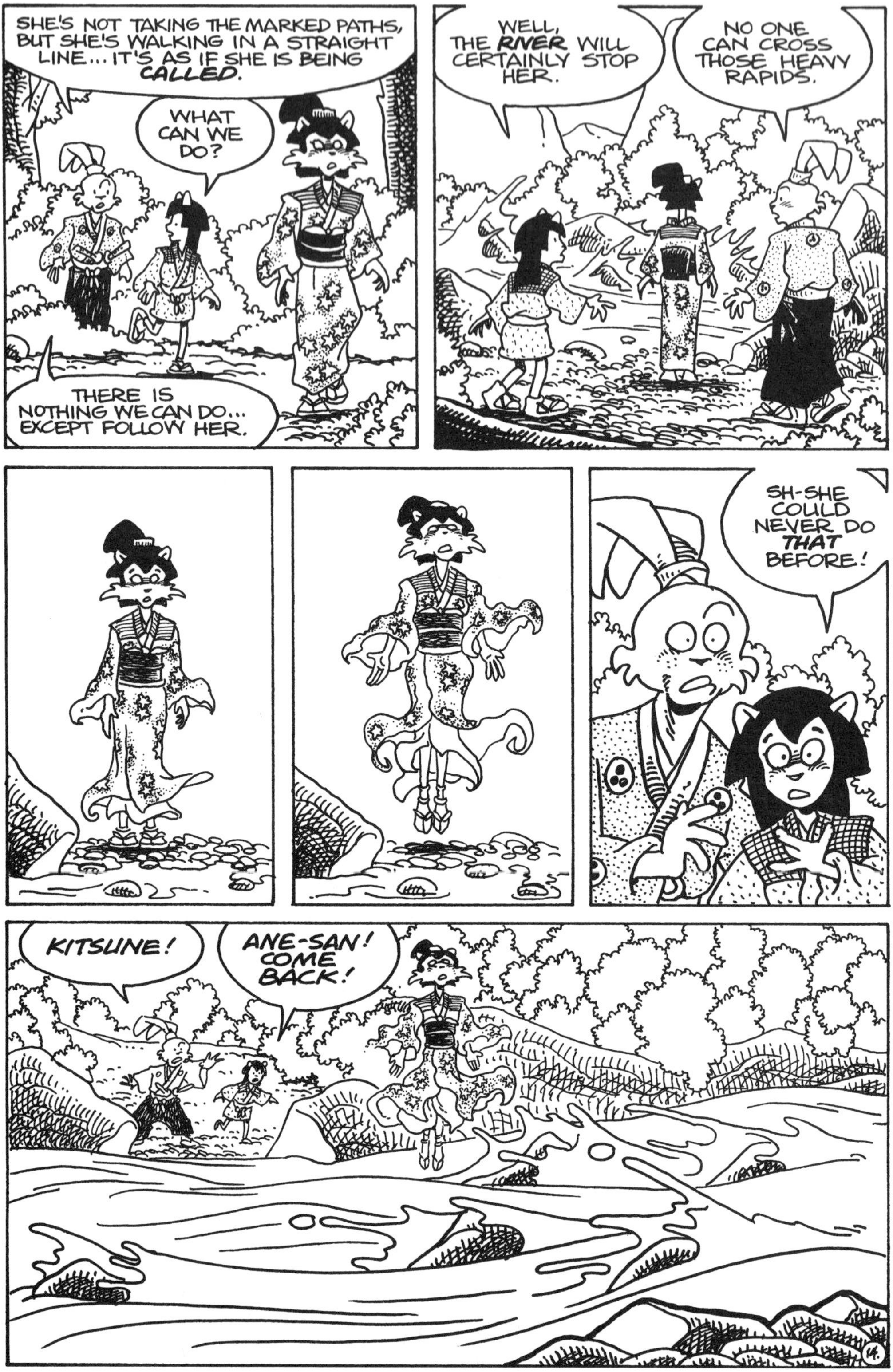
SHE'S NOT TAKING THE MARKED PATHS, BUT SHE'S WALKING IN A STRAIGHT LINE... IT'S AS IF SHE IS BEING CALLED.
WHAT CAN WE DO?
THERE IS NOTHING WE CAN DO... EXCEPT FOLLOW HER.
WELL, THE RIVER WILL CERTAINLY STOP HER.
NO ONE CAN CROSS THOSE HEAVY RAPIDS.
SH-SHE COULD NEVER DO THAT BEFORE!
KITSUNE!
ANE-SAN! COME BACK!
14.

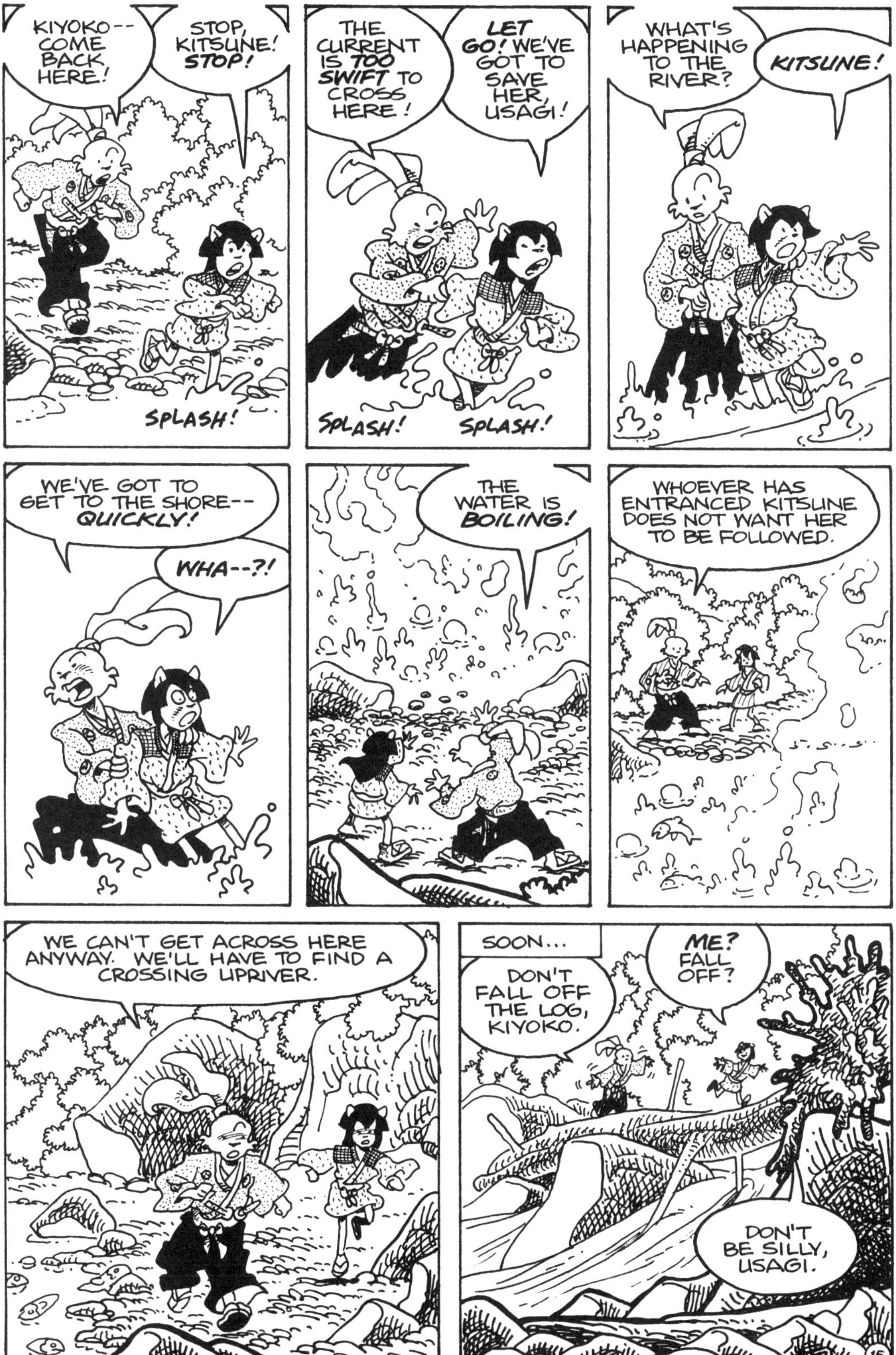
KIYOKO-- COME BACK HERE!
STOP, KITSUNE! STOP!
SPLASH!
THE CURRENT IS TOO SWIFT TO CROSS HERE!
LET GO! WE'VE GOT TO SAVE HER, USAGI!
SPLASH!
SPLASH!
WHAT'S HAPPENING TO THE RIVER?
KITSUNE!
WE'VE GOT TO GET TO THE SHORE-- QUICKLY!
WHA--?!
THE WATER IS BOILING!
WHOEVER HAS ENTRANCED KITSUNE DOES NOT WANT HER TO BE FOLLOWED.
WE CAN'T GET ACROSS HERE ANYWAY. WE'LL HAVE TO FIND A CROSSING UPRIVER.
SOON...
DON'T FALL OFF THE LOG, KIYOKO.
ME? FALL OFF?
DON'T BE SILLY, USAGI.
15.

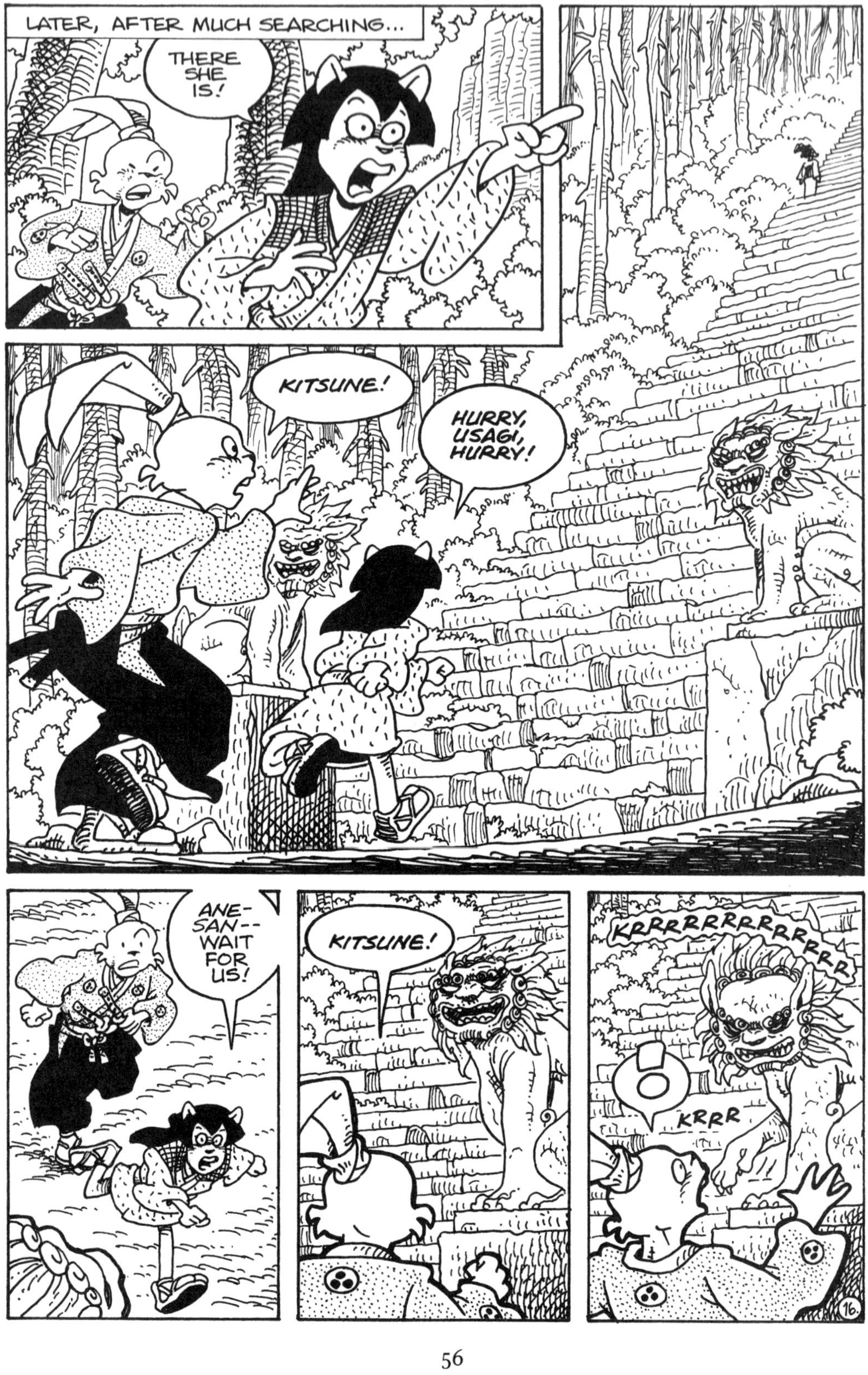
LATER, AFTER MUCH SEARCHING...
THERE SHE IS!
KITSUNE!
HURRY, USAGI, HURRY!
ANE-SAN-- WAIT FOR US!
KITSUNE!
KRRRRRRRRRRRRR
!
KRRR
16.

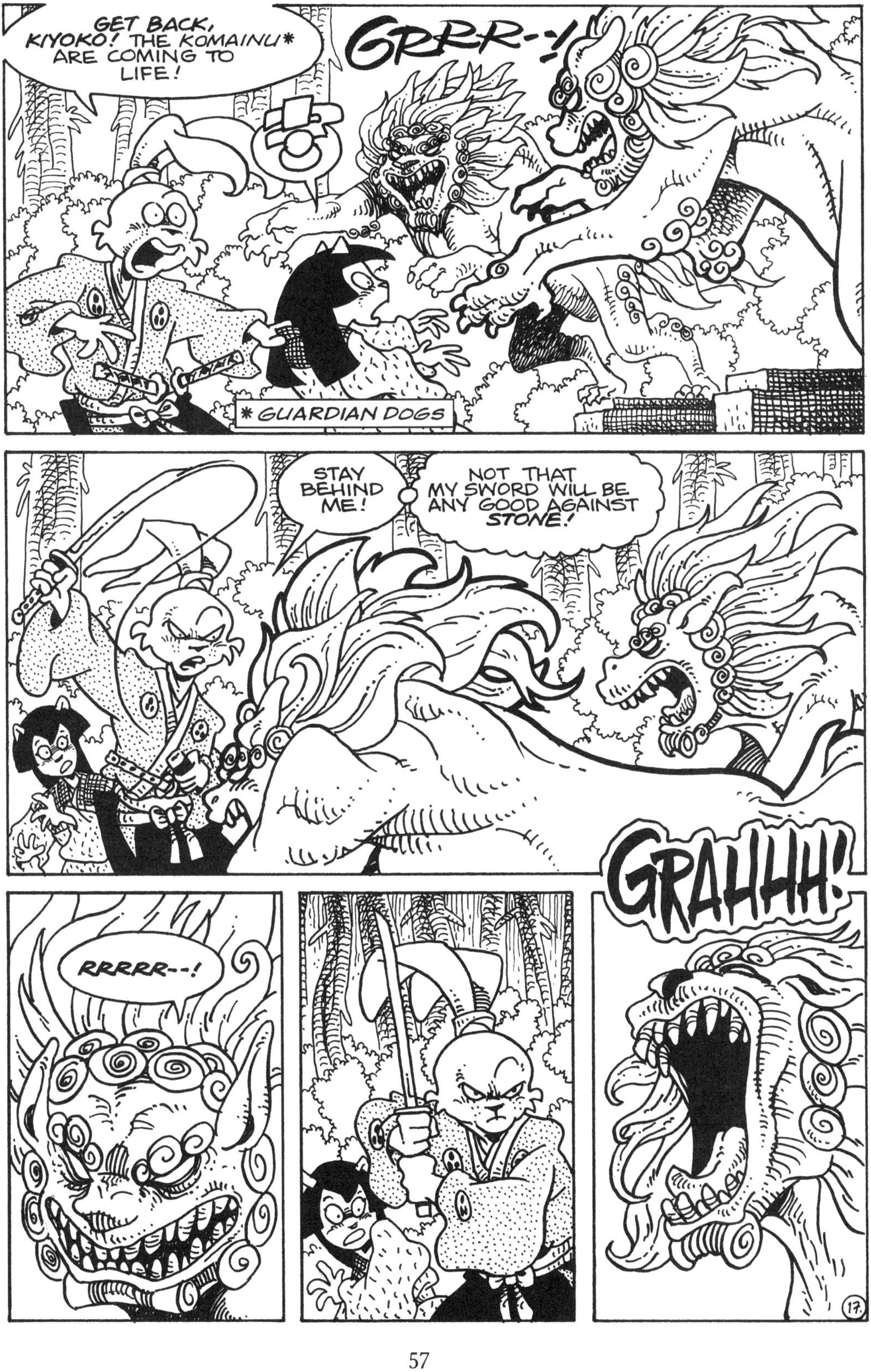
GET BACK, KIYOKO! THE KOMAINU* ARE COMING TO LIFE!
GRRR--!
* GUARDIAN DOGS
STAY BEHIND ME!
NOT THAT MY SWORD WILL BE ANY GOOD AGAINST STONE!
GRAHHH!
RRRRR--!
17.

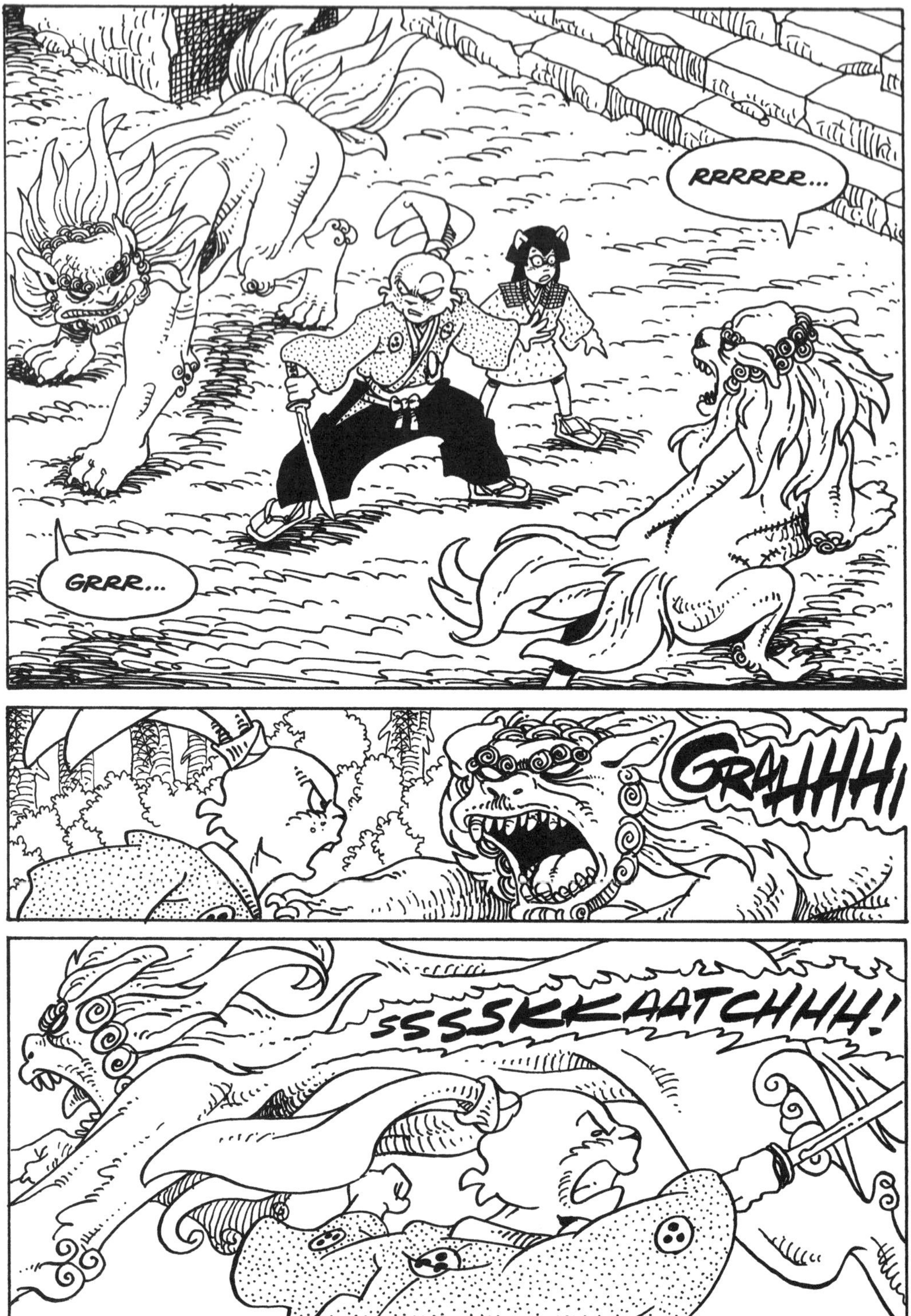
RRRRRR...
GRRR...
GRAHHH
SSSSKKAATCHHH!
18.

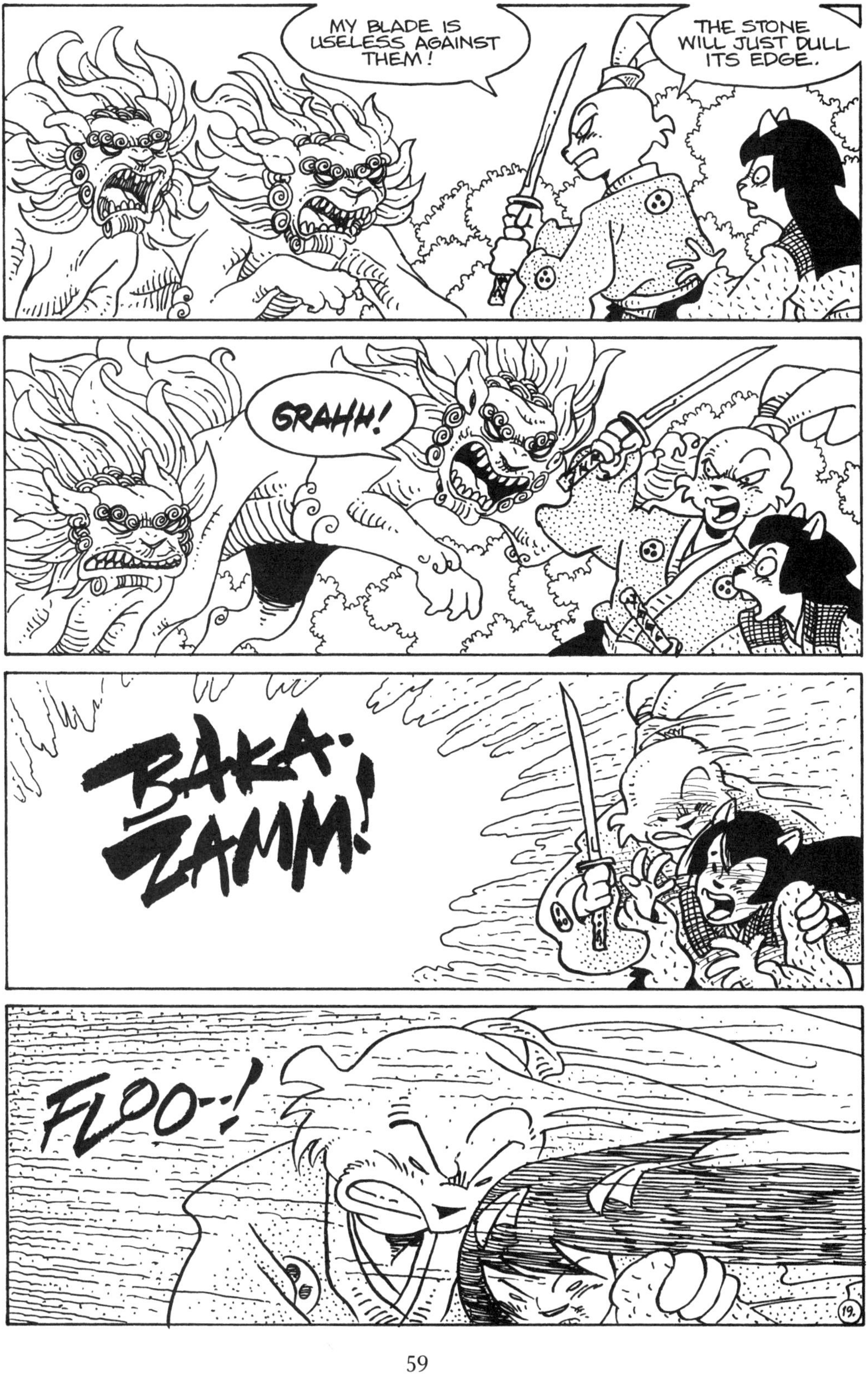
MY BLADE IS USELESS AGAINST THEM!
THE STONE WILL JUST DULL ITS EDGE.
GRAHH!
BAKA-ZAMM!
FLOO--!
19.

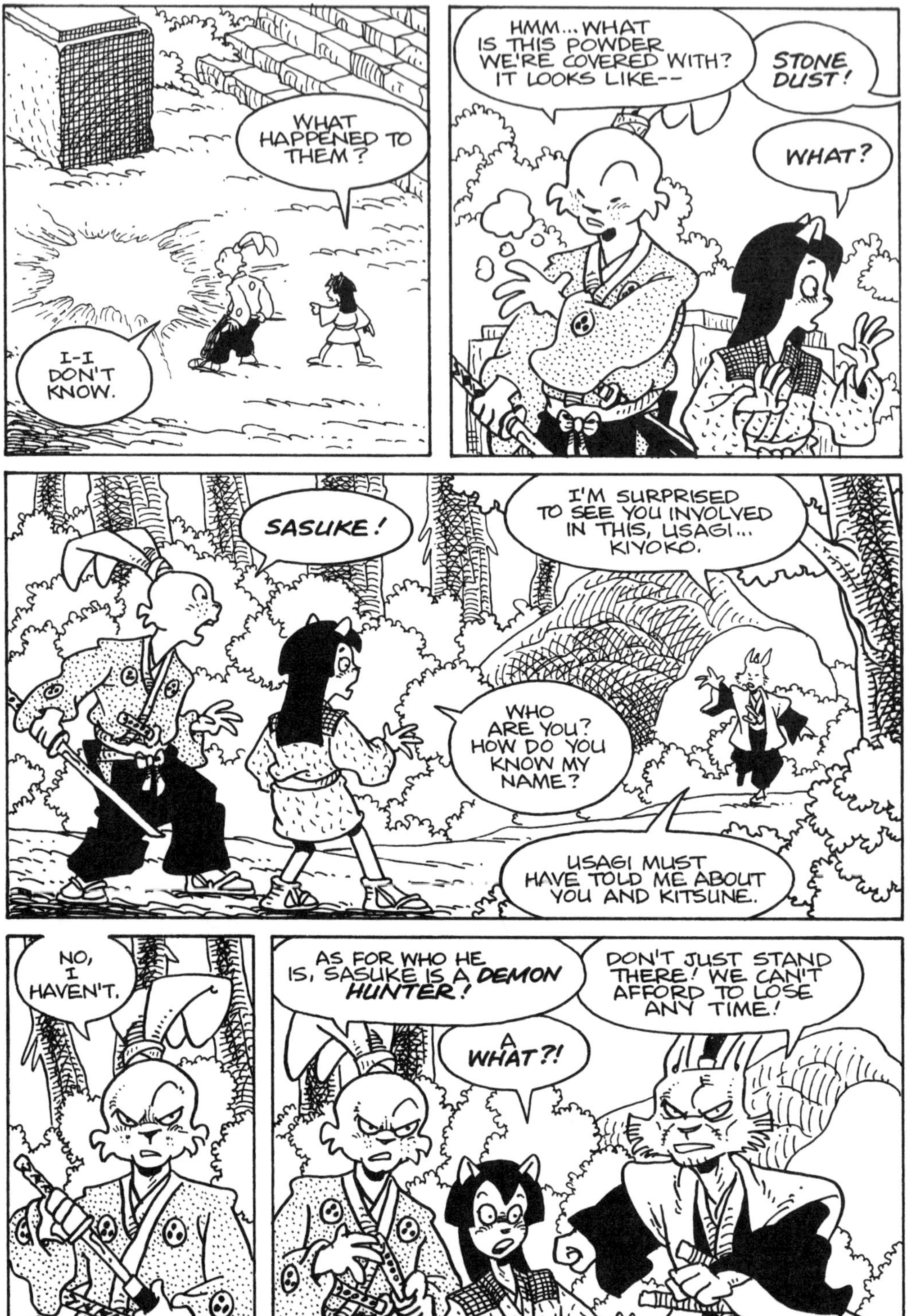
WHAT HAPPENED TO THEM?
I-I DON'T KNOW.
HMM... WHAT IS THIS POWDER WE'RE COVERED WITH? IT LOOKS LIKE--
STONE DUST!
WHAT?
SASUKE!
I'M SURPRISED TO SEE YOU INVOLVED IN THIS, USAGI... KIYOKO.
WHO ARE YOU? HOW DO YOU KNOW MY NAME?
USAGI MUST HAVE TOLD ME ABOUT YOU AND KITSUNE.
NO, I HAVEN'T.
AS FOR WHO HE IS, SASUKE IS A **DEMON HUNTER!**
DON'T JUST STAND THERE! WE CAN'T AFFORD TO LOSE ANY TIME!
A **WHAT?!**
20.

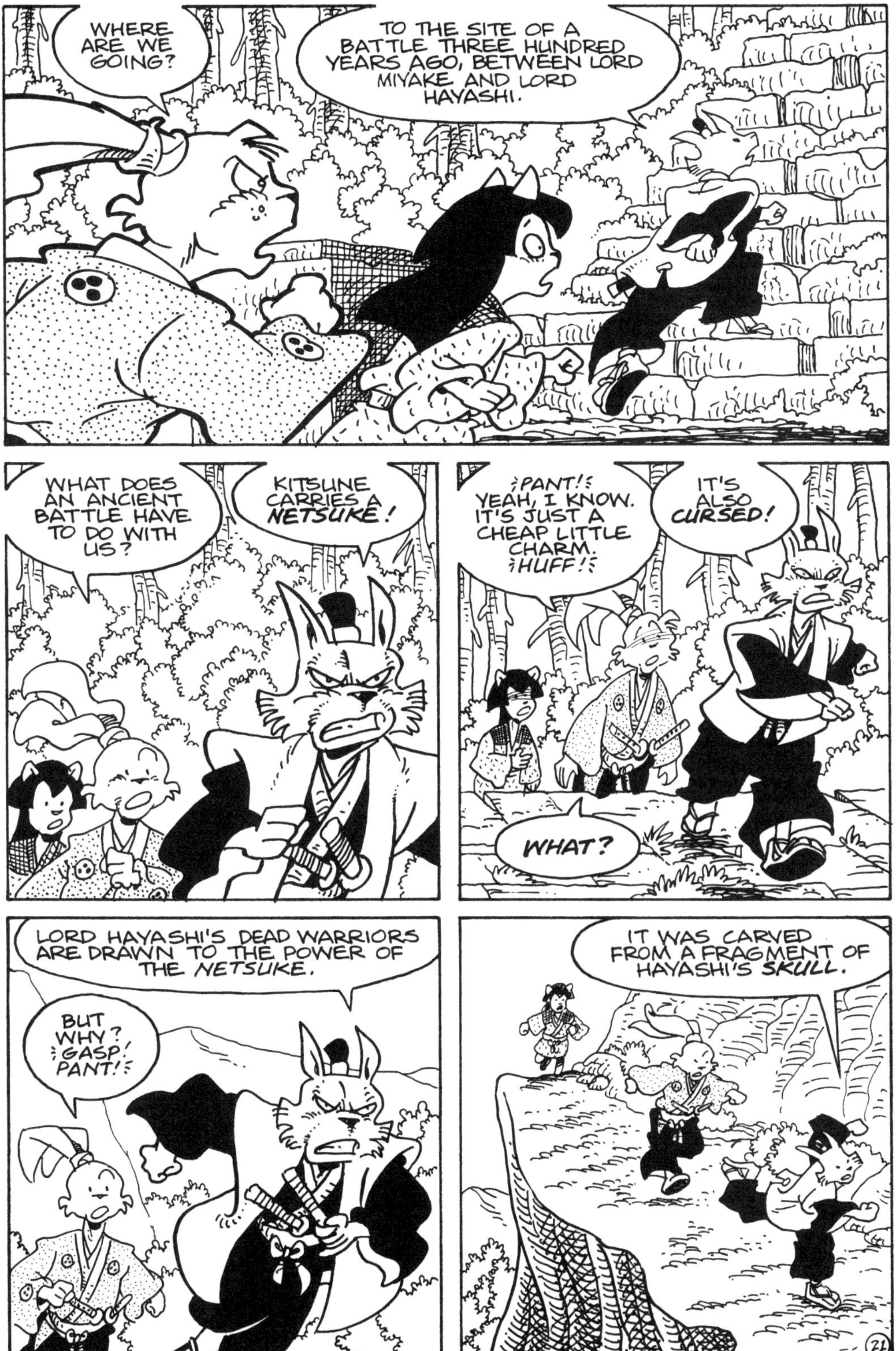
WHERE ARE WE GOING?
TO THE SITE OF A BATTLE THREE HUNDRED YEARS AGO, BETWEEN LORD MIYAKE AND LORD HAYASHI.
WHAT DOES AN ANCIENT BATTLE HAVE TO DO WITH US?
KITSUNE CARRIES A NETSUKE!
PANT! YEAH, I KNOW. IT'S JUST A CHEAP LITTLE CHARM. HUFF!
IT'S ALSO CURSED!
WHAT?
LORD HAYASHI'S DEAD WARRIORS ARE DRAWN TO THE POWER OF THE NETSUKE.
BUT WHY? GASP! PANT!
IT WAS CARVED FROM A FRAGMENT OF HAYASHI'S SKULL.
21

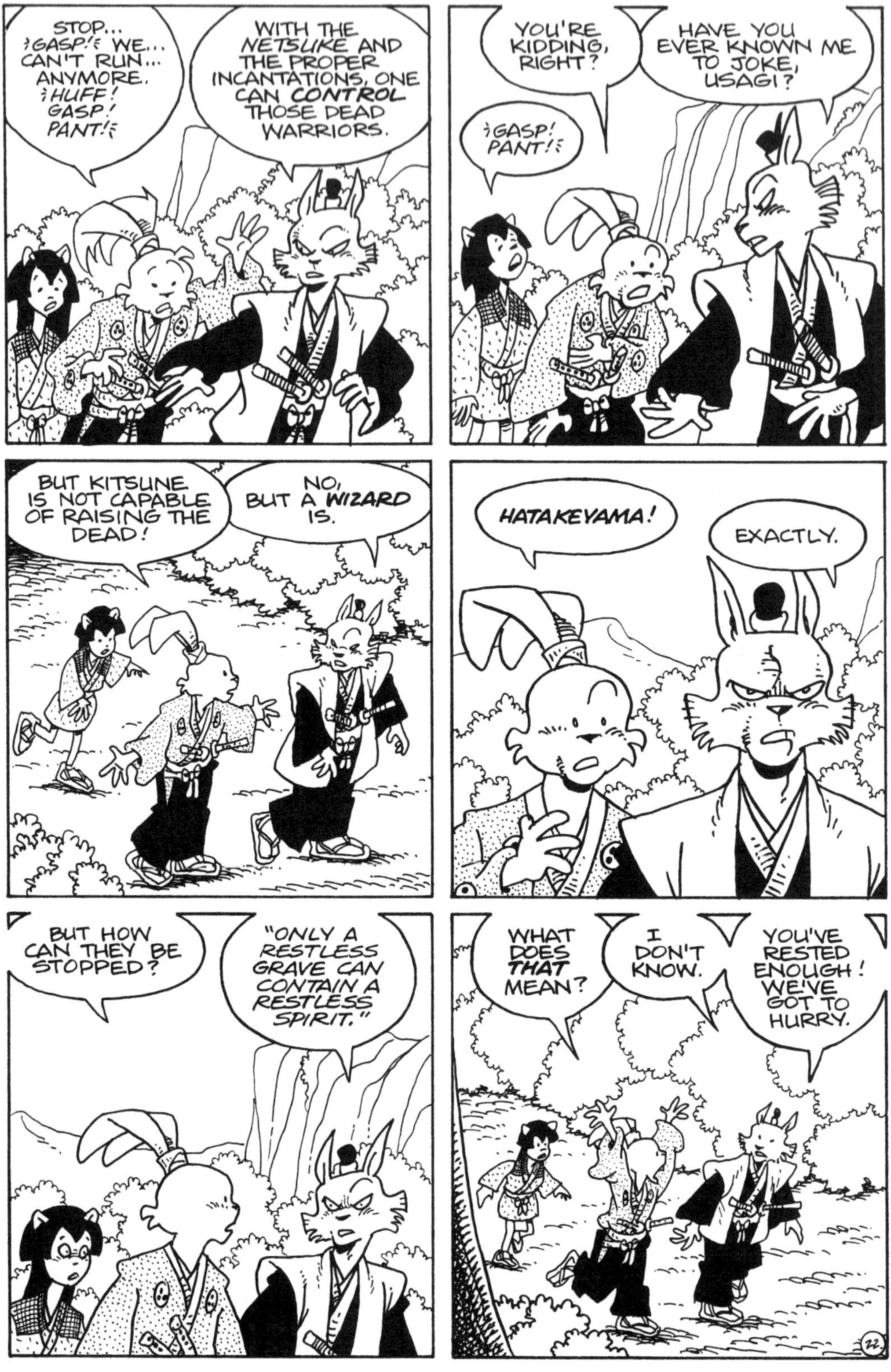
STOP... ≷GASP!≶ WE... CAN'T RUN... ANYMORE. ≷HUFF! GASP! PANT!≶
WITH THE *NETSUKE* AND THE PROPER INCANTATIONS, ONE CAN **CONTROL** THOSE DEAD WARRIORS.
YOU'RE KIDDING, RIGHT?
≷GASP! PANT!≶
HAVE YOU EVER KNOWN ME TO JOKE, USAGI?
BUT KITSUNE IS NOT CAPABLE OF RAISING THE DEAD!
NO, BUT A ***WIZARD*** IS.
HATAKEYAMA!
EXACTLY.
BUT HOW CAN THEY BE STOPPED?
"ONLY A RESTLESS GRAVE CAN CONTAIN A RESTLESS SPIRIT."
WHAT DOES ***THAT*** MEAN?
I DON'T KNOW.
YOU'VE RESTED ENOUGH! WE'VE GOT TO HURRY.
22

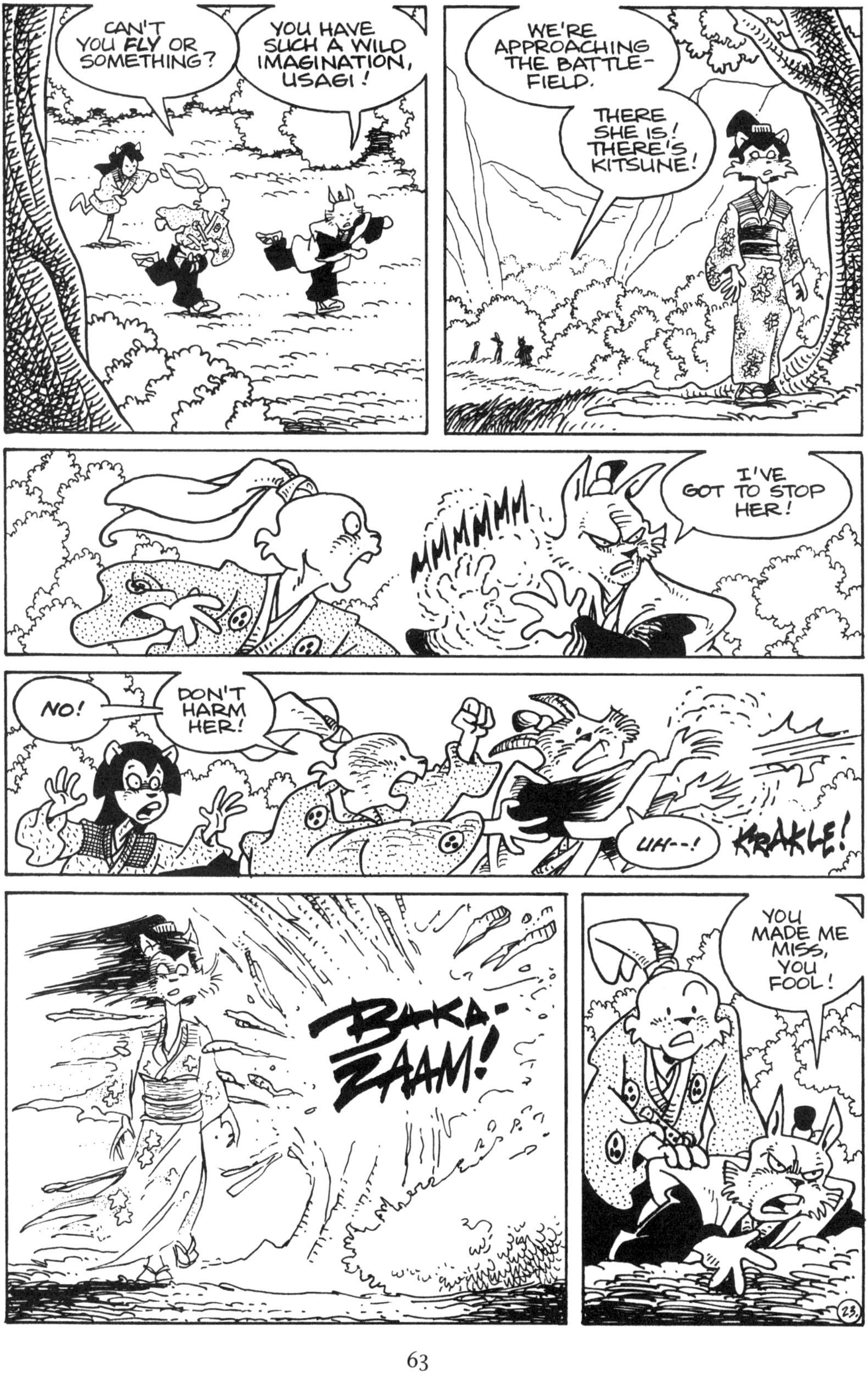
CAN'T YOU FLY OR SOMETHING?
YOU HAVE SUCH A WILD IMAGINATION, USAGI!
WE'RE APPROACHING THE BATTLE-FIELD.
THERE SHE IS! THERE'S KITSUNE!
MMMMMM
I'VE GOT TO STOP HER!
NO!
DON'T HARM HER!
UH--!
KRAKLE!
BAKA-ZAAM!
YOU MADE ME MISS, YOU FOOL!
23.

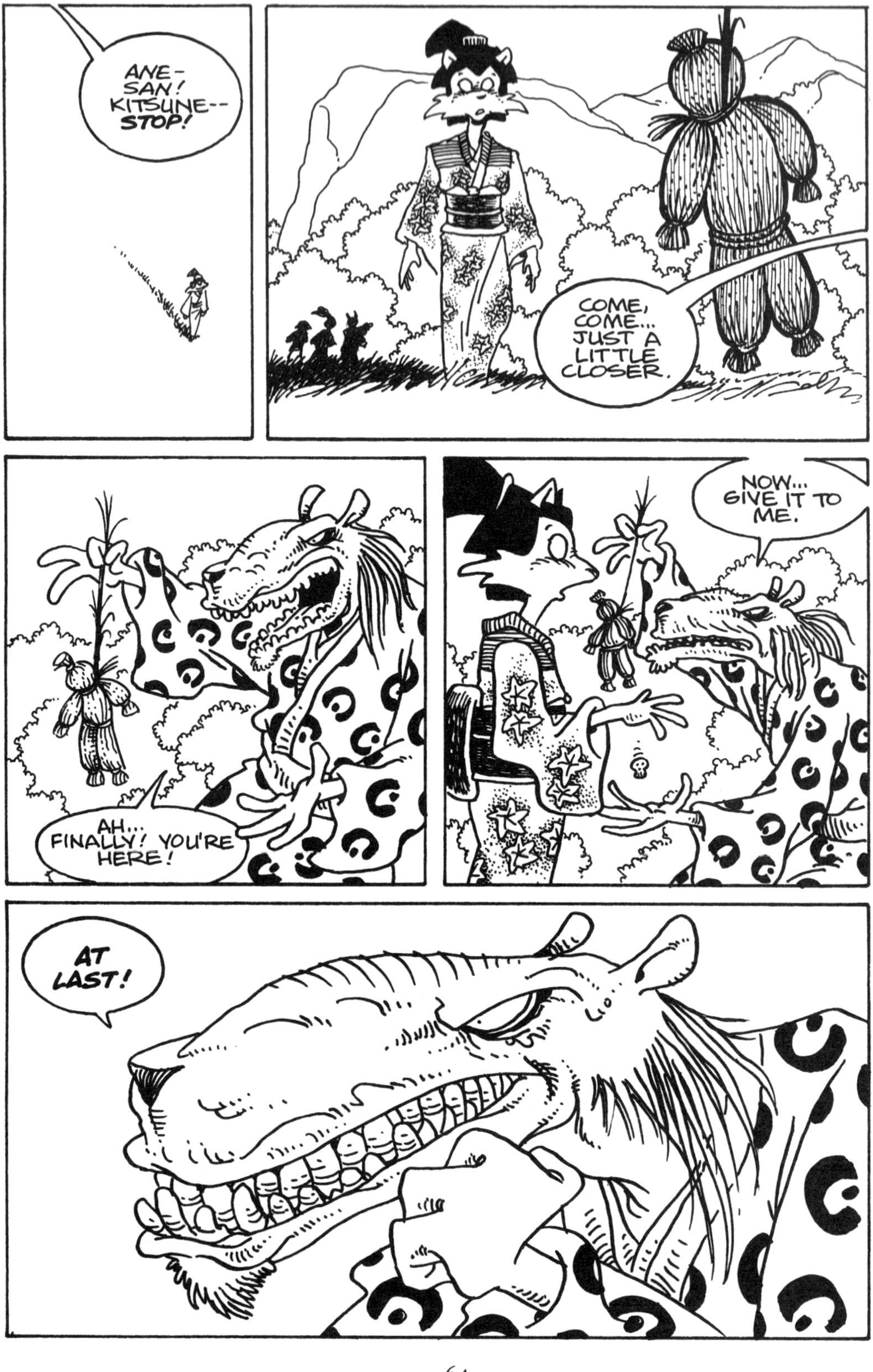
ANE-SAN! KITSUNE-- STOP!
COME, COME... JUST A LITTLE CLOSER.
AH... FINALLY! YOU'RE HERE!
NOW... GIVE IT TO ME.
AT LAST!

TRAITORS OF THE EARTH PART THREE

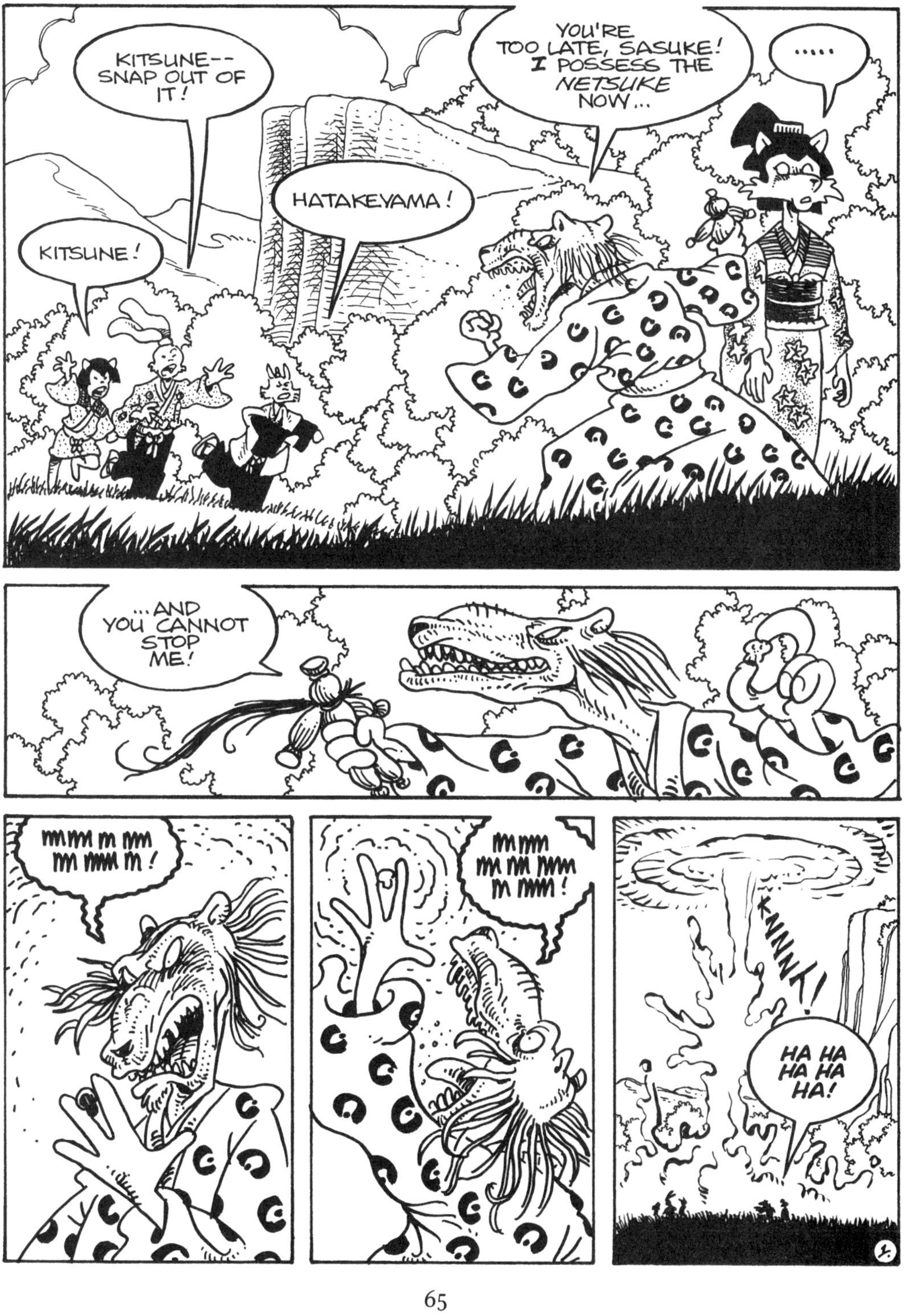

KITSUNE!
KITSUNE-- SNAP OUT OF IT!
HATAKEYAMA!
YOU'RE TOO LATE, SASUKE! I POSSESS THE *NETSUKE* NOW...
.....
...AND YOU CANNOT STOP ME!
mmm m mm mm mmm m!
mmm mm mm mmm m mmm!
KNNNT!
HA HA HA HA HA!

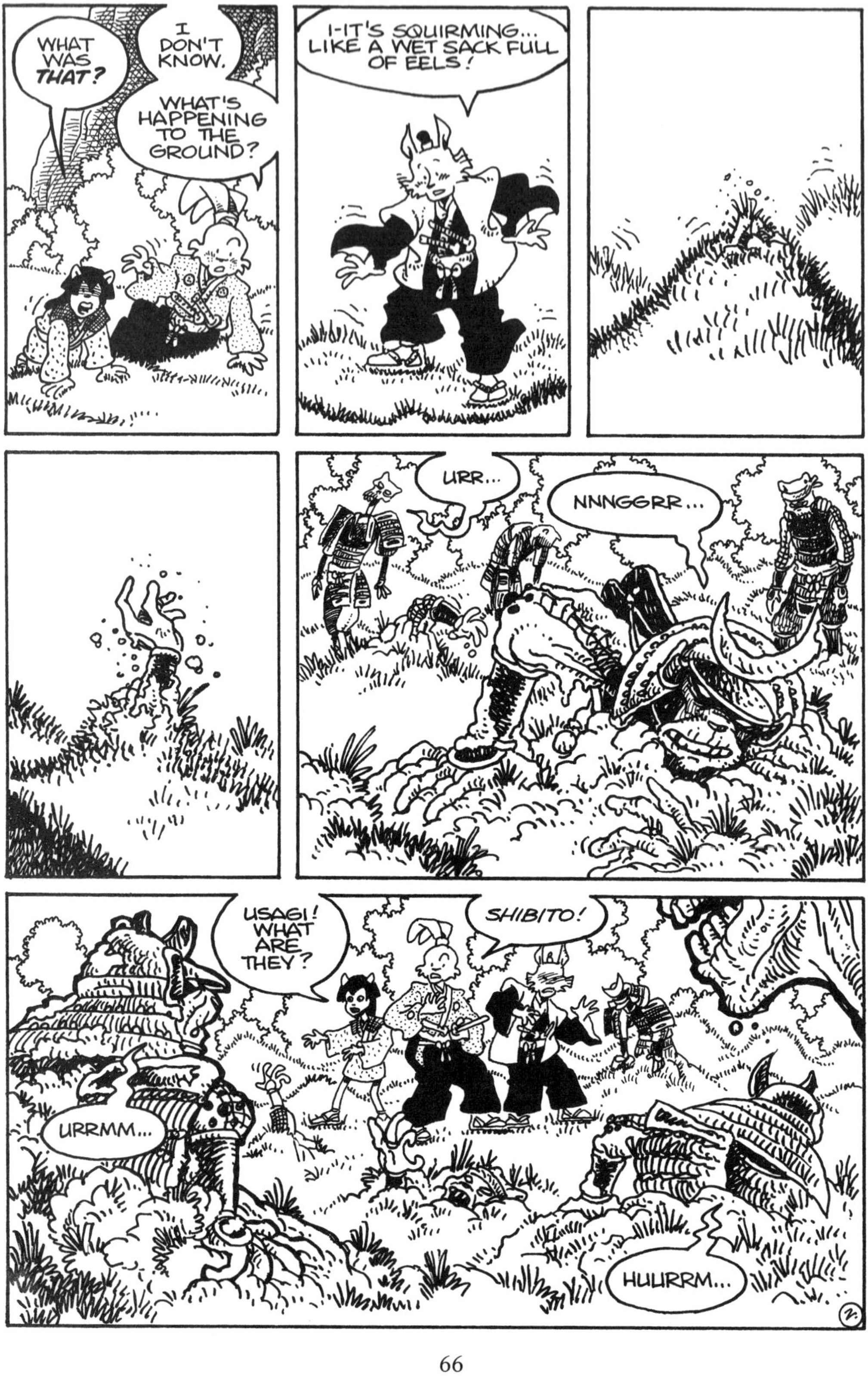
WHAT WAS *THAT*?
I DON'T KNOW.
WHAT'S HAPPENING TO THE GROUND?
I-IT'S SQUIRMING... LIKE A WET SACK FULL OF EELS!
URR...
NNNGGRR...
USAGI! WHAT ARE THEY?
SHIBITO!
URRMM...
HUURRM...

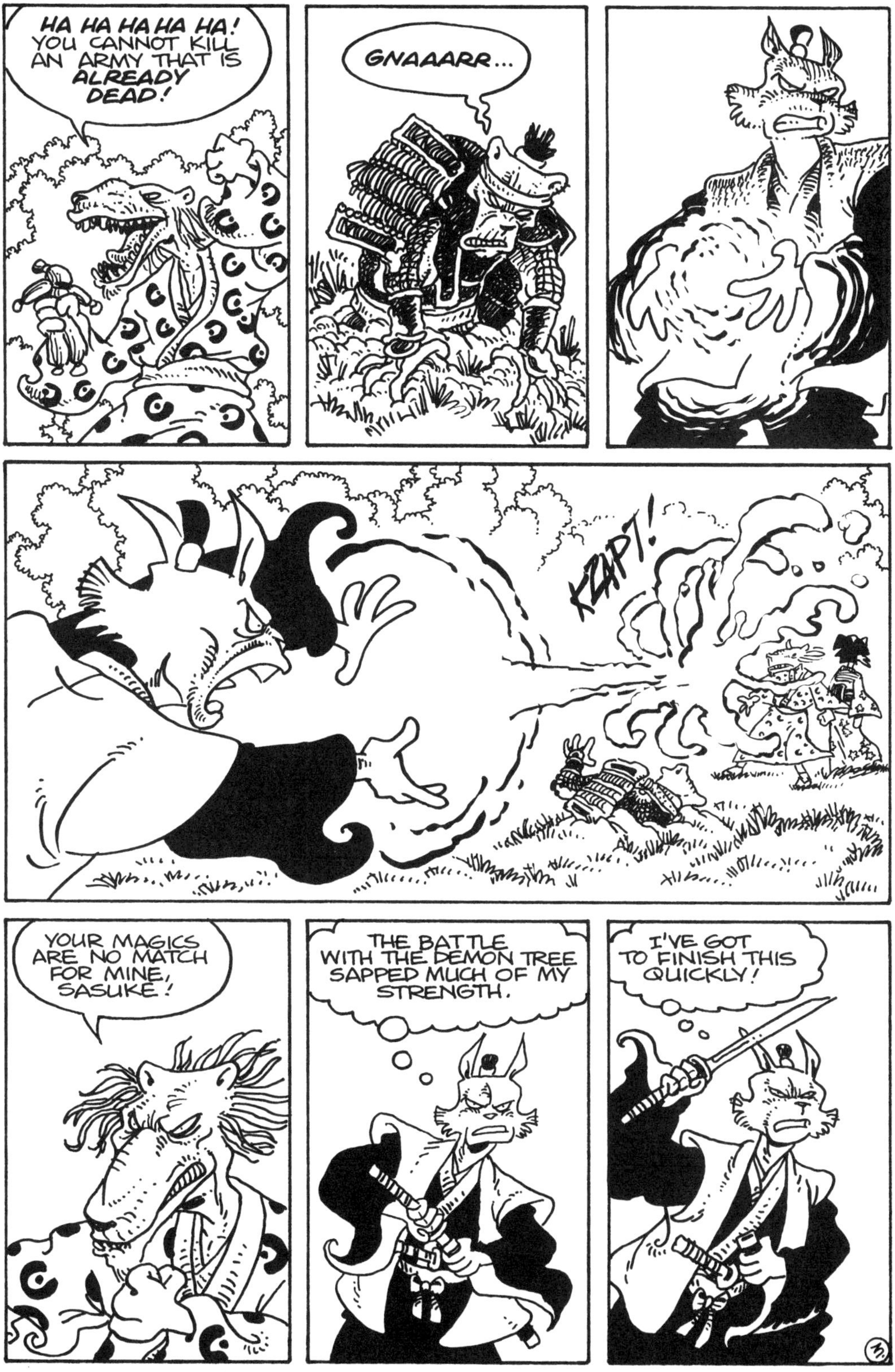
HA HA HA HA HA! YOU CANNOT KILL AN ARMY THAT IS ALREADY DEAD!
GNAAARR...
KZAPT!
YOUR MAGICS ARE NO MATCH FOR MINE, SASUKE!
THE BATTLE WITH THE DEMON TREE SAPPED MUCH OF MY STRENGTH.
I'VE GOT TO FINISH THIS QUICKLY!
3

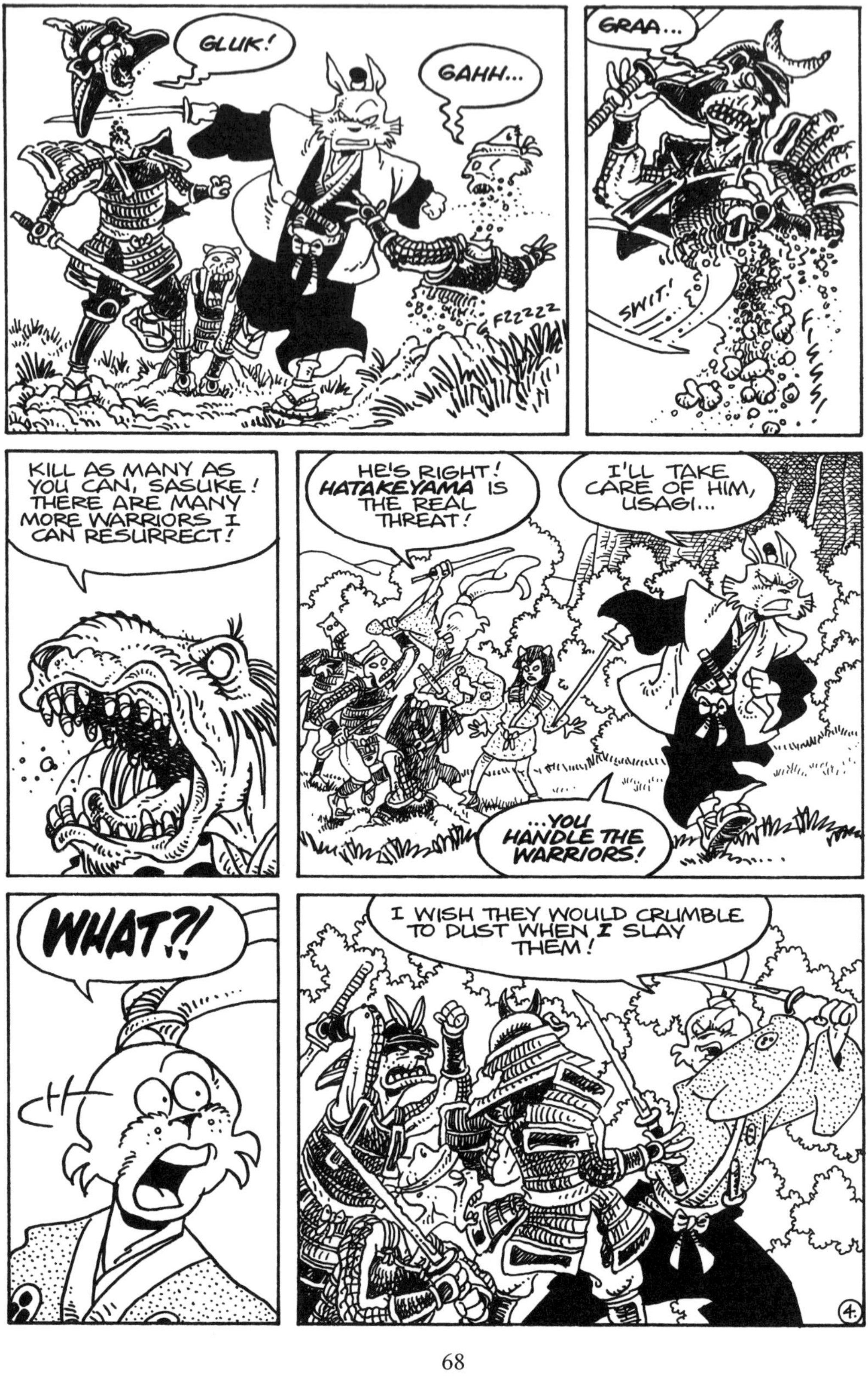
GLUK!
GAHH...
F'ZZZZZ
GRAA...
SWIT!
KILL AS MANY AS YOU CAN, SASUKE! THERE ARE MANY MORE WARRIORS I CAN RESURRECT!
HE'S RIGHT! HATAKEYAMA IS THE REAL THREAT!
I'LL TAKE CARE OF HIM, USAGI...
...YOU HANDLE THE WARRIORS!
WHAT?!
I WISH THEY WOULD CRUMBLE TO DUST WHEN I SLAY THEM!
4.

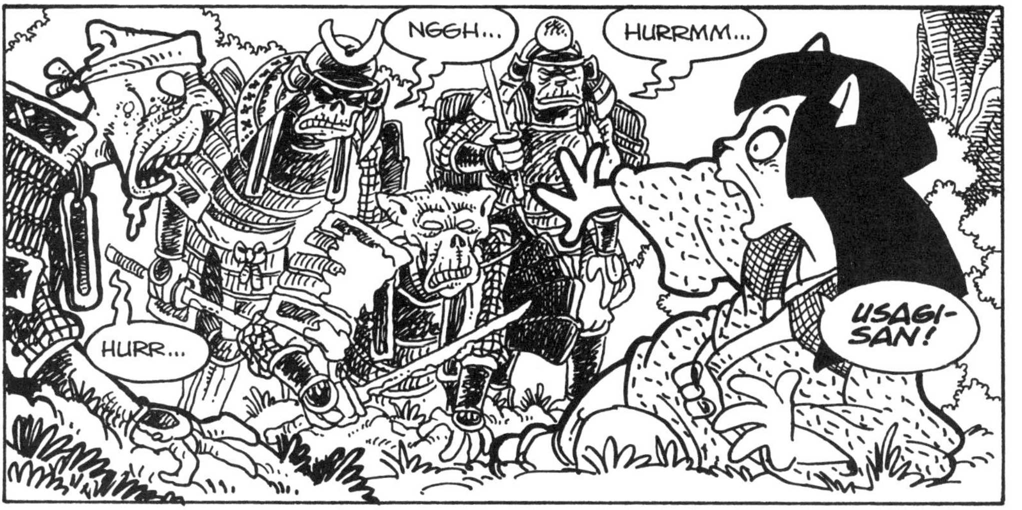
NGGH...
HURRMM...
HURR...
USAGI-SAN!
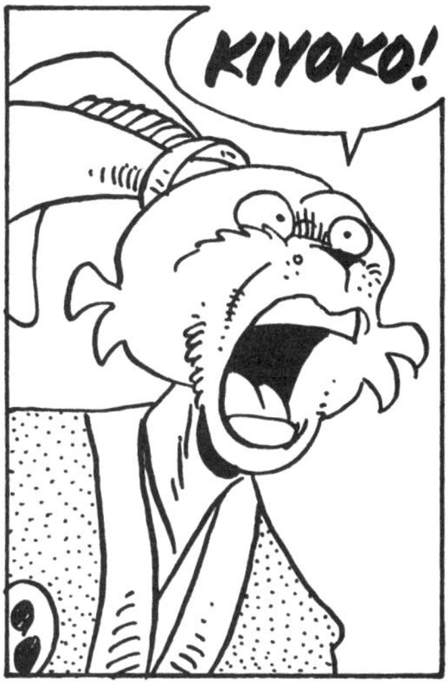
KIYOKO!
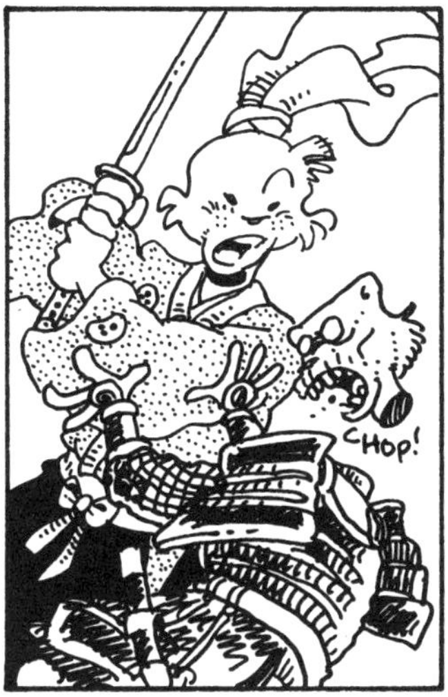
CHOP!
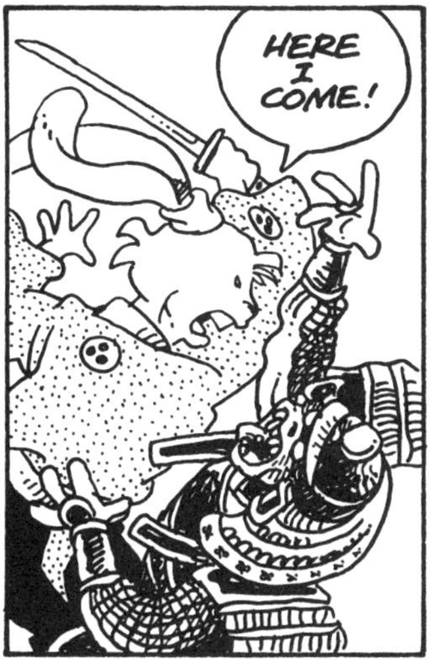
HERE I COME!
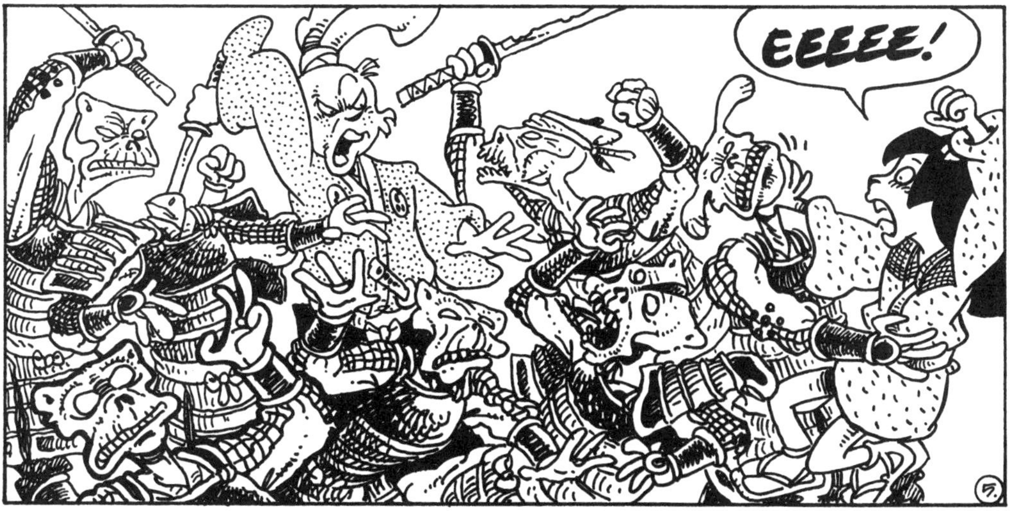
EEEEE!

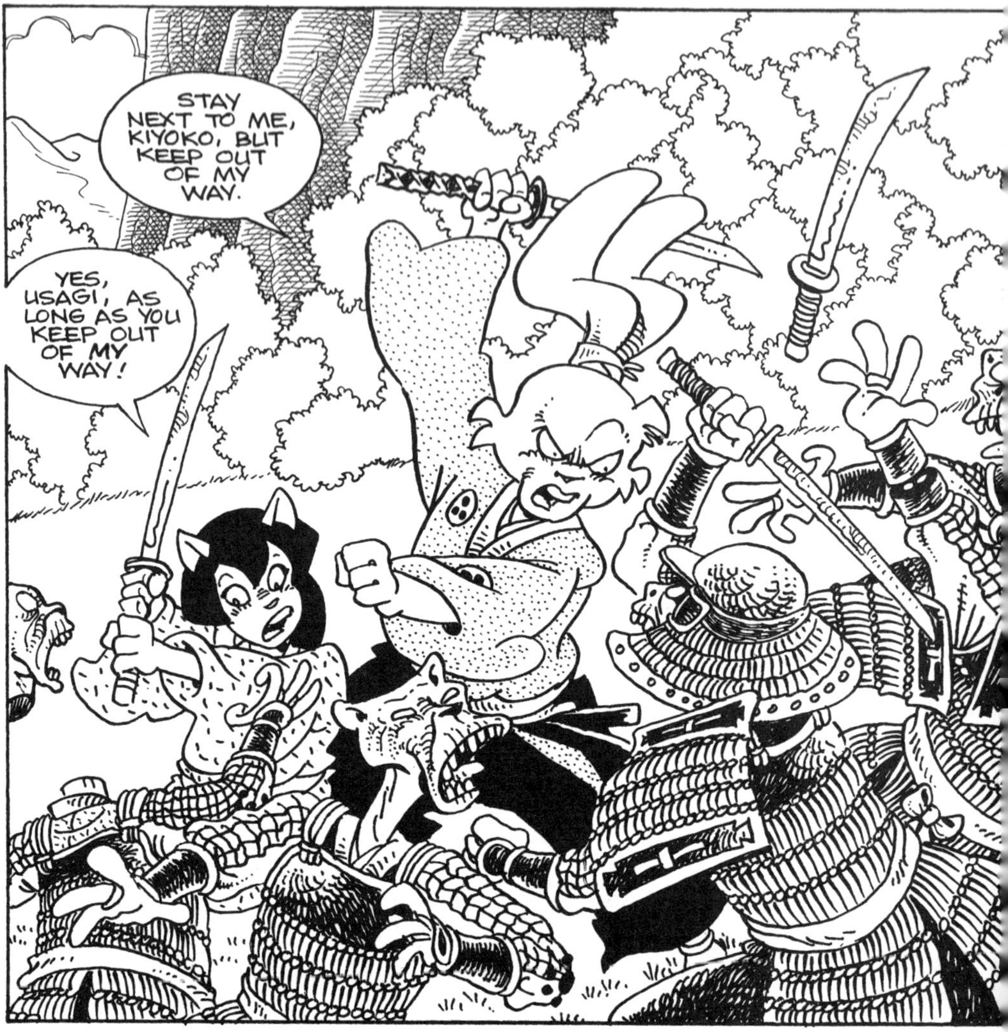
STAY NEXT TO ME, KIYOKO, BUT KEEP OUT OF MY WAY.
YES, USAGI, AS LONG AS YOU KEEP OUT OF MY WAY!

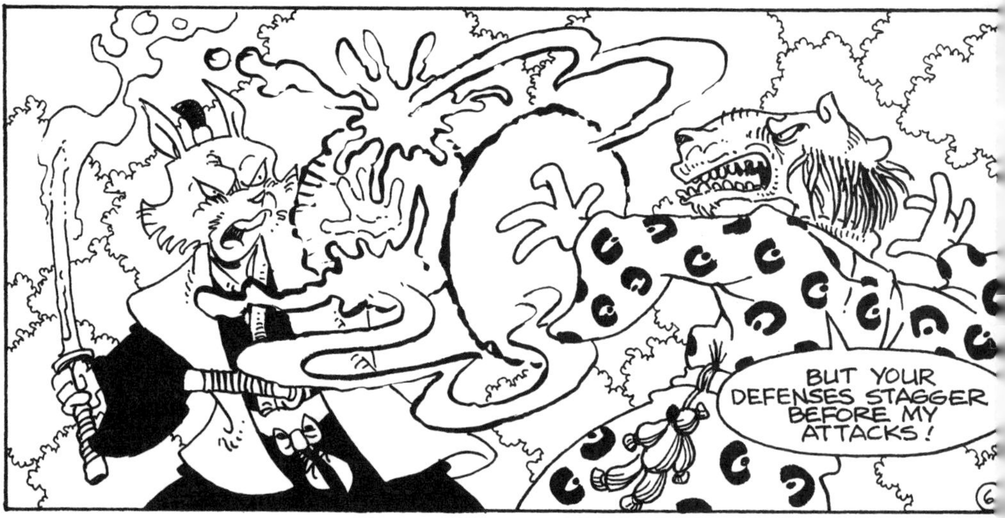
BUT YOUR DEFENSES STAGGER BEFORE MY ATTACKS!

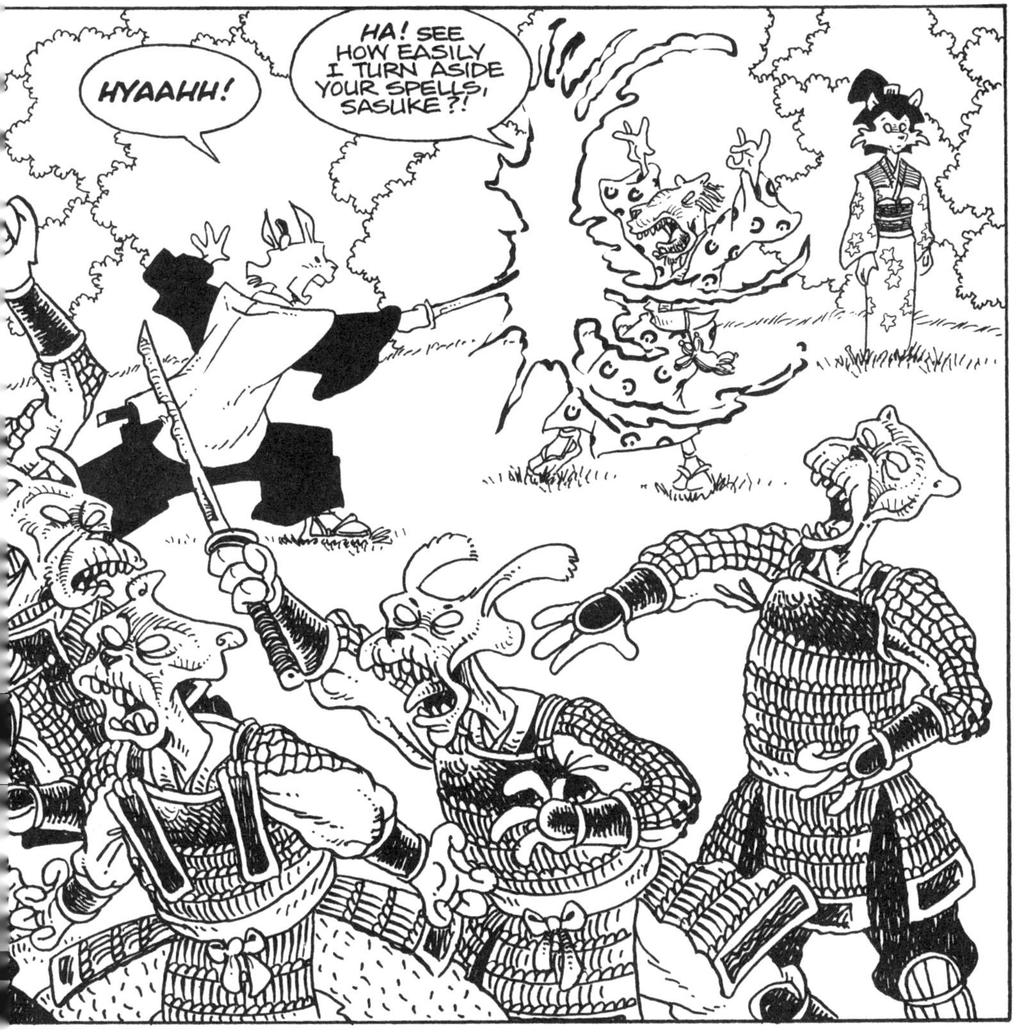
HYAAHH!
HA! SEE HOW EASILY I TURN ASIDE YOUR SPELLS, SASUKE?!

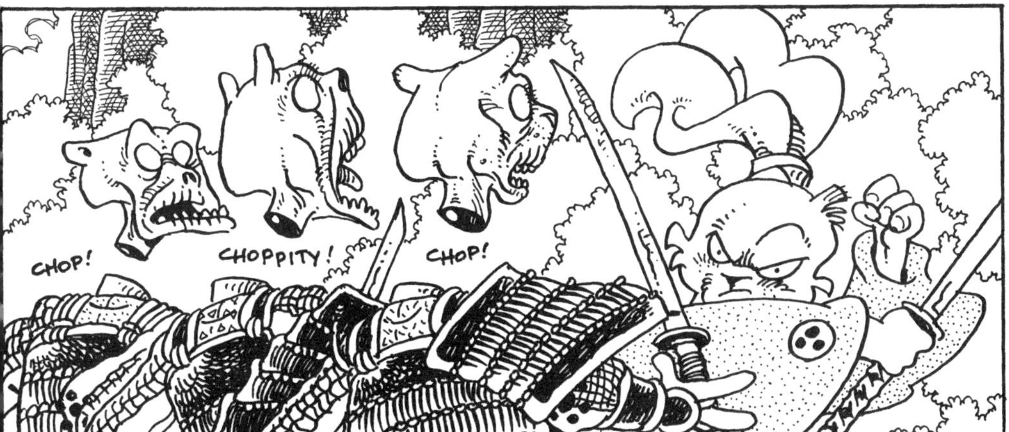
CHOP!
CHOPPITY!
CHOP!

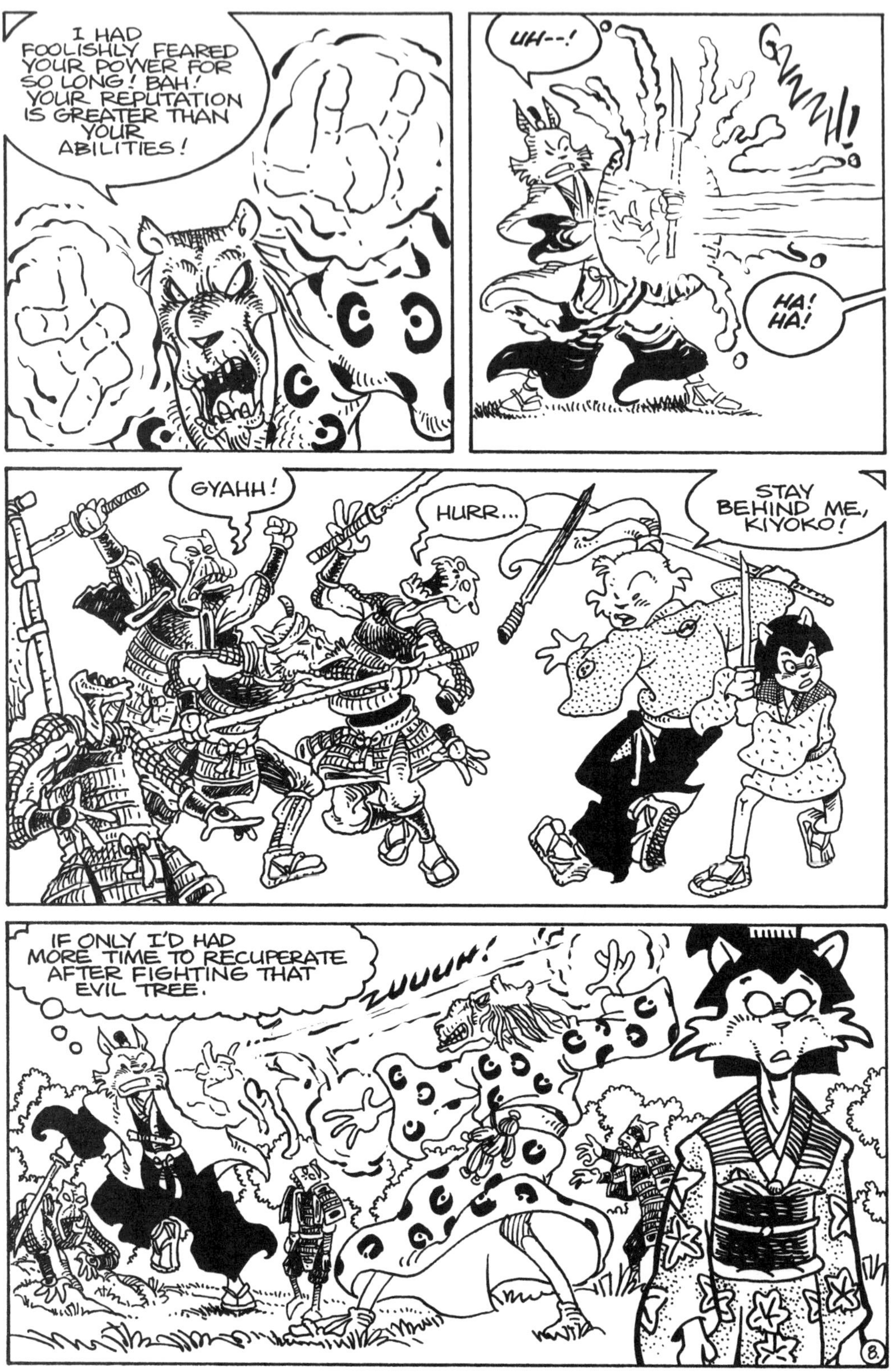
I HAD FOOLISHLY FEARED YOUR POWER FOR SO LONG! BAH! YOUR REPUTATION IS GREATER THAN YOUR ABILITIES!
UH--!
HA! HA!
GYAHH!
HURR...
STAY BEHIND ME, KIYOKO!
IF ONLY I'D HAD MORE TIME TO RECUPERATE AFTER FIGHTING THAT EVIL TREE.
ZUUUH!
8.

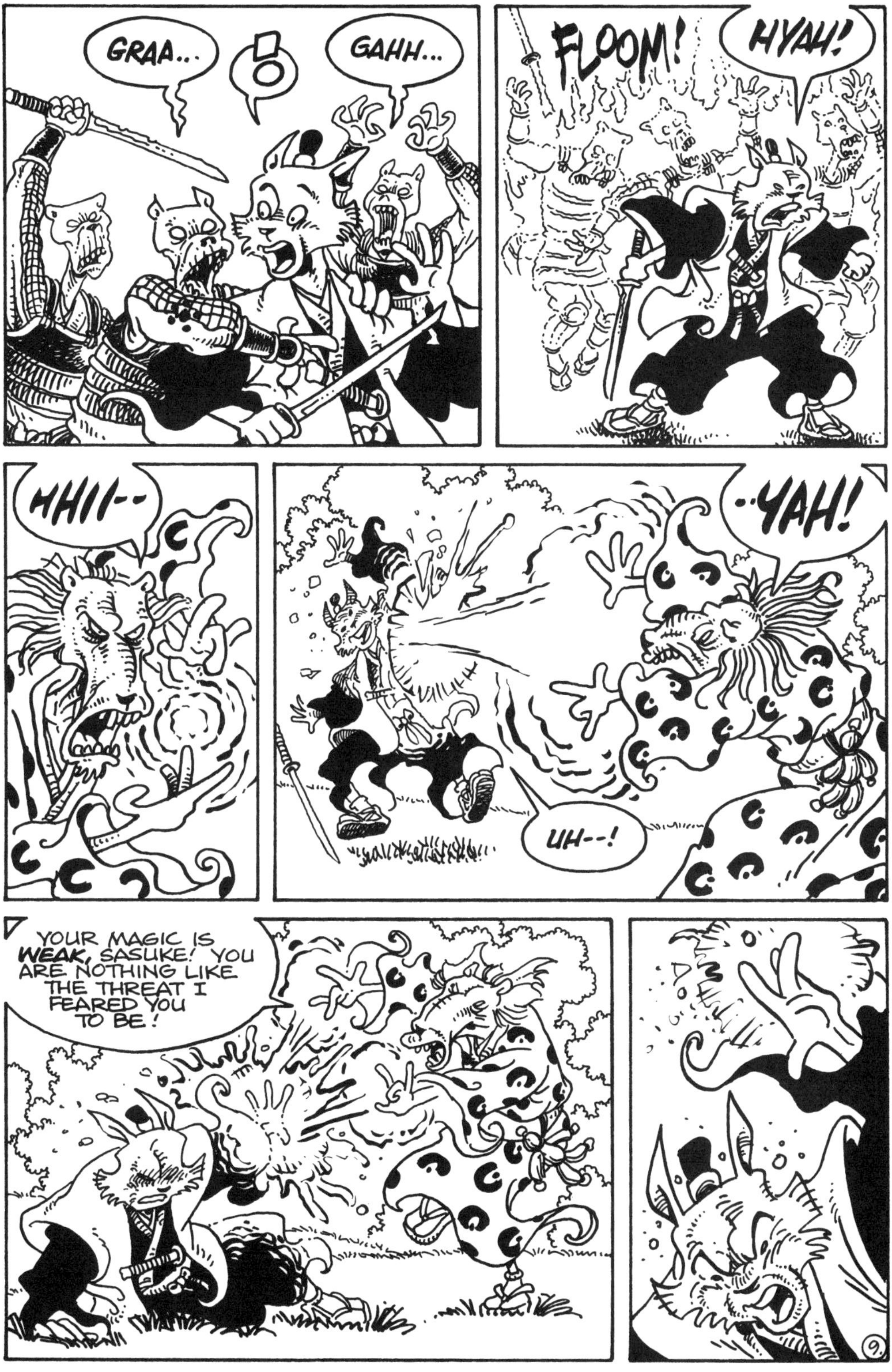
GRAA...
GAHH...
FLOOM!
HYAH!
HHII--
--YAH!
UH--!
YOUR MAGIC IS **WEAK**, SASUKE! YOU ARE NOTHING LIKE THE THREAT I FEARED YOU TO BE!

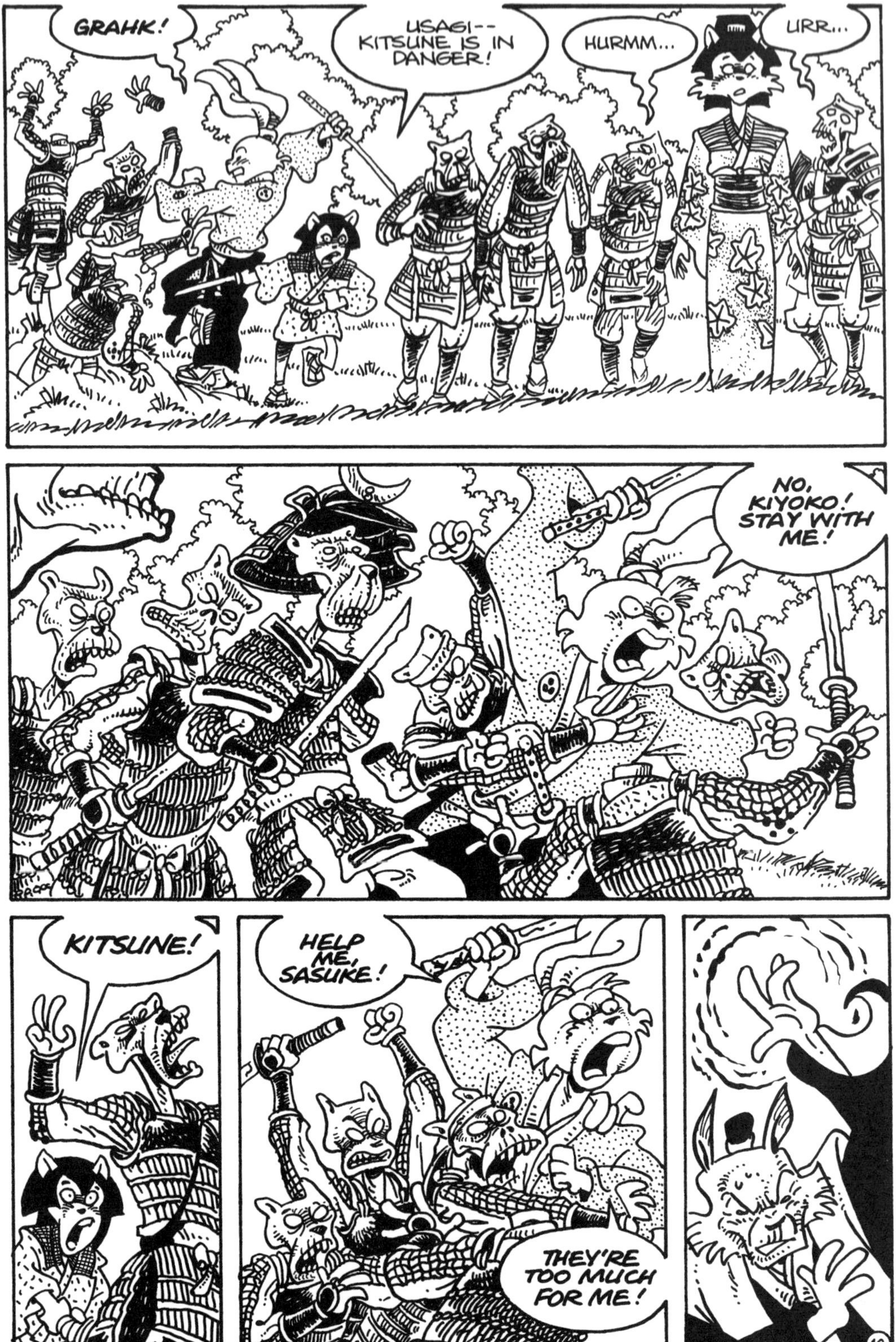
GRAHK!
USAGI-- KITSUNE IS IN DANGER!
HURMM...
URR...
NO, KIYOKO! STAY WITH ME!
KITSUNE!
HELP ME, SASUKE!
THEY'RE TOO MUCH FOR ME!
10.

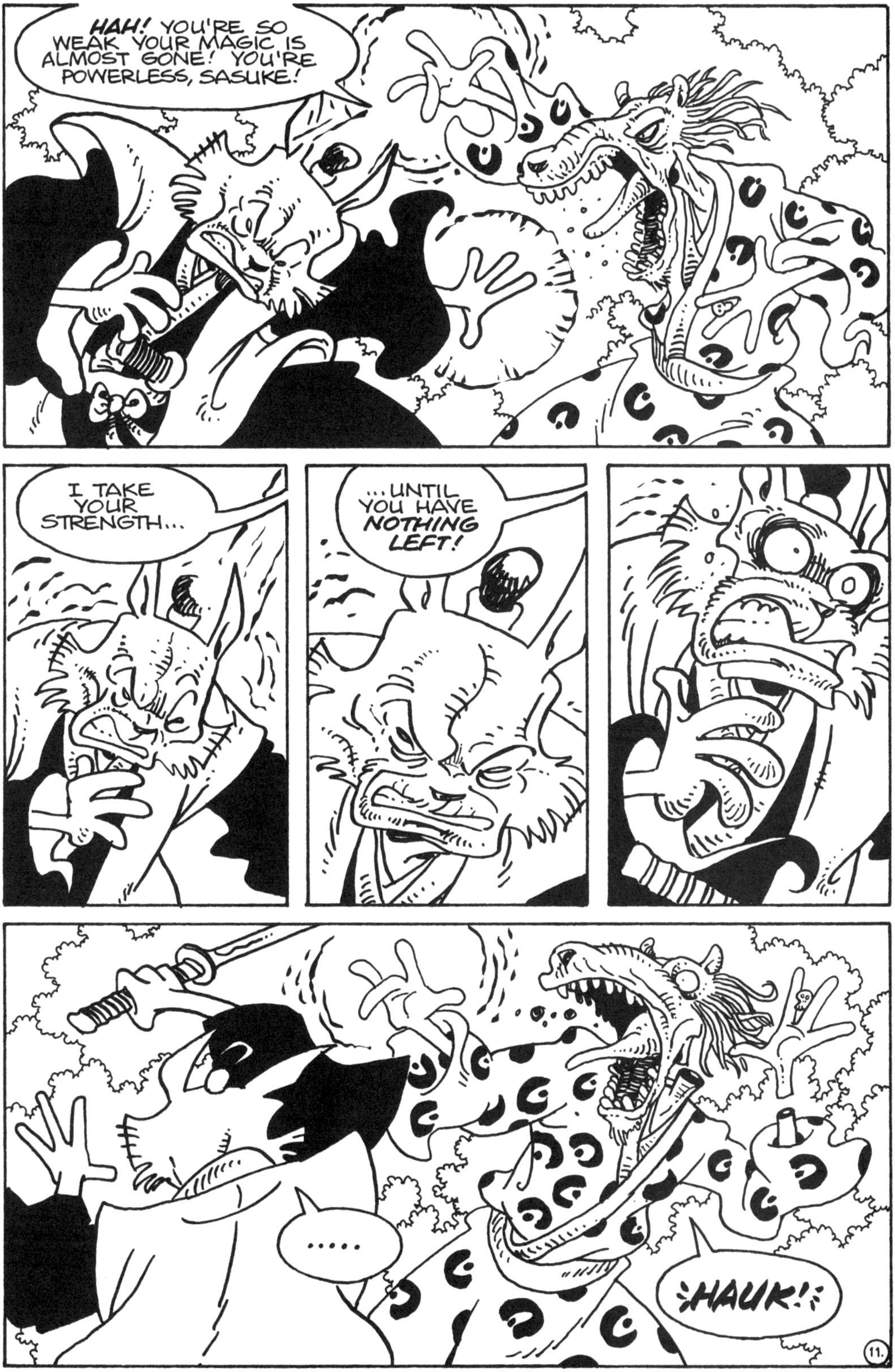
HAH! YOU'RE SO WEAK YOUR MAGIC IS ALMOST GONE! YOU'RE POWERLESS, SASUKE!
I TAKE YOUR STRENGTH...
...UNTIL YOU HAVE NOTHING LEFT!
.....
HAUK!
11.

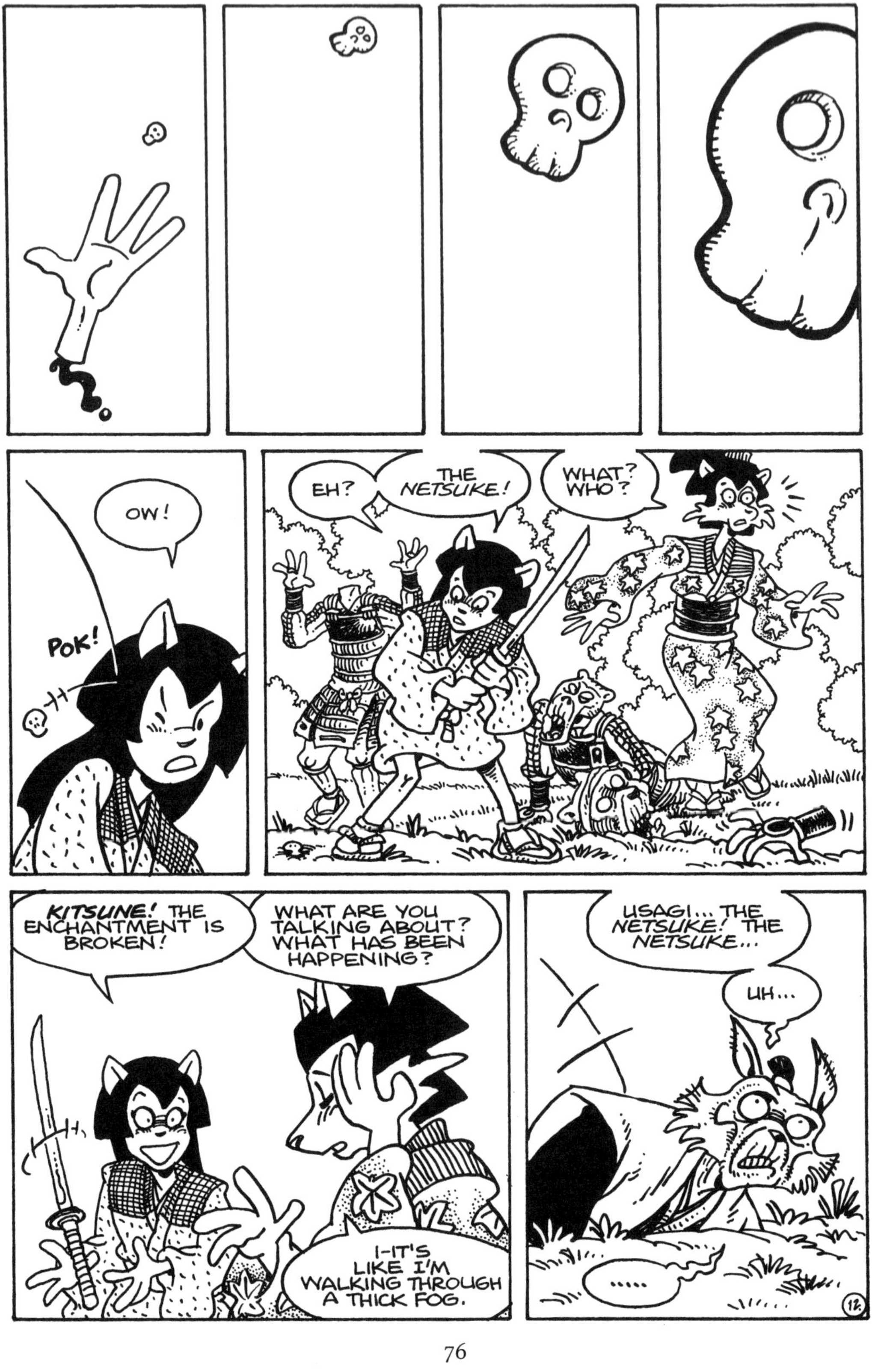
OW!
POK!
EH?
THE NETSUKE!
WHAT? WHO?
KITSUNE! THE ENCHANTMENT IS BROKEN!
WHAT ARE YOU TALKING ABOUT? WHAT HAS BEEN HAPPENING?
I-IT'S LIKE I'M WALKING THROUGH A THICK FOG.
USAGI... THE NETSUKE! THE NETSUKE...
UH...
.....
12.

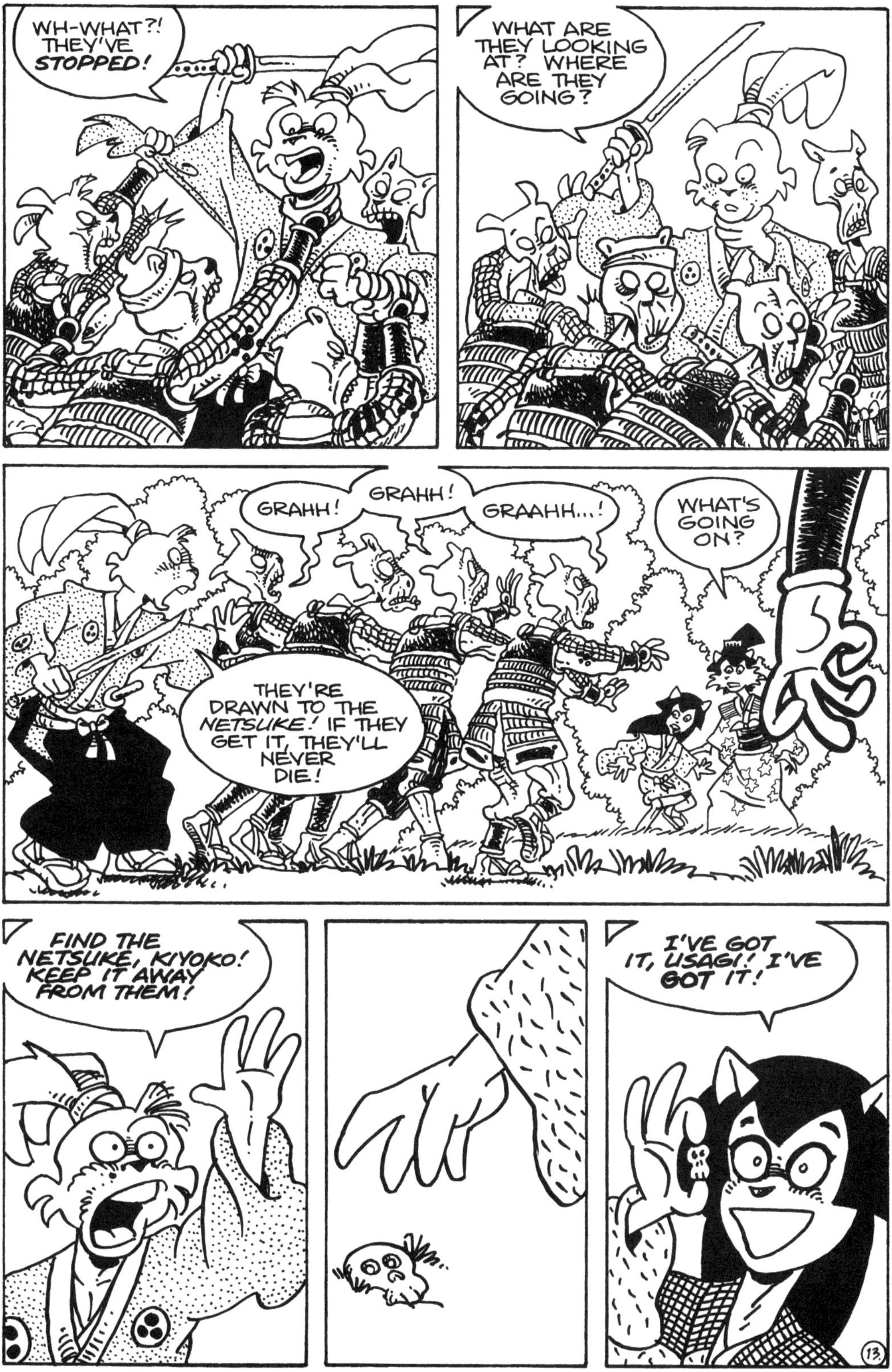
WH-WHAT?! THEY'VE STOPPED!
WHAT ARE THEY LOOKING AT? WHERE ARE THEY GOING?
GRAHH!
GRAHH!
GRAAHH...!
WHAT'S GOING ON?
THEY'RE DRAWN TO THE NETSUKE! IF THEY GET IT, THEY'LL NEVER DIE!
FIND THE NETSUKE, KIYOKO! KEEP IT AWAY FROM THEM!
I'VE GOT IT, USAGI! I'VE GOT IT!
13

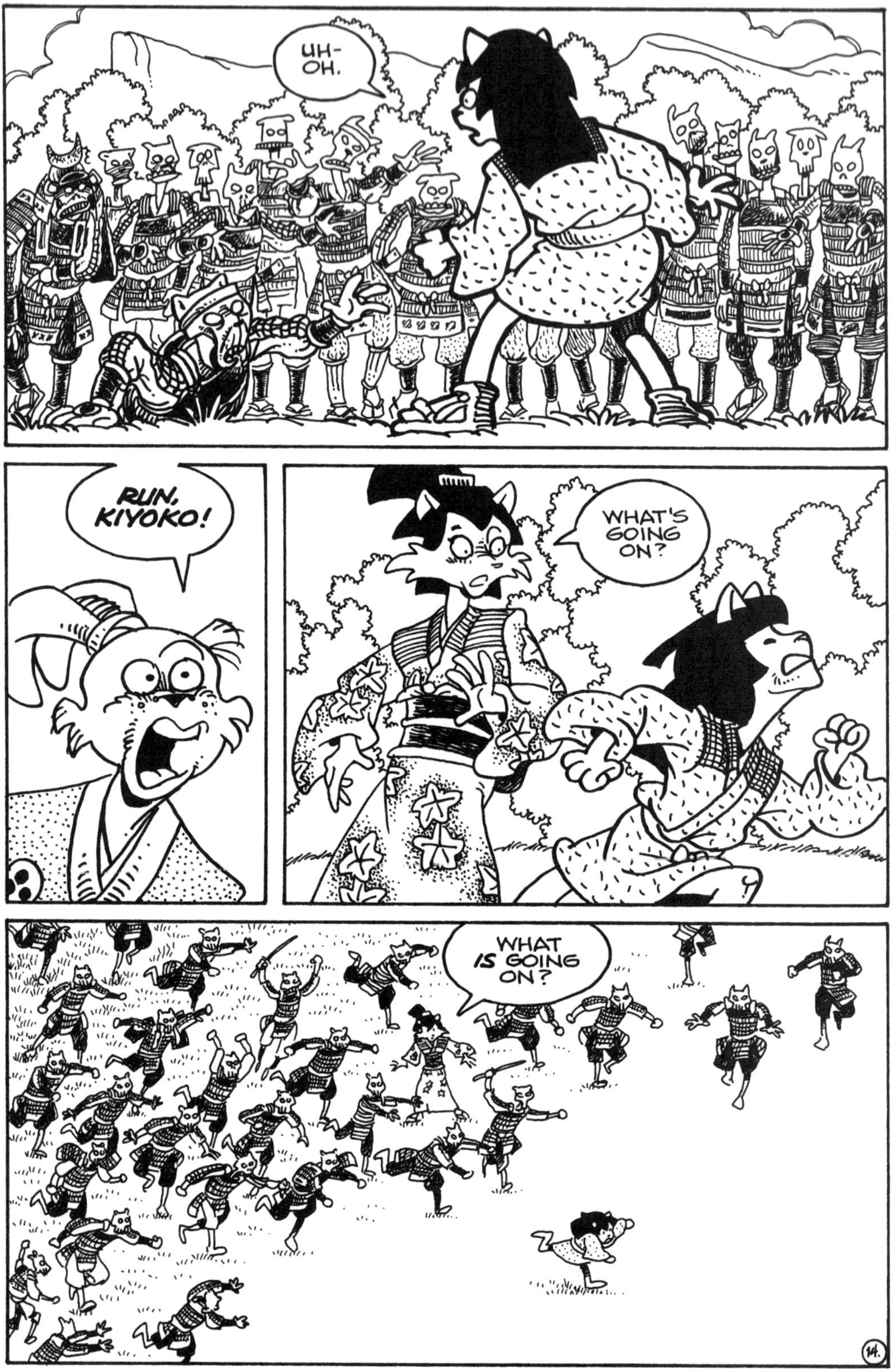
UH-OH.
RUN, KIYOKO!
WHAT'S GOING ON?
WHAT *IS* GOING ON?
14.

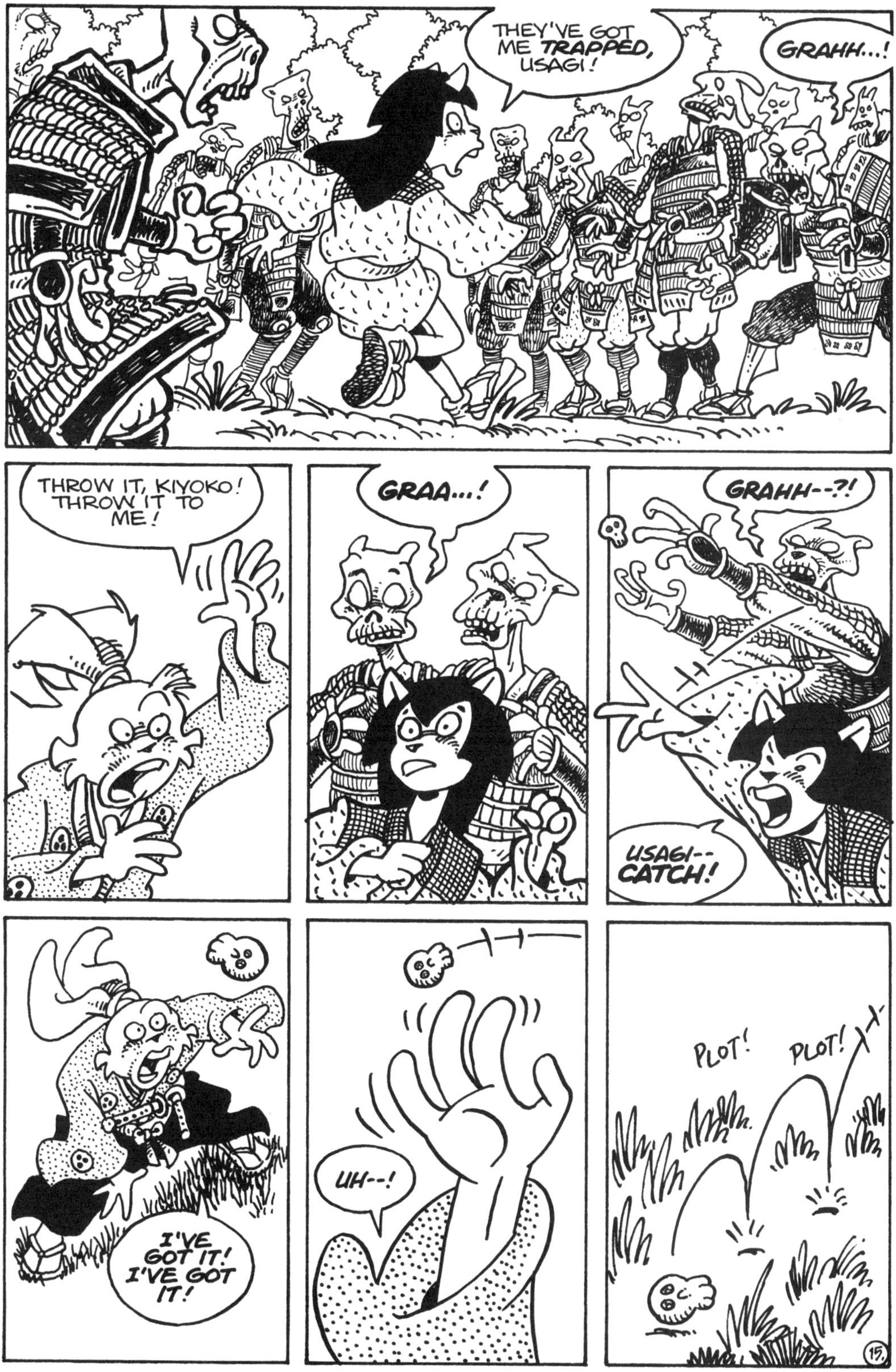
THEY'VE GOT ME **TRAPPED**, USAGI!
GRAHH...!
THROW IT, KIYOKO! THROW IT TO ME!
GRAA...!
GRAHH--?!
USAGI-- CATCH!
I'VE GOT IT! I'VE GOT IT!
UH--!
PLOT!
PLOT!
15

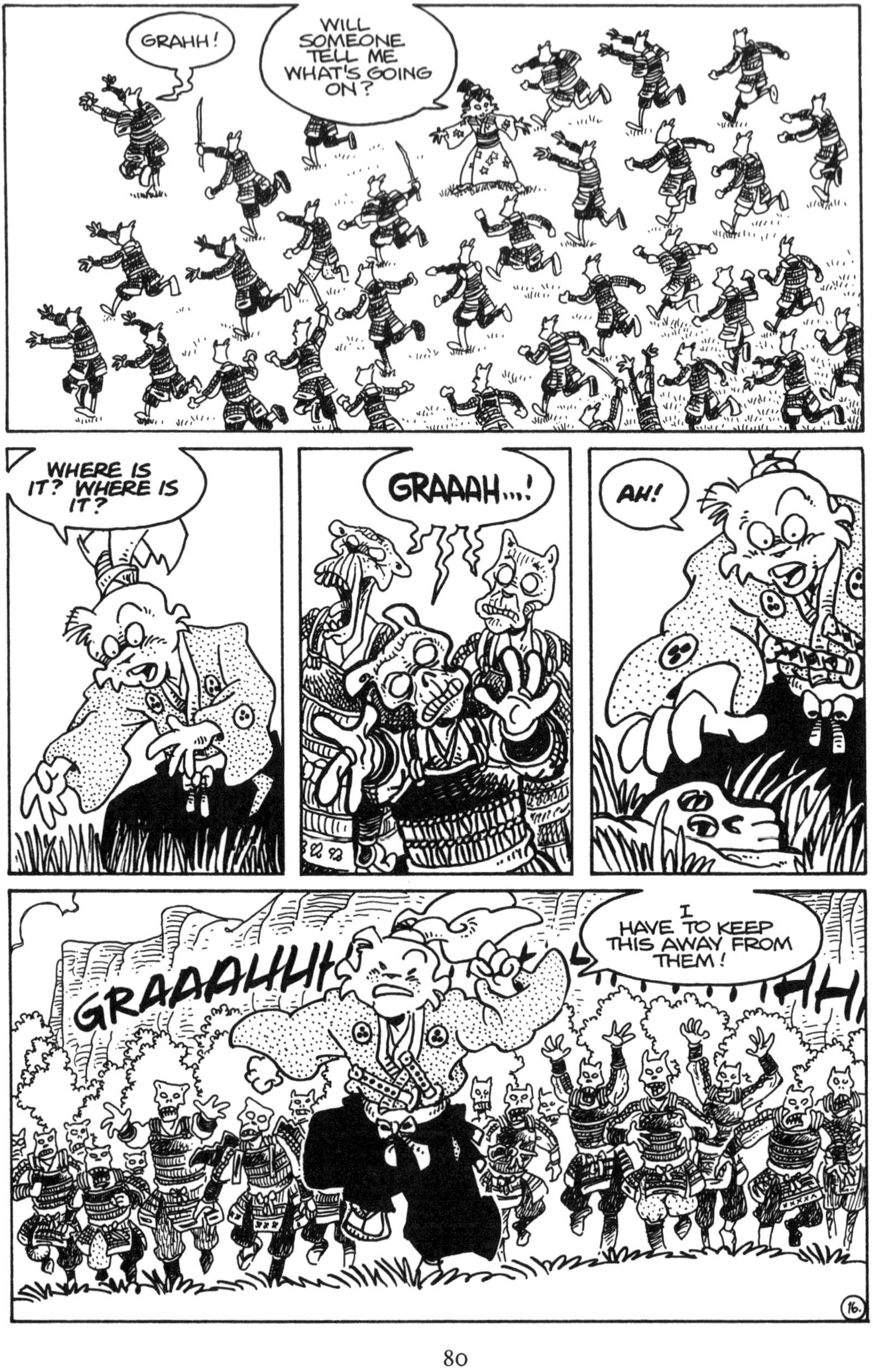
GRAHH!
WILL SOMEONE TELL ME WHAT'S GOING ON?
WHERE IS IT? WHERE IS IT?
GRAAAH...!
AH!
GRAAAHHH
I HAVE TO KEEP THIS AWAY FROM THEM!
16.

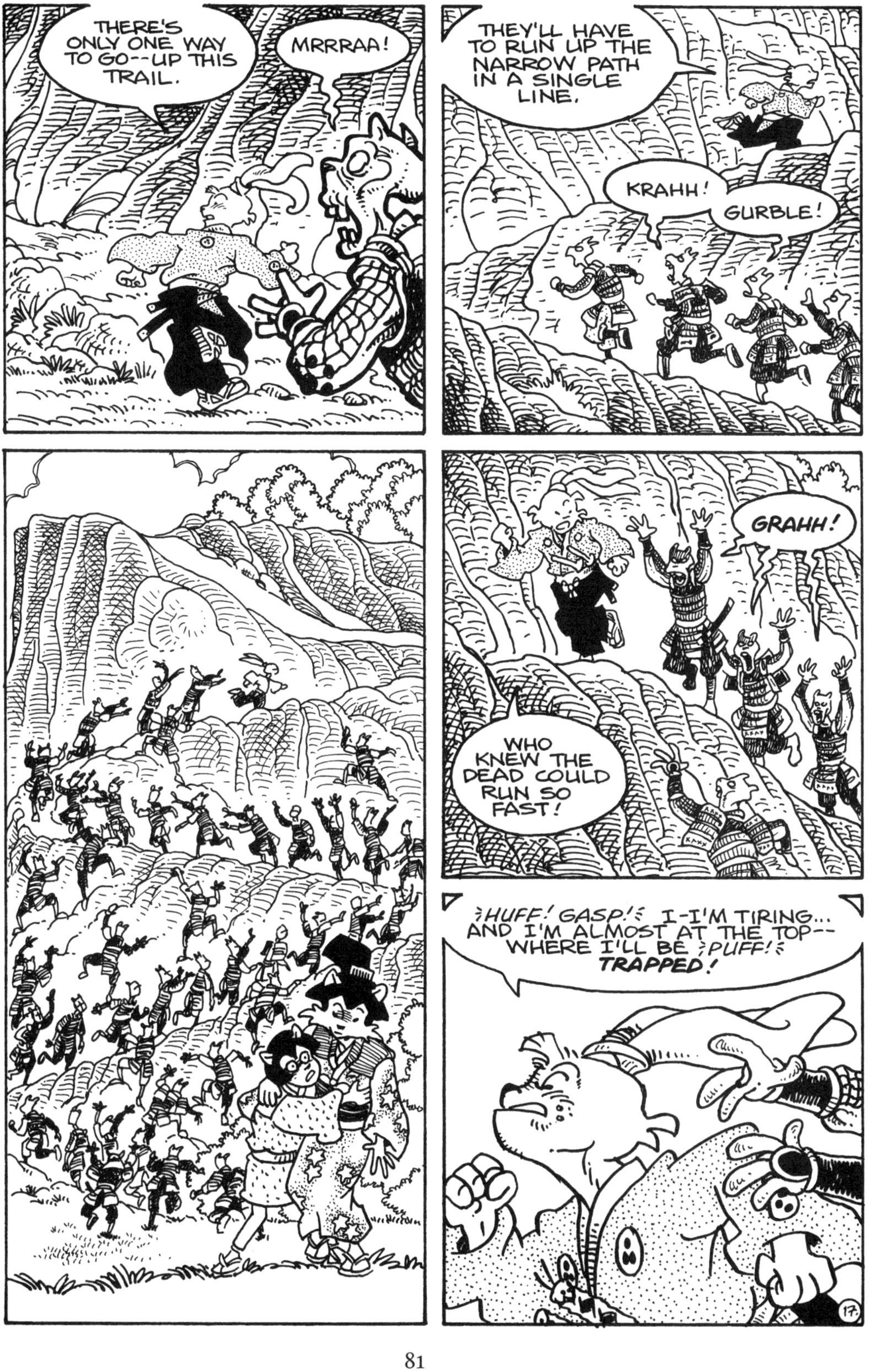
THERE'S ONLY ONE WAY TO GO--UP THIS TRAIL.
MRRRAA!
THEY'LL HAVE TO RUN UP THE NARROW PATH IN A SINGLE LINE.
KRAHH!
GURBLE!
GRAHH!
WHO KNEW THE DEAD COULD RUN SO FAST!
HUFF! GASP! I-I'M TIRING... AND I'M ALMOST AT THE TOP-- WHERE I'LL BE PUFF! TRAPPED!
17.

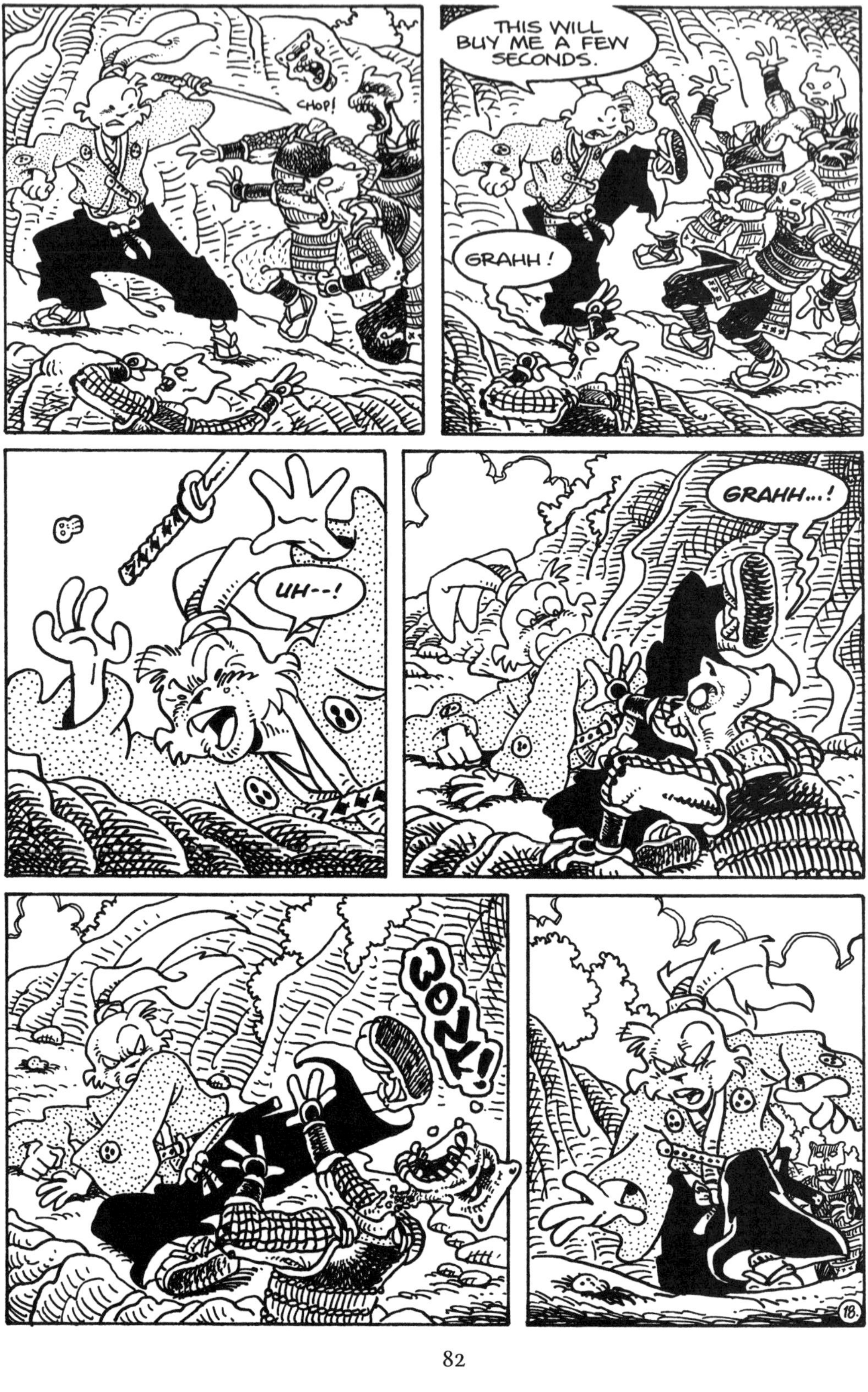
CHOP!
THIS WILL BUY ME A FEW SECONDS.
GRAHH!
UH--!
GRAHH...!
WONK!
18.

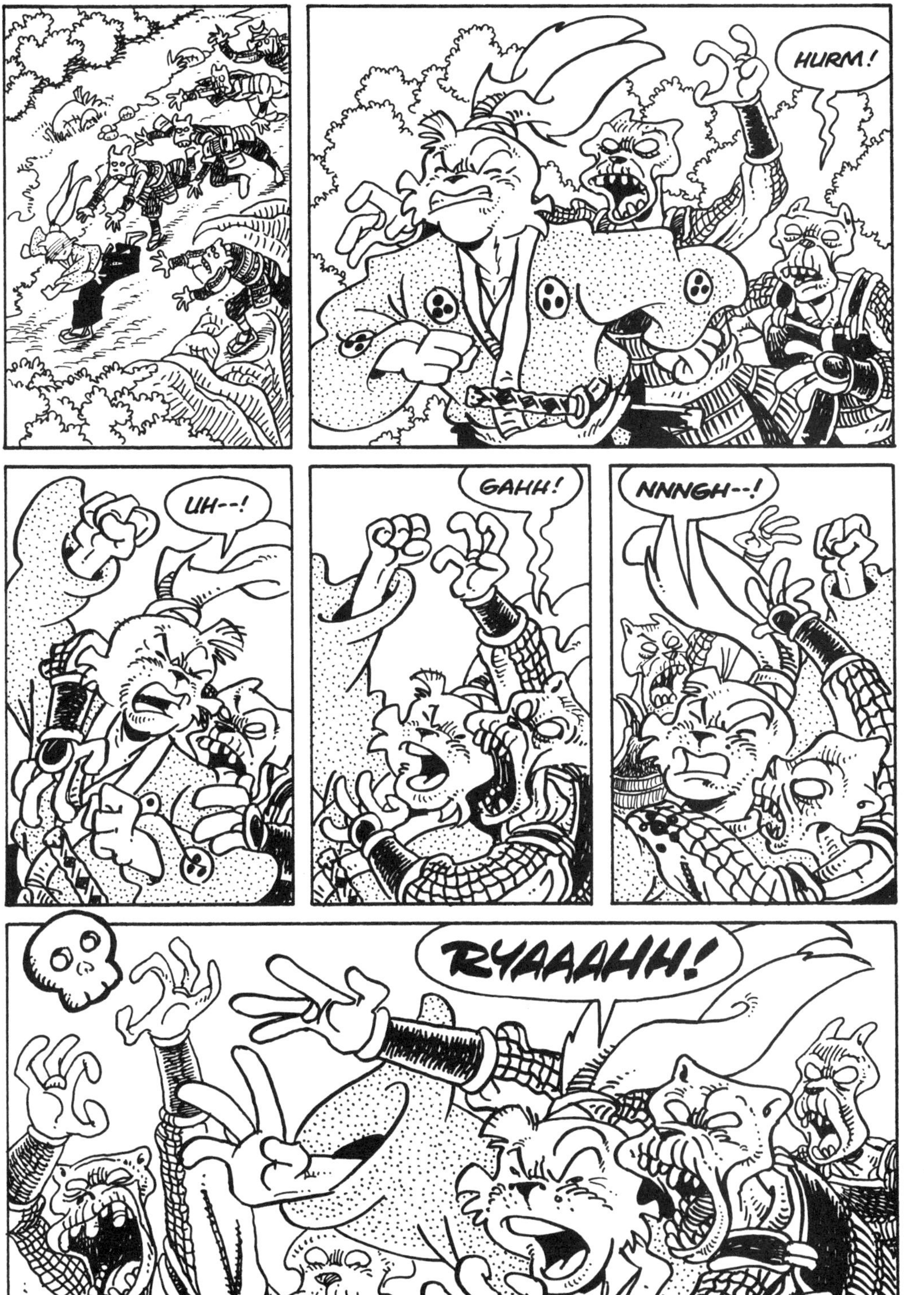
HURM!
UH--!
GAHH!
NNNGH--!
RYAAAHH!
19

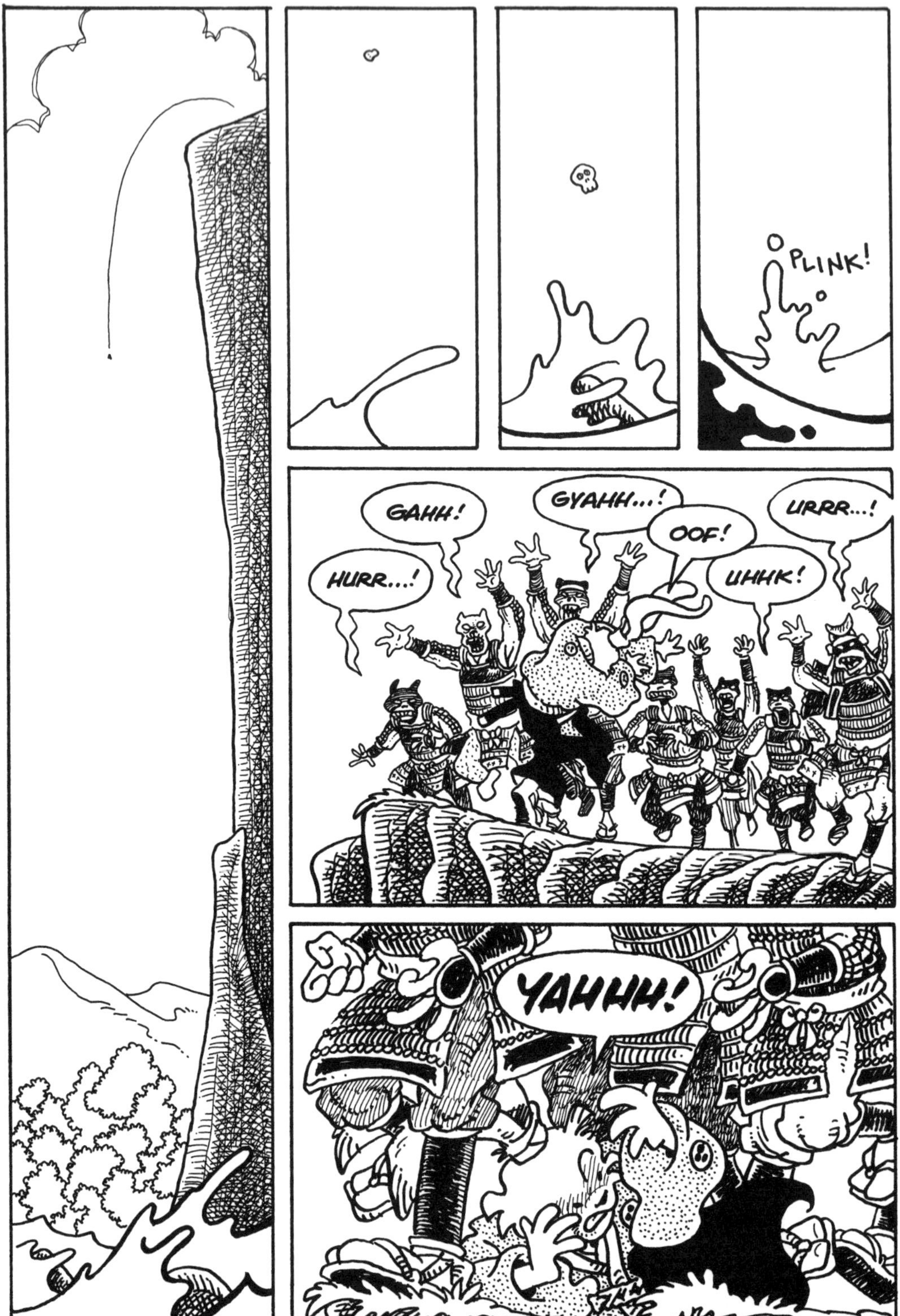
PLINK!
GAHH!
GYAHH...!
URRR...!
OOF!
HURR...!
UHHK!
YAHHH!
20.

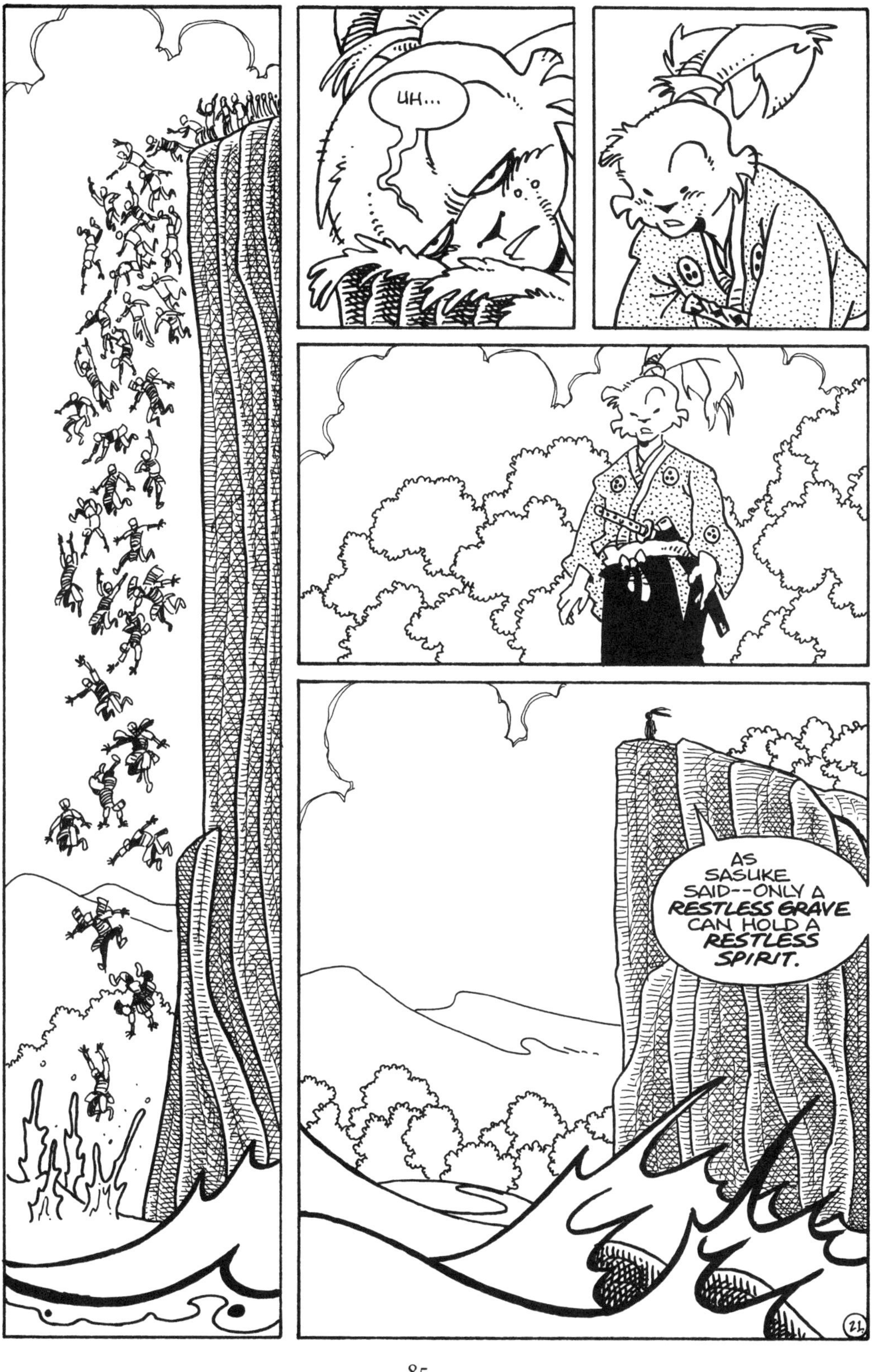
UH...
AS SASUKE SAID--ONLY A RESTLESS GRAVE CAN HOLD A RESTLESS SPIRIT.
21

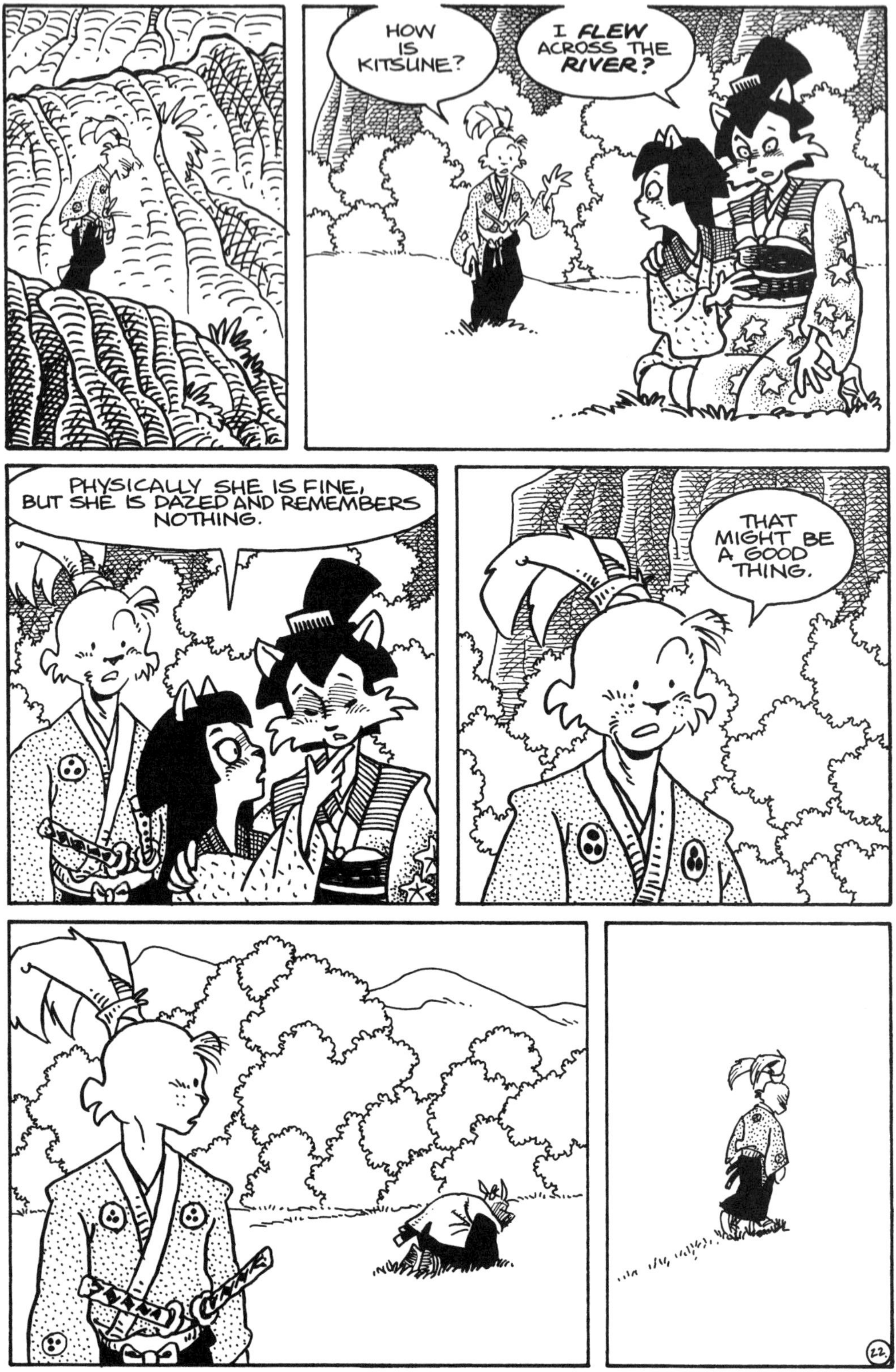
HOW IS KITSUNE?
I FLEW ACROSS THE RIVER?
PHYSICALLY SHE IS FINE, BUT SHE IS DAZED AND REMEMBERS NOTHING.
THAT MIGHT BE A GOOD THING.
22.

SASUKE-- ARE YOU ALL RIGHT?

GODS!

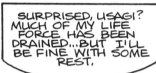

SURPRISED, USAGI? MUCH OF MY LIFE FORCE HAS BEEN DRAINED...BUT I'LL BE FINE WITH SOME REST.

SASUKE...

SHOKI!

SHOKI?!

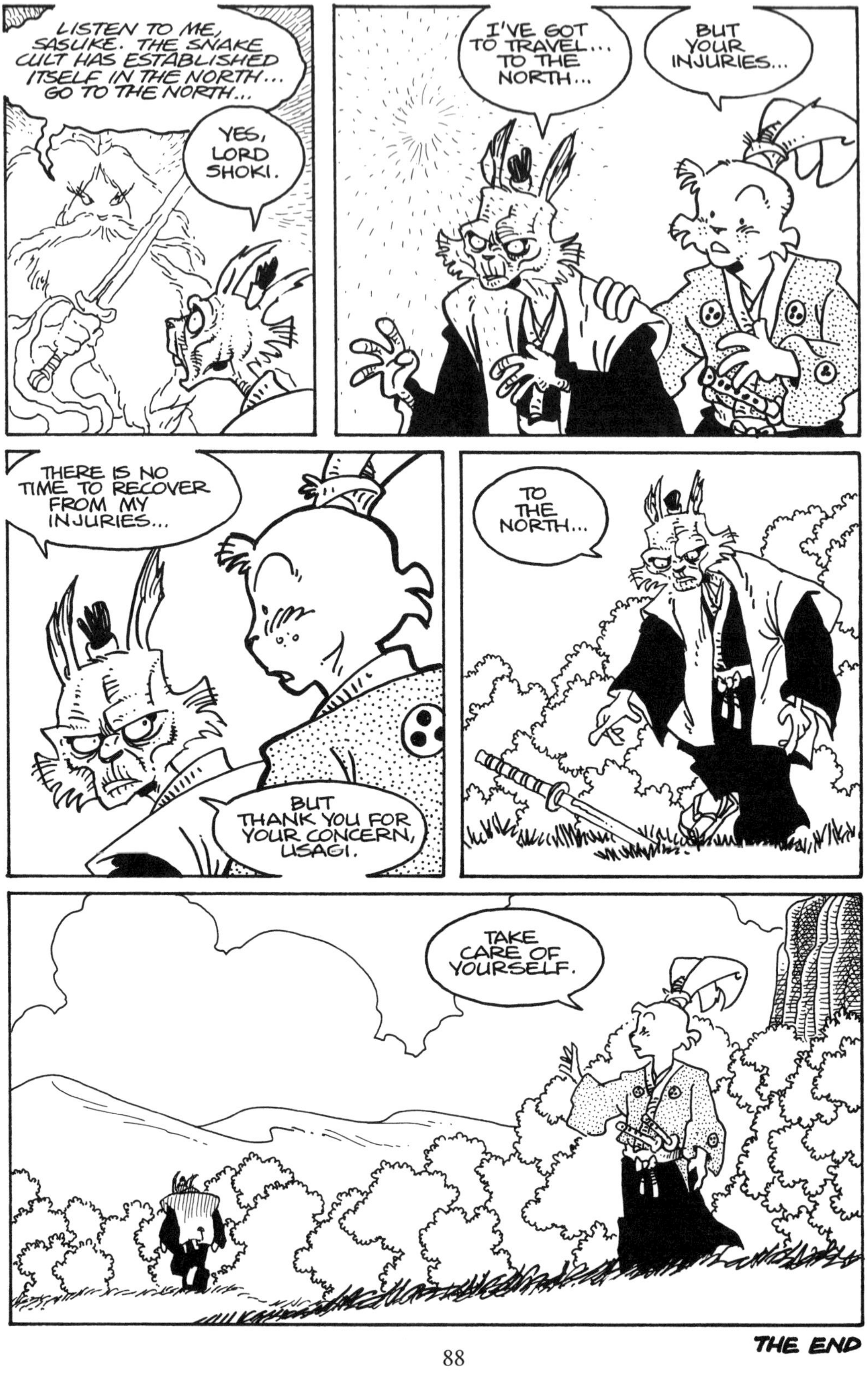
LISTEN TO ME, SASUKE. THE SNAKE CULT HAS ESTABLISHED ITSELF IN THE NORTH... GO TO THE NORTH...
YES, LORD SHOKI.
I'VE GOT TO TRAVEL... TO THE NORTH...
BUT YOUR INJURIES...
THERE IS NO TIME TO RECOVER FROM MY INJURIES...
BUT THANK YOU FOR YOUR CONCERN, USAGI.
TO THE NORTH...
TAKE CARE OF YOURSELF.
THE END

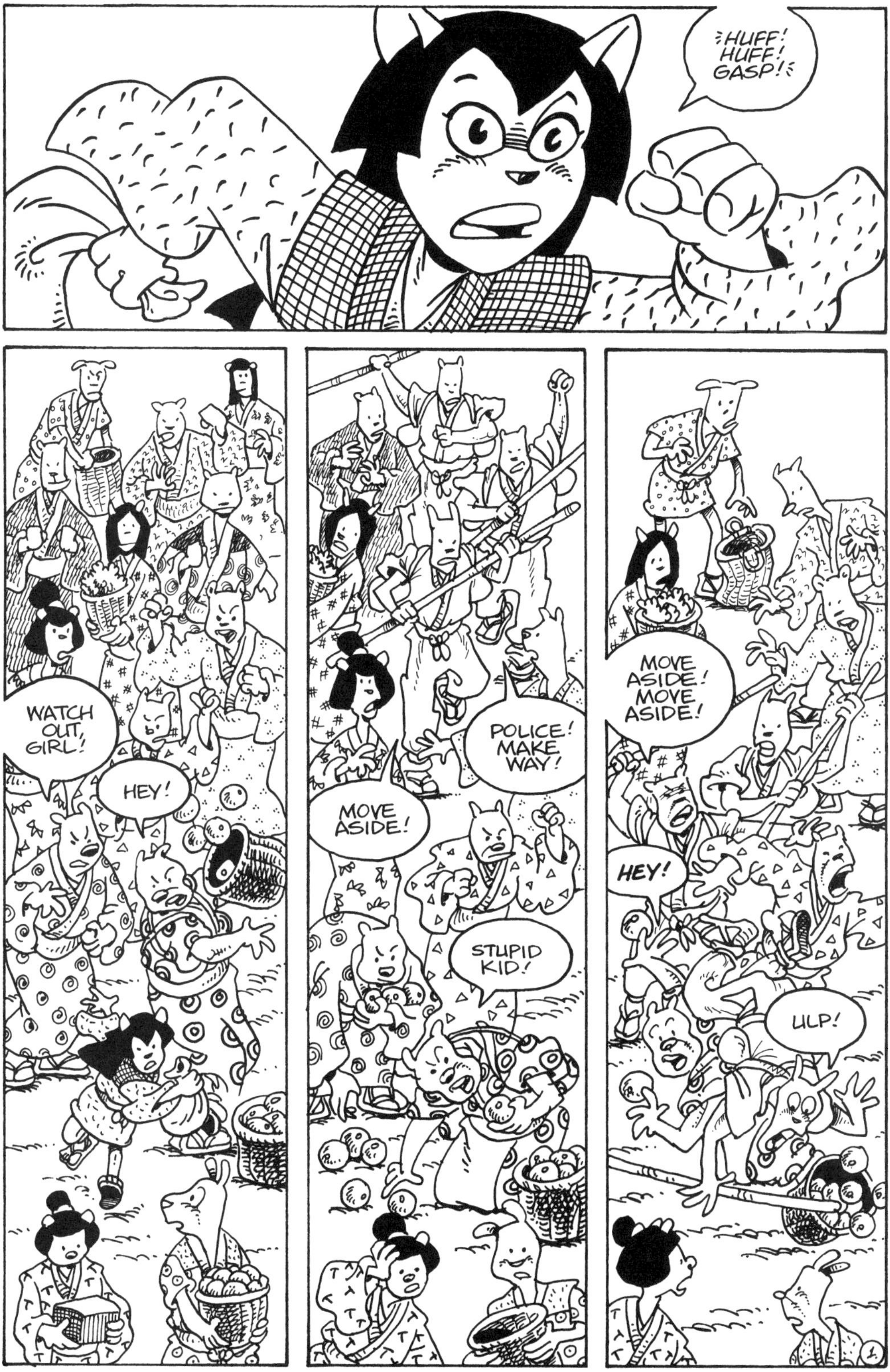
HUFF! HUFF! GASP!
WATCH OUT, GIRL!
HEY!
POLICE! MAKE WAY!
MOVE ASIDE!
STUPID KID!
MOVE ASIDE! MOVE ASIDE!
HEY!
ULP!

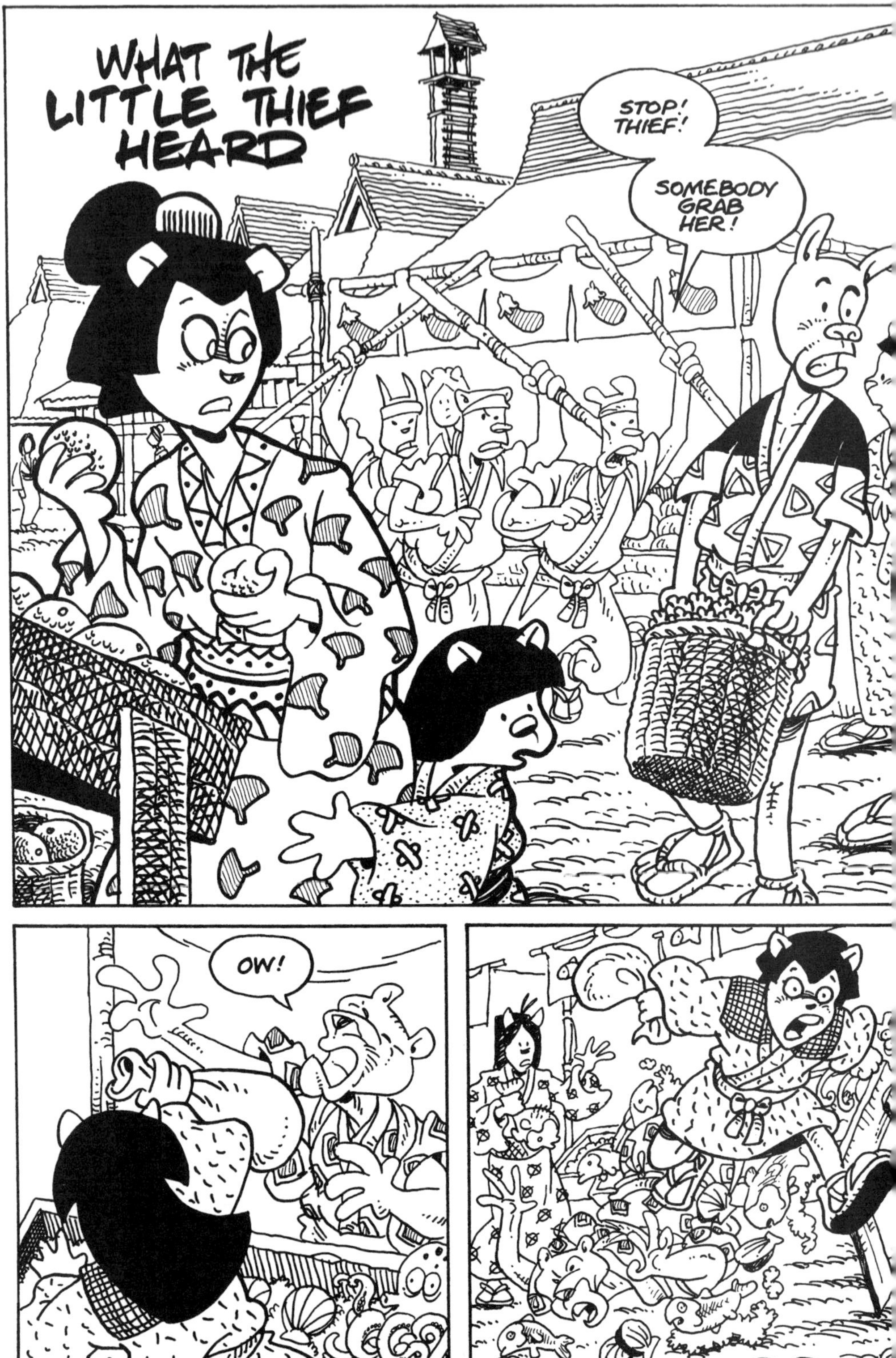
WHAT THE LITTLE THIEF HEARD
STOP! THIEF!
SOMEBODY GRAB HER!
OW!

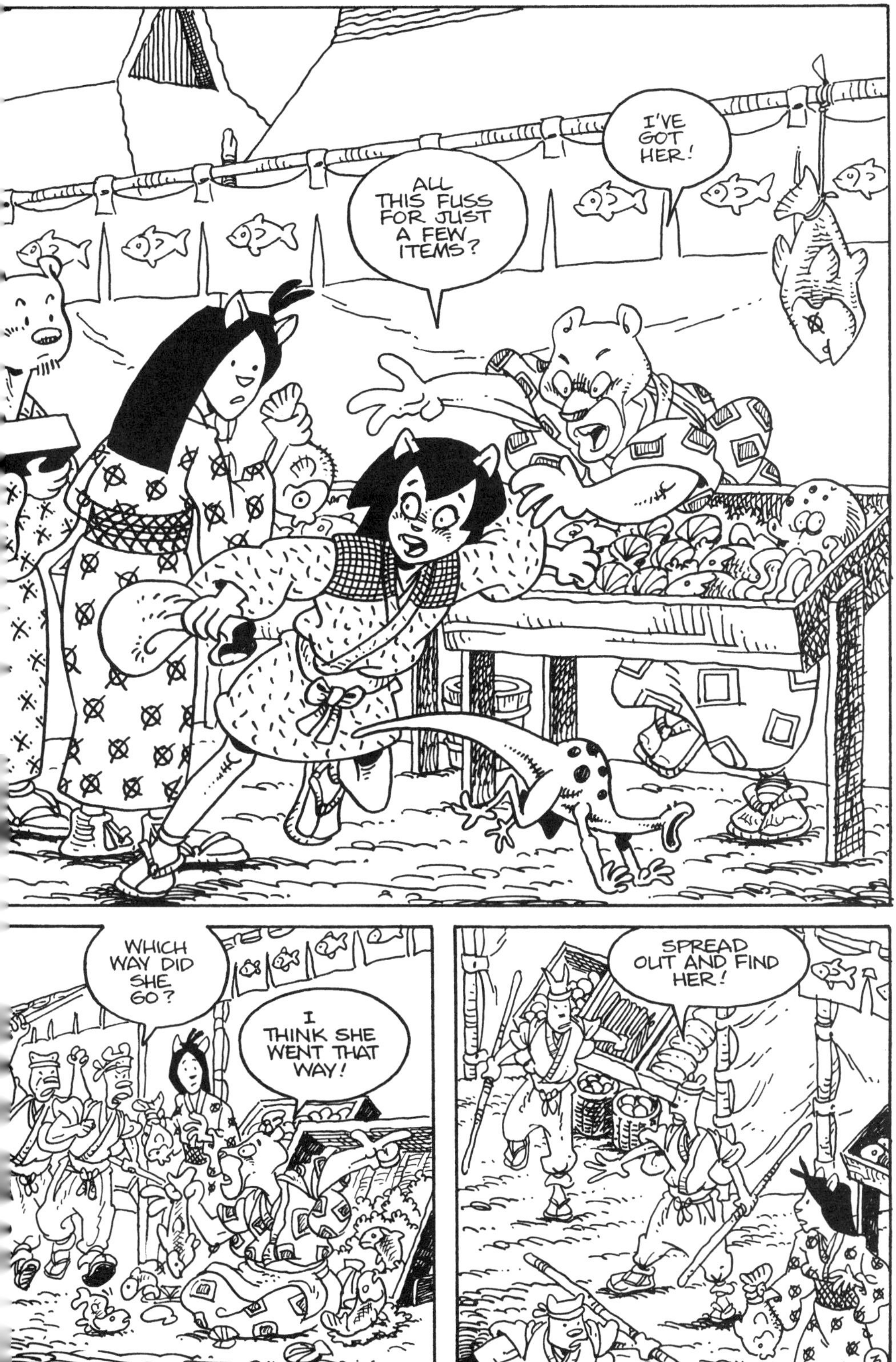

ALL THIS FUSS FOR JUST A FEW ITEMS?
I'VE GOT HER!
WHICH WAY DID SHE GO?
I THINK SHE WENT THAT WAY!
SPREAD OUT AND FIND HER!

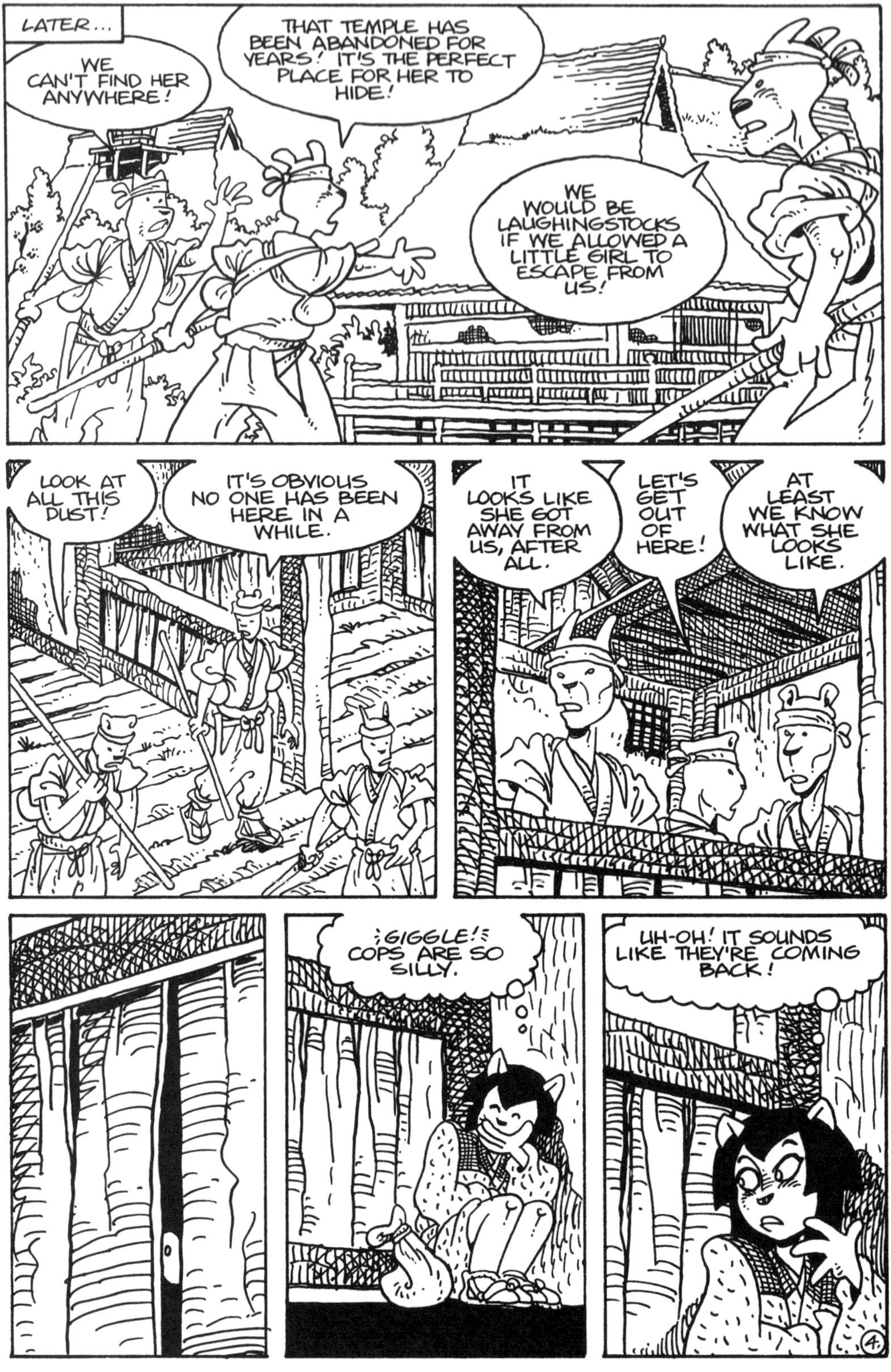
LATER...
WE CAN'T FIND HER ANYWHERE!
THAT TEMPLE HAS BEEN ABANDONED FOR YEARS! IT'S THE PERFECT PLACE FOR HER TO HIDE!
WE WOULD BE LAUGHINGSTOCKS IF WE ALLOWED A LITTLE GIRL TO ESCAPE FROM US!
LOOK AT ALL THIS DUST!
IT'S OBVIOUS NO ONE HAS BEEN HERE IN A WHILE.
IT LOOKS LIKE SHE GOT AWAY FROM US, AFTER ALL.
LET'S GET OUT OF HERE!
AT LEAST WE KNOW WHAT SHE LOOKS LIKE.
:GIGGLE!: COPS ARE SO SILLY.
UH-OH! IT SOUNDS LIKE THEY'RE COMING BACK!
4

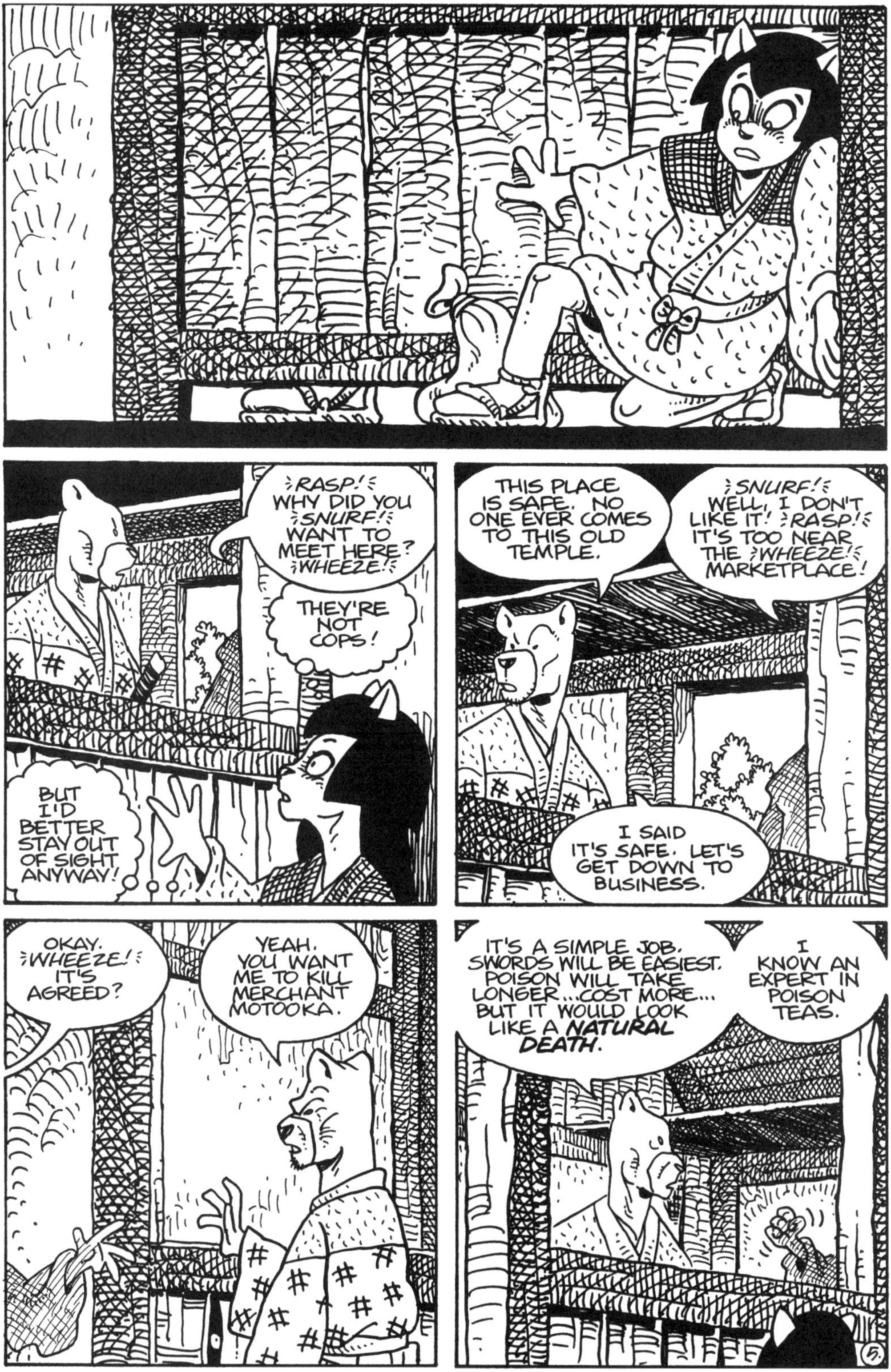
RASP! WHY DID YOU SNURF! WANT TO MEET HERE? WHEEZE!
THEY'RE NOT COPS!
BUT I'D BETTER STAY OUT OF SIGHT ANYWAY!
THIS PLACE IS SAFE. NO ONE EVER COMES TO THIS OLD TEMPLE.
SNURF! WELL, I DON'T LIKE IT! RASP! IT'S TOO NEAR THE WHEEZE! MARKETPLACE!
I SAID IT'S SAFE. LET'S GET DOWN TO BUSINESS.
OKAY. WHEEZE! IT'S AGREED?
YEAH. YOU WANT ME TO KILL MERCHANT MOTOOKA.
IT'S A SIMPLE JOB. SWORDS WILL BE EASIEST. POISON WILL TAKE LONGER...COST MORE... BUT IT WOULD LOOK LIKE A **NATURAL DEATH**.
I KNOW AN EXPERT IN POISON TEAS.
5

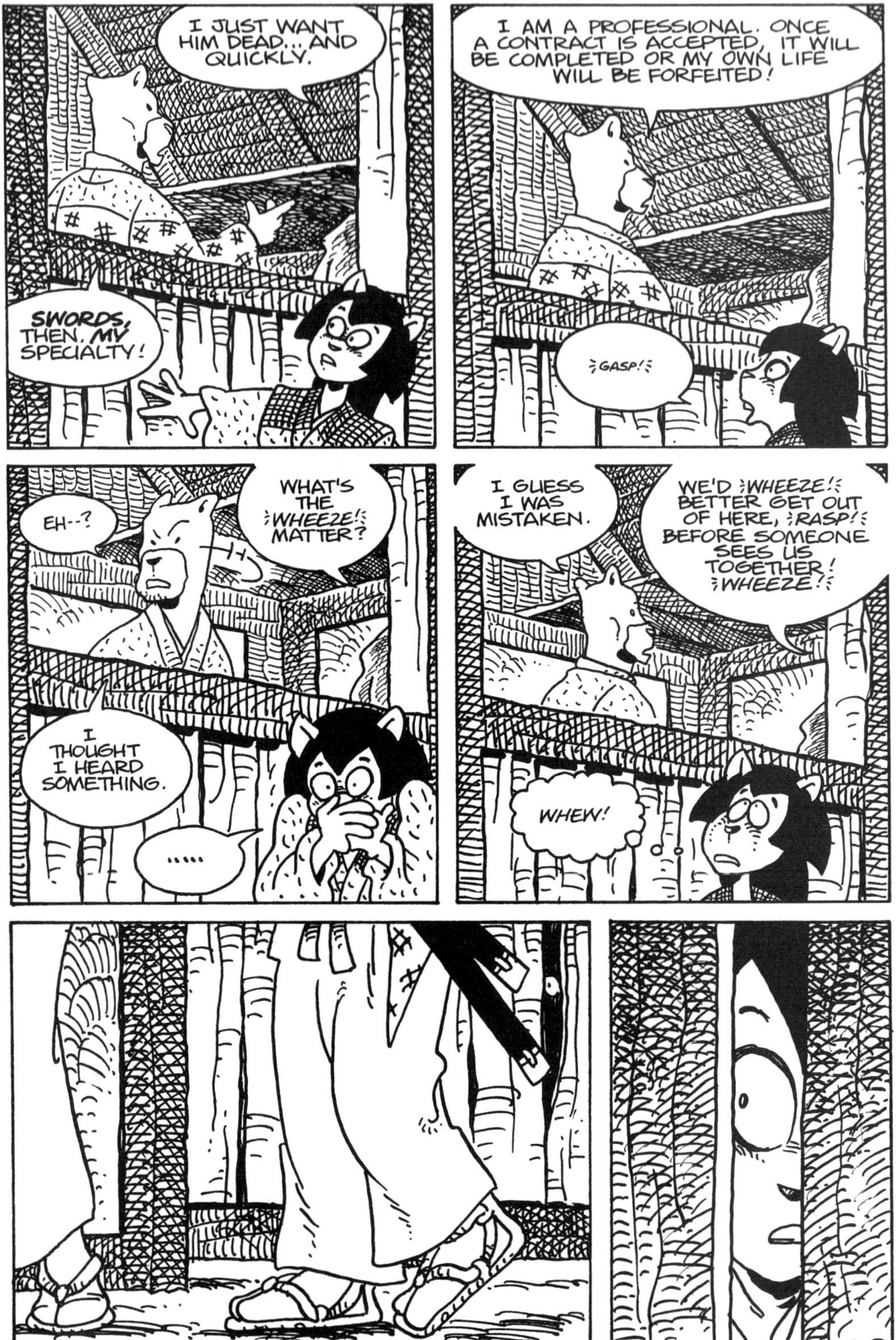
I JUST WANT HIM DEAD... AND QUICKLY.
SWORDS, THEN, MY SPECIALTY!
I AM A PROFESSIONAL. ONCE A CONTRACT IS ACCEPTED, IT WILL BE COMPLETED OR MY OWN LIFE WILL BE FORFEITED!
GASP!
EH--?
WHAT'S THE WHEEZE! MATTER?
I THOUGHT I HEARD SOMETHING.
.....
I GUESS I WAS MISTAKEN.
WE'D WHEEZE! BETTER GET OUT OF HERE, RASP! BEFORE SOMEONE SEES US TOGETHER! WHEEZE!
WHEW!
6.

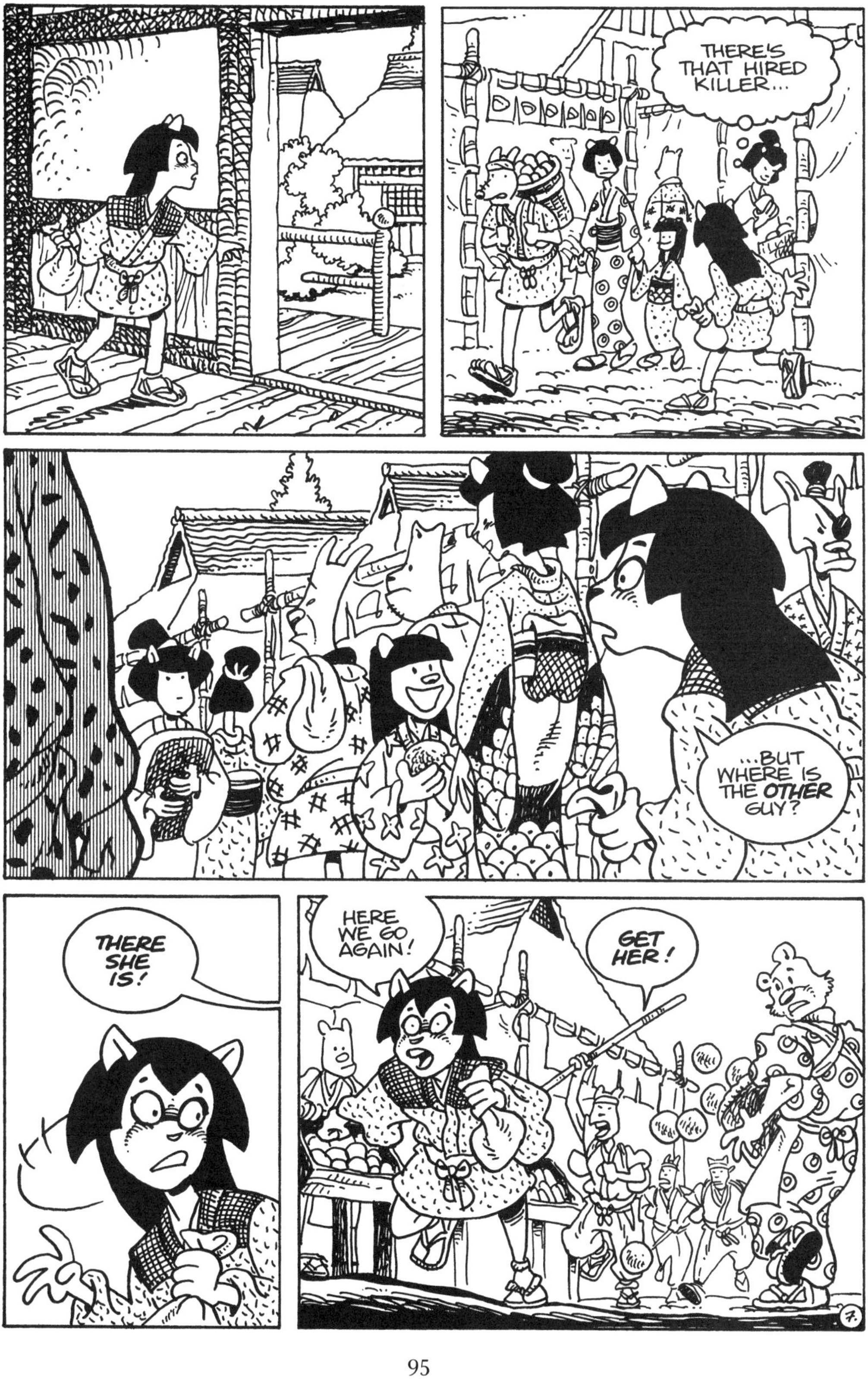
THERE'S THAT HIRED KILLER...
...BUT WHERE IS THE OTHER GUY?
THERE SHE IS!
HERE WE GO AGAIN!
GET HER!

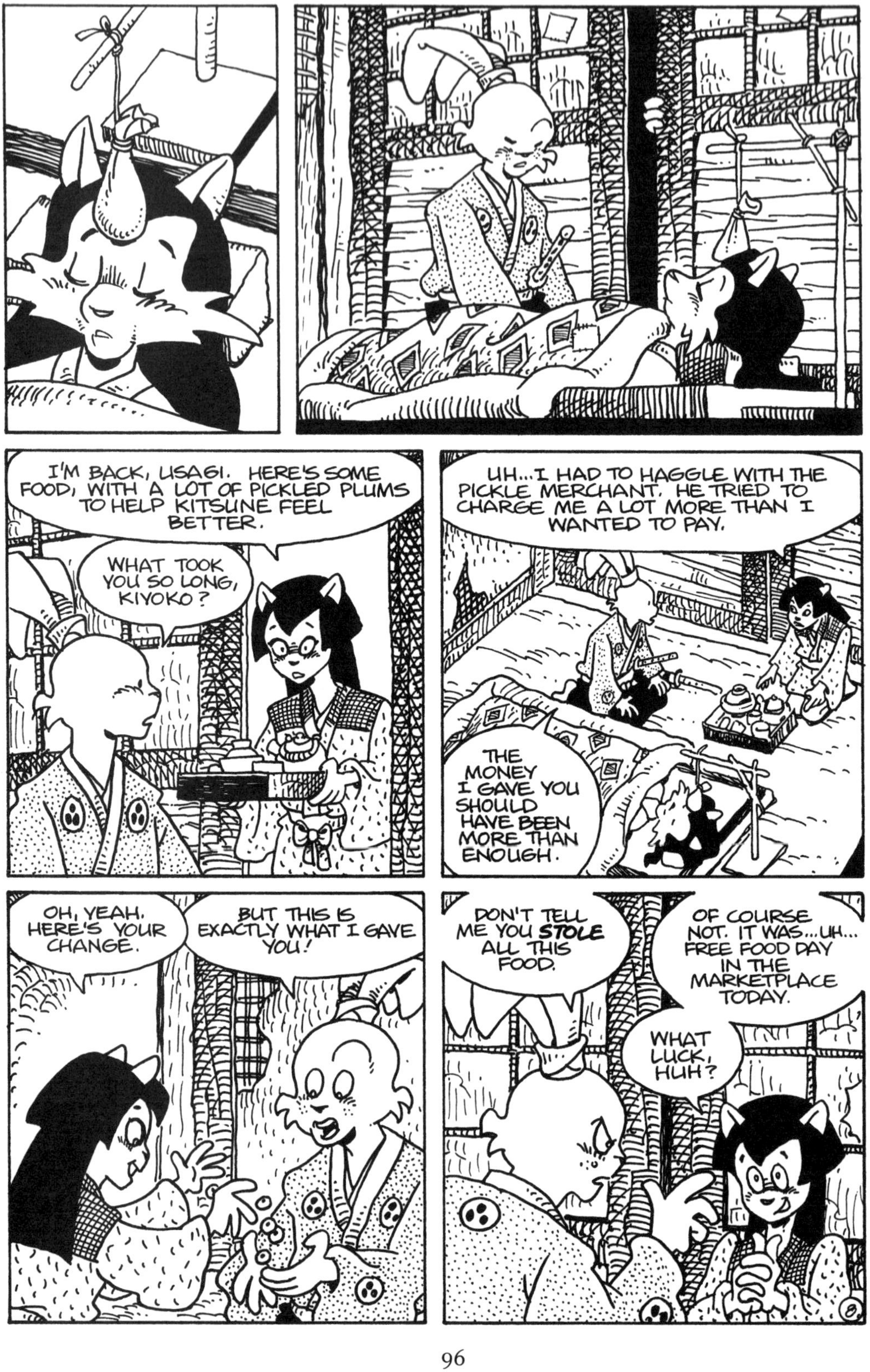
I'M BACK, USAGI. HERE'S SOME FOOD, WITH A LOT OF PICKLED PLUMS TO HELP KITSUNE FEEL BETTER.
WHAT TOOK YOU SO LONG, KIYOKO?
UH...I HAD TO HAGGLE WITH THE PICKLE MERCHANT. HE TRIED TO CHARGE ME A LOT MORE THAN I WANTED TO PAY.
THE MONEY I GAVE YOU SHOULD HAVE BEEN MORE THAN ENOUGH.
OH, YEAH. HERE'S YOUR CHANGE.
BUT THIS IS EXACTLY WHAT I GAVE YOU!
DON'T TELL ME YOU **STOLE** ALL THIS FOOD.
OF COURSE NOT. IT WAS...UH... FREE FOOD DAY IN THE MARKETPLACE TODAY.
WHAT LUCK, HUH?

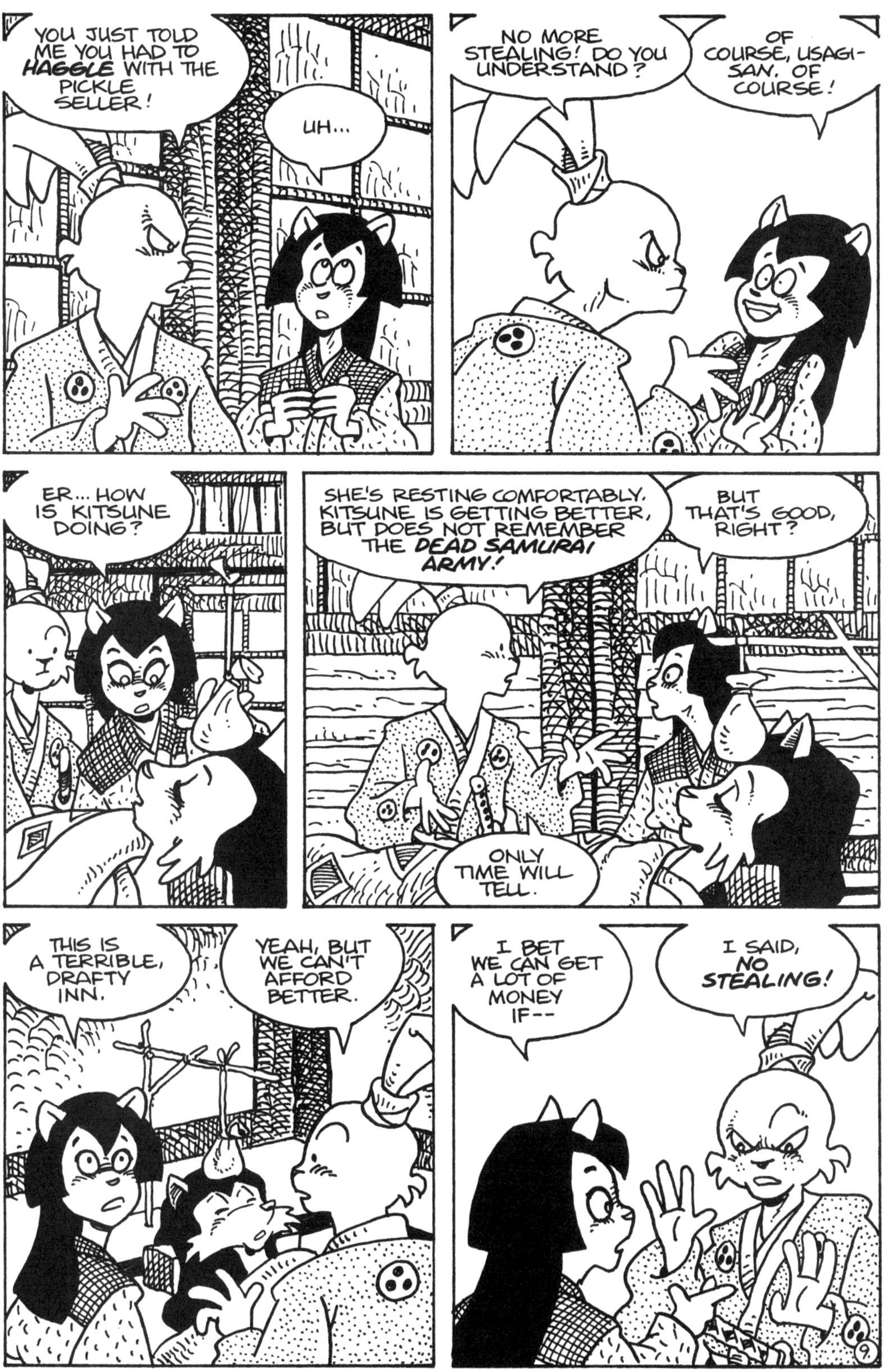
YOU JUST TOLD ME YOU HAD TO **HAGGLE** WITH THE PICKLE SELLER!
UH...
NO MORE STEALING! DO YOU UNDERSTAND?
OF COURSE, USAGI-SAN. OF COURSE!
ER... HOW IS KITSUNE DOING?
SHE'S RESTING COMFORTABLY. KITSUNE IS GETTING BETTER, BUT DOES NOT REMEMBER THE **DEAD SAMURAI ARMY!**
BUT THAT'S GOOD, RIGHT?
ONLY TIME WILL TELL.
THIS IS A TERRIBLE, DRAFTY INN.
YEAH, BUT WE CAN'T AFFORD BETTER.
I BET WE CAN GET A LOT OF MONEY IF--
I SAID, **NO STEALING!**
9.

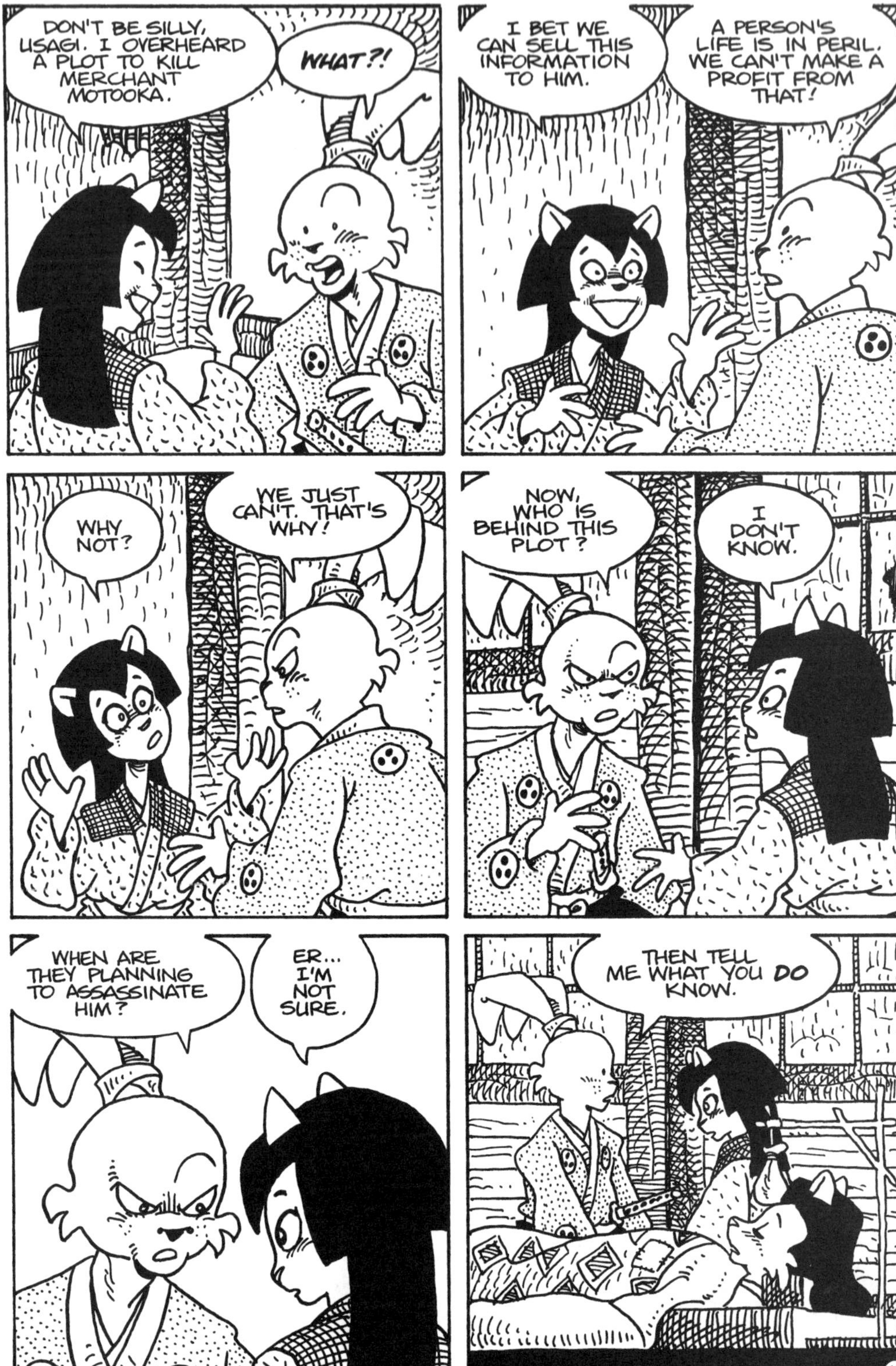
DON'T BE SILLY, USAGI. I OVERHEARD A PLOT TO KILL MERCHANT MOTOOKA.
WHAT?!
I BET WE CAN SELL THIS INFORMATION TO HIM.
A PERSON'S LIFE IS IN PERIL. WE CAN'T MAKE A PROFIT FROM THAT!
WHY NOT?
WE JUST CAN'T. THAT'S WHY!
NOW, WHO IS BEHIND THIS PLOT?
I DON'T KNOW.
WHEN ARE THEY PLANNING TO ASSASSINATE HIM?
ER... I'M NOT SURE.
THEN TELL ME WHAT YOU DO KNOW.
10.

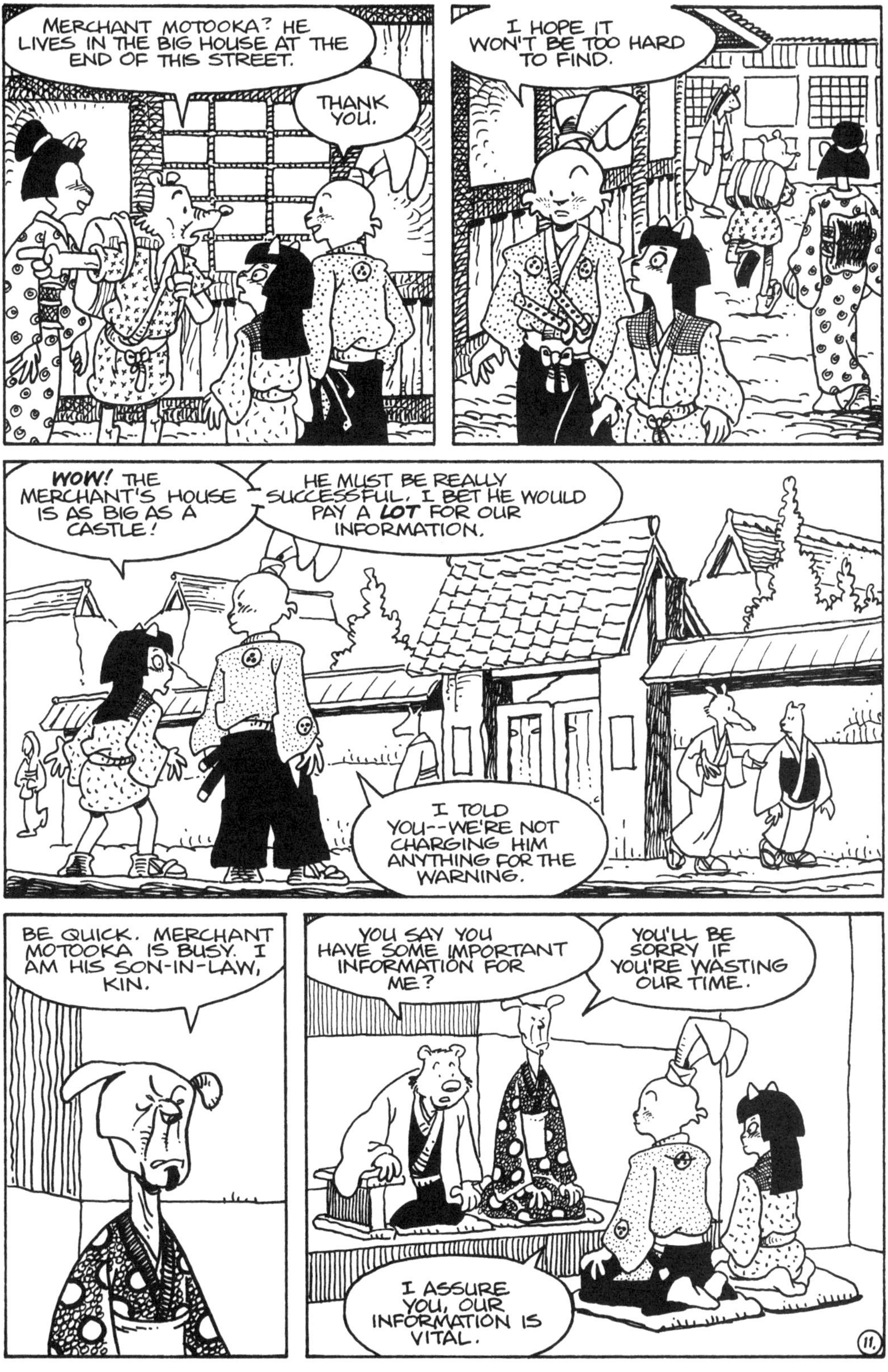
MERCHANT MOTOOKA? HE LIVES IN THE BIG HOUSE AT THE END OF THIS STREET.
THANK YOU.
I HOPE IT WON'T BE TOO HARD TO FIND.
WOW! THE MERCHANT'S HOUSE IS AS BIG AS A CASTLE!
HE MUST BE REALLY SUCCESSFUL. I BET HE WOULD PAY A LOT FOR OUR INFORMATION.
I TOLD YOU--WE'RE NOT CHARGING HIM ANYTHING FOR THE WARNING.
BE QUICK. MERCHANT MOTOOKA IS BUSY. I AM HIS SON-IN-LAW, KIN.
YOU SAY YOU HAVE SOME IMPORTANT INFORMATION FOR ME?
YOU'LL BE SORRY IF YOU'RE WASTING OUR TIME.
I ASSURE YOU, OUR INFORMATION IS VITAL.
11.

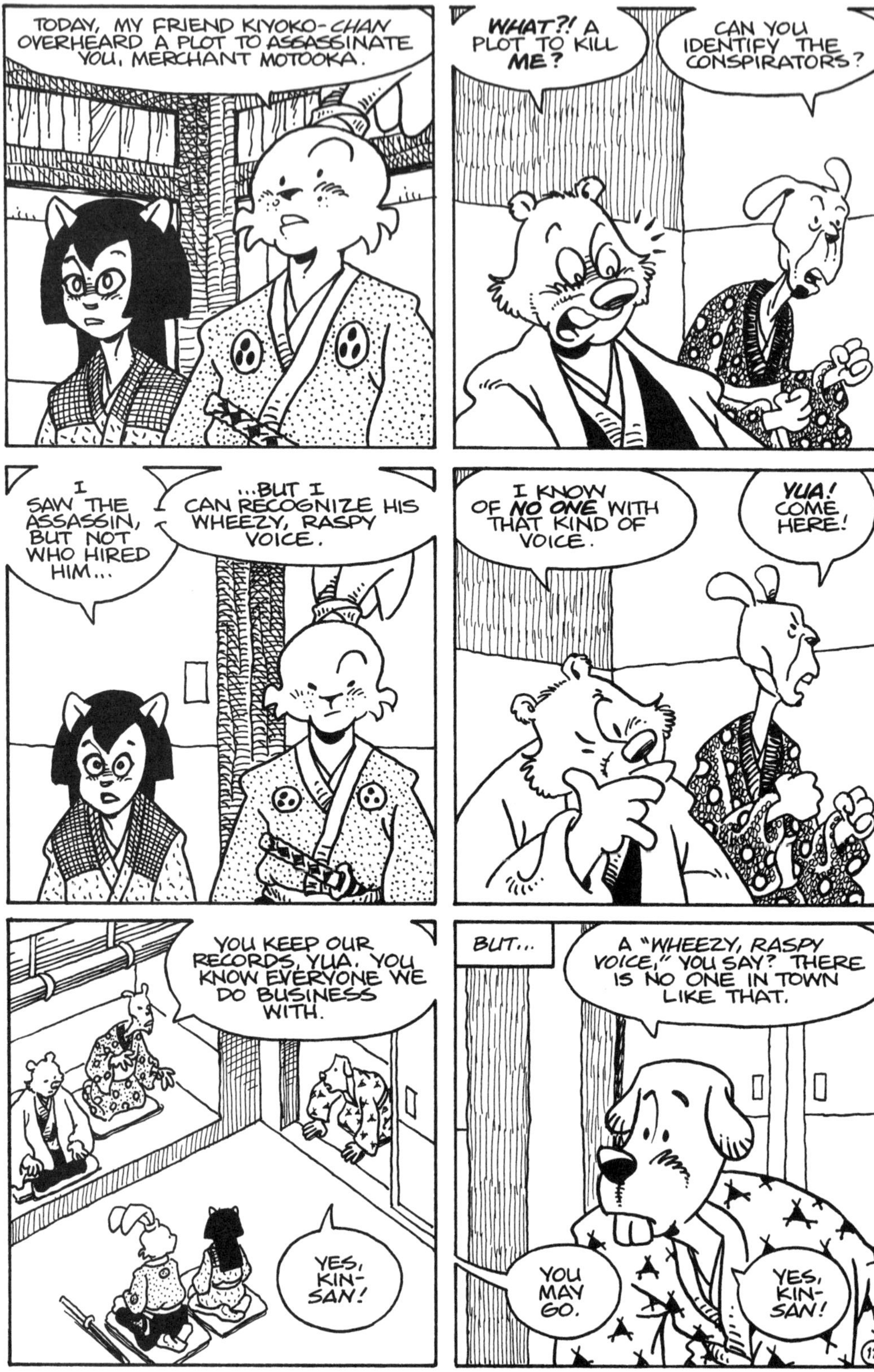
TODAY, MY FRIEND KIYOKO-*CHAN* OVERHEARD A PLOT TO ASSASSINATE YOU, MERCHANT MOTOOKA.
WHAT?! A PLOT TO KILL ***ME?***
CAN YOU IDENTIFY THE CONSPIRATORS?
I SAW THE ASSASSIN, BUT NOT WHO HIRED HIM...
...BUT I CAN RECOGNIZE HIS WHEEZY, RASPY VOICE.
I KNOW OF ***NO ONE*** WITH THAT KIND OF VOICE.
YUA! COME HERE!
YOU KEEP OUR RECORDS, YUA. YOU KNOW EVERYONE WE DO BUSINESS WITH.
YES, KIN-SAN!
BUT...
A "WHEEZY, RASPY VOICE," YOU SAY? THERE IS NO ONE IN TOWN LIKE THAT.
YOU MAY GO.
YES, KIN-SAN!
12.

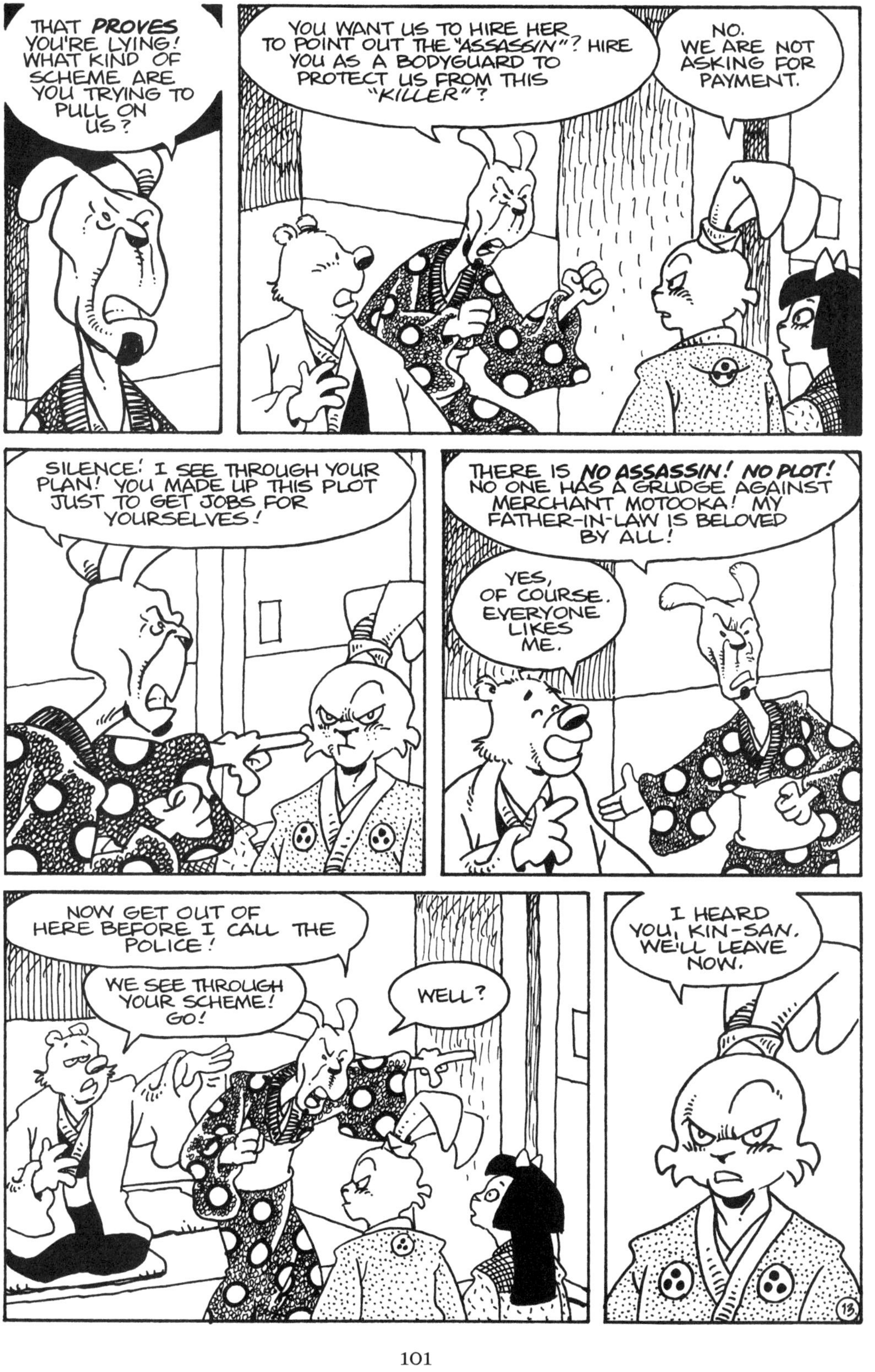
THAT **PROVES** YOU'RE LYING! WHAT KIND OF SCHEME ARE YOU TRYING TO PULL ON US?
YOU WANT US TO HIRE HER TO POINT OUT THE "ASSASSIN"? HIRE YOU AS A BODYGUARD TO PROTECT US FROM THIS "KILLER"?
NO. WE ARE NOT ASKING FOR PAYMENT.
SILENCE! I SEE THROUGH YOUR PLAN! YOU MADE UP THIS PLOT JUST TO GET JOBS FOR YOURSELVES!
THERE IS **NO ASSASSIN! NO PLOT!** NO ONE HAS A GRUDGE AGAINST MERCHANT MOTOOKA! MY FATHER-IN-LAW IS BELOVED BY ALL!
YES, OF COURSE. EVERYONE LIKES ME.
NOW GET OUT OF HERE BEFORE I CALL THE POLICE!
WE SEE THROUGH YOUR SCHEME! GO!
WELL?
I HEARD YOU, KIN-SAN. WE'LL LEAVE NOW.
13

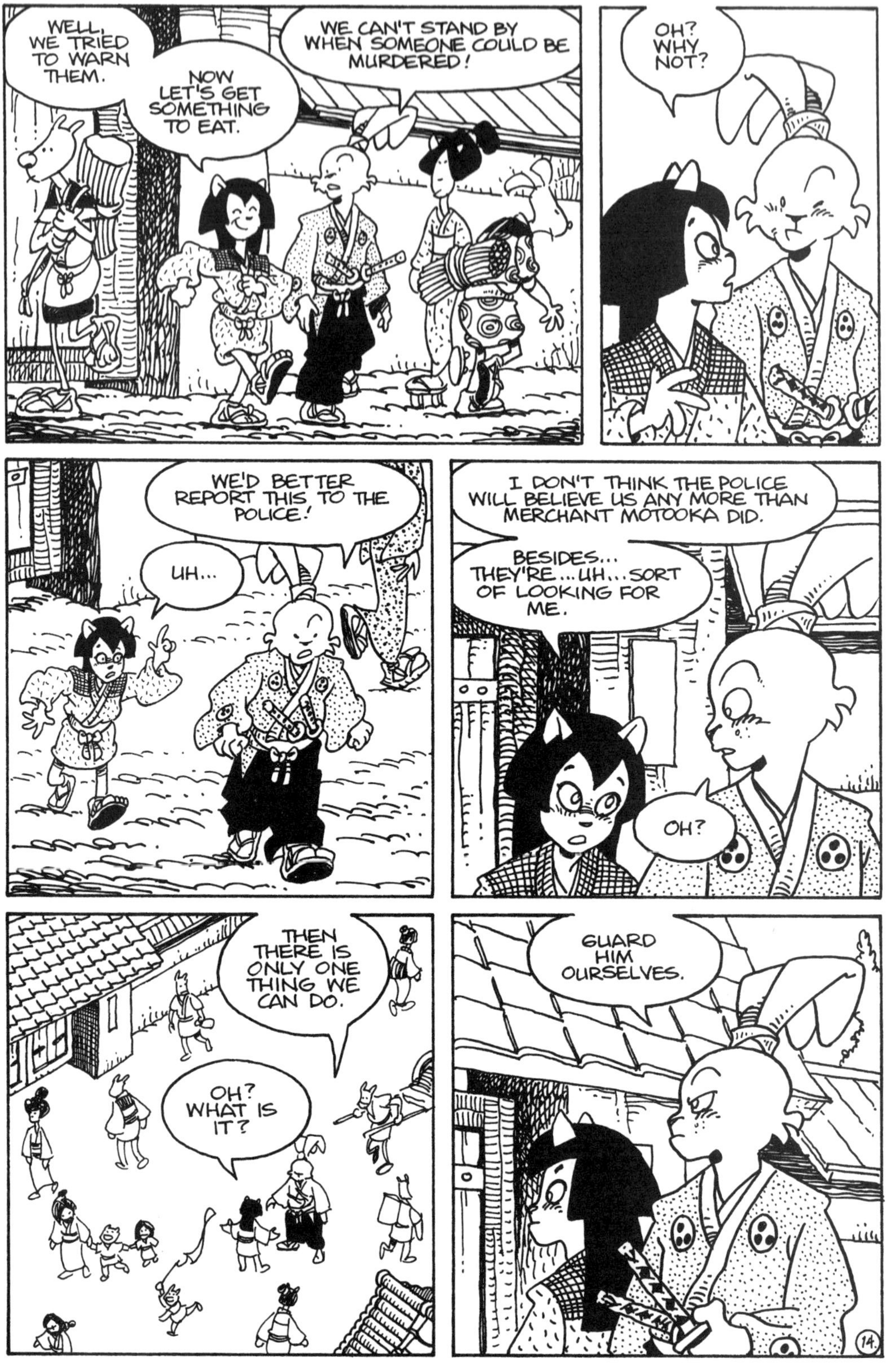
WELL, WE TRIED TO WARN THEM.
NOW LET'S GET SOMETHING TO EAT.
WE CAN'T STAND BY WHEN SOMEONE COULD BE MURDERED!
OH? WHY NOT?
WE'D BETTER REPORT THIS TO THE POLICE!
UH...
I DON'T THINK THE POLICE WILL BELIEVE US ANY MORE THAN MERCHANT MOTOOKA DID.
BESIDES... THEY'RE...UH...SORT OF LOOKING FOR ME.
OH?
THEN THERE IS ONLY ONE THING WE CAN DO.
OH? WHAT IS IT?
GUARD HIM OURSELVES.
14.

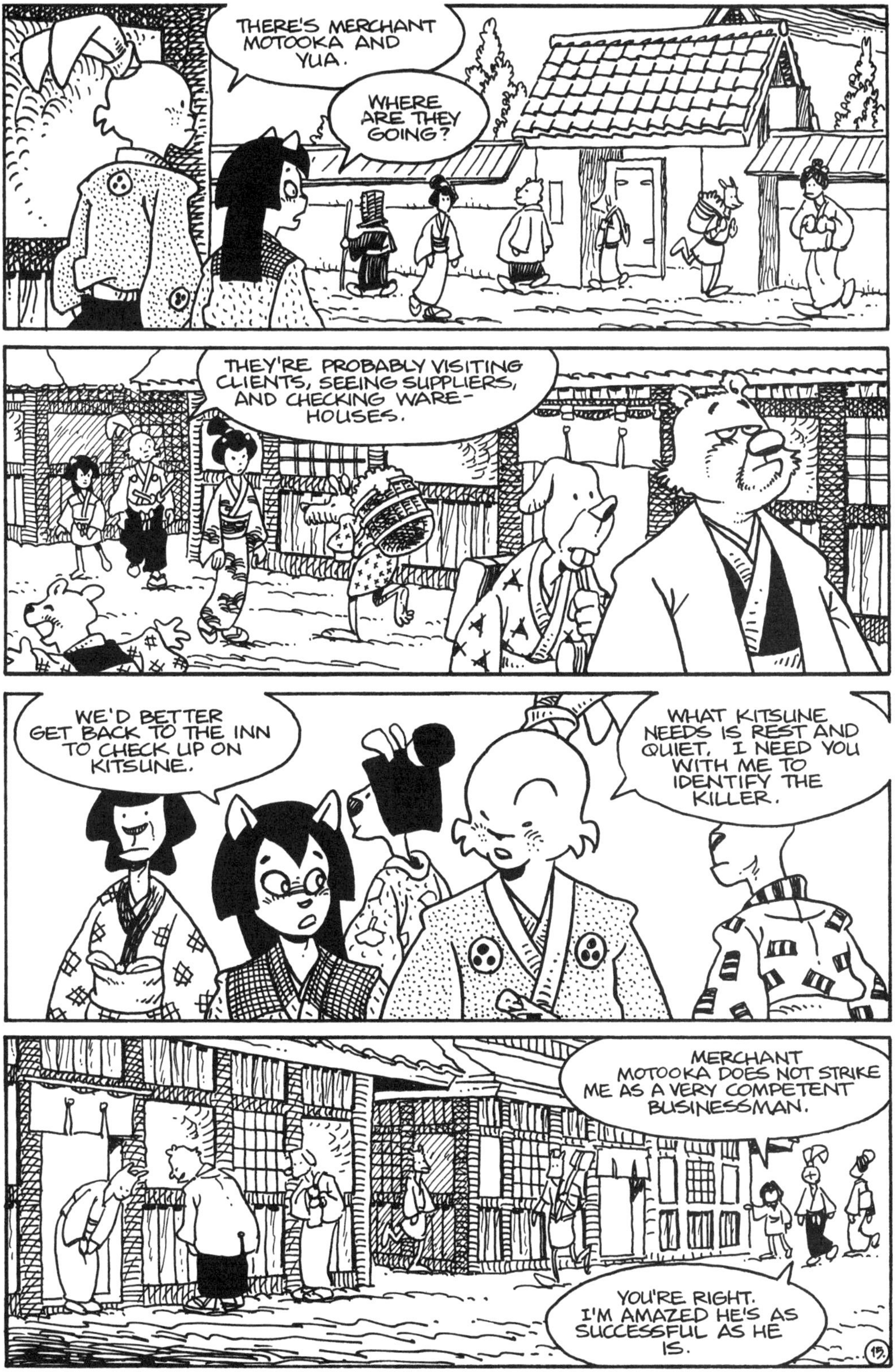
THERE'S MERCHANT MOTOOKA AND YUA.
WHERE ARE THEY GOING?
THEY'RE PROBABLY VISITING CLIENTS, SEEING SUPPLIERS, AND CHECKING WARE-HOUSES.
WE'D BETTER GET BACK TO THE INN TO CHECK UP ON KITSUNE.
WHAT KITSUNE NEEDS IS REST AND QUIET. I NEED YOU WITH ME TO IDENTIFY THE KILLER.
MERCHANT MOTOOKA DOES NOT STRIKE ME AS A VERY COMPETENT BUSINESSMAN.
YOU'RE RIGHT. I'M AMAZED HE'S AS SUCCESSFUL AS HE IS.
13.

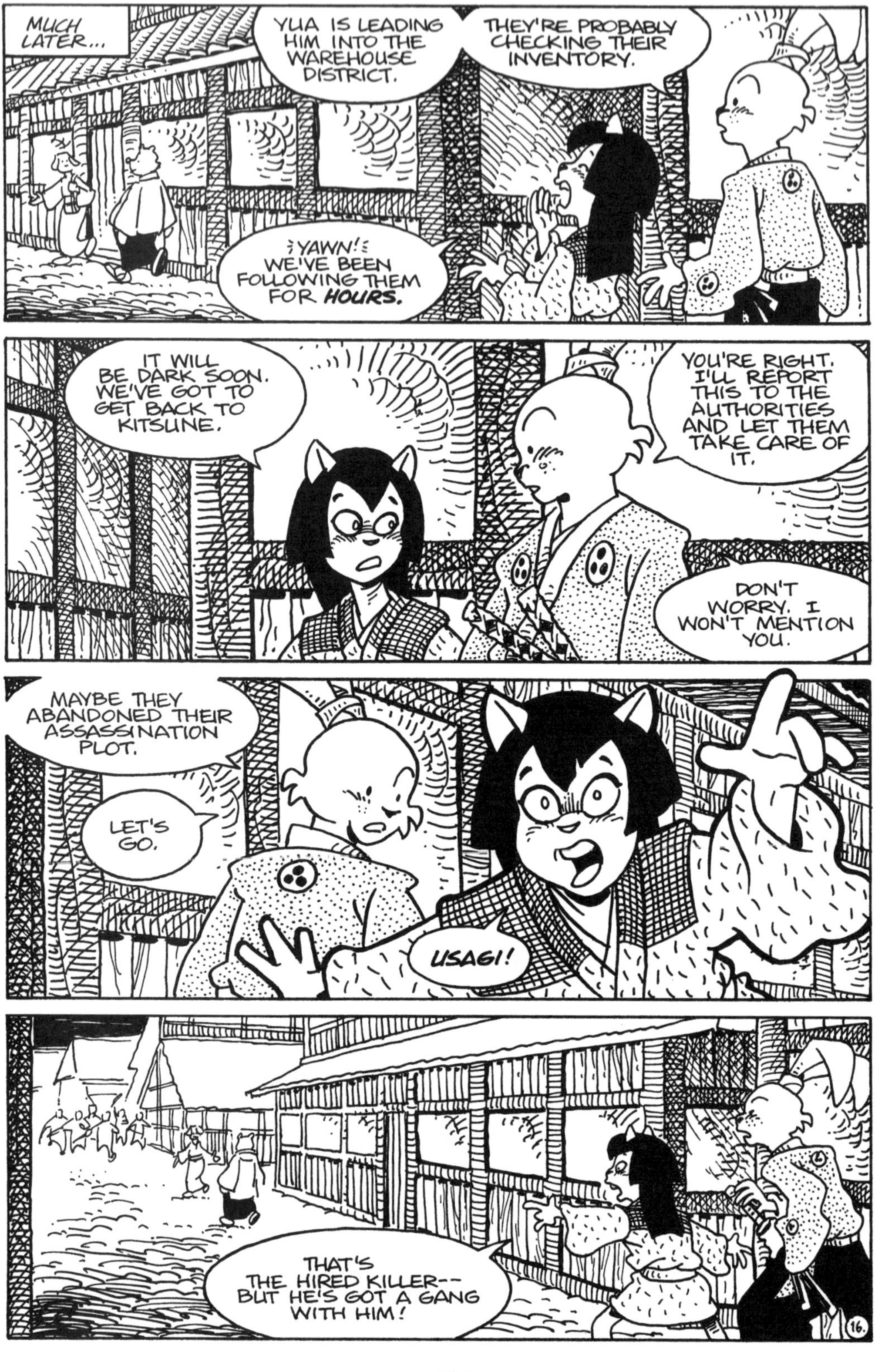
MUCH LATER...
YUA IS LEADING HIM INTO THE WAREHOUSE DISTRICT.
THEY'RE PROBABLY CHECKING THEIR INVENTORY.
YAWN! WE'VE BEEN FOLLOWING THEM FOR HOURS.
IT WILL BE DARK SOON. WE'VE GOT TO GET BACK TO KITSUNE.
YOU'RE RIGHT. I'LL REPORT THIS TO THE AUTHORITIES AND LET THEM TAKE CARE OF IT.
DON'T WORRY. I WON'T MENTION YOU.
MAYBE THEY ABANDONED THEIR ASSASSINATION PLOT.
LET'S GO.
USAGI!
THAT'S THE HIRED KILLER-- BUT HE'S GOT A GANG WITH HIM!
16.

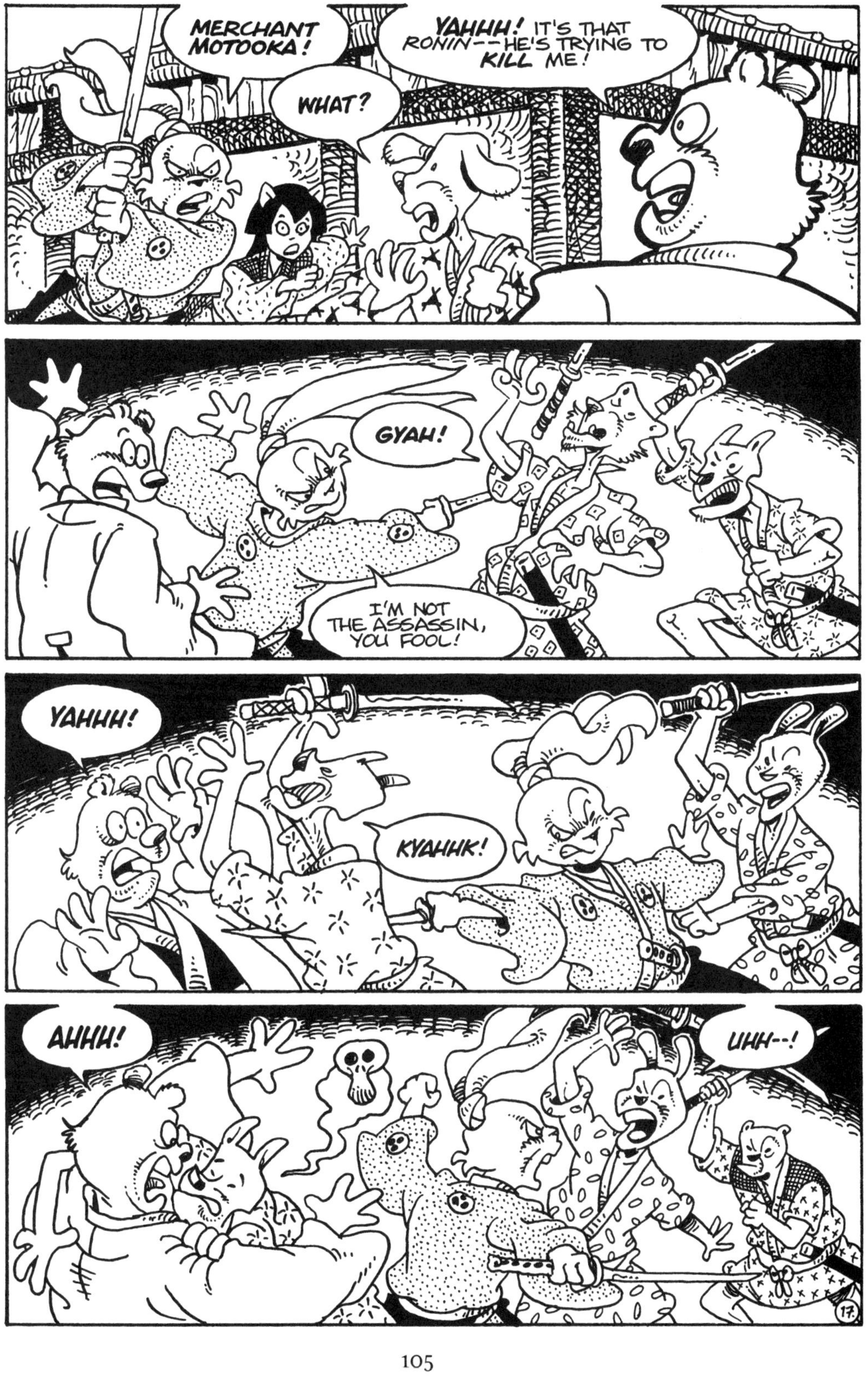
MERCHANT MOTOOKA!
WHAT?
YAHHH! IT'S THAT RONIN-- HE'S TRYING TO KILL ME!
GYAH!
I'M NOT THE ASSASSIN, YOU FOOL!
YAHHH!
KYAHHK!
AHHH!
UHH--!
17

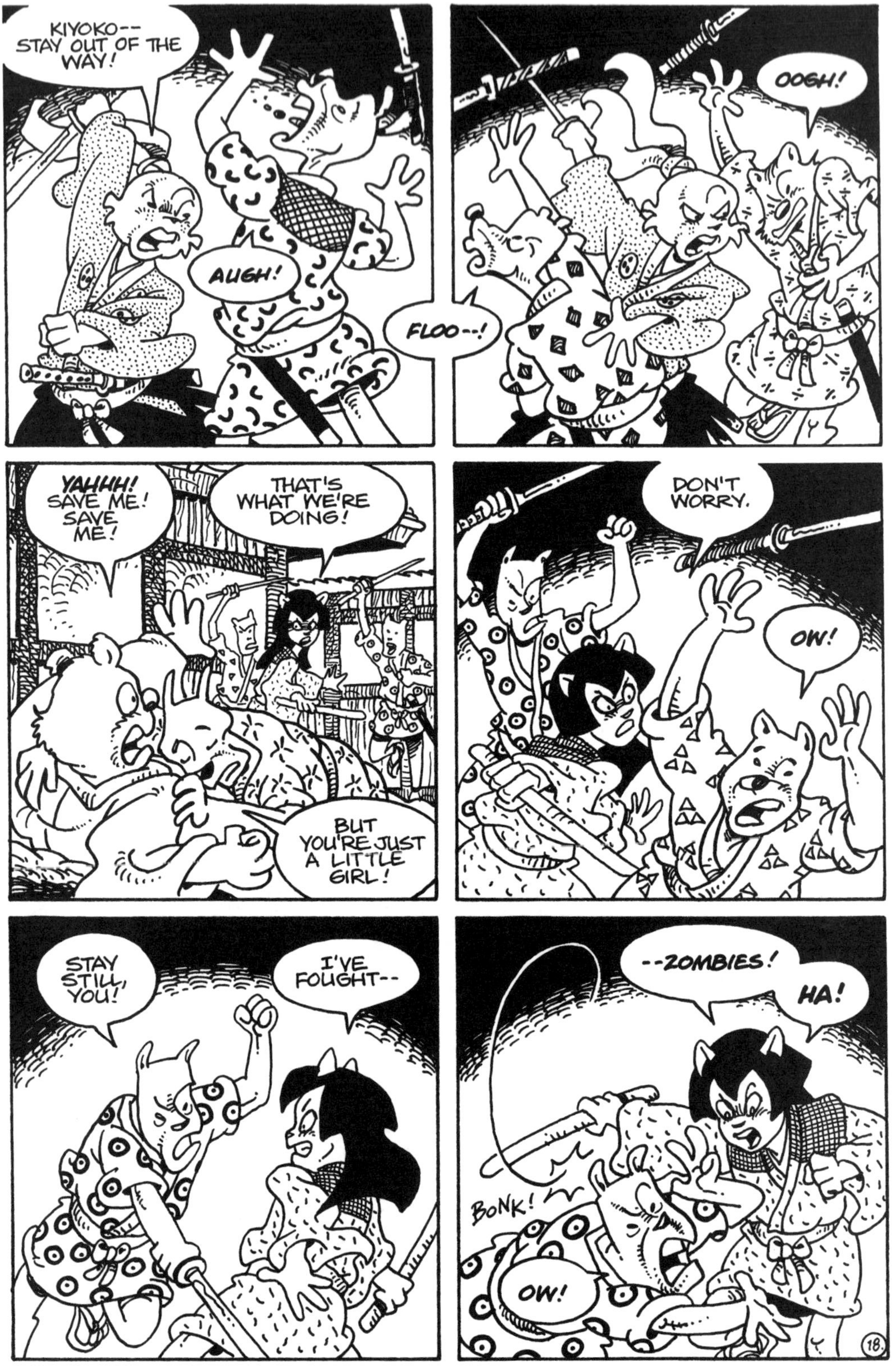
KIYOKO-- STAY OUT OF THE WAY!
AUGH!
OOGH!
FLOO--!
YAHHH! SAVE ME! SAVE ME!
THAT'S WHAT WE'RE DOING!
BUT YOU'RE JUST A LITTLE GIRL!
DON'T WORRY.
OW!
STAY STILL, YOU!
I'VE FOUGHT--
--ZOMBIES!
HA!
BONK!
OW!
18.

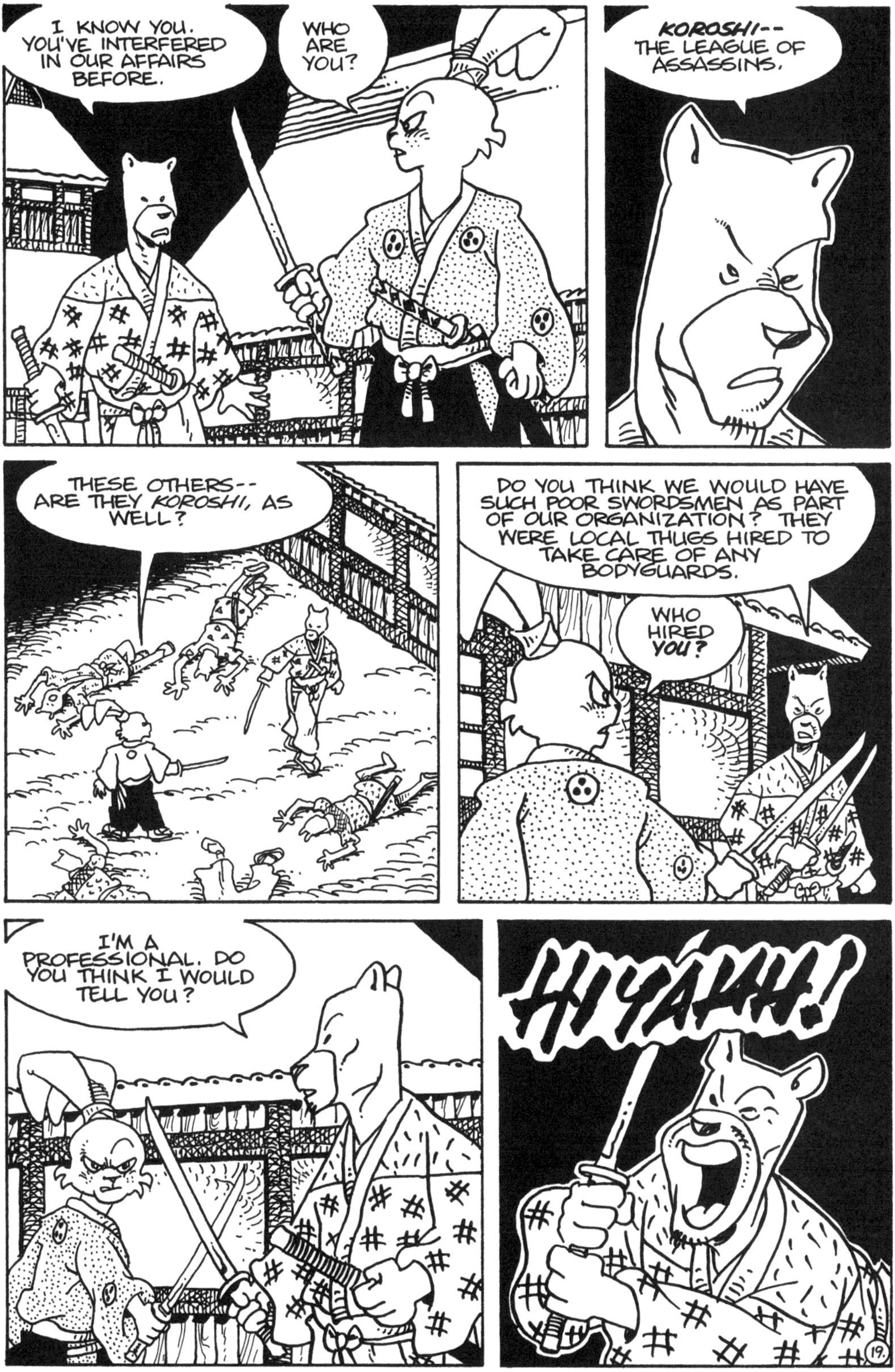
I KNOW YOU. YOU'VE INTERFERED IN OUR AFFAIRS BEFORE.
WHO ARE YOU?
KOROSHI-- THE LEAGUE OF ASSASSINS.
THESE OTHERS-- ARE THEY KOROSHI, AS WELL?
DO YOU THINK WE WOULD HAVE SUCH POOR SWORDSMEN AS PART OF OUR ORGANIZATION? THEY WERE LOCAL THUGS HIRED TO TAKE CARE OF ANY BODYGUARDS.
WHO HIRED YOU?
I'M A PROFESSIONAL. DO YOU THINK I WOULD TELL YOU?
HI YAAAH!
19.

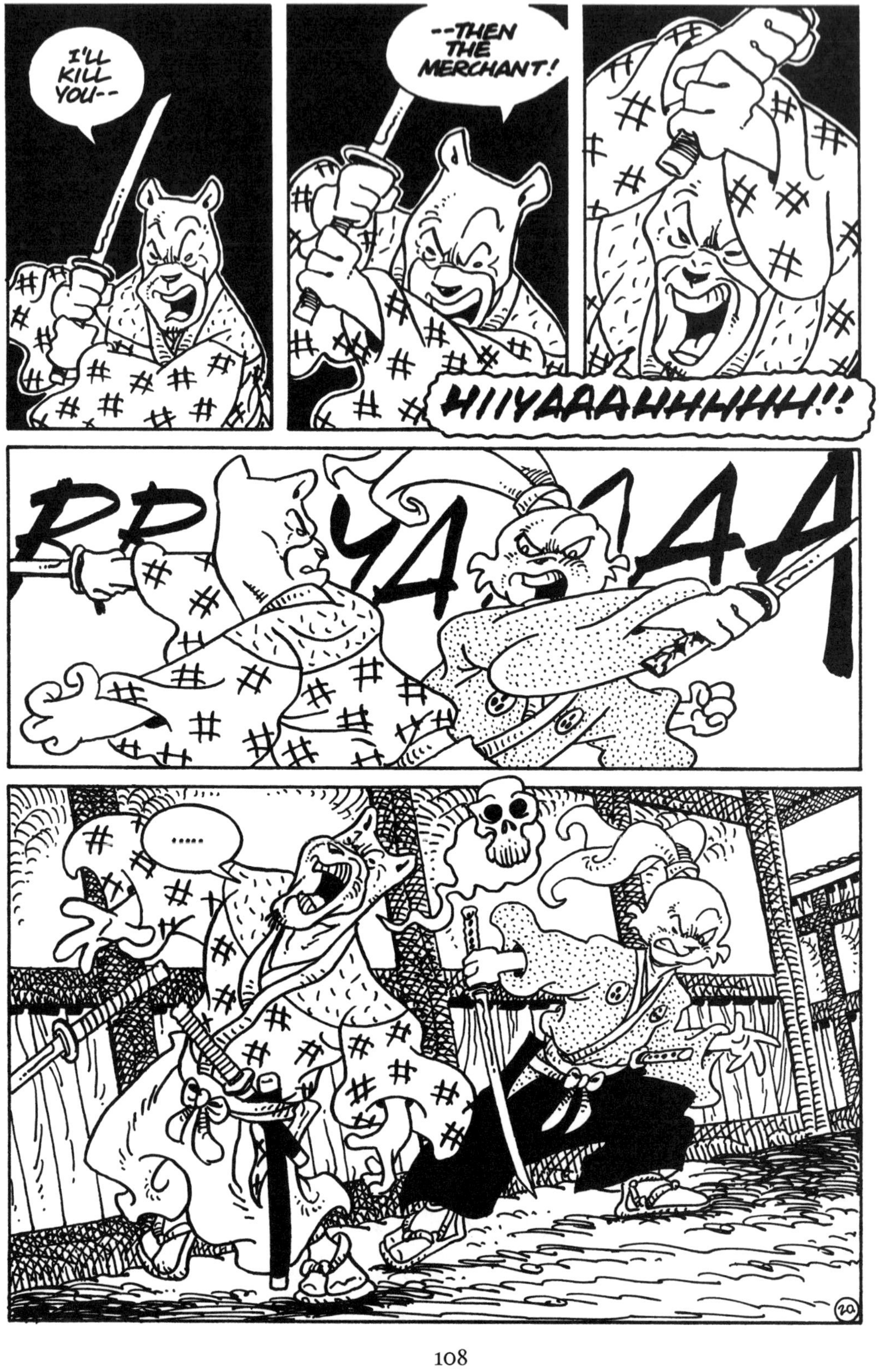
I'LL KILL YOU--
--THEN THE MERCHANT!
HIIYAAAHHHHHH!!
RRYAAAA
.....
20

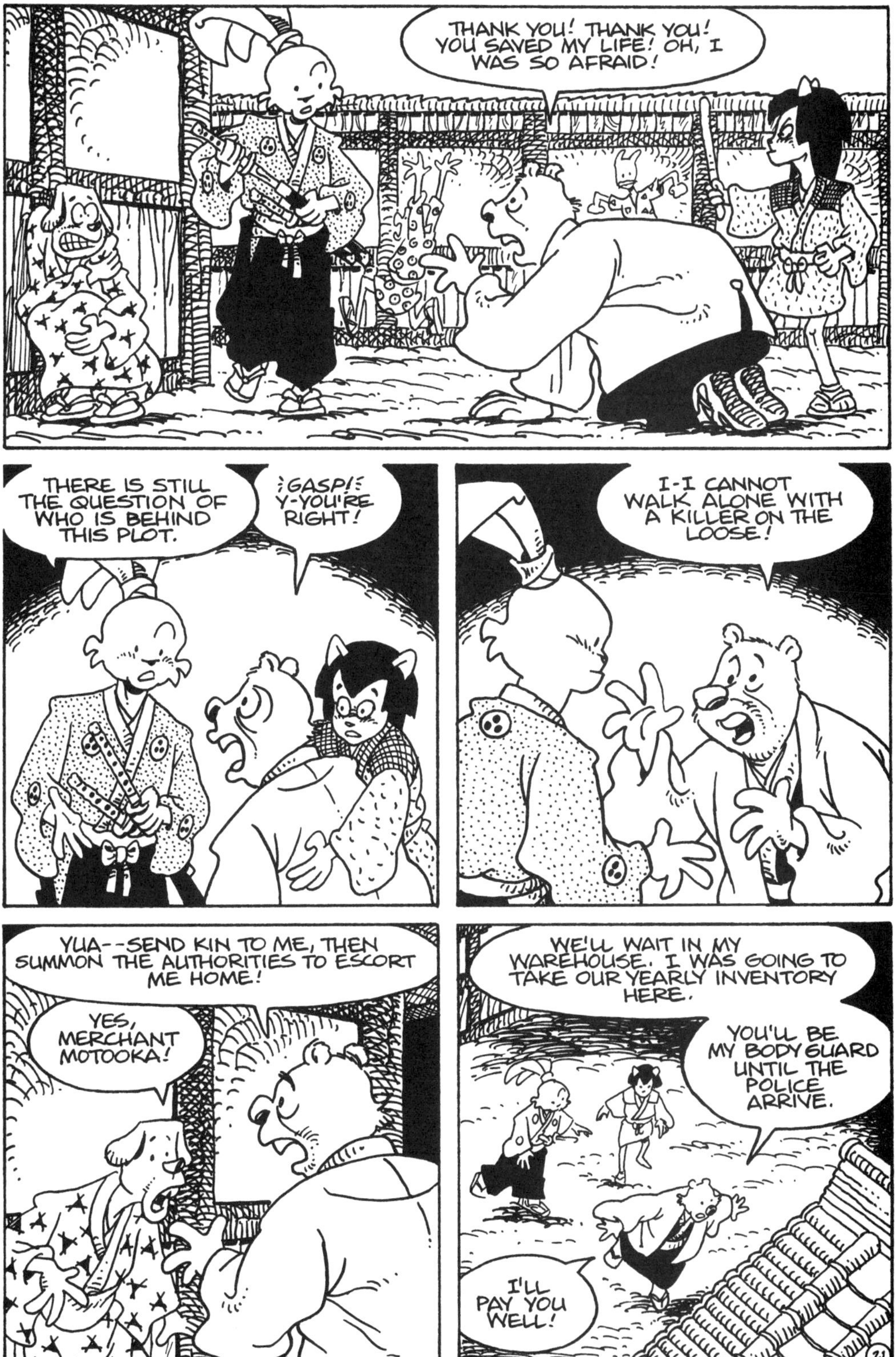
THANK YOU! THANK YOU! YOU SAVED MY LIFE! OH, I WAS SO AFRAID!
THERE IS STILL THE QUESTION OF WHO IS BEHIND THIS PLOT.
GASP! Y-YOU'RE RIGHT!
I-I CANNOT WALK ALONE WITH A KILLER ON THE LOOSE!
YUA--SEND KIN TO ME, THEN SUMMON THE AUTHORITIES TO ESCORT ME HOME!
YES, MERCHANT MOTOOKA!
WE'LL WAIT IN MY WAREHOUSE. I WAS GOING TO TAKE OUR YEARLY INVENTORY HERE.
YOU'LL BE MY BODYGUARD UNTIL THE POLICE ARRIVE.
I'LL PAY YOU WELL!
21

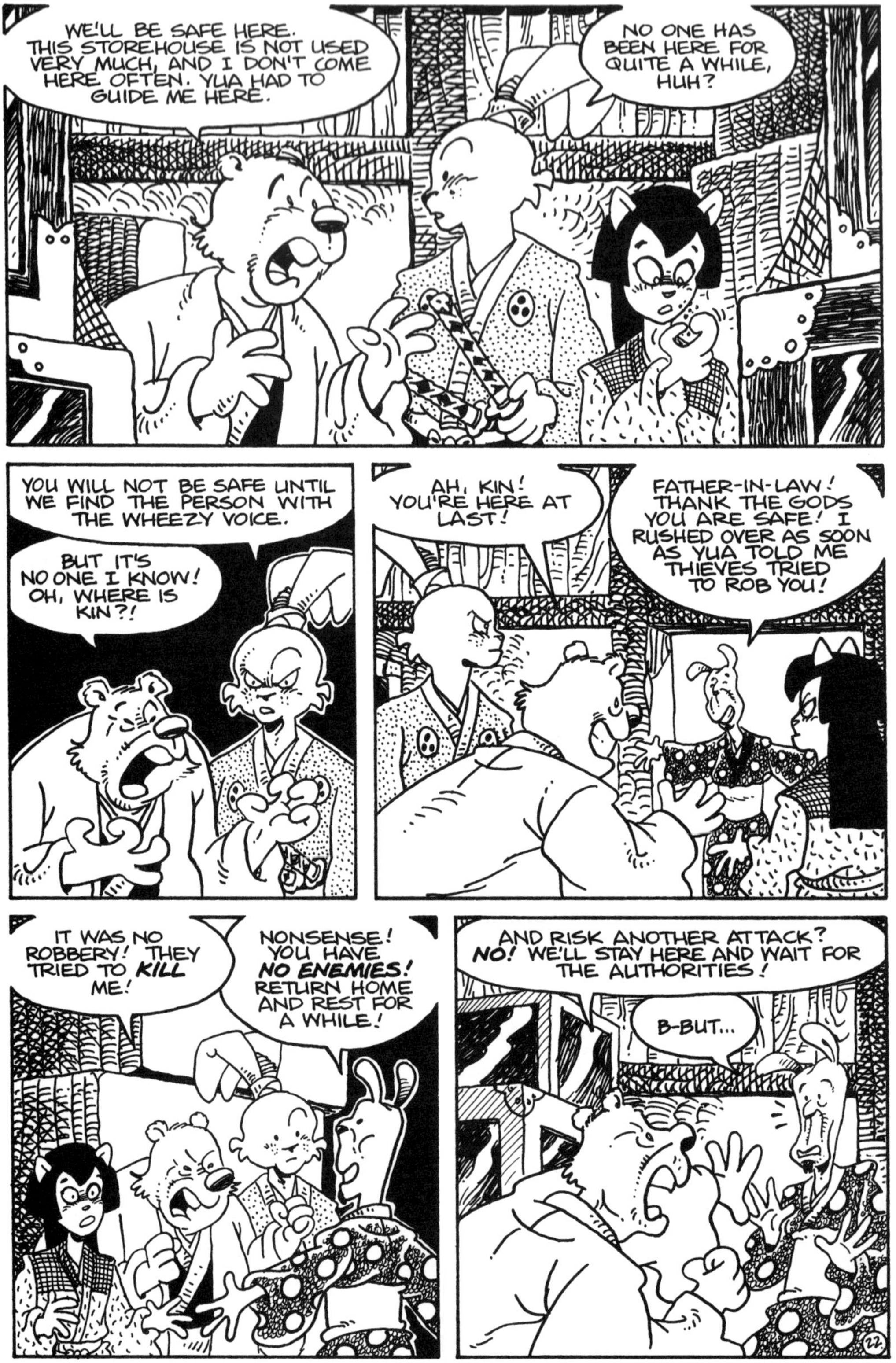
WE'LL BE SAFE HERE. THIS STOREHOUSE IS NOT USED VERY MUCH, AND I DON'T COME HERE OFTEN. YUA HAD TO GUIDE ME HERE.
NO ONE HAS BEEN HERE FOR QUITE A WHILE, HUH?
YOU WILL NOT BE SAFE UNTIL WE FIND THE PERSON WITH THE WHEEZY VOICE.
BUT IT'S NO ONE I KNOW! OH, WHERE IS KIN?!
AH, KIN! YOU'RE HERE AT LAST!
FATHER-IN-LAW! THANK THE GODS YOU ARE SAFE! I RUSHED OVER AS SOON AS YUA TOLD ME THIEVES TRIED TO ROB YOU!
IT WAS NO ROBBERY! THEY TRIED TO ***KILL*** ME!
NONSENSE! YOU HAVE ***NO ENEMIES!*** RETURN HOME AND REST FOR A WHILE!
AND RISK ANOTHER ATTACK? ***NO!*** WE'LL STAY HERE AND WAIT FOR THE AUTHORITIES!
B-BUT...
22

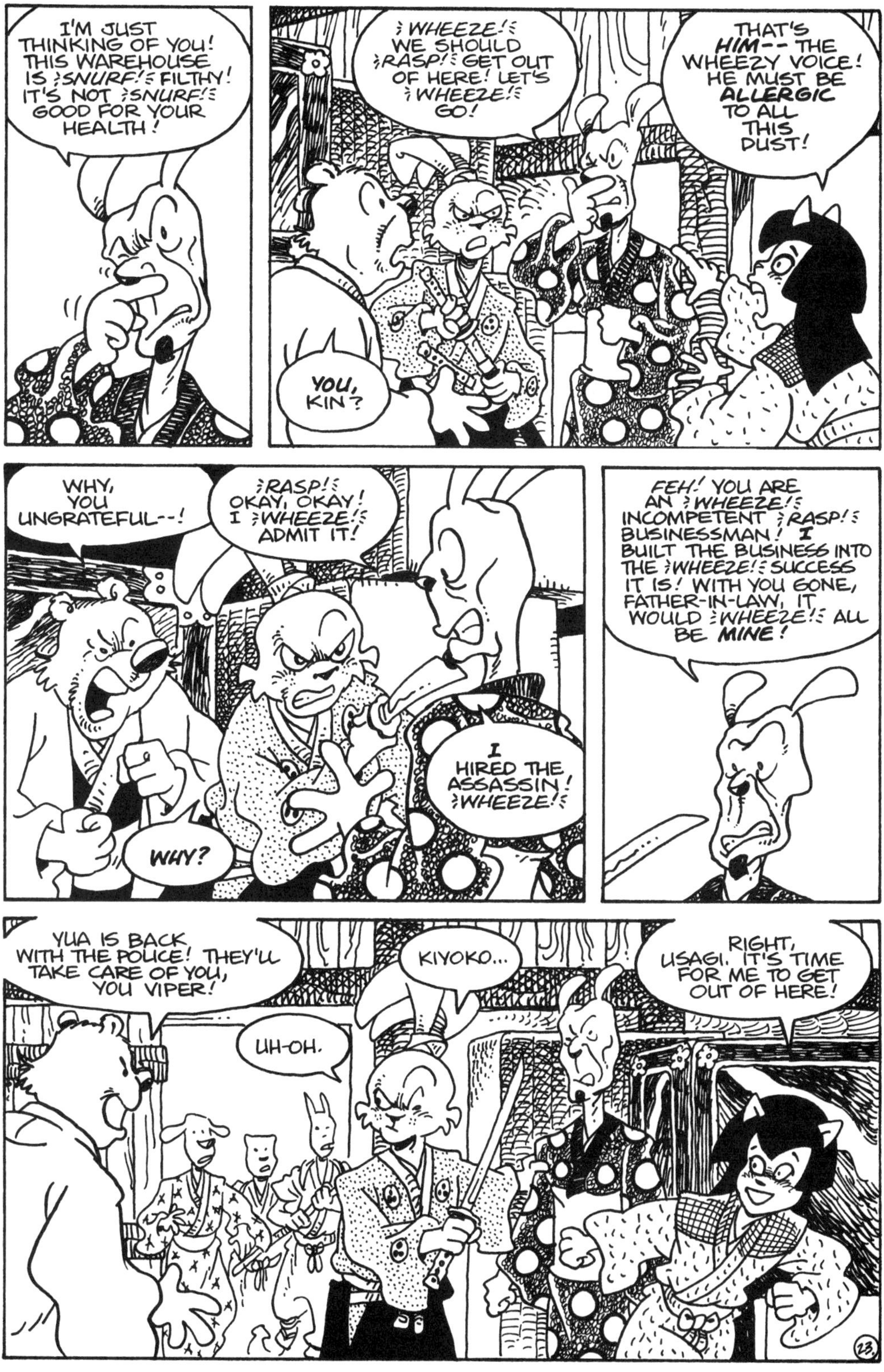
I'M JUST THINKING OF YOU! THIS WAREHOUSE IS ⁝SNURF!⁝ FILTHY! IT'S NOT ⁝SNURF!⁝ GOOD FOR YOUR HEALTH!
⁝WHEEZE!⁝ WE SHOULD ⁝RASP!⁝ GET OUT OF HERE! LET'S ⁝WHEEZE!⁝ GO!
THAT'S HIM-- THE WHEEZY VOICE! HE MUST BE ALLERGIC TO ALL THIS DUST!
YOU, KIN?
WHY, YOU UNGRATEFUL--!
⁝RASP!⁝ OKAY, OKAY! I ⁝WHEEZE!⁝ ADMIT IT!
I HIRED THE ASSASSIN! ⁝WHEEZE!⁝
WHY?
FEH! YOU ARE AN ⁝WHEEZE!⁝ INCOMPETENT ⁝RASP!⁝ BUSINESSMAN! I BUILT THE BUSINESS INTO THE ⁝WHEEZE!⁝ SUCCESS IT IS! WITH YOU GONE, FATHER-IN-LAW, IT WOULD ⁝WHEEZE!⁝ ALL BE MINE!
YUA IS BACK WITH THE POLICE! THEY'LL TAKE CARE OF YOU, YOU VIPER!
KIYOKO...
UH-OH.
RIGHT, USAGI. IT'S TIME FOR ME TO GET OUT OF HERE!
23.

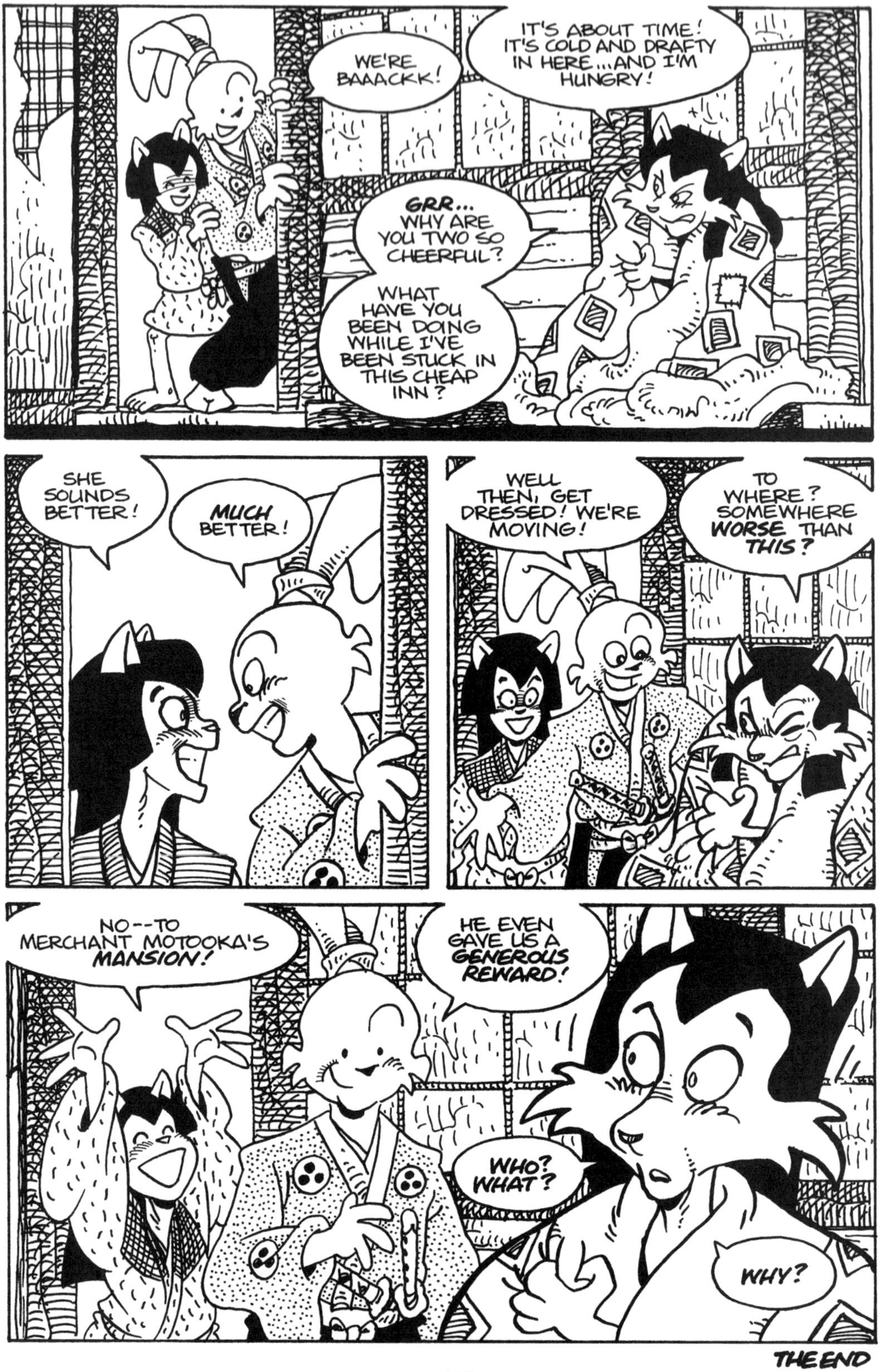
WE'RE BAAACKK!
IT'S ABOUT TIME! IT'S COLD AND DRAFTY IN HERE...AND I'M HUNGRY!
GRR... WHY ARE YOU TWO SO CHEERFUL?
WHAT HAVE YOU BEEN DOING WHILE I'VE BEEN STUCK IN THIS CHEAP INN?
SHE SOUNDS BETTER!
MUCH BETTER!
WELL THEN, GET DRESSED! WE'RE MOVING!
TO WHERE? SOMEWHERE WORSE THAN THIS?
NO--TO MERCHANT MOTOOKA'S MANSION!
HE EVEN GAVE US A GENEROUS REWARD!
WHO? WHAT?
WHY?
THE END

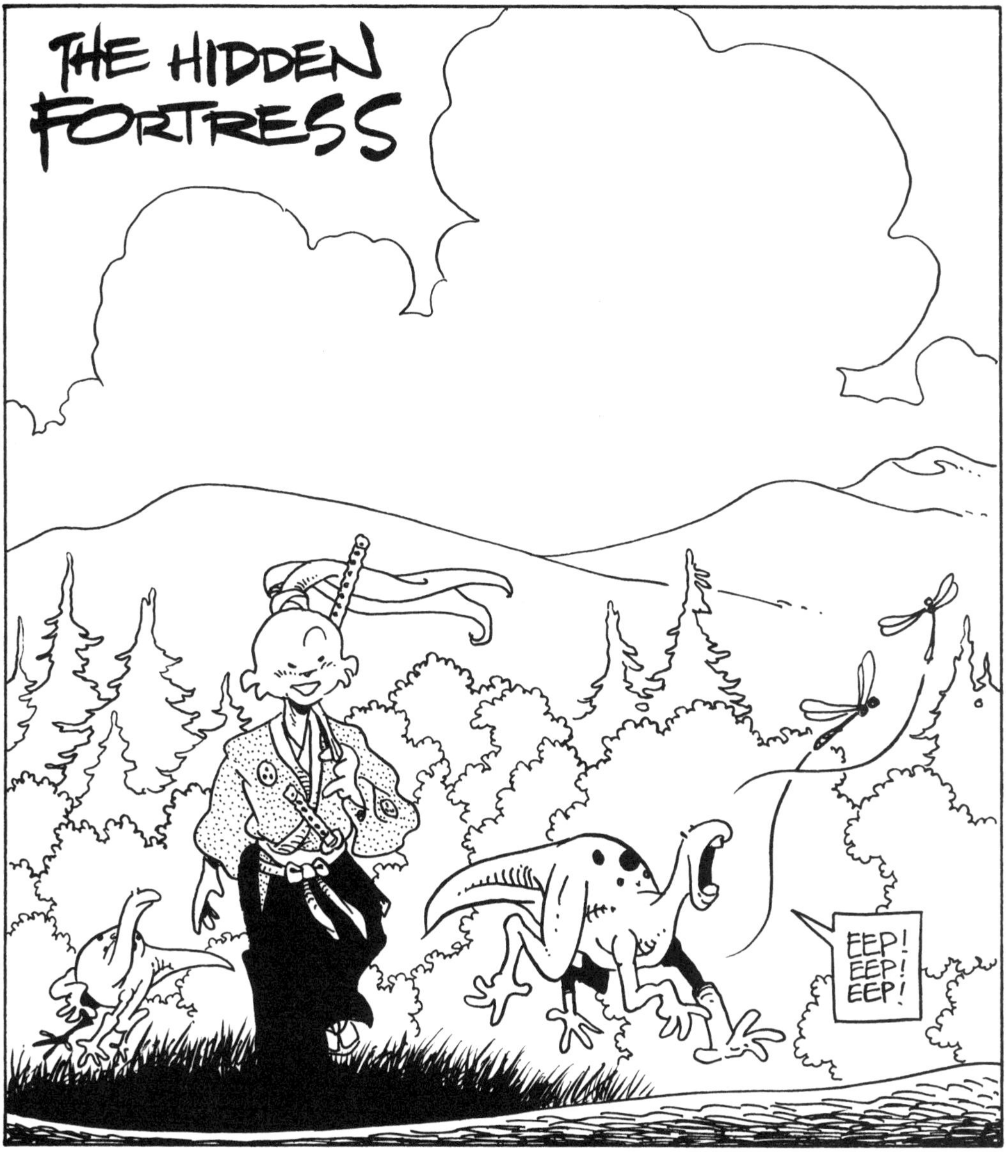
THE HIDDEN FORTRESS
EEP! EEP! EEP!

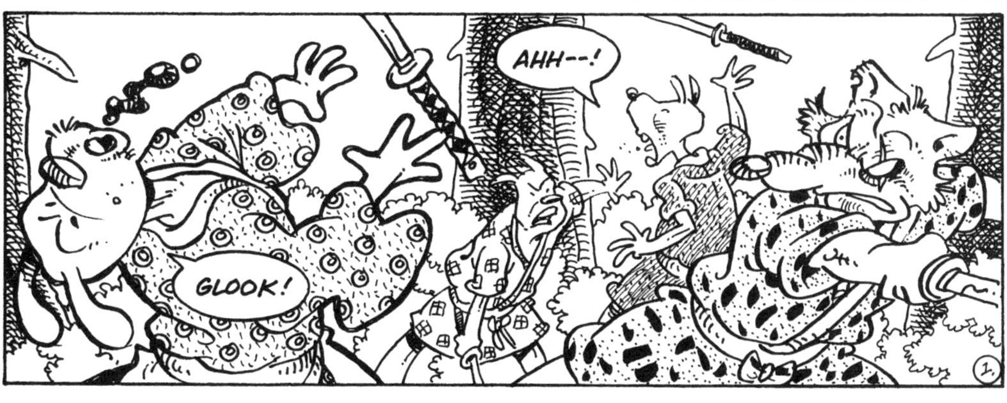
AHH--!
GLOOK!
1.

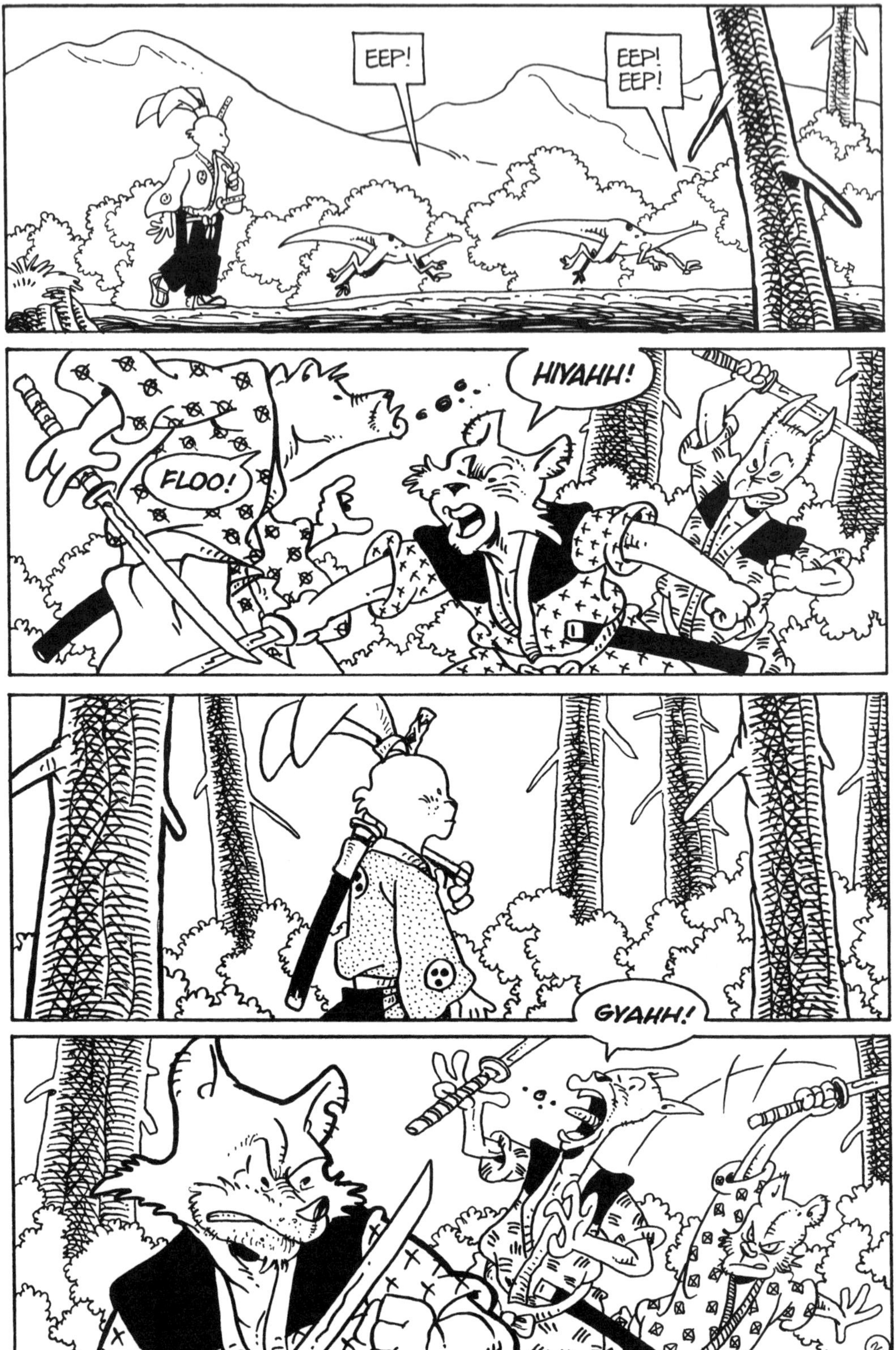
EEP!
EEP! EEP!
HIYAHH!
FLOO!
GYAHH!
2.

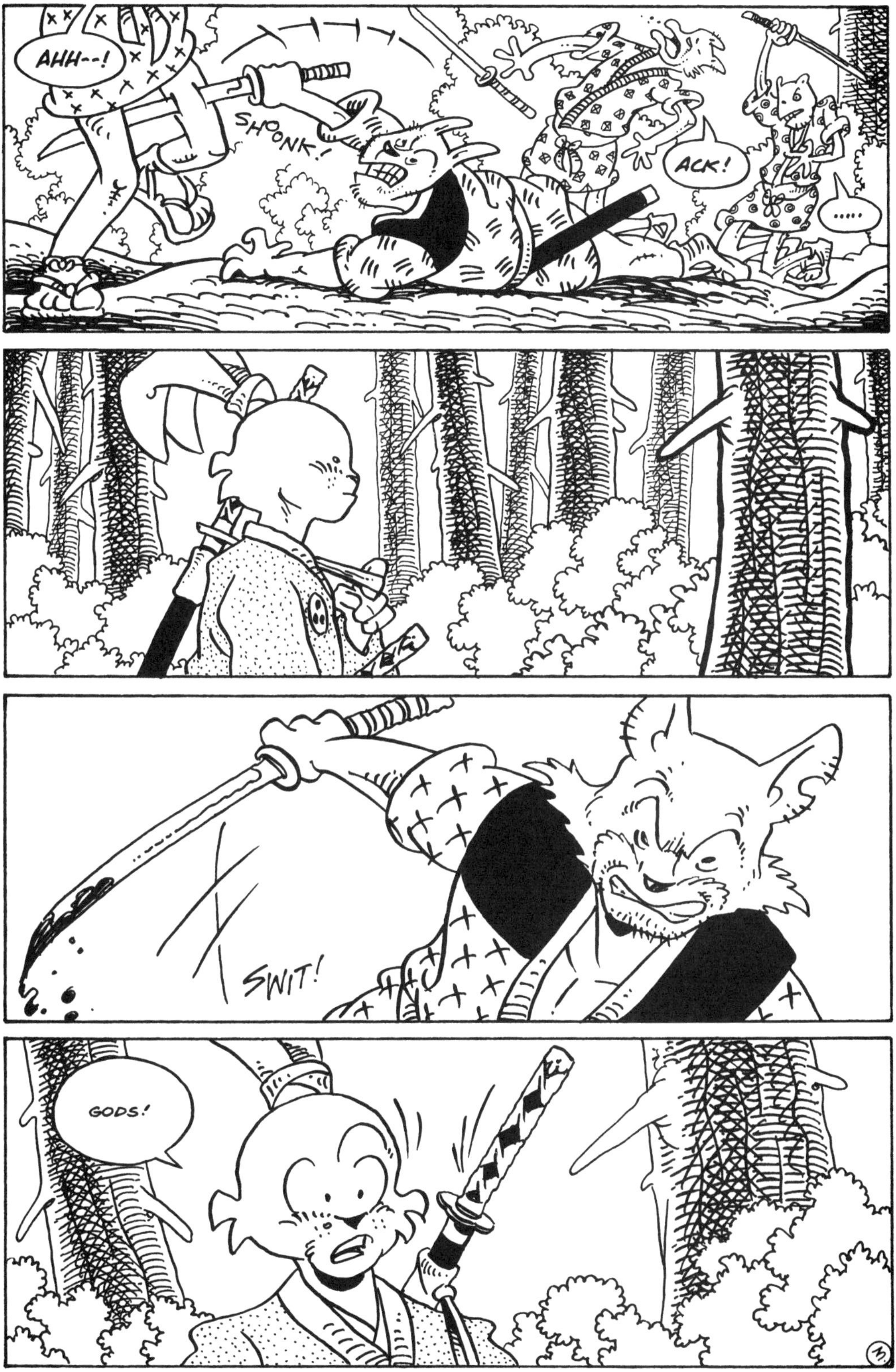
AHH--!
SHPONK!
ACK!
.....
SWIT!
GODS!

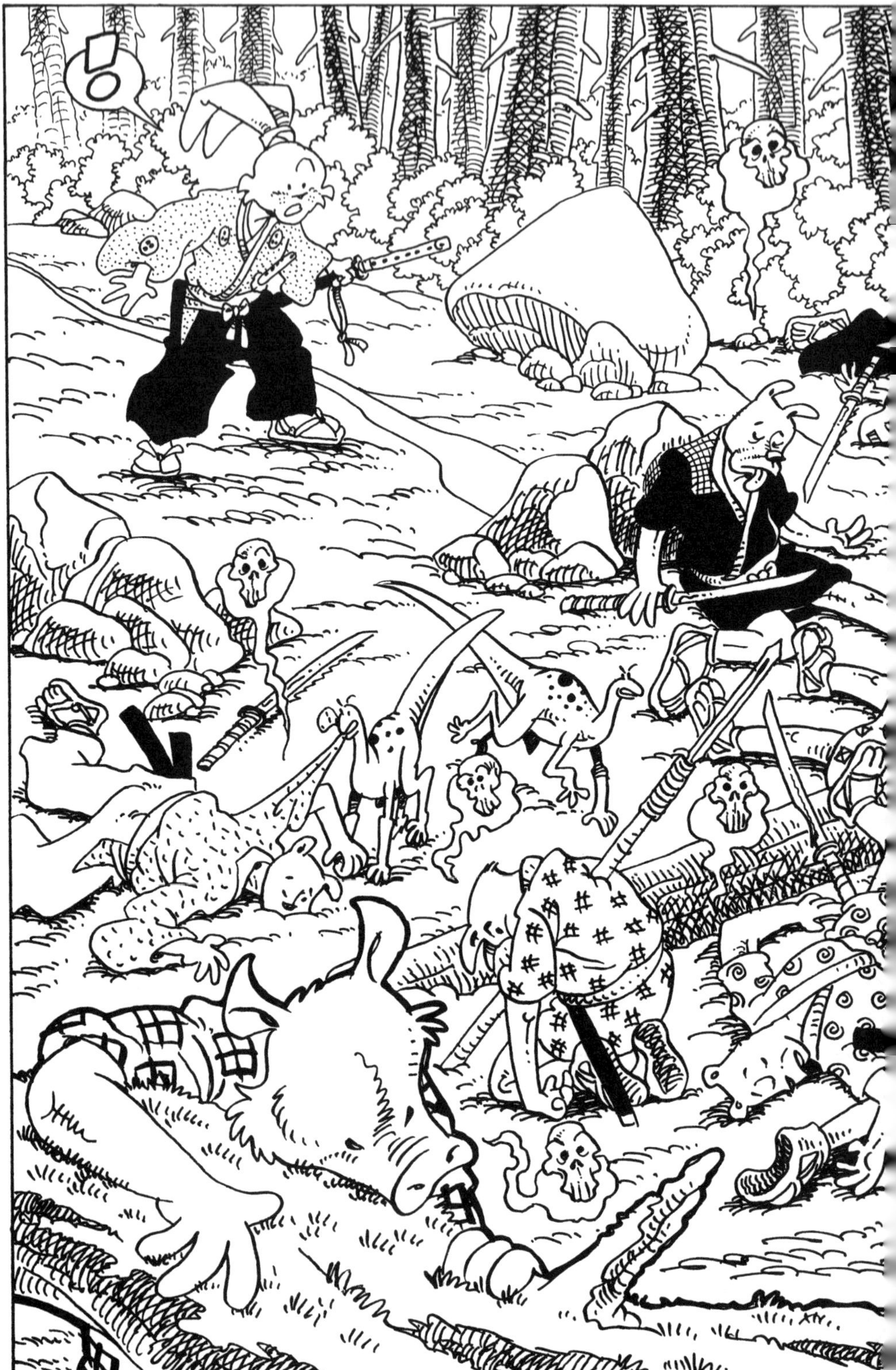
!

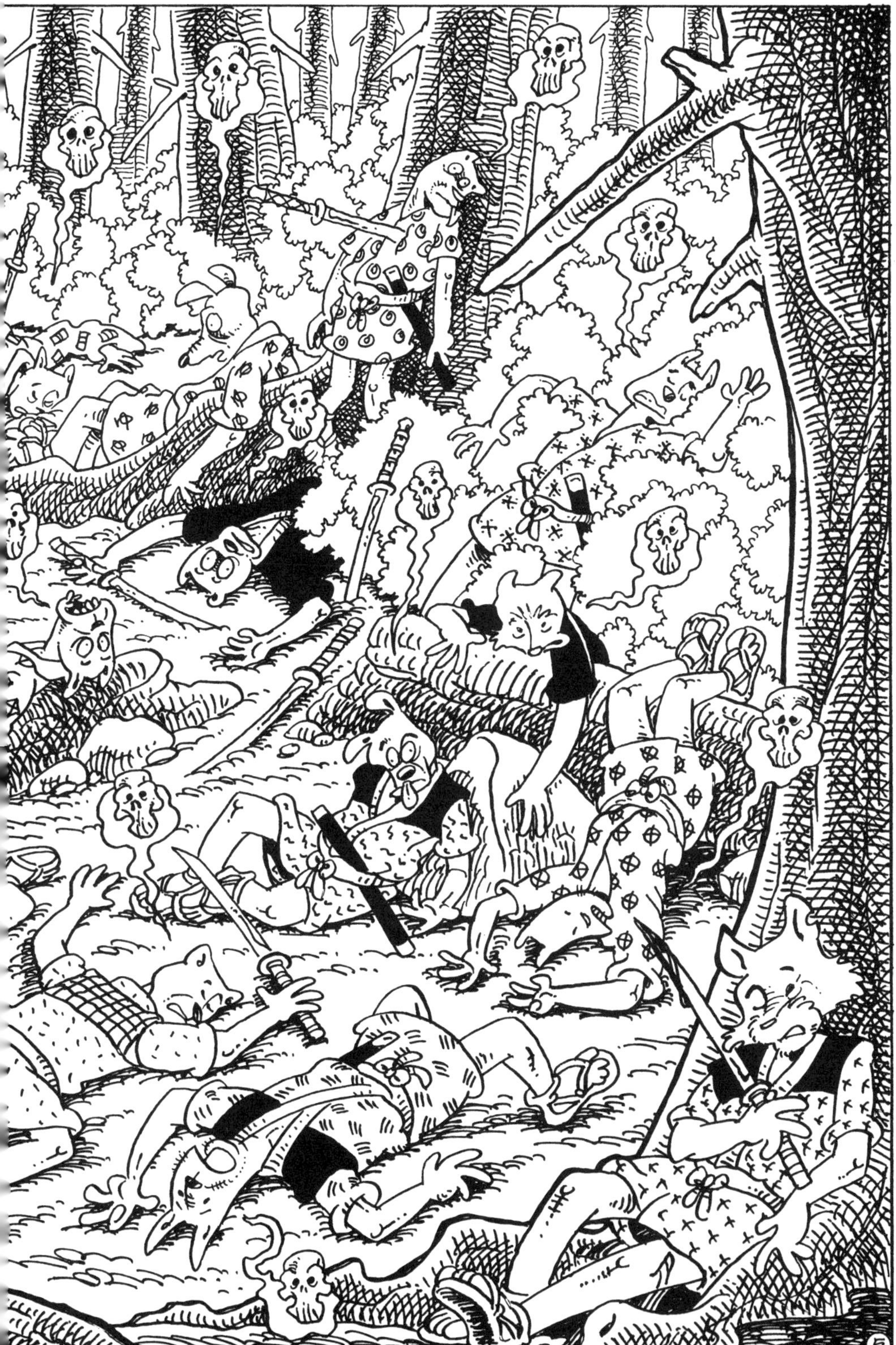

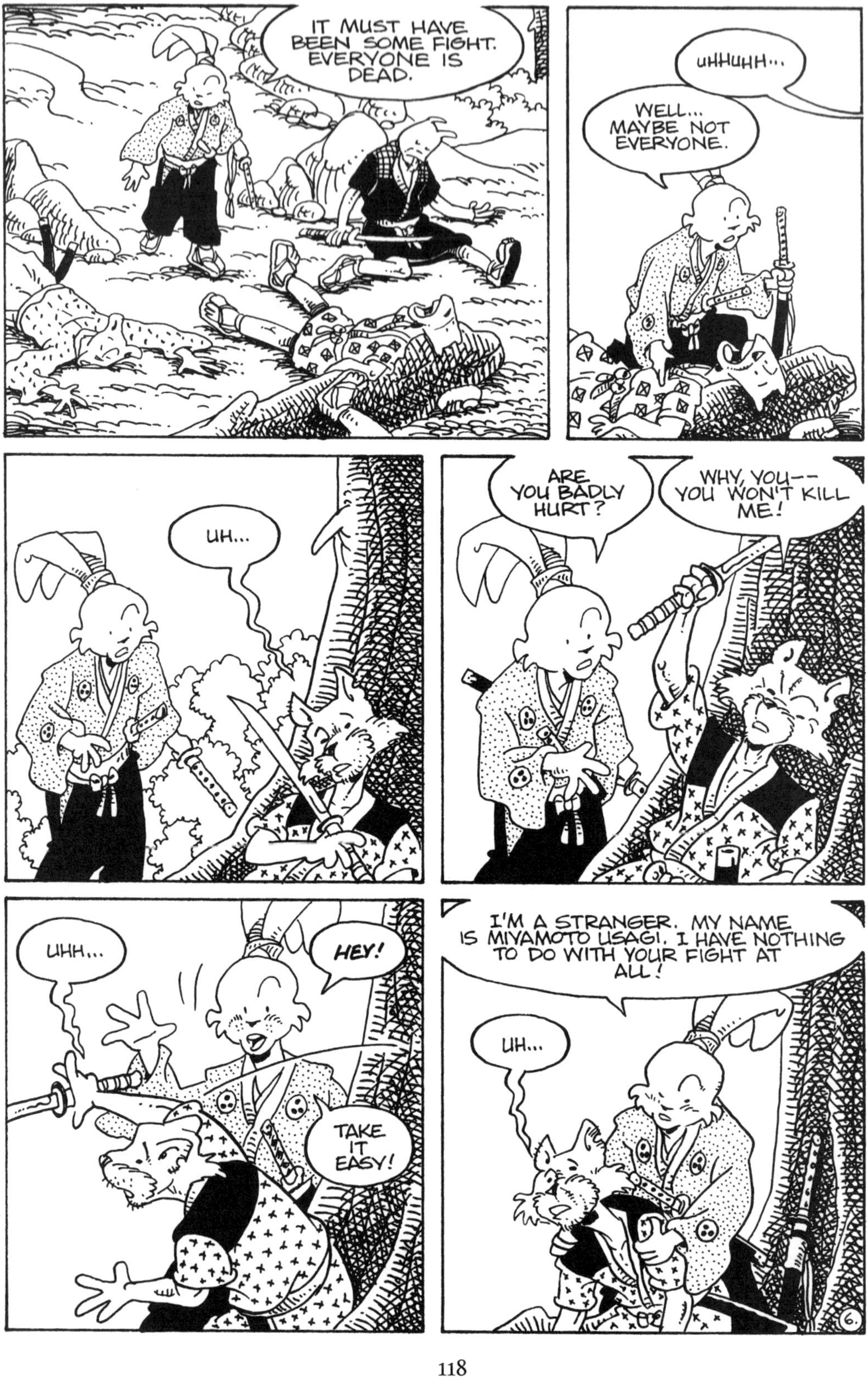
IT MUST HAVE BEEN SOME FIGHT. EVERYONE IS DEAD.
uHHuHH...
WELL... MAYBE NOT EVERYONE.
UH...
ARE YOU BADLY HURT?
WHY, YOU-- YOU WON'T KILL ME!
UHH...
HEY!
TAKE IT EASY!
I'M A STRANGER. MY NAME IS MIYAMOTO USAGI. I HAVE NOTHING TO DO WITH YOUR FIGHT AT ALL!
UH...
6.

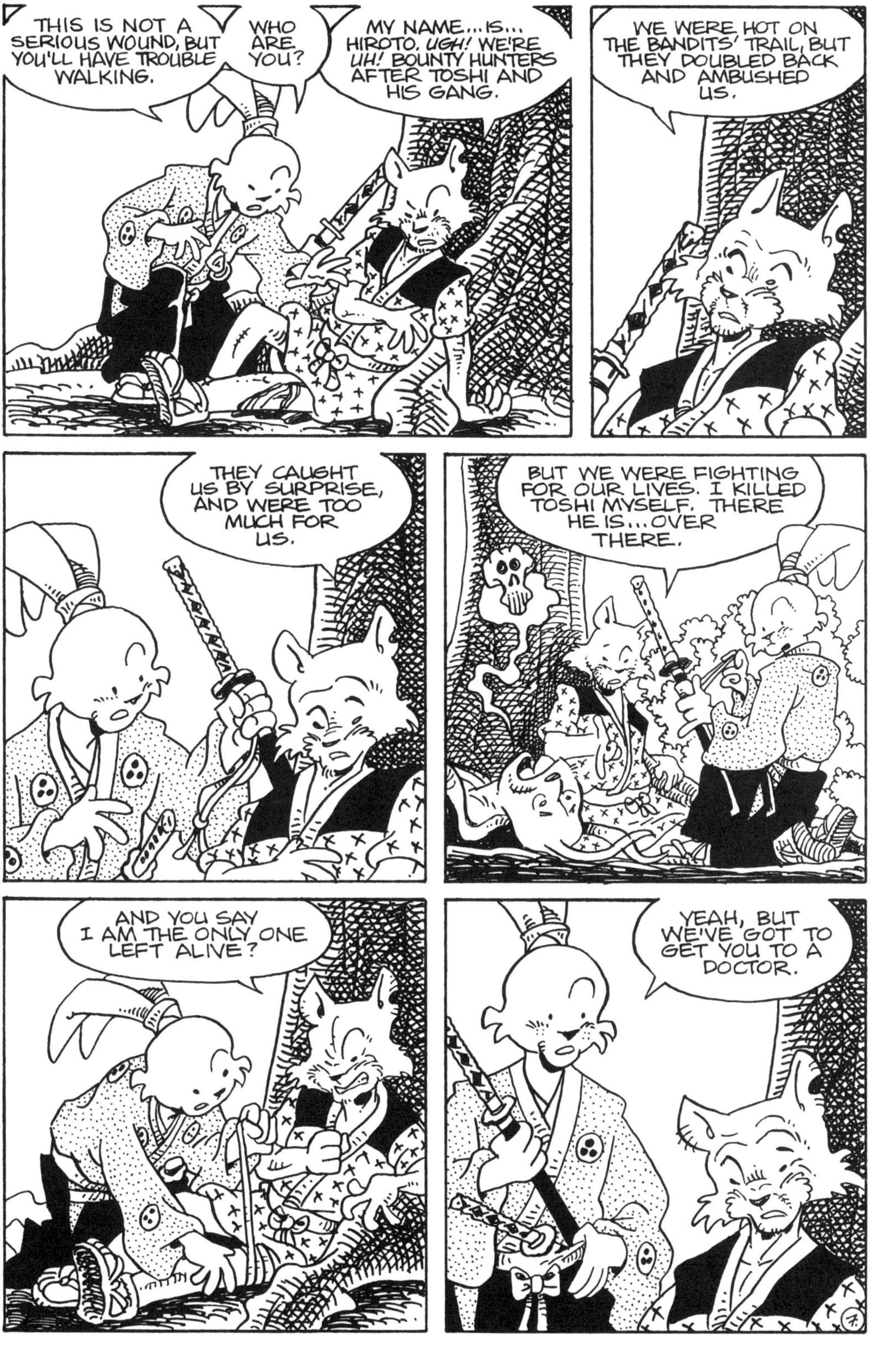
THIS IS NOT A SERIOUS WOUND, BUT YOU'LL HAVE TROUBLE WALKING.
WHO ARE YOU?
MY NAME...IS... HIROTO. *UGH!* WE'RE *UH!* BOUNTY HUNTERS AFTER TOSHI AND HIS GANG.
WE WERE HOT ON THE BANDITS' TRAIL, BUT THEY DOUBLED BACK AND AMBUSHED US.
THEY CAUGHT US BY SURPRISE, AND WERE TOO MUCH FOR US.
BUT WE WERE FIGHTING FOR OUR LIVES. I KILLED TOSHI MYSELF. THERE HE IS...OVER THERE.
AND YOU SAY I AM THE ONLY ONE LEFT ALIVE?
YEAH, BUT WE'VE GOT TO GET YOU TO A DOCTOR.

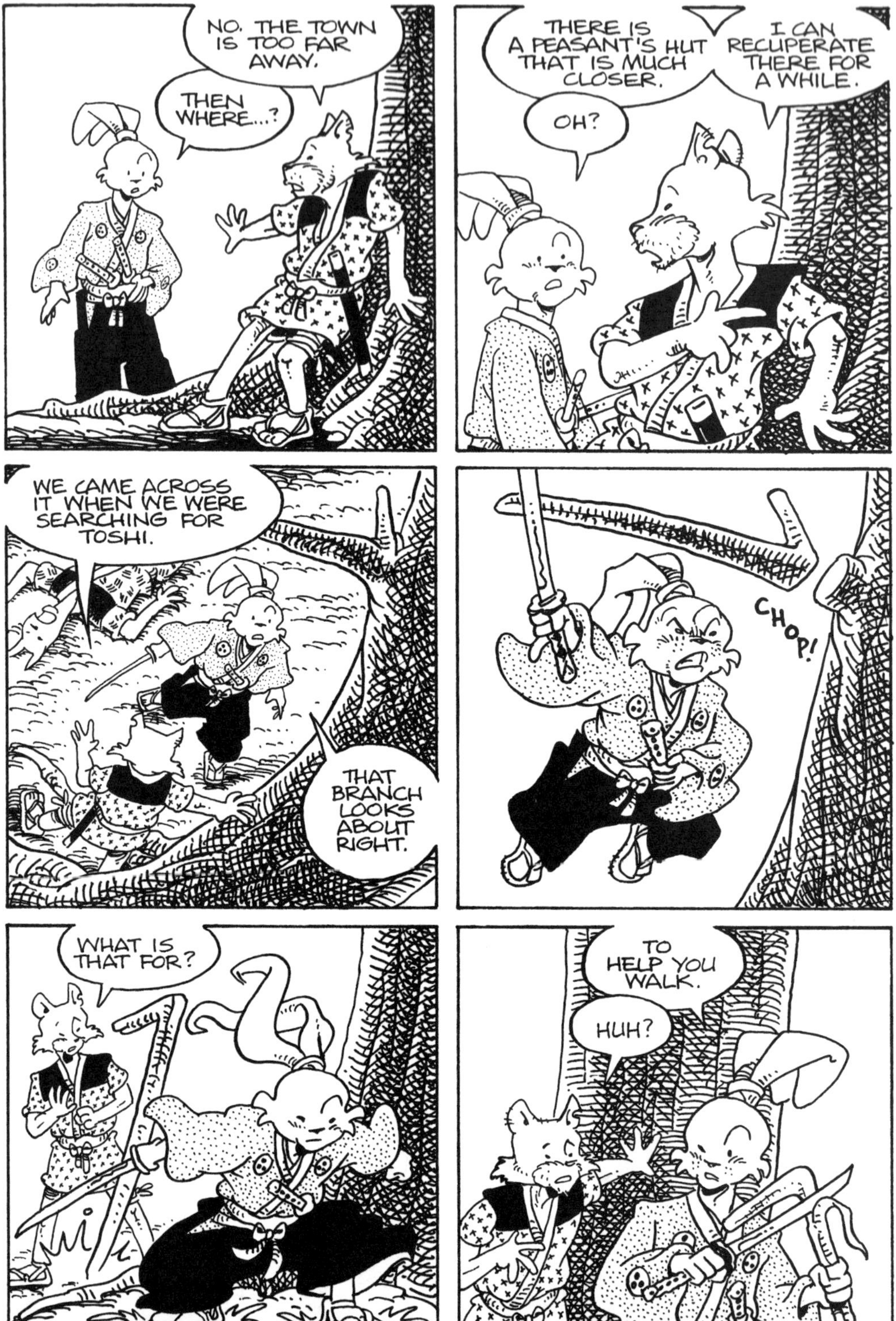
NO. THE TOWN IS TOO FAR AWAY.
THEN WHERE...?
THERE IS A PEASANT'S HUT THAT IS MUCH CLOSER.
I CAN RECUPERATE THERE FOR A WHILE.
OH?
WE CAME ACROSS IT WHEN WE WERE SEARCHING FOR TOSHI.
THAT BRANCH LOOKS ABOUT RIGHT.
CHOP!
WHAT IS THAT FOR?
TO HELP YOU WALK.
HUH?
8

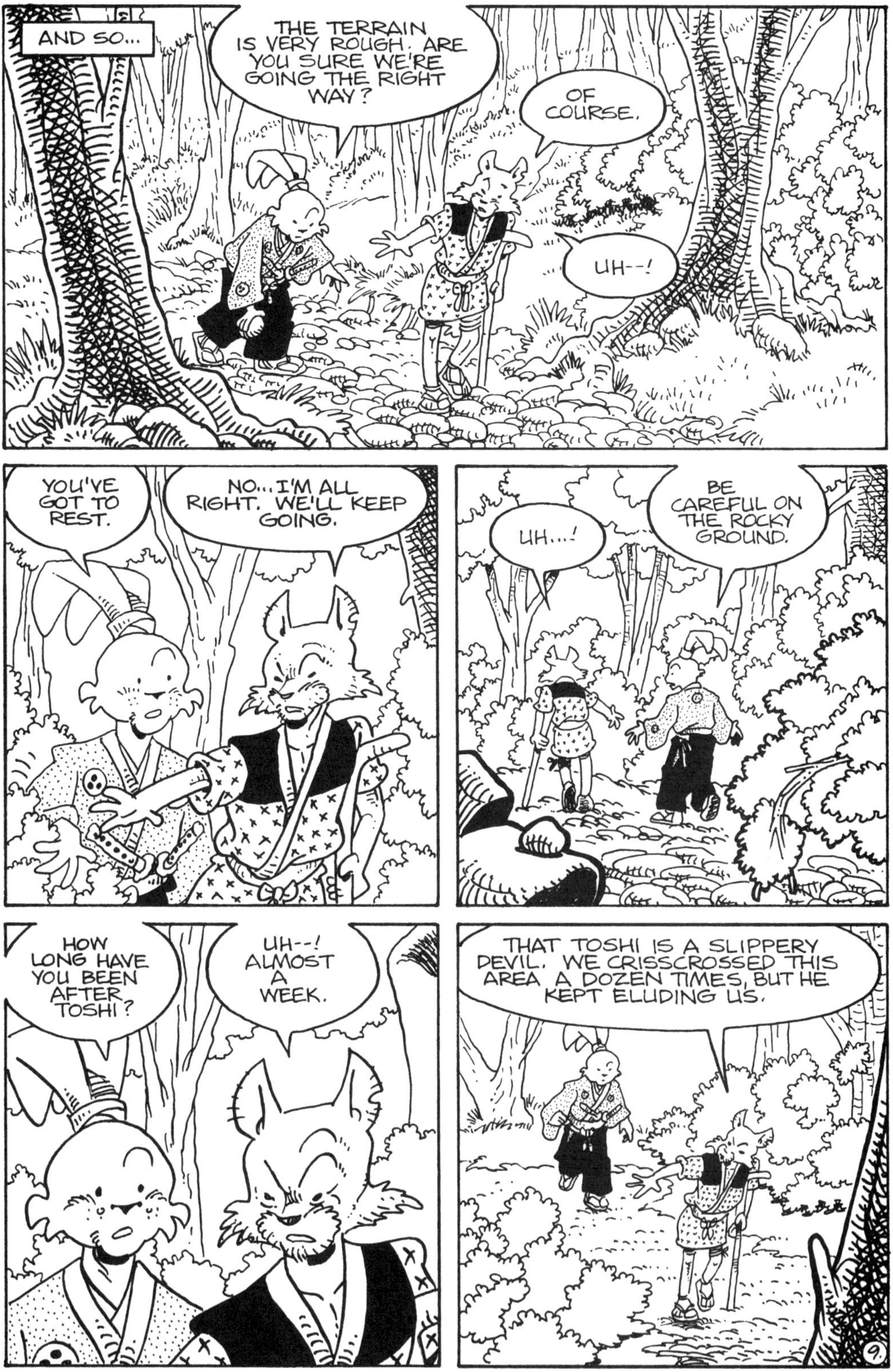
AND SO...
THE TERRAIN IS VERY ROUGH. ARE YOU SURE WE'RE GOING THE RIGHT WAY?
OF COURSE.
UH--!
YOU'VE GOT TO REST.
NO... I'M ALL RIGHT. WE'LL KEEP GOING.
UH...!
BE CAREFUL ON THE ROCKY GROUND.
HOW LONG HAVE YOU BEEN AFTER TOSHI?
UH--! ALMOST A WEEK.
THAT TOSHI IS A SLIPPERY DEVIL. WE CRISSCROSSED THIS AREA A DOZEN TIMES, BUT HE KEPT ELUDING US.
9.

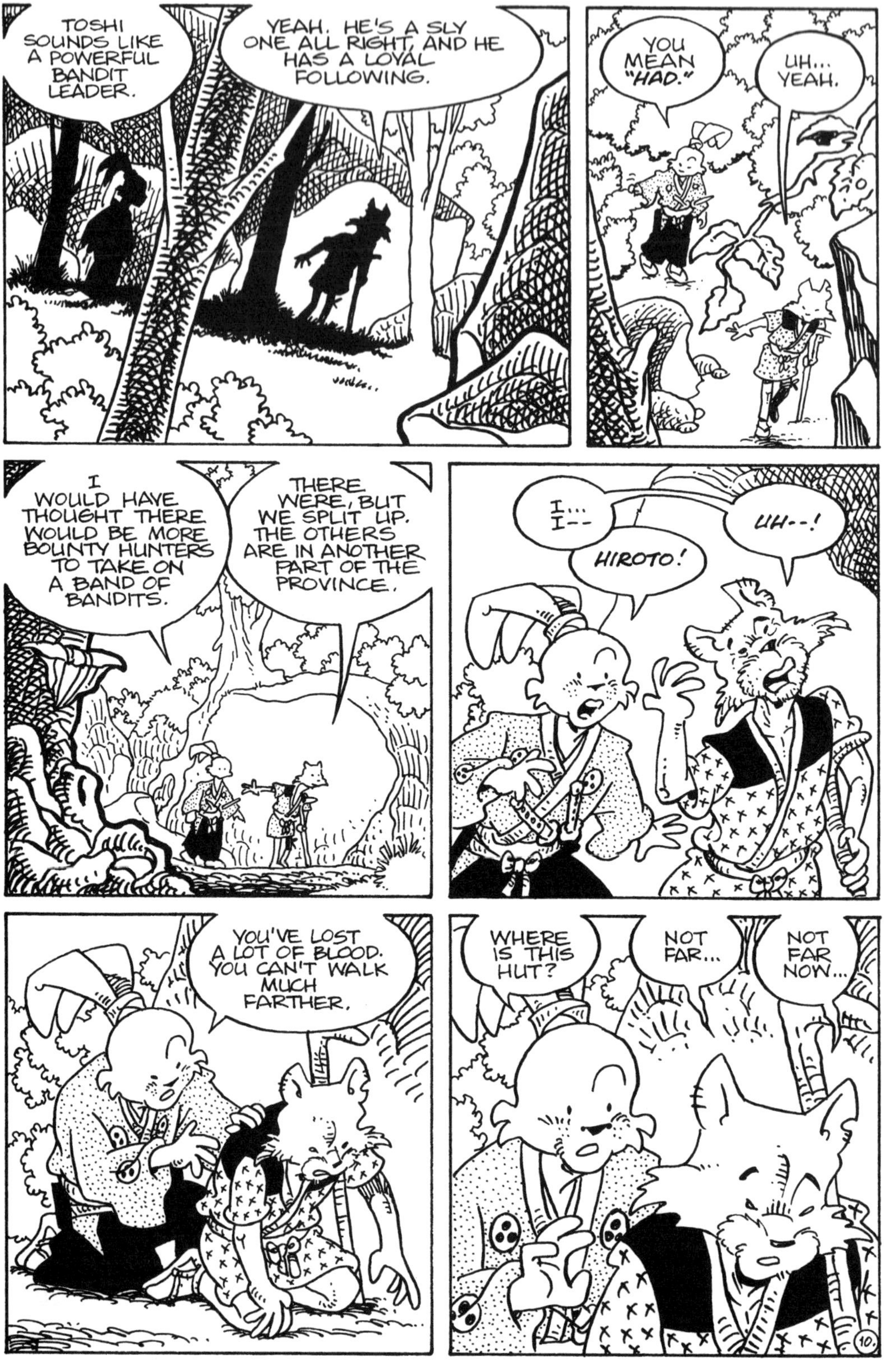
TOSHI SOUNDS LIKE A POWERFUL BANDIT LEADER.
YEAH. HE'S A SLY ONE ALL RIGHT, AND HE HAS A LOYAL FOLLOWING.
YOU MEAN "HAD."
UH... YEAH.
I WOULD HAVE THOUGHT THERE WOULD BE MORE BOUNTY HUNTERS TO TAKE ON A BAND OF BANDITS.
THERE WERE, BUT WE SPLIT UP. THE OTHERS ARE IN ANOTHER PART OF THE PROVINCE.
I... I--
HIROTO!
UH--!
YOU'VE LOST A LOT OF BLOOD. YOU CAN'T WALK MUCH FARTHER.
WHERE IS THIS HUT?
NOT FAR...
NOT FAR NOW...
10.

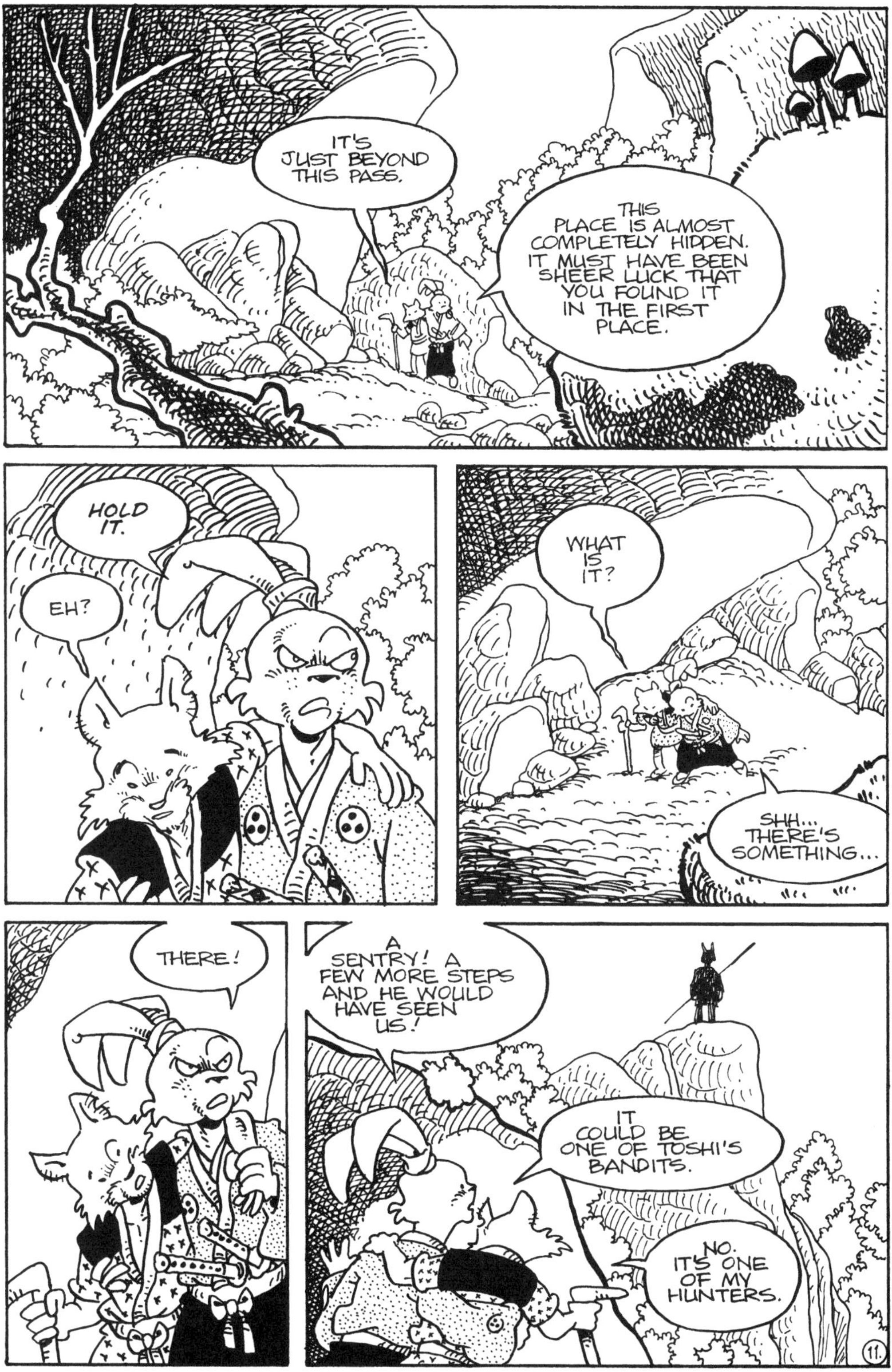
IT'S JUST BEYOND THIS PASS.
THIS PLACE IS ALMOST COMPLETELY HIDDEN. IT MUST HAVE BEEN SHEER LUCK THAT YOU FOUND IT IN THE FIRST PLACE.
HOLD IT.
EH?
WHAT IS IT?
SHH... THERE'S SOMETHING...
THERE!
A SENTRY! A FEW MORE STEPS AND HE WOULD HAVE SEEN US!
IT COULD BE ONE OF TOSHI'S BANDITS.
NO. IT'S ONE OF MY HUNTERS.
11.

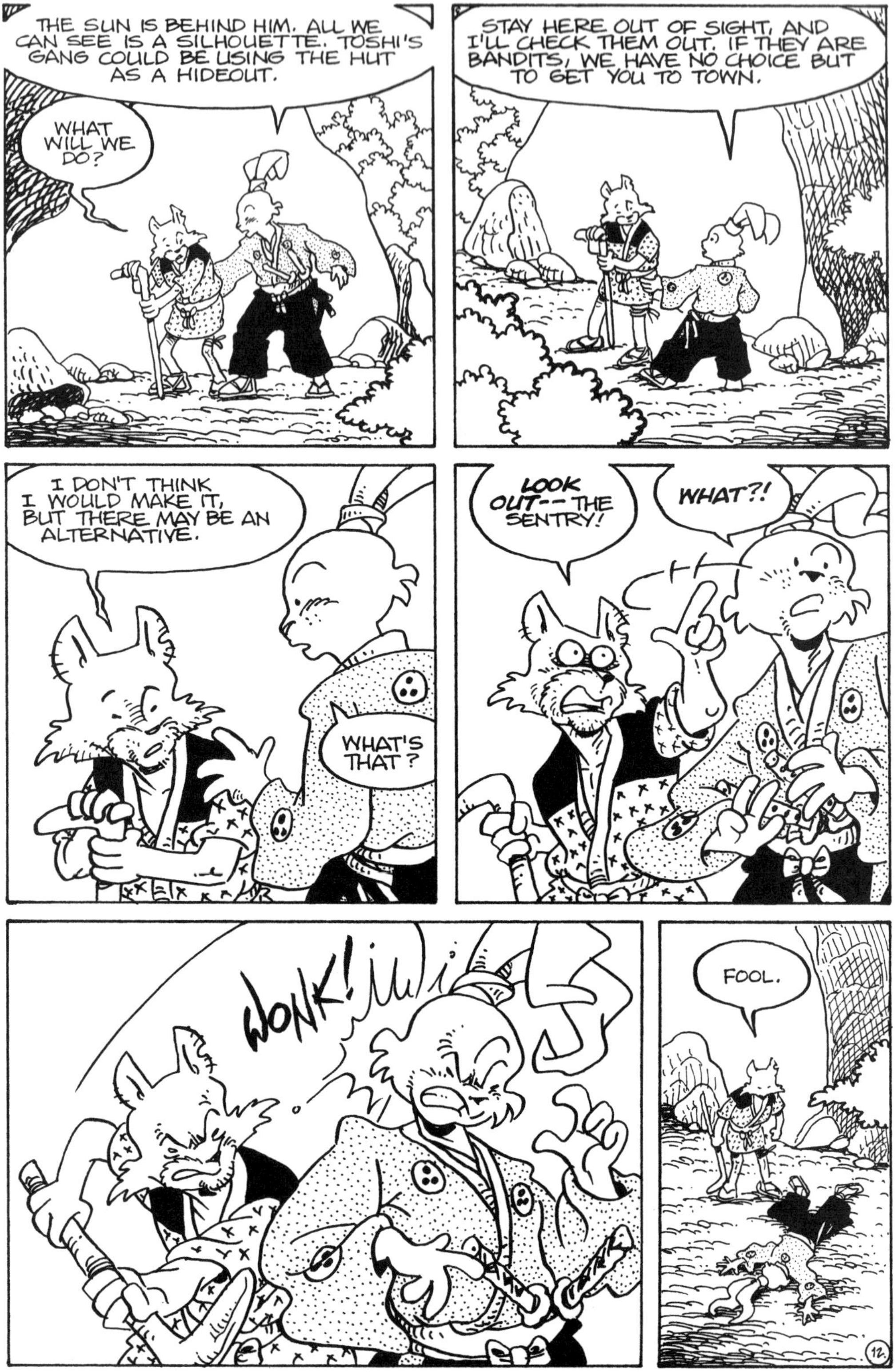
THE SUN IS BEHIND HIM. ALL WE CAN SEE IS A SILHOUETTE. TOSHI'S GANG COULD BE USING THE HUT AS A HIDEOUT.
WHAT WILL WE DO?
STAY HERE OUT OF SIGHT, AND I'LL CHECK THEM OUT. IF THEY ARE BANDITS, WE HAVE NO CHOICE BUT TO GET YOU TO TOWN.
I DON'T THINK I WOULD MAKE IT, BUT THERE MAY BE AN ALTERNATIVE.
WHAT'S THAT?
LOOK OUT-- THE SENTRY!
WHAT?!
WONK!
FOOL.
12.

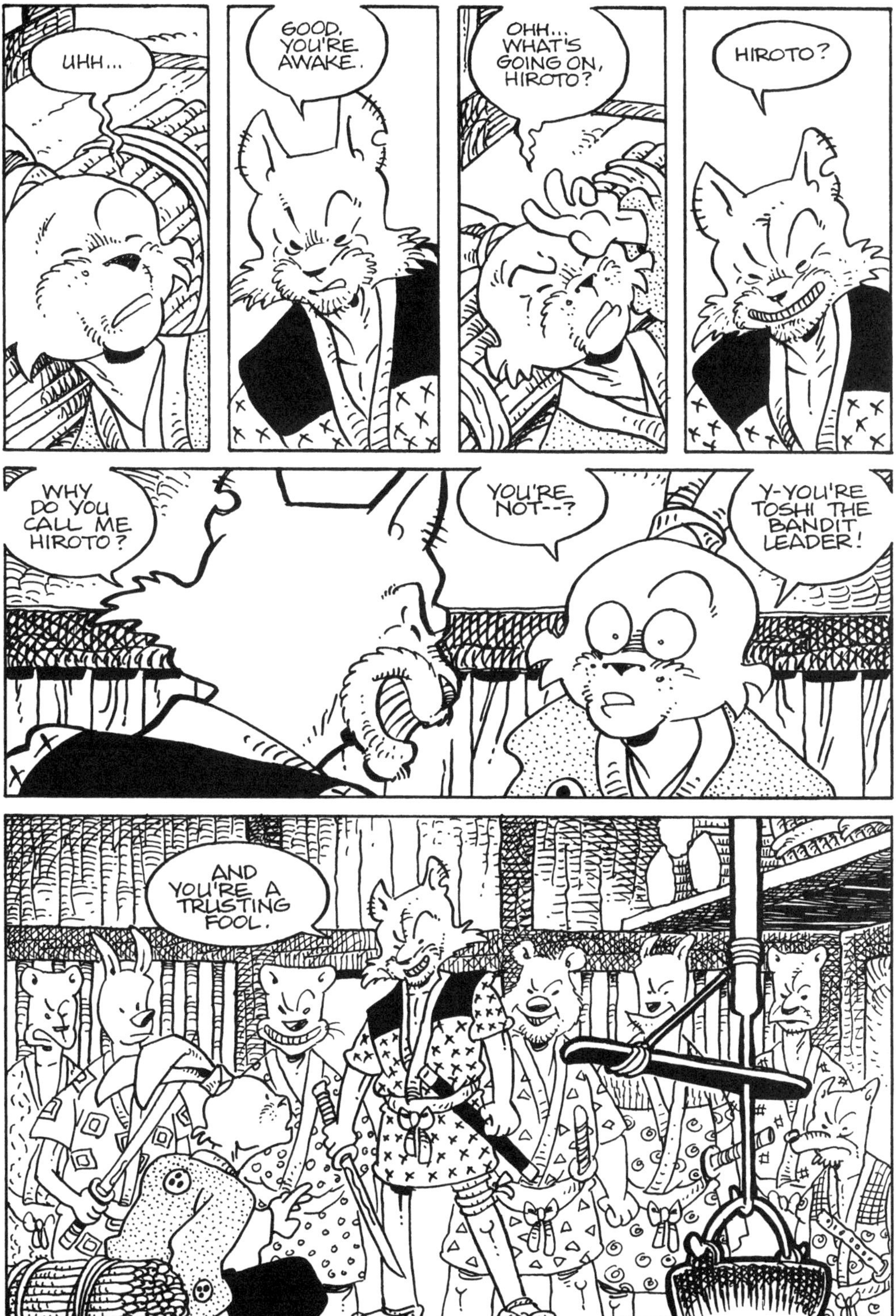
UHH...
GOOD. YOU'RE AWAKE.
OHH... WHAT'S GOING ON, HIROTO?
HIROTO?
WHY DO YOU CALL ME HIROTO?
YOU'RE NOT--?
Y-YOU'RE TOSHI THE BANDIT LEADER!
AND YOU'RE A TRUSTING FOOL.
13

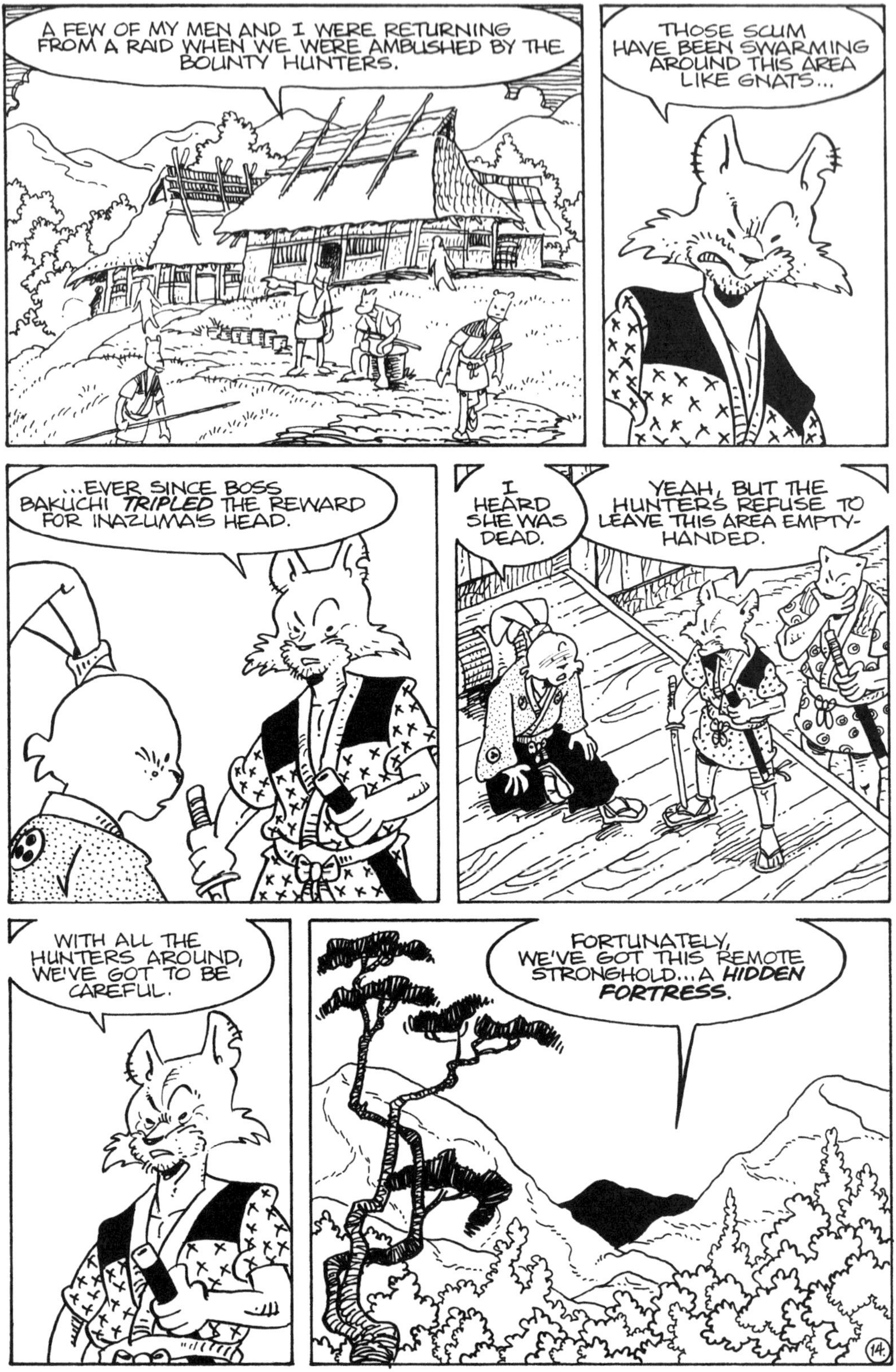
A FEW OF MY MEN AND I WERE RETURNING FROM A RAID WHEN WE WERE AMBUSHED BY THE BOUNTY HUNTERS.
THOSE SCUM HAVE BEEN SWARMING AROUND THIS AREA LIKE GNATS...
...EVER SINCE BOSS BAKUCHI TRIPLED THE REWARD FOR INAZUMA'S HEAD.
I HEARD SHE WAS DEAD.
YEAH, BUT THE HUNTERS REFUSE TO LEAVE THIS AREA EMPTY-HANDED.
WITH ALL THE HUNTERS AROUND, WE'VE GOT TO BE CAREFUL.
FORTUNATELY, WE'VE GOT THIS REMOTE STRONGHOLD...A HIDDEN FORTRESS.
14.

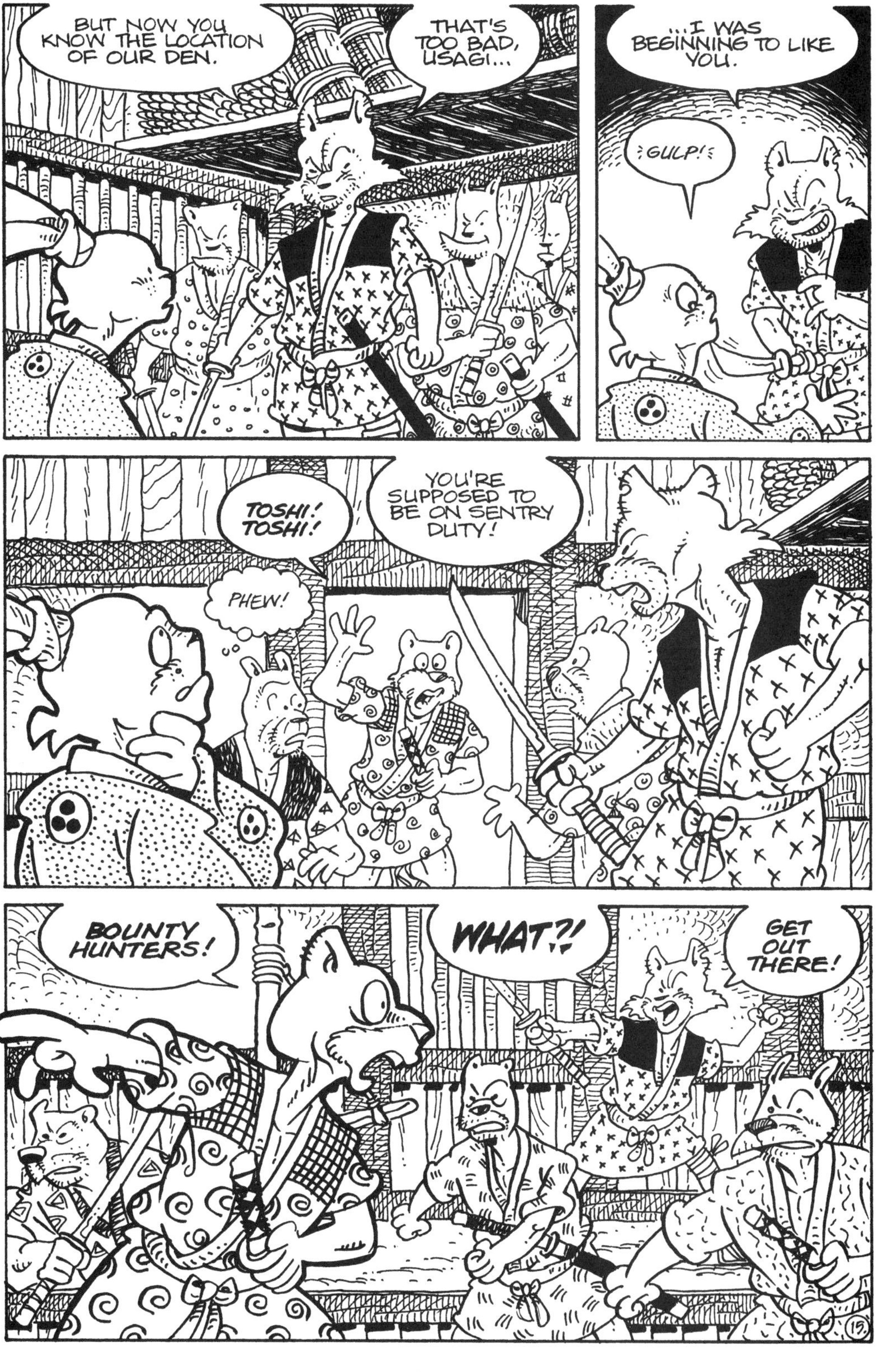
BUT NOW YOU KNOW THE LOCATION OF OUR DEN.
THAT'S TOO BAD, USAGI...
...I WAS BEGINNING TO LIKE YOU.
GULP!
TOSHI! TOSHI!
PHEW!
YOU'RE SUPPOSED TO BE ON SENTRY DUTY!
BOUNTY HUNTERS!
WHAT?!
GET OUT THERE!
15

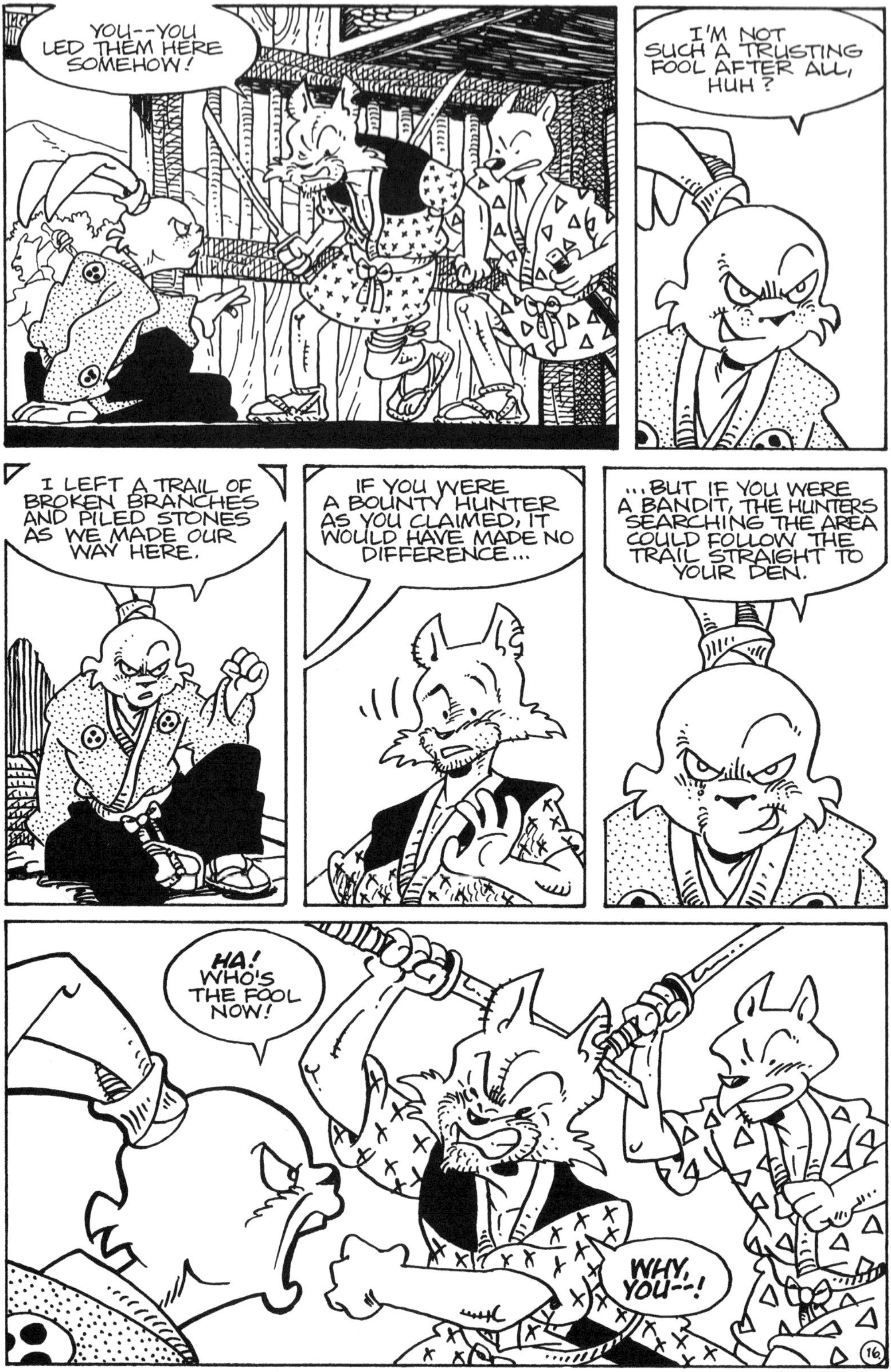
YOU--YOU LED THEM HERE SOMEHOW!
I'M NOT SUCH A TRUSTING FOOL AFTER ALL, HUH?
I LEFT A TRAIL OF BROKEN BRANCHES AND PILED STONES AS WE MADE OUR WAY HERE.
IF YOU WERE A BOUNTY HUNTER AS YOU CLAIMED, IT WOULD HAVE MADE NO DIFFERENCE...
...BUT IF YOU WERE A BANDIT, THE HUNTERS SEARCHING THE AREA COULD FOLLOW THE TRAIL STRAIGHT TO YOUR DEN.
HA! WHO'S THE FOOL NOW!
WHY, YOU--!
16.

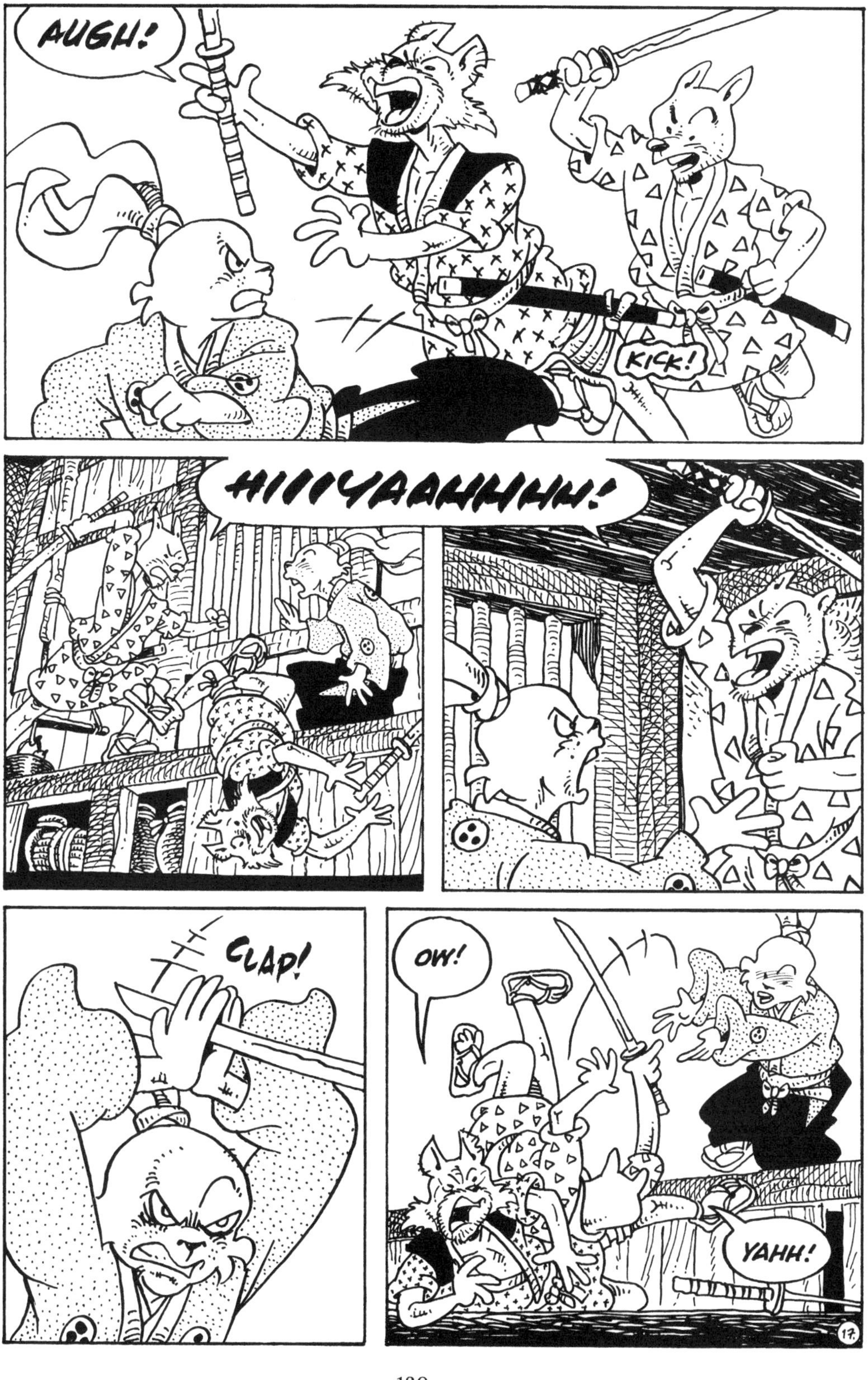
AUGH!
KICK!
HIIIYAAHHHH!
CLAP!
OW!
YAHH!
17.

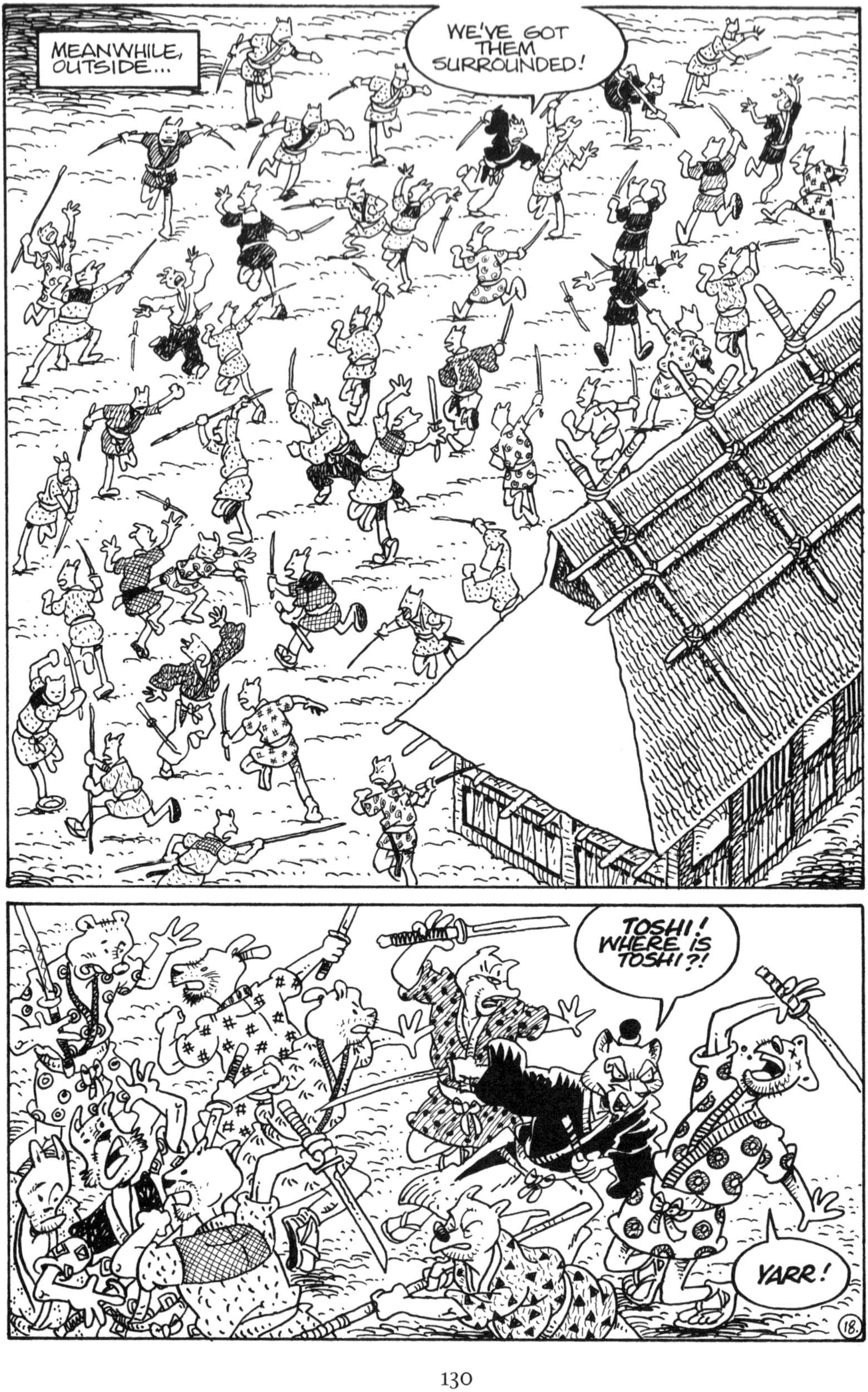
MEANWHILE, OUTSIDE...
WE'VE GOT THEM SURROUNDED!
TOSHI! WHERE IS TOSHI?!
YARR!
18.

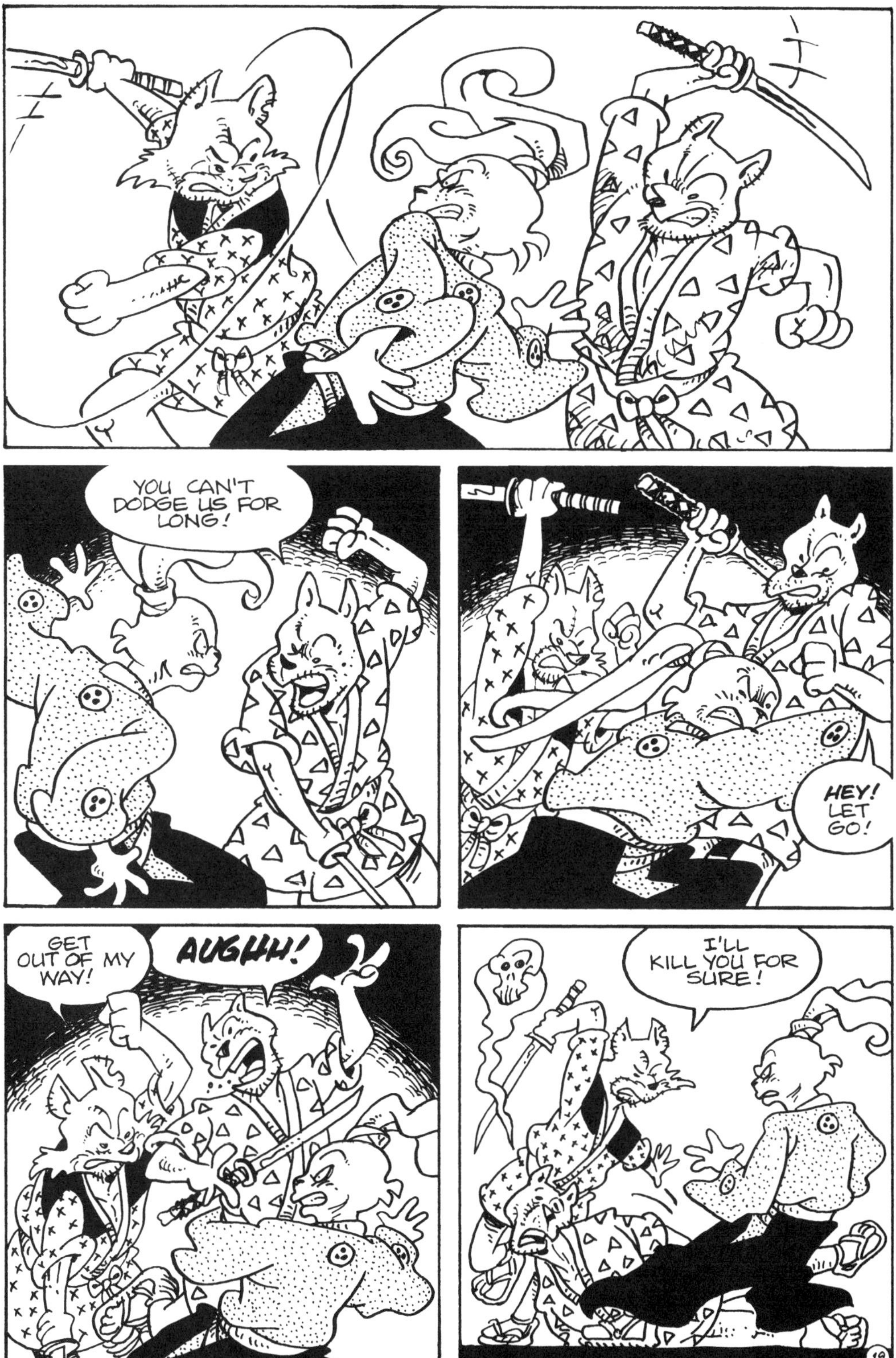
YOU CAN'T DODGE US FOR LONG!
HEY! LET GO!
GET OUT OF MY WAY!
AUGHH!
I'LL KILL YOU FOR SURE!
19

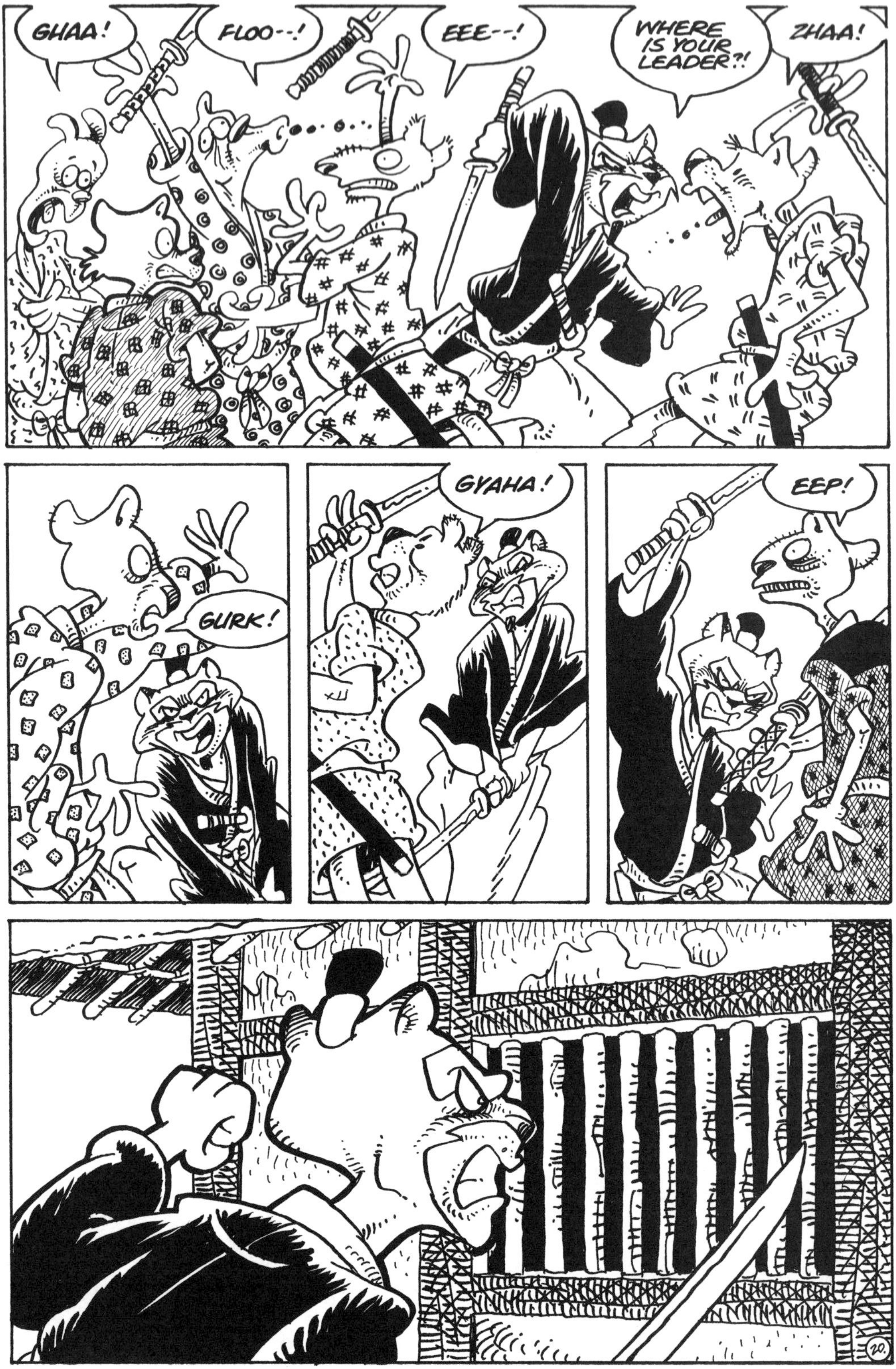
GHAA!
FLOO--!
EEE--!
WHERE IS YOUR LEADER?!
ZHAA!
GURK!
GYAHA!
EEP!
20.

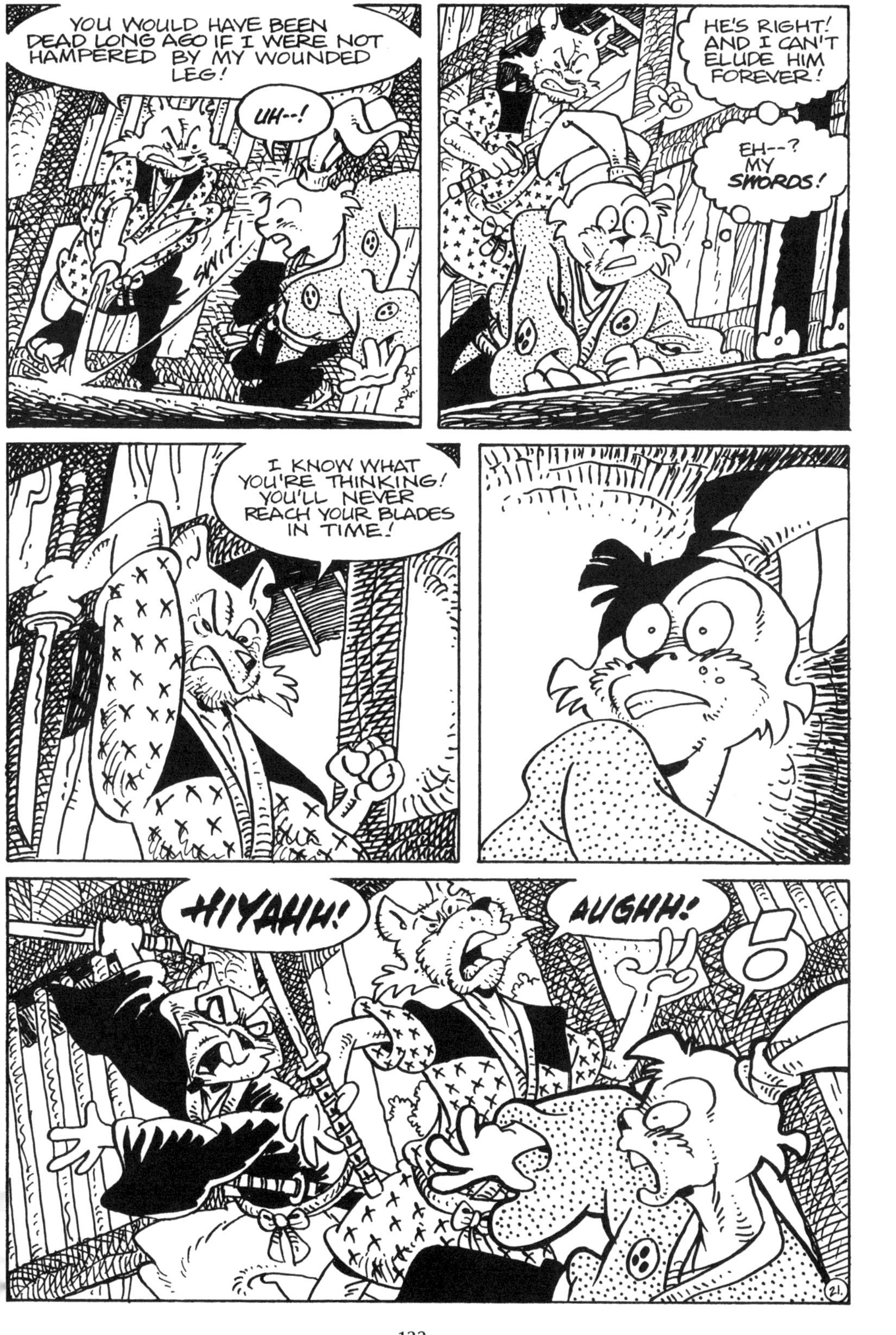
YOU WOULD HAVE BEEN DEAD LONG AGO IF I WERE NOT HAMPERED BY MY WOUNDED LEG!
UH--!
SWIT!
HE'S RIGHT! AND I CAN'T ELUDE HIM FOREVER!
EH--? MY SWORDS!
I KNOW WHAT YOU'RE THINKING! YOU'LL NEVER REACH YOUR BLADES IN TIME!
HIYAHH!
AUGHH!
21.

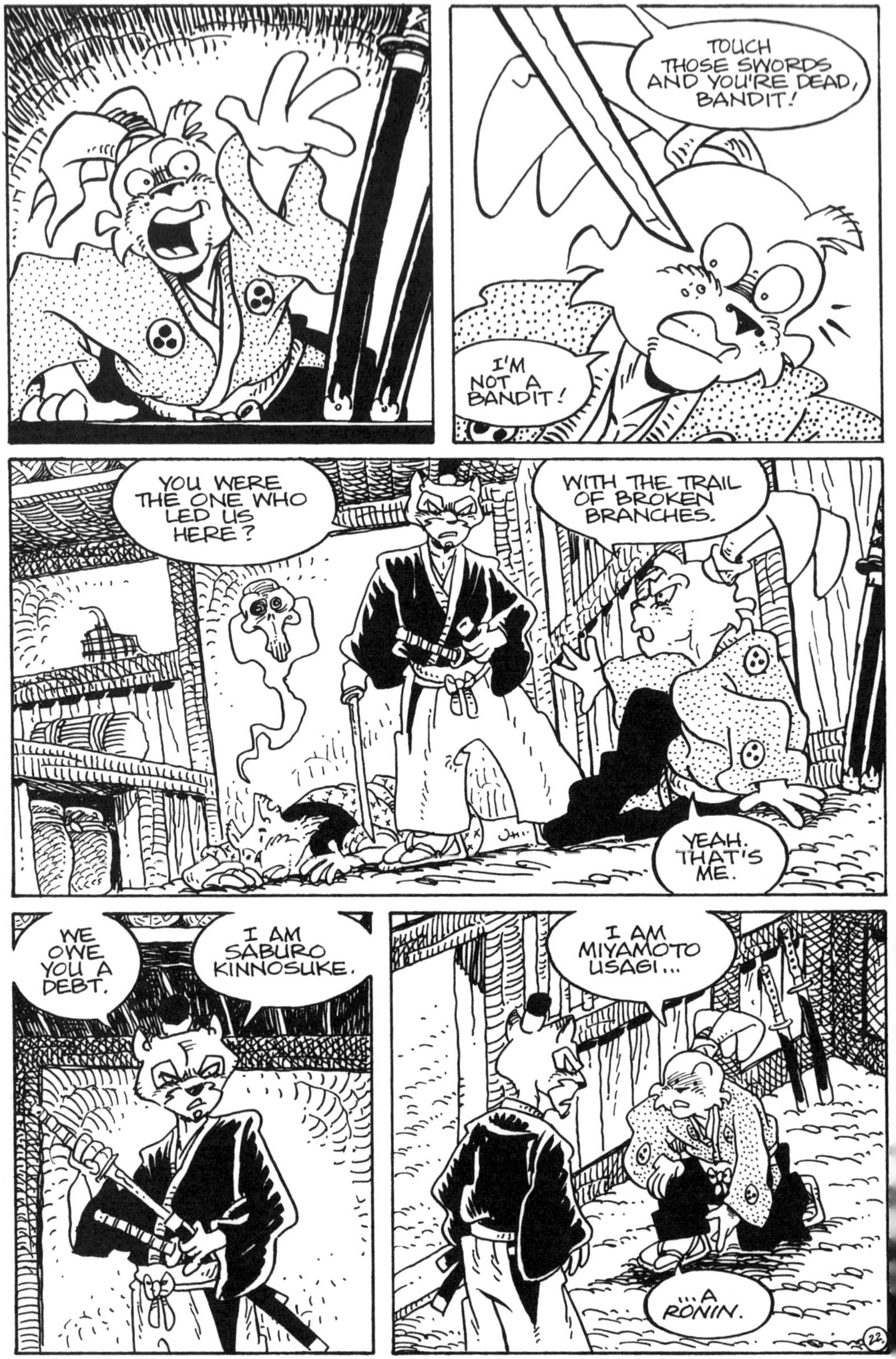
TOUCH THOSE SWORDS AND YOU'RE DEAD, BANDIT!
I'M NOT A BANDIT!
YOU WERE THE ONE WHO LED US HERE?
WITH THE TRAIL OF BROKEN BRANCHES.
YEAH. THAT'S ME.
WE OWE YOU A DEBT.
I AM SABURO KINNOSUKE.
I AM MIYAMOTO USAGI...
...A RONIN.
22.

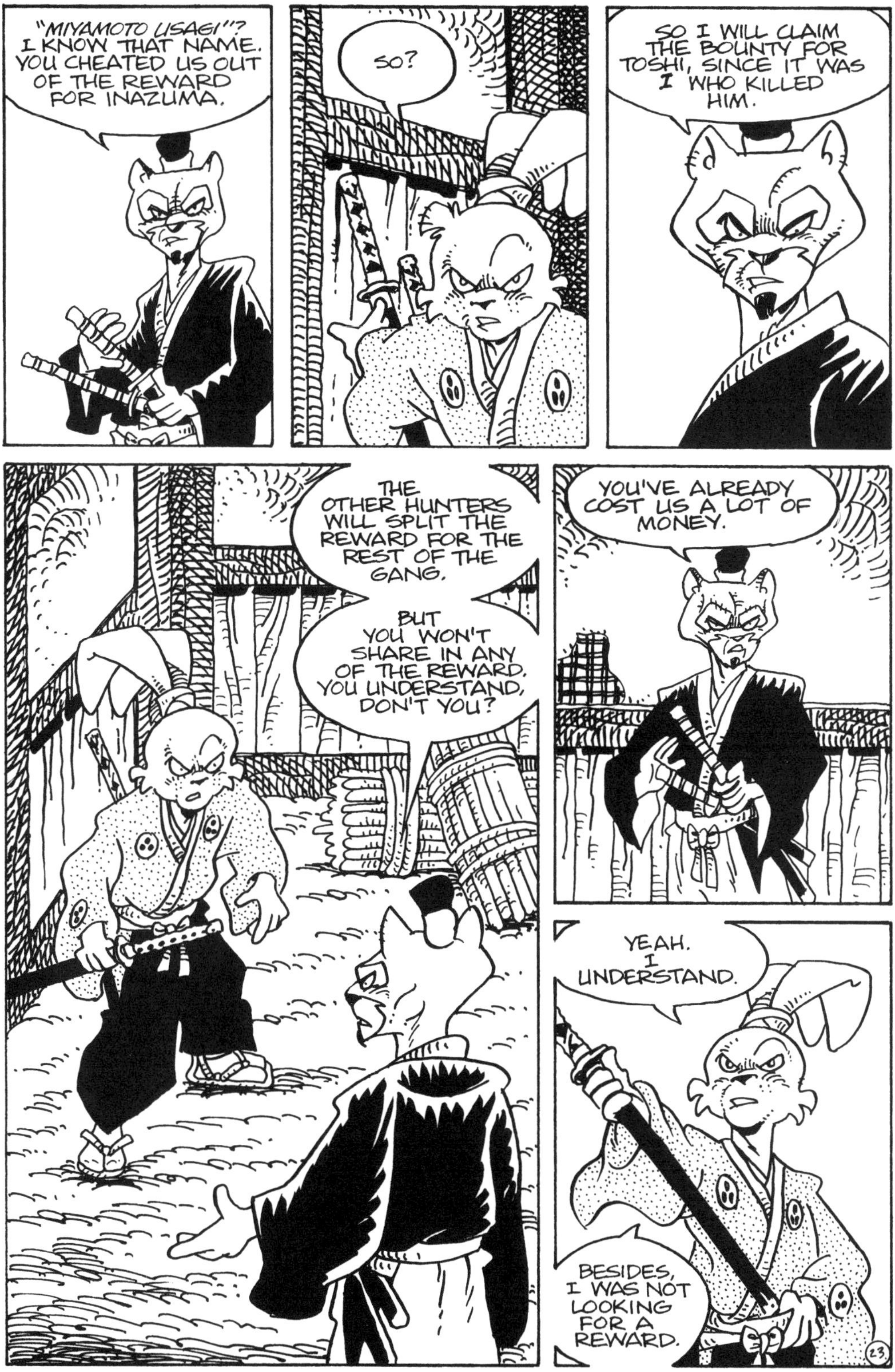
"MIYAMOTO USAGI"? I KNOW THAT NAME. YOU CHEATED US OUT OF THE REWARD FOR INAZUMA.
SO?
SO I WILL CLAIM THE BOUNTY FOR TOSHI, SINCE IT WAS I WHO KILLED HIM.
THE OTHER HUNTERS WILL SPLIT THE REWARD FOR THE REST OF THE GANG.
BUT YOU WON'T SHARE IN ANY OF THE REWARD. YOU UNDERSTAND, DON'T YOU?
YOU'VE ALREADY COST US A LOT OF MONEY.
YEAH. I UNDERSTAND.
BESIDES, I WAS NOT LOOKING FOR A REWARD.
23.

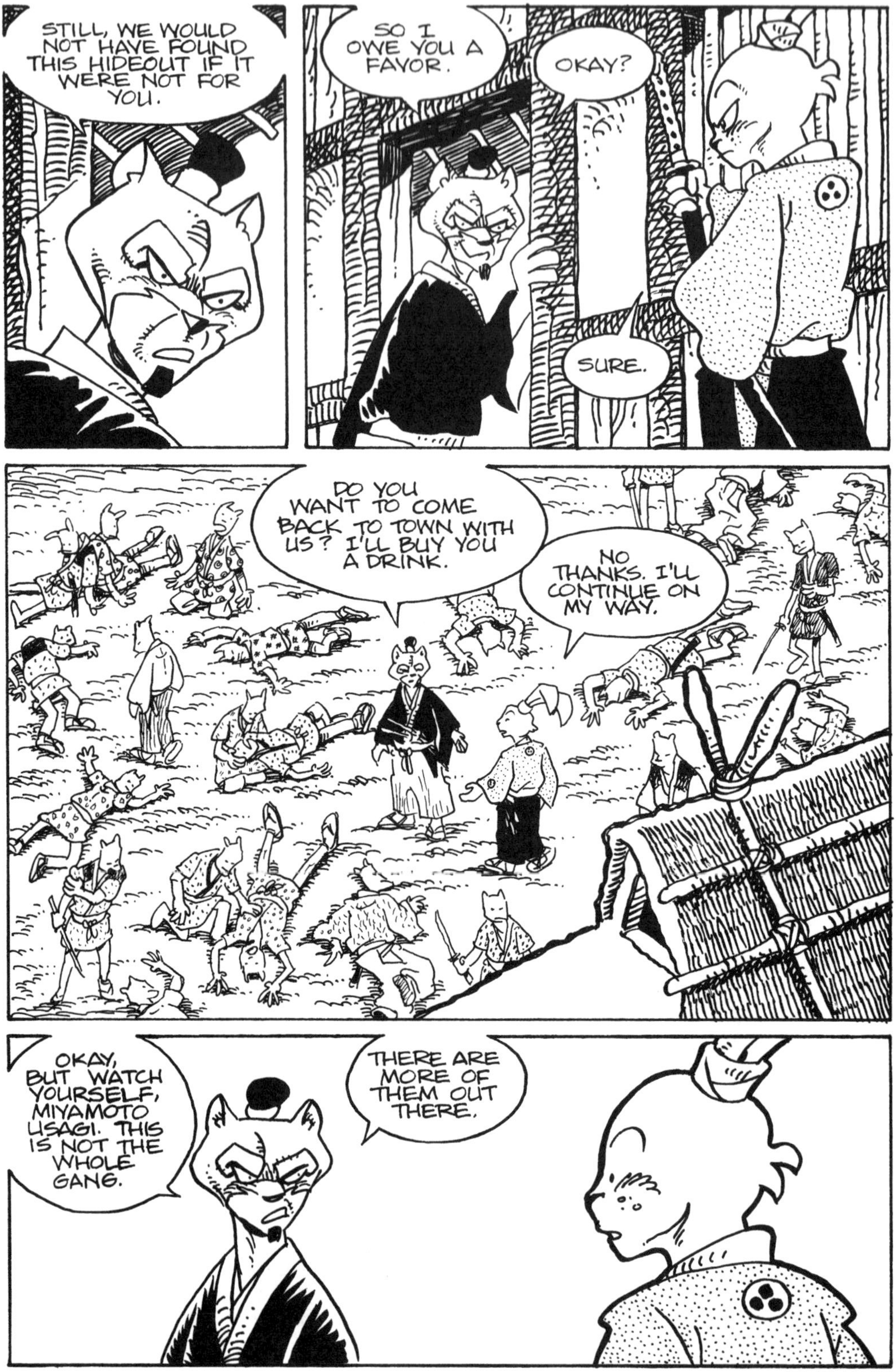
STILL, WE WOULD NOT HAVE FOUND THIS HIDEOUT IF IT WERE NOT FOR YOU.
SO I OWE YOU A FAVOR.
OKAY?
SURE.
DO YOU WANT TO COME BACK TO TOWN WITH US? I'LL BUY YOU A DRINK.
NO THANKS. I'LL CONTINUE ON MY WAY.
OKAY, BUT WATCH YOURSELF, MIYAMOTO USAGI. THIS IS NOT THE WHOLE GANG.
THERE ARE MORE OF THEM OUT THERE.

THE END

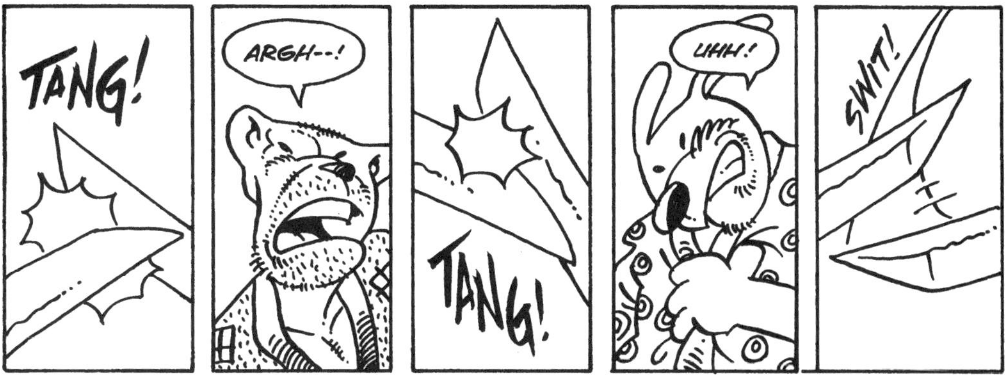
TANG!
ARGH--!
TANG!
UHH!
SWIT!

A PLACE TO STAY

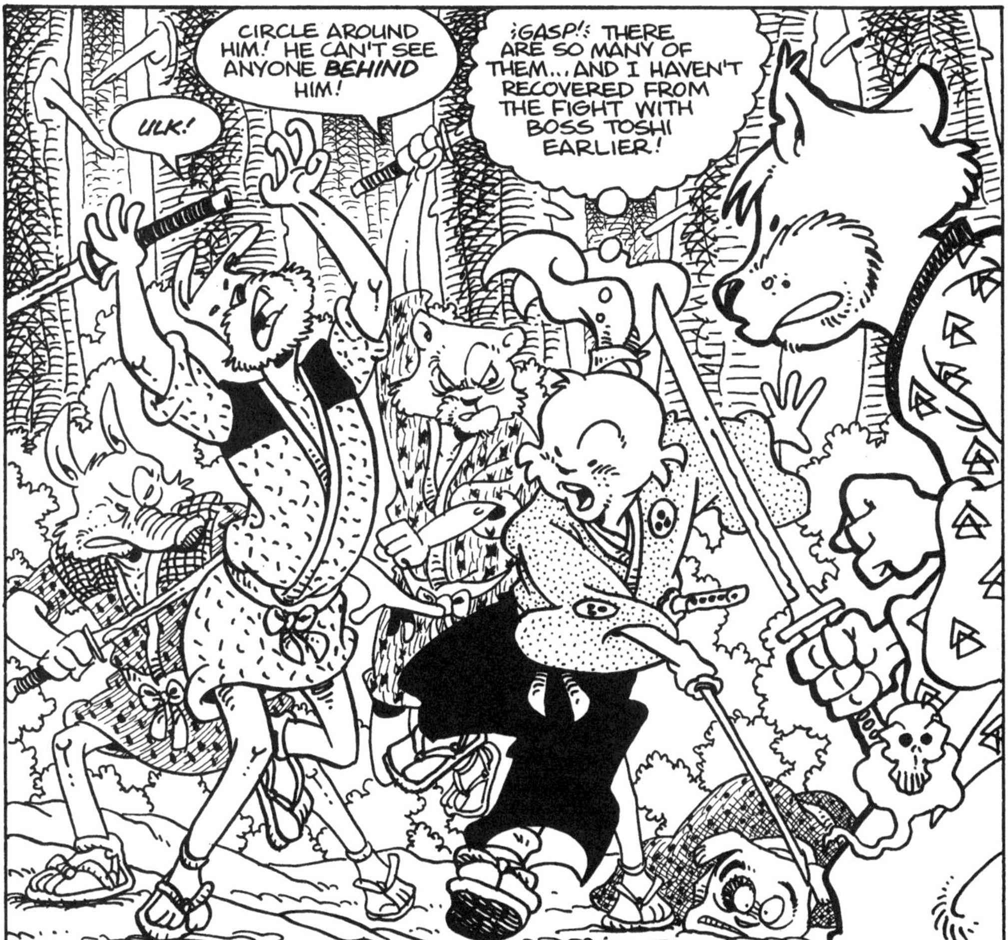
ULK!
CIRCLE AROUND HIM! HE CAN'T SEE ANYONE *BEHIND* HIM!
¡GASP!¡ THERE ARE SO MANY OF THEM... AND I HAVEN'T RECOVERED FROM THE FIGHT WITH BOSS TOSHI EARLIER!
1.

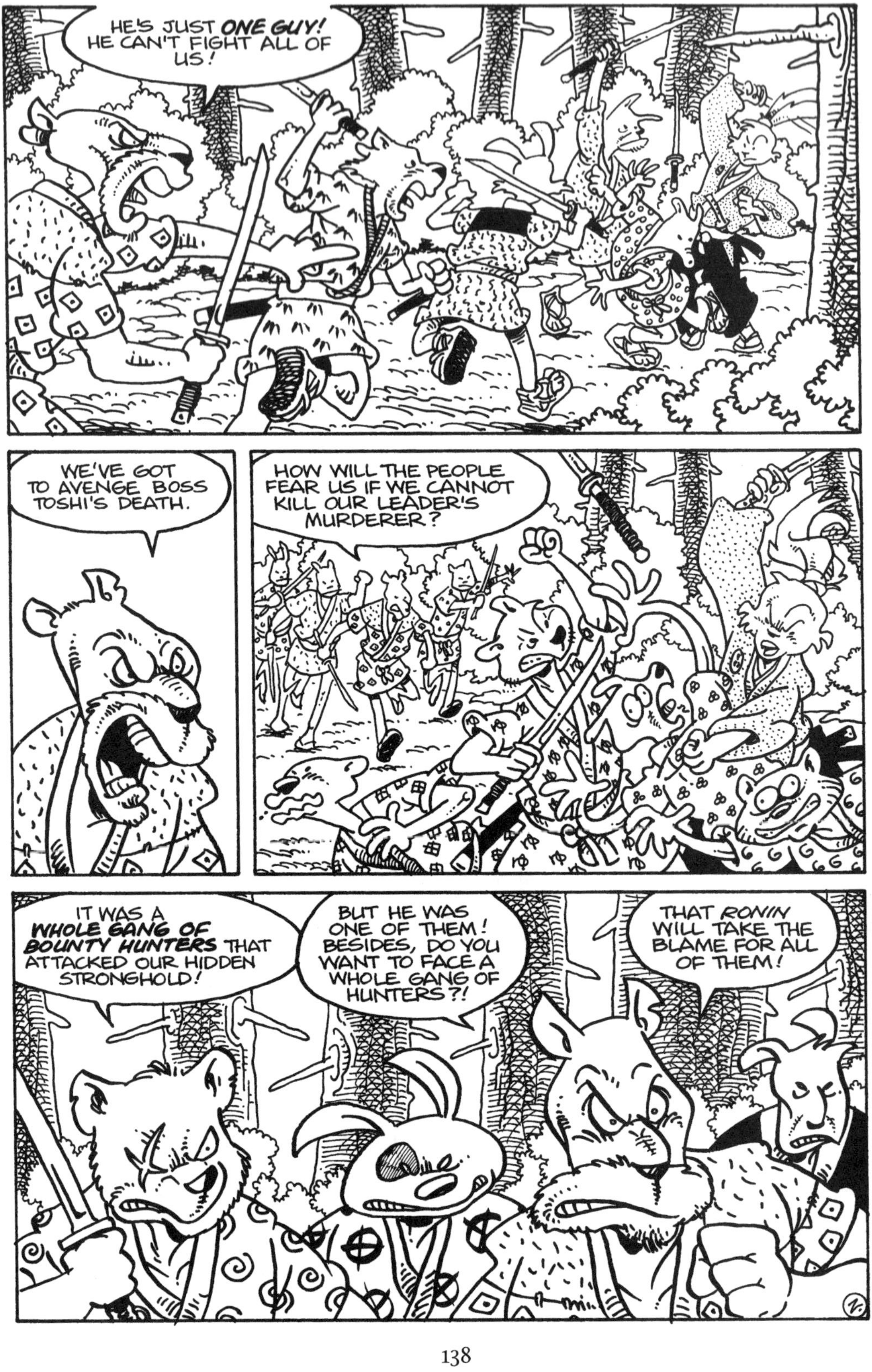

HE'S JUST **ONE GUY!** HE CAN'T FIGHT ALL OF US!
WE'VE GOT TO AVENGE BOSS TOSHI'S DEATH.
HOW WILL THE PEOPLE FEAR US IF WE CANNOT KILL OUR LEADER'S MURDERER?
IT WAS A **WHOLE GANG OF BOUNTY HUNTERS** THAT ATTACKED OUR HIDDEN STRONGHOLD!
BUT HE WAS ONE OF THEM! BESIDES, DO YOU WANT TO FACE A WHOLE GANG OF HUNTERS?!
THAT *RONIN* WILL TAKE THE BLAME FOR ALL OF THEM!

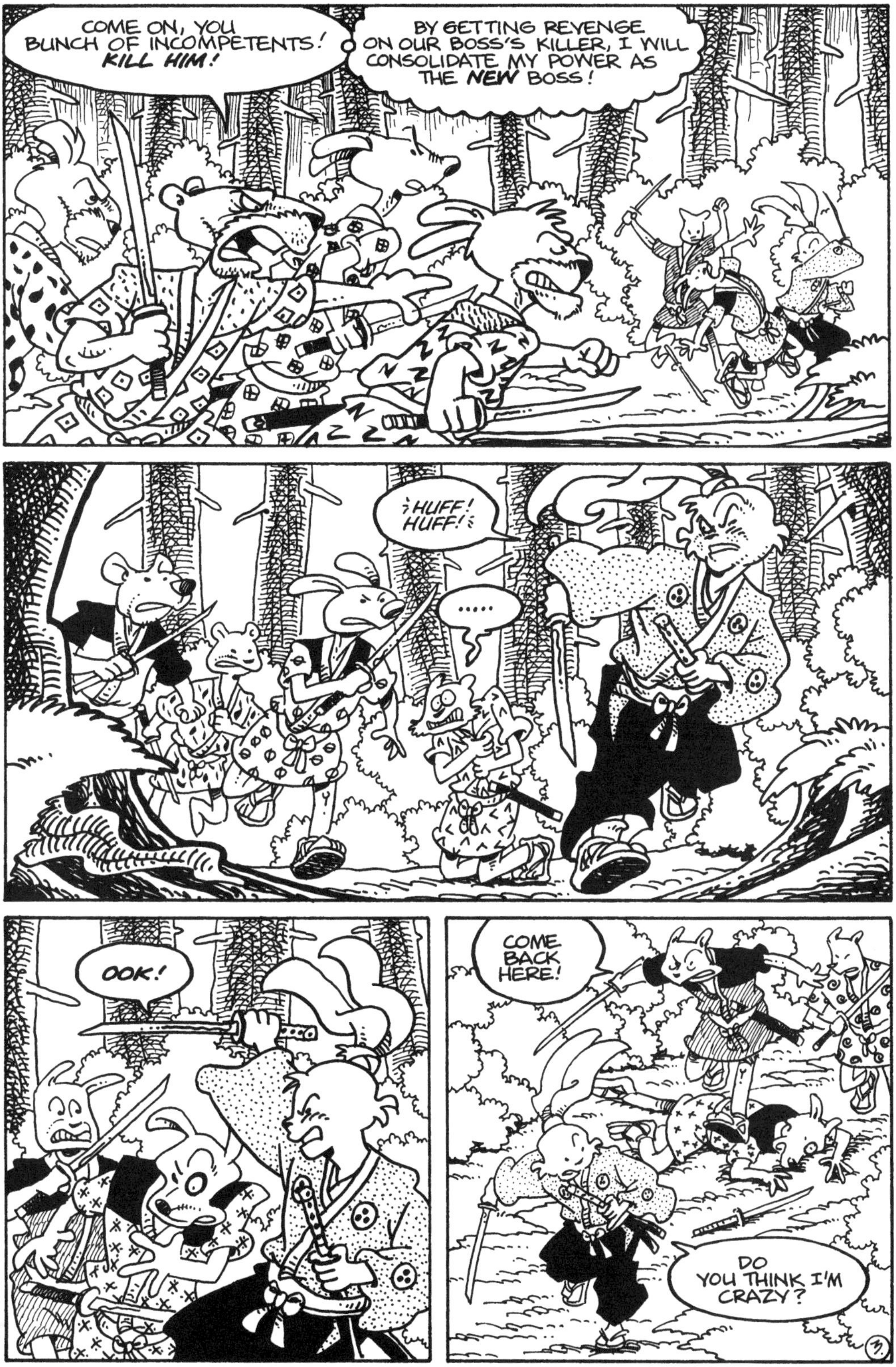

COME ON, YOU BUNCH OF INCOMPETENTS! KILL HIM!
BY GETTING REVENGE ON OUR BOSS'S KILLER, I WILL CONSOLIDATE MY POWER AS THE NEW BOSS!
HUFF! HUFF!
......
OOK!
COME BACK HERE!
DO YOU THINK I'M CRAZY?

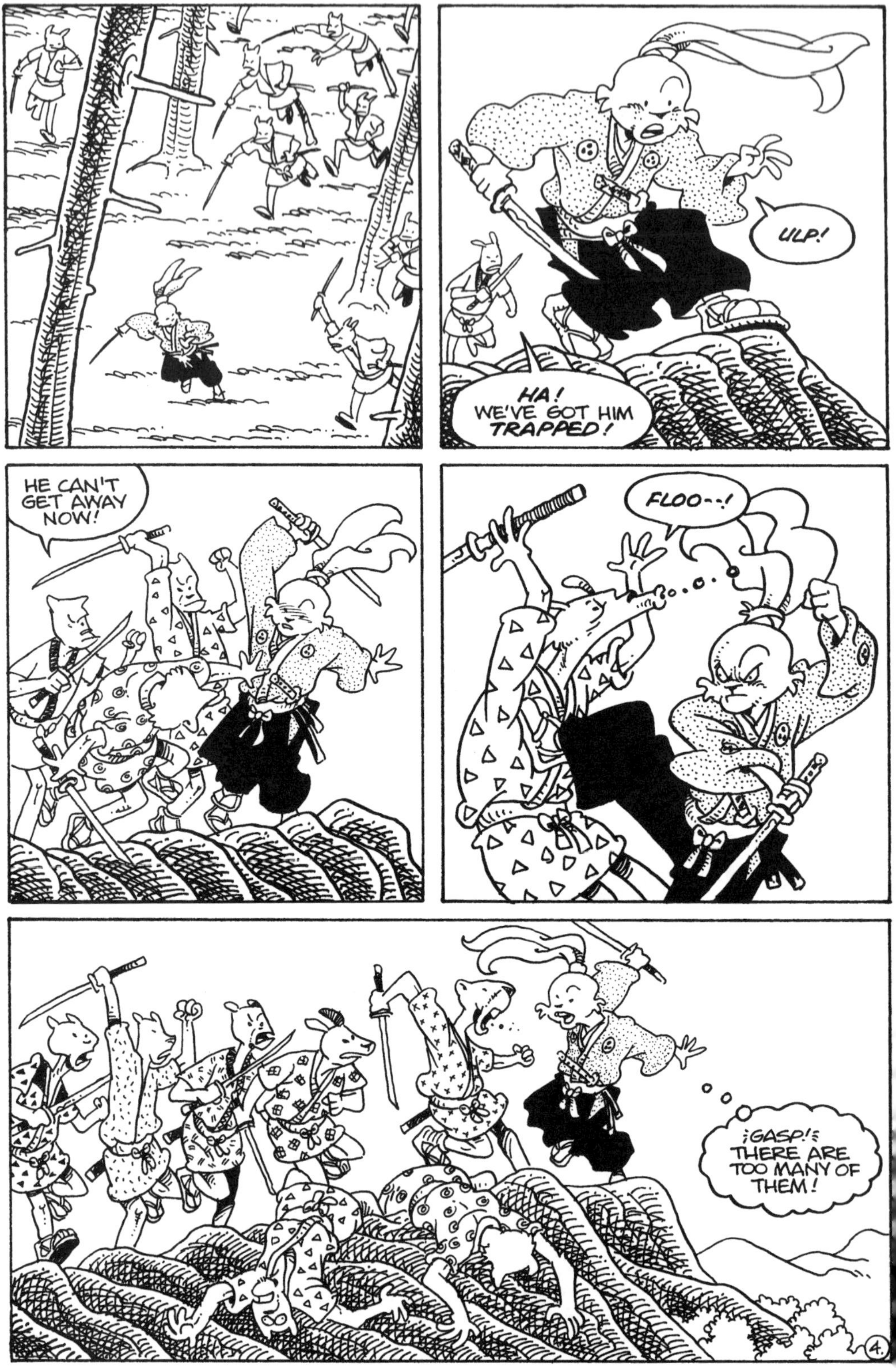
ULP!
HA! WE'VE GOT HIM TRAPPED!
HE CAN'T GET AWAY NOW!
FLOO--!
¡GASP!¡ THERE ARE TOO MANY OF THEM!
4.

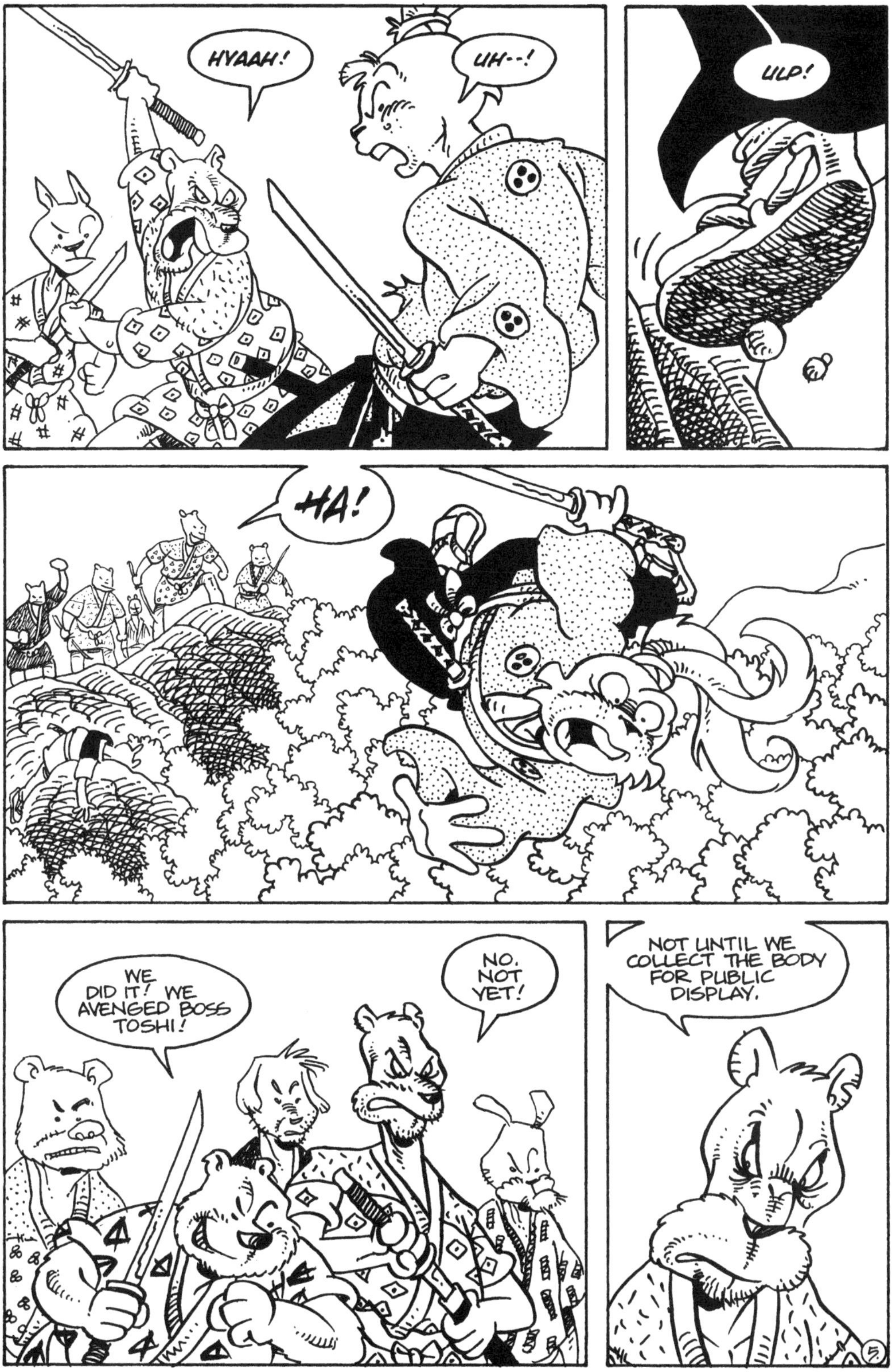
HYAAH!
UH--!
ULP!
HA!
WE DID IT! WE AVENGED BOSS TOSHI!
NO. NOT YET!
NOT UNTIL WE COLLECT THE BODY FOR PUBLIC DISPLAY.
5

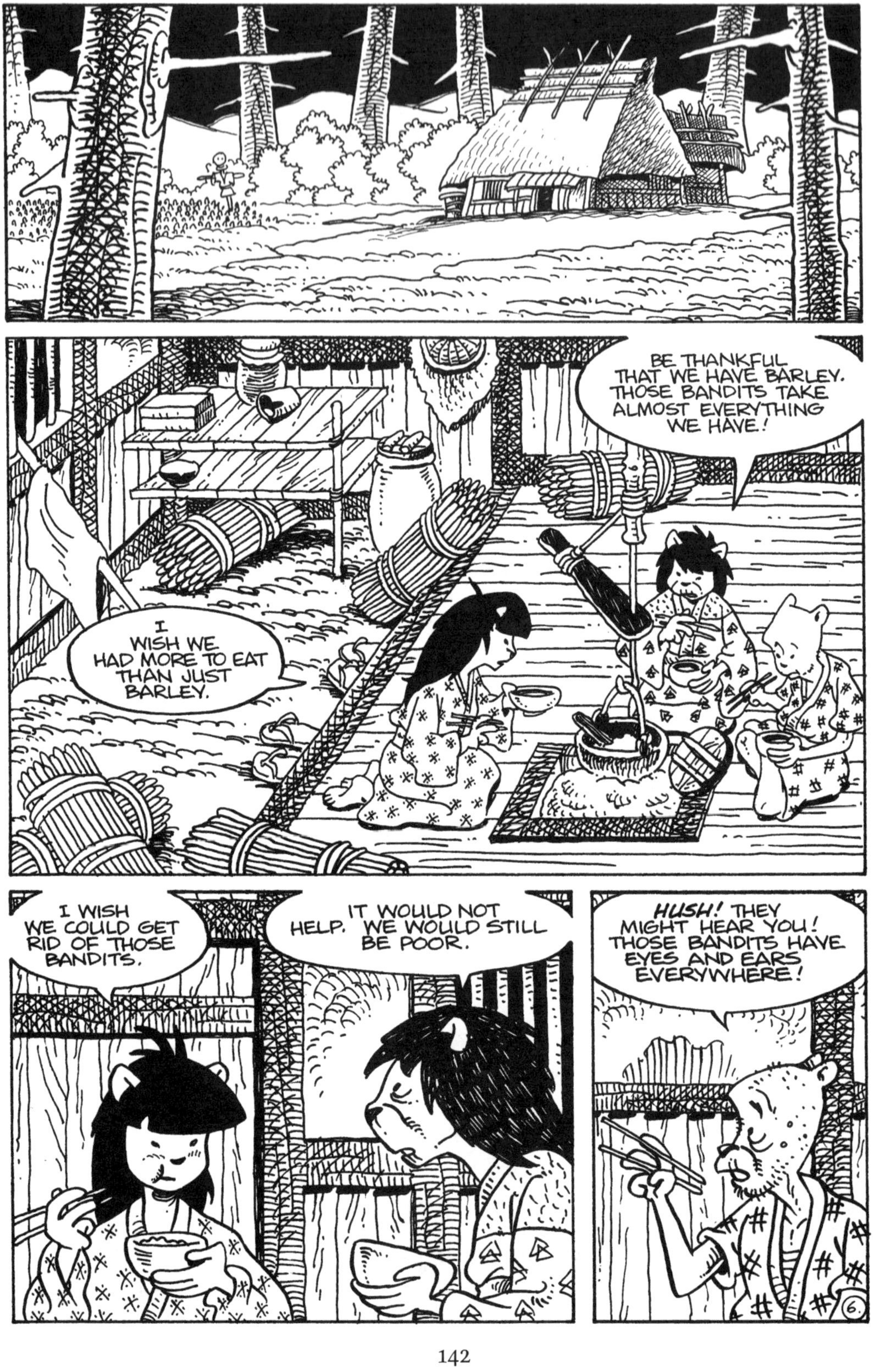
BE THANKFUL THAT WE HAVE BARLEY. THOSE BANDITS TAKE ALMOST EVERYTHING WE HAVE!
I WISH WE HAD MORE TO EAT THAN JUST BARLEY.
I WISH WE COULD GET RID OF THOSE BANDITS.
IT WOULD NOT HELP. WE WOULD STILL BE POOR.
HUSH! THEY MIGHT HEAR YOU! THOSE BANDITS HAVE EYES AND EARS EVERYWHERE!
6.

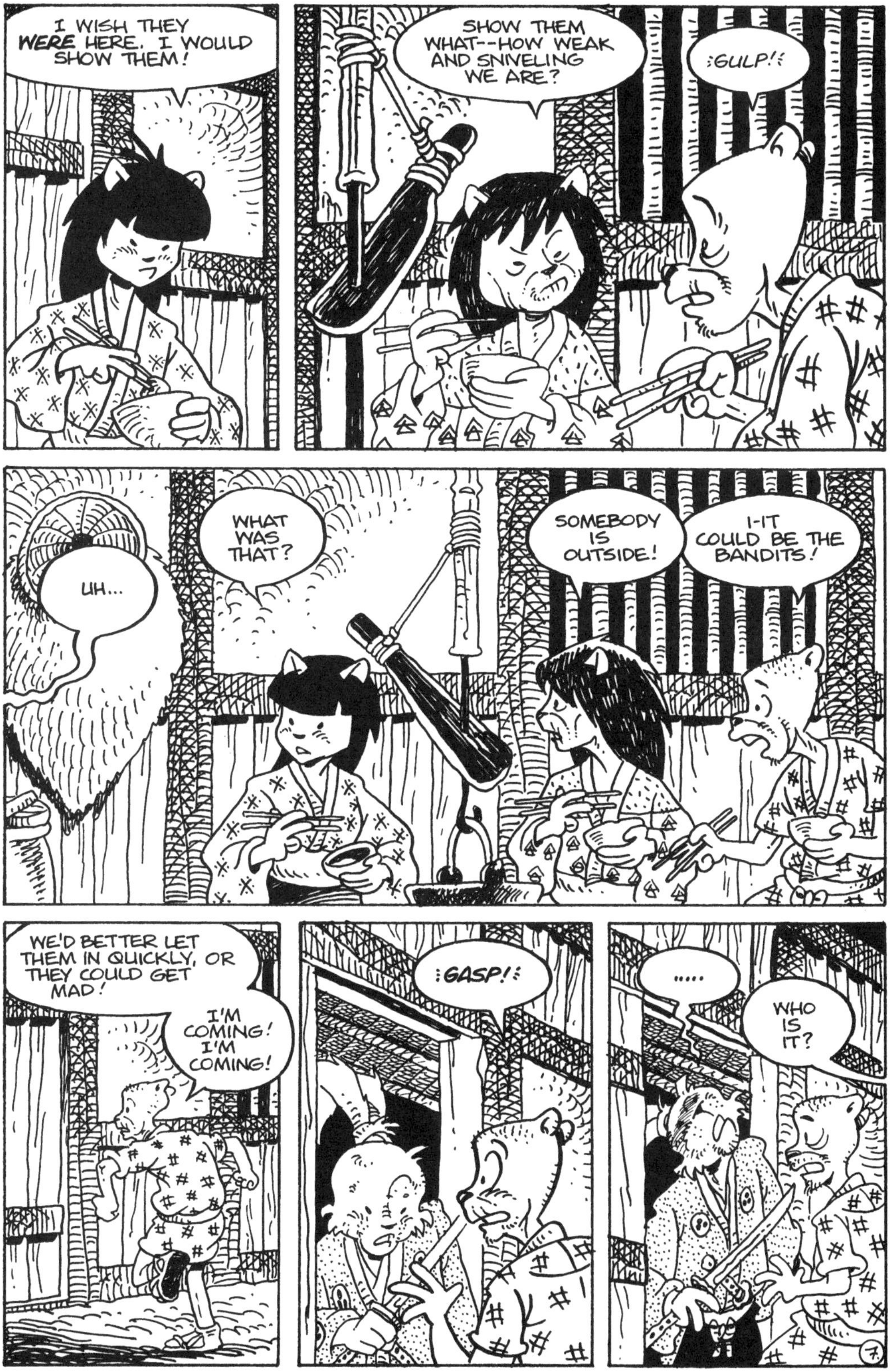
I WISH THEY **WERE** HERE. I WOULD SHOW THEM!
SHOW THEM WHAT--HOW WEAK AND SNIVELING WE ARE?
GULP!
UH...
WHAT WAS THAT?
SOMEBODY IS OUTSIDE!
I-IT COULD BE THE BANDITS!
WE'D BETTER LET THEM IN QUICKLY, OR THEY COULD GET MAD!
I'M COMING! I'M COMING!
GASP!
.....
WHO IS IT?

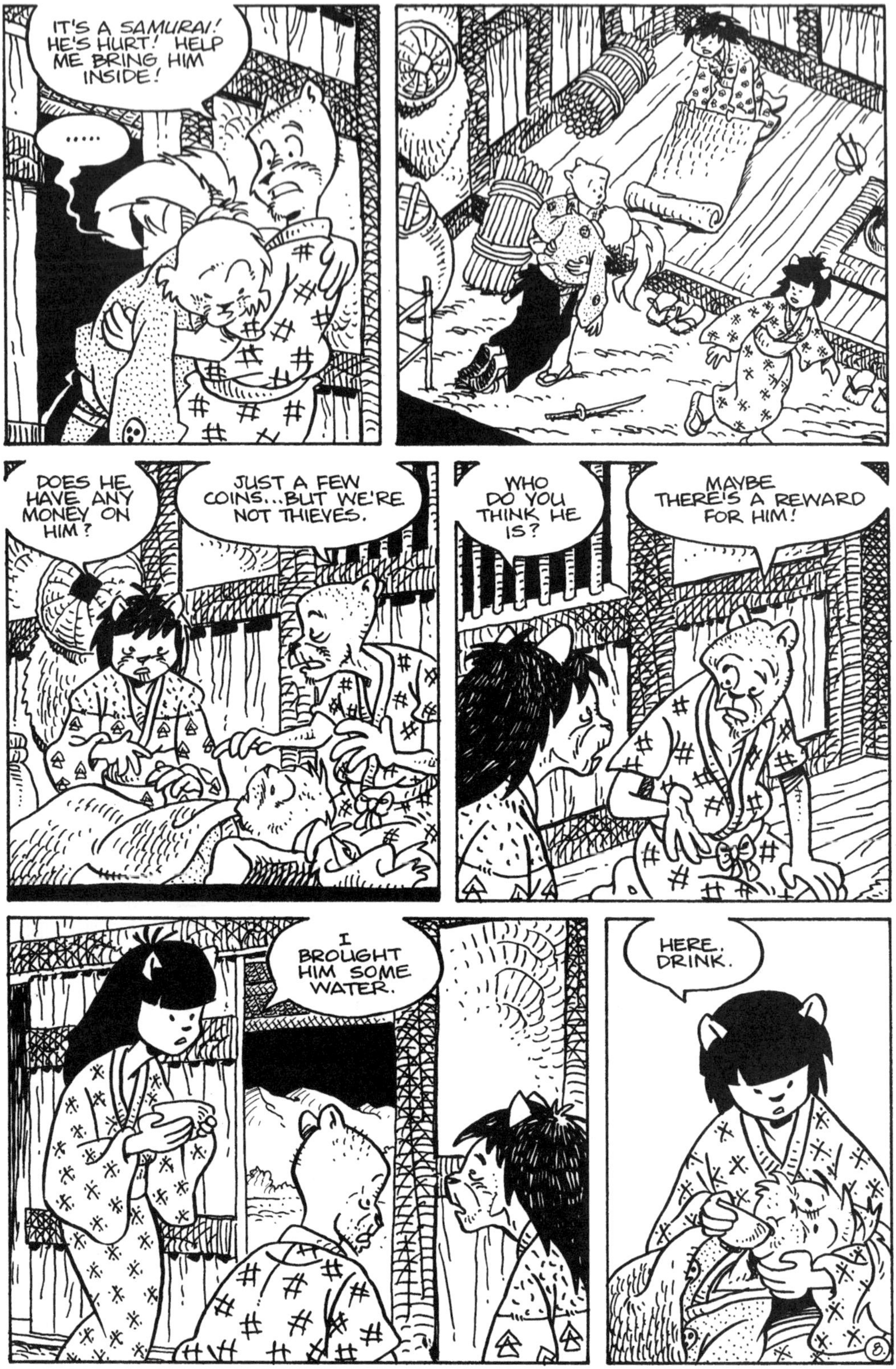
IT'S A SAMURAI! HE'S HURT! HELP ME BRING HIM INSIDE!
.....
DOES HE HAVE ANY MONEY ON HIM?
JUST A FEW COINS...BUT WE'RE NOT THIEVES.
WHO DO YOU THINK HE IS?
MAYBE THERE'S A REWARD FOR HIM!
I BROUGHT HIM SOME WATER.
HERE. DRINK.
8.

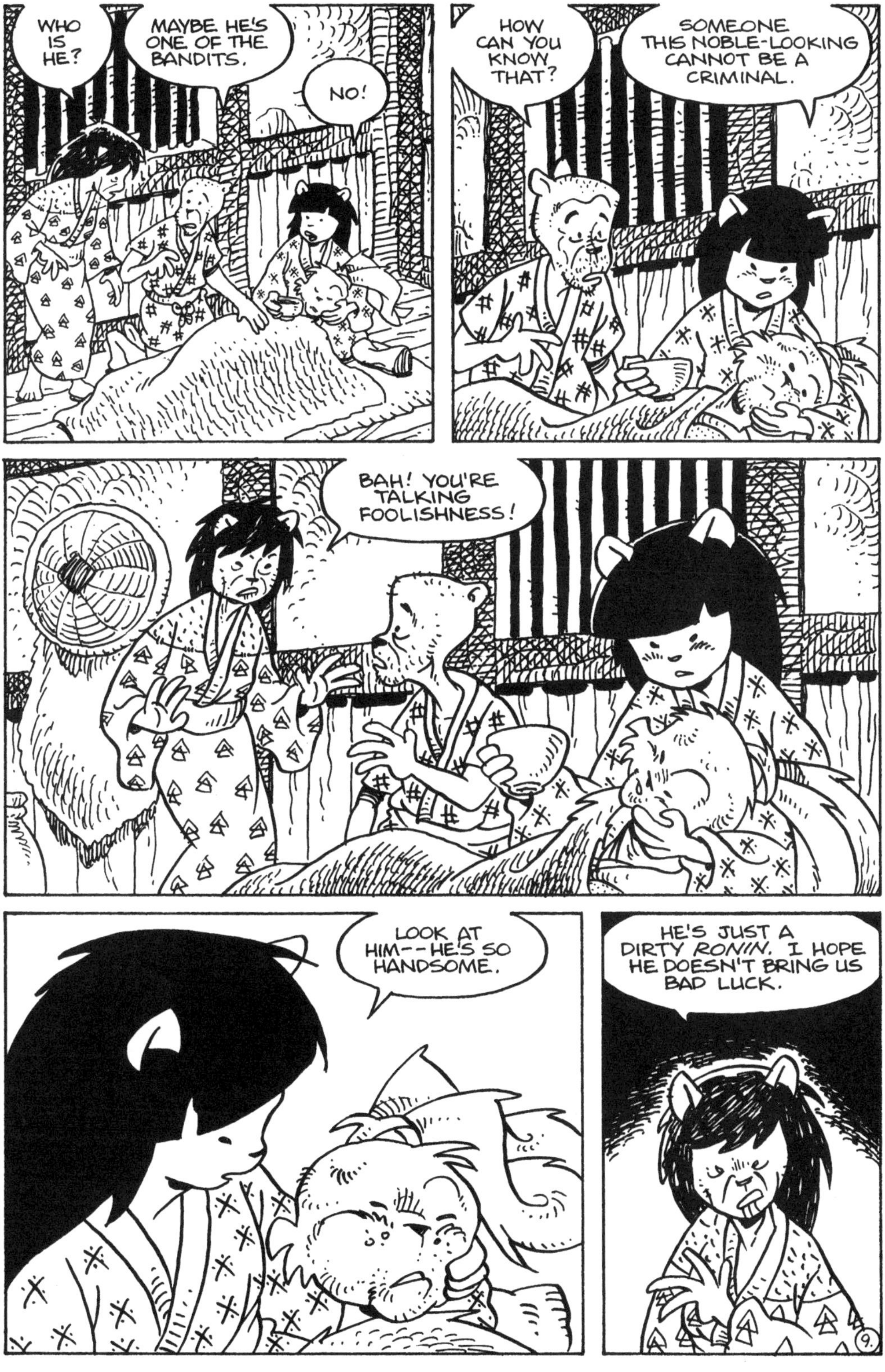
WHO IS HE?
MAYBE HE'S ONE OF THE BANDITS.
NO!
HOW CAN YOU KNOW THAT?
SOMEONE THIS NOBLE-LOOKING CANNOT BE A CRIMINAL.
BAH! YOU'RE TALKING FOOLISHNESS!
LOOK AT HIM--HE'S SO HANDSOME.
HE'S JUST A DIRTY *RONIN*. I HOPE HE DOESN'T BRING US BAD LUCK.
9.

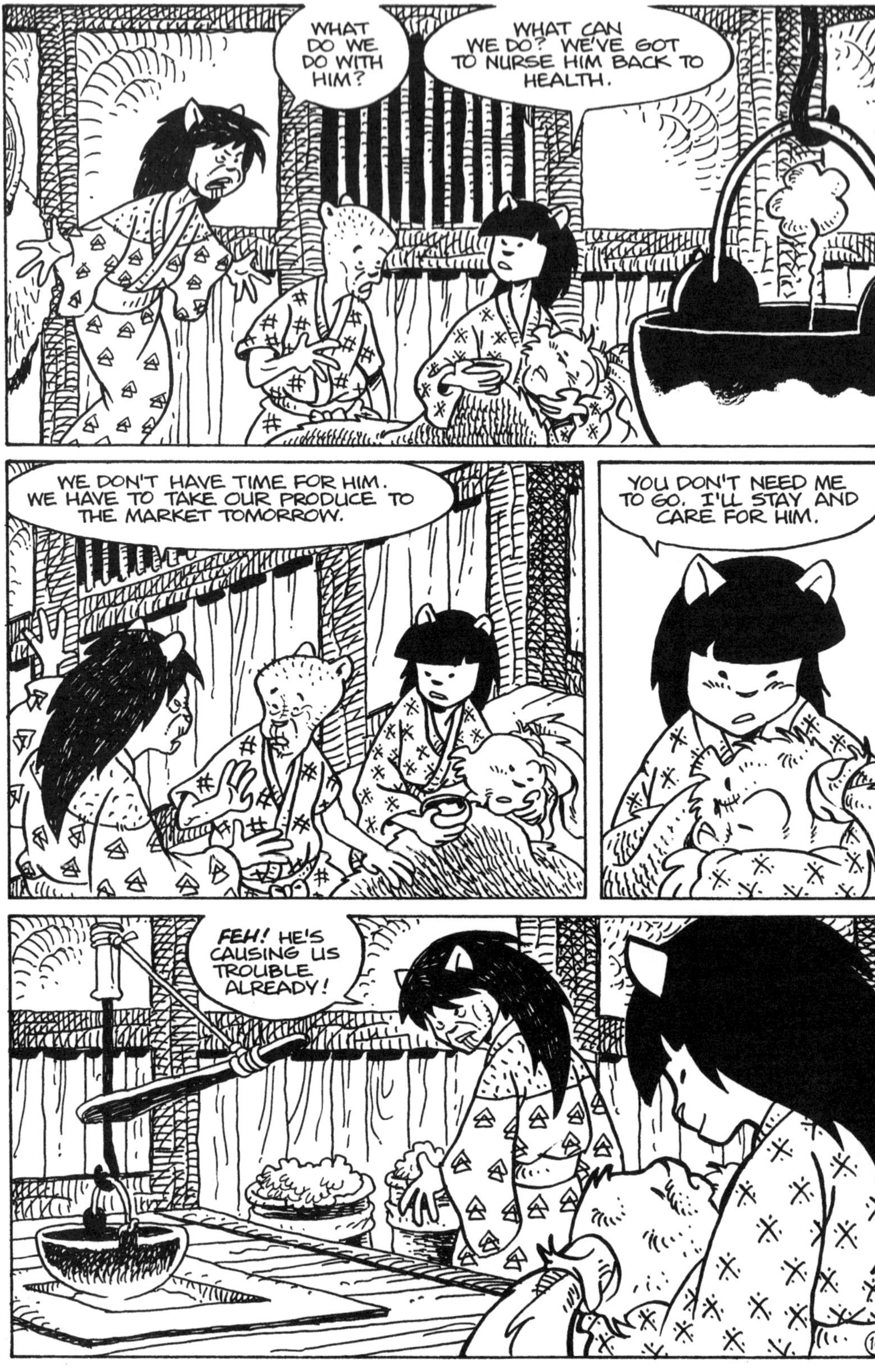
WHAT DO WE DO WITH HIM?
WHAT CAN WE DO? WE'VE GOT TO NURSE HIM BACK TO HEALTH.
WE DON'T HAVE TIME FOR HIM. WE HAVE TO TAKE OUR PRODUCE TO THE MARKET TOMORROW.
YOU DON'T NEED ME TO GO. I'LL STAY AND CARE FOR HIM.
FEH! HE'S CAUSING US TROUBLE ALREADY!
10.

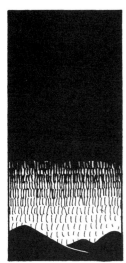

UHH...

OH, YOU'RE AWAKE. I WAS GETTING WORRIED. YOU HAVEN'T MOVED SINCE YOU GOT HERE.

WHO...?

I AM YOKO. YOU STUMBLED INTO OUR HOME LAST NIGHT.

I REMEMBER-- I FELL OFF THAT CLIFF.

YOU SHOULD BE MORE CAREFUL WHERE YOU WALK.

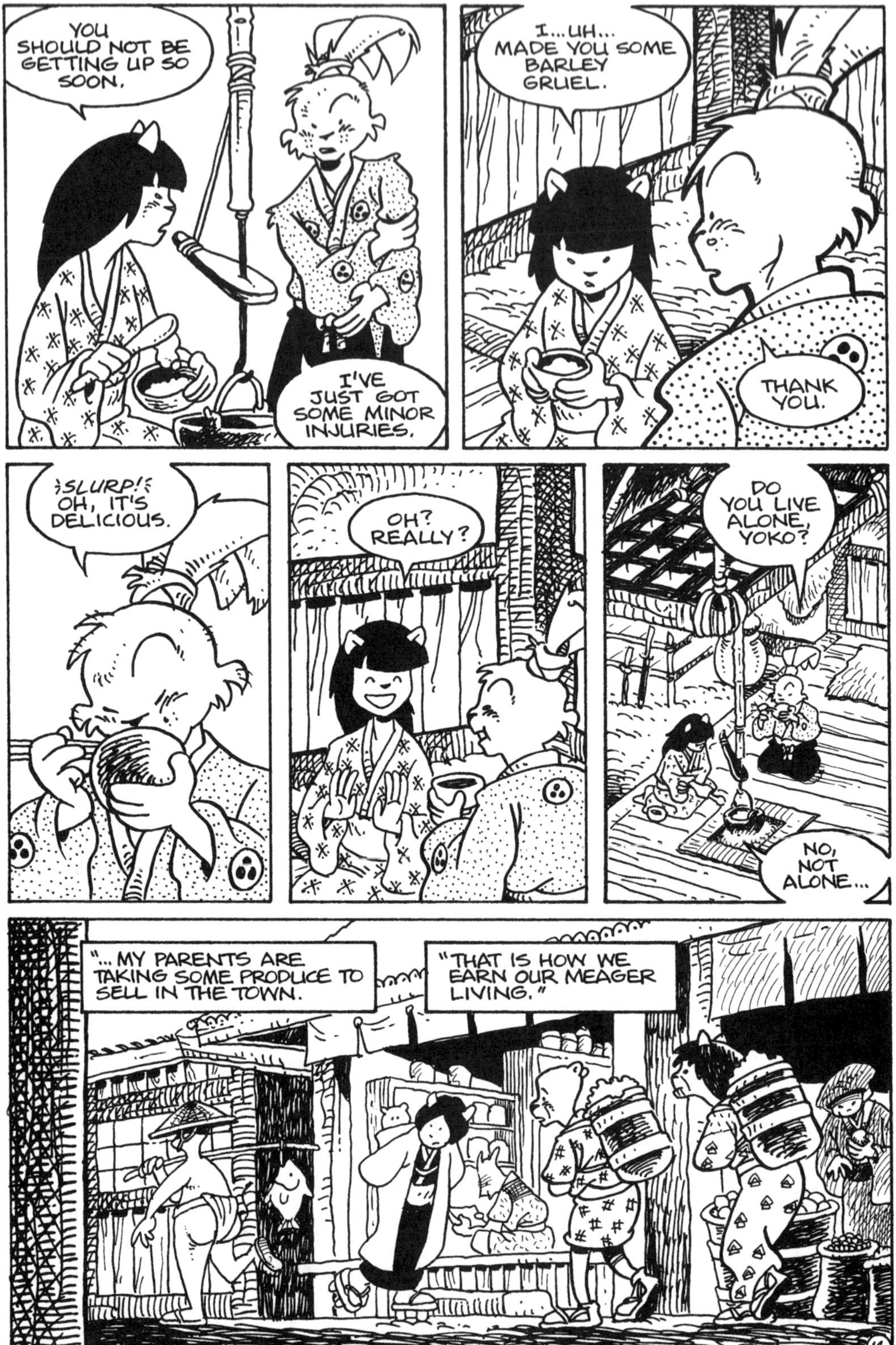
YOU SHOULD NOT BE GETTING UP SO SOON.
I'VE JUST GOT SOME MINOR INJURIES.
I...UH... MADE YOU SOME BARLEY GRUEL.
THANK YOU.
SLURP! OH, IT'S DELICIOUS.
OH? REALLY?
DO YOU LIVE ALONE, YOKO?
NO, NOT ALONE...
"...MY PARENTS ARE TAKING SOME PRODUCE TO SELL IN THE TOWN.
"THAT IS HOW WE EARN OUR MEAGER LIVING."
12.

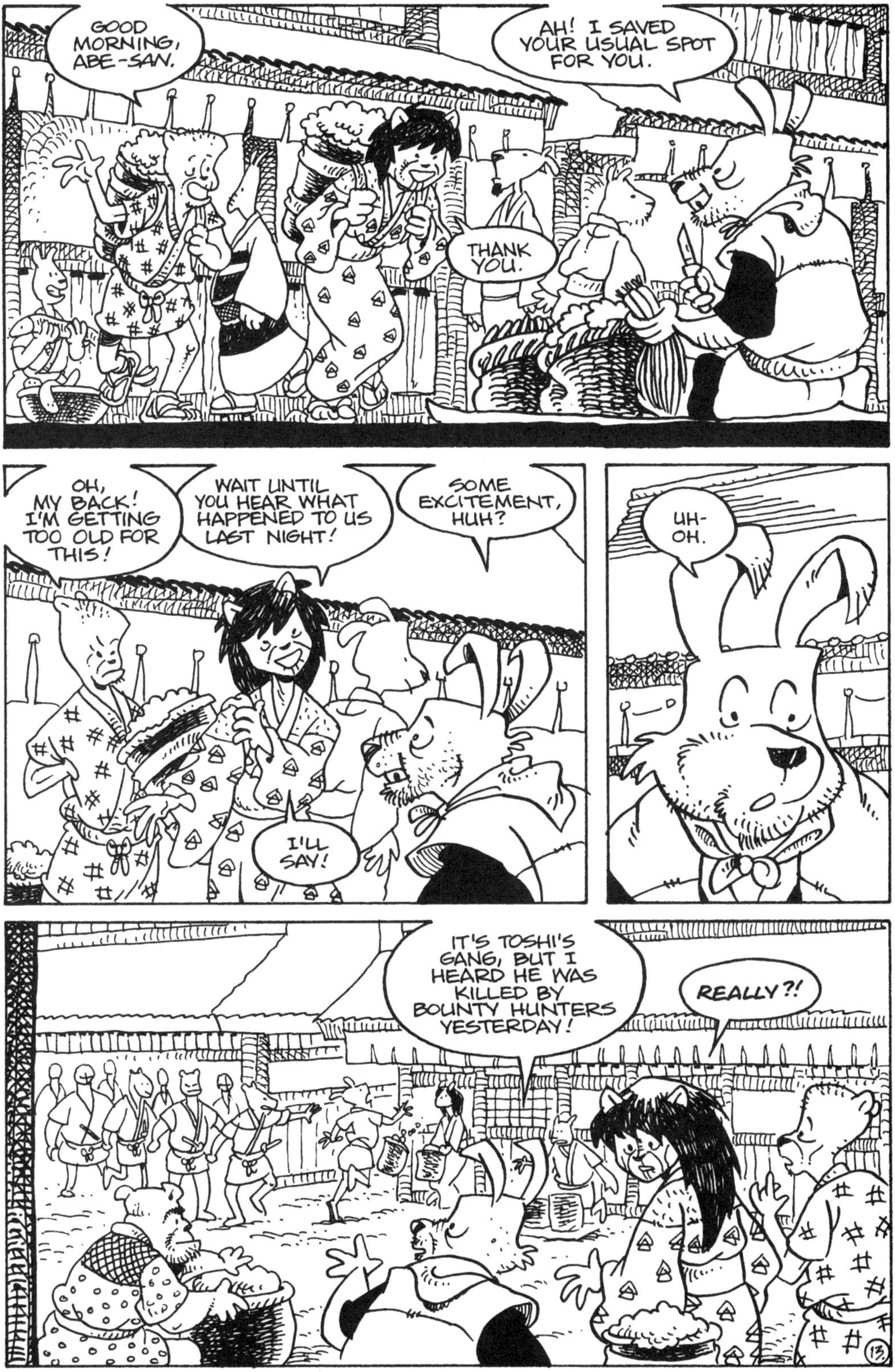
GOOD MORNING, ABE-SAN.
AH! I SAVED YOUR USUAL SPOT FOR YOU.
THANK YOU.
OH, MY BACK! I'M GETTING TOO OLD FOR THIS!
WAIT UNTIL YOU HEAR WHAT HAPPENED TO US LAST NIGHT!
SOME EXCITEMENT, HUH?
I'LL SAY!
UH-OH.
IT'S TOSHI'S GANG, BUT I HEARD HE WAS KILLED BY BOUNTY HUNTERS YESTERDAY!
REALLY?!
13.

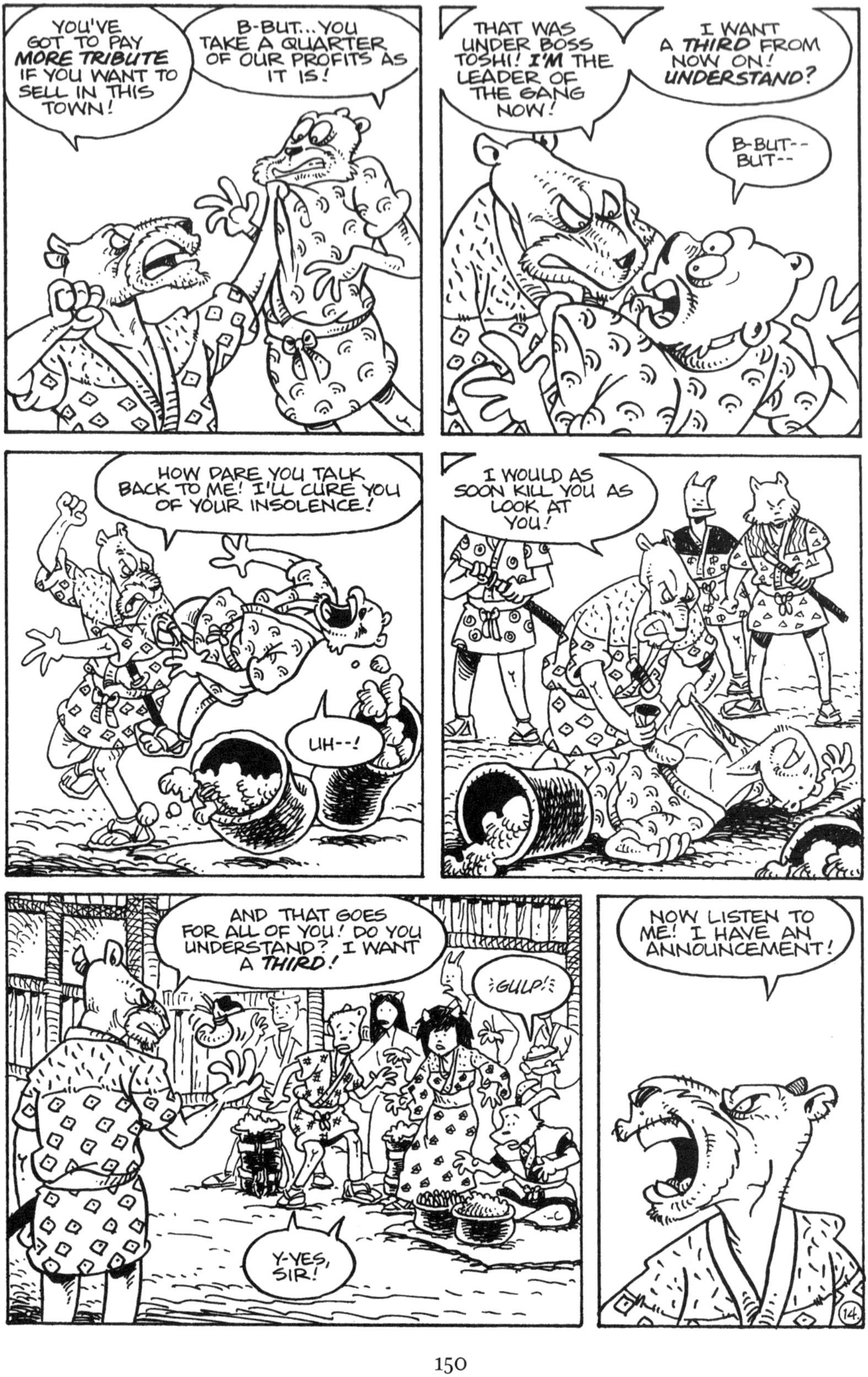
YOU'VE GOT TO PAY MORE TRIBUTE IF YOU WANT TO SELL IN THIS TOWN!
B-BUT...YOU TAKE A QUARTER OF OUR PROFITS AS IT IS!
THAT WAS UNDER BOSS TOSHI! I'M THE LEADER OF THE GANG NOW!
I WANT A THIRD FROM NOW ON! UNDERSTAND?
B-BUT-- BUT--
HOW DARE YOU TALK BACK TO ME! I'LL CURE YOU OF YOUR INSOLENCE!
UH--!
I WOULD AS SOON KILL YOU AS LOOK AT YOU!
AND THAT GOES FOR ALL OF YOU! DO YOU UNDERSTAND? I WANT A THIRD!
¡GULP!
Y-YES, SIR!
NOW LISTEN TO ME! I HAVE AN ANNOUNCEMENT!
14.

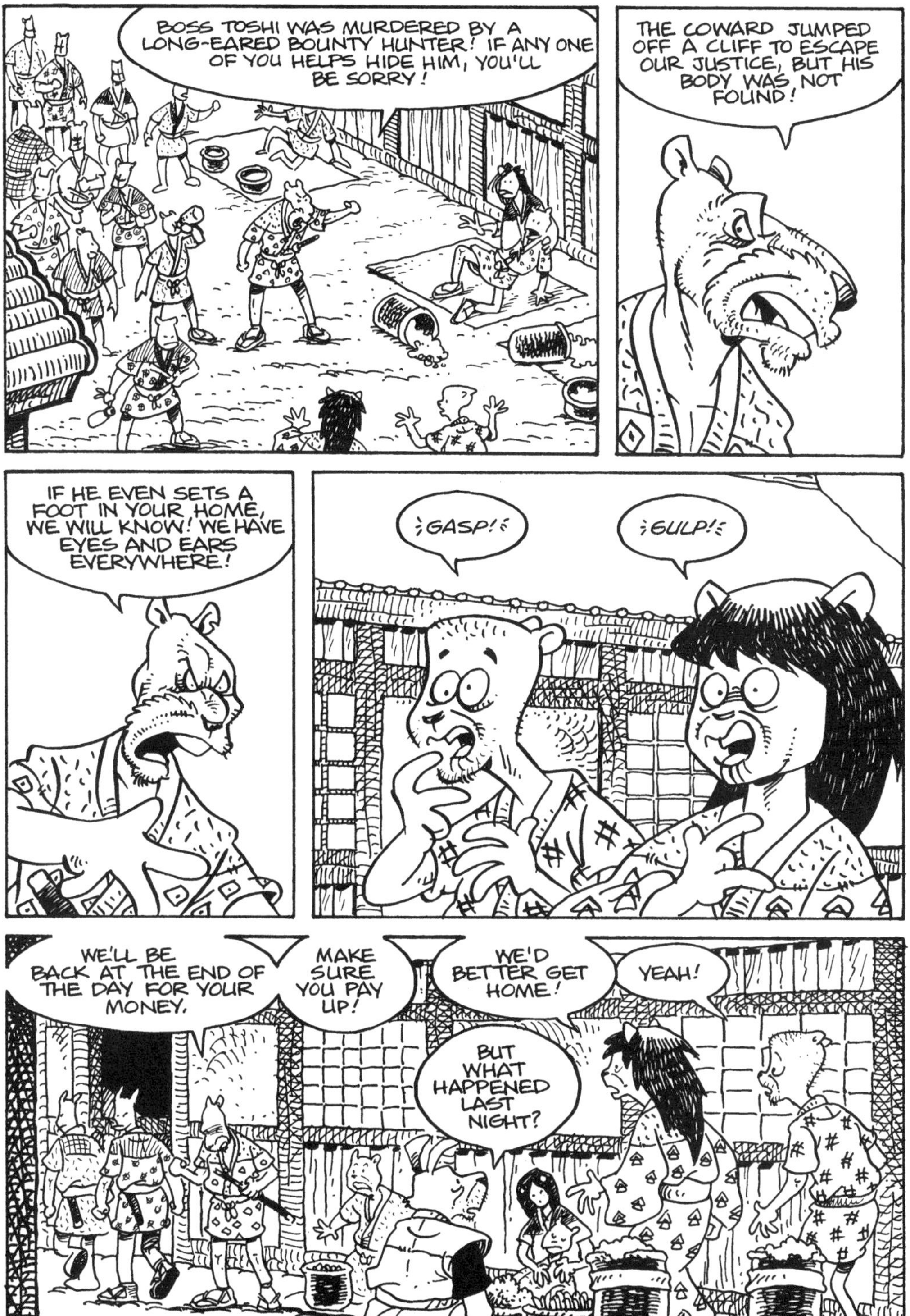
BOSS TOSHI WAS MURDERED BY A LONG-EARED BOUNTY HUNTER! IF ANY ONE OF YOU HELPS HIDE HIM, YOU'LL BE SORRY!
THE COWARD JUMPED OFF A CLIFF TO ESCAPE OUR JUSTICE, BUT HIS BODY WAS NOT FOUND!
IF HE EVEN SETS A FOOT IN YOUR HOME, WE WILL KNOW! WE HAVE EYES AND EARS EVERYWHERE!
GASP!
GULP!
WE'LL BE BACK AT THE END OF THE DAY FOR YOUR MONEY.
MAKE SURE YOU PAY UP!
WE'D BETTER GET HOME!
YEAH!
BUT WHAT HAPPENED LAST NIGHT?
13.

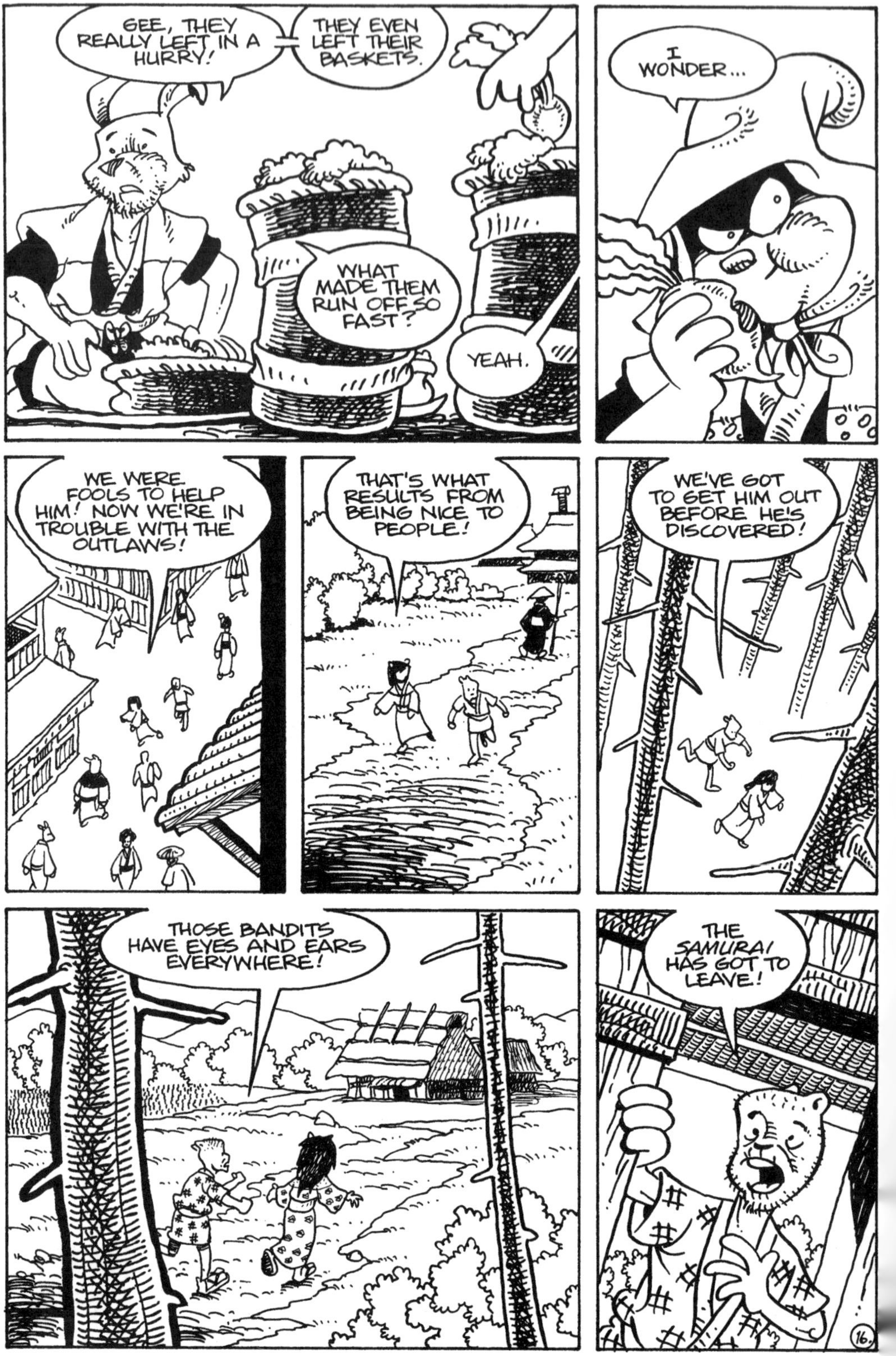
GEE, THEY REALLY LEFT IN A HURRY!
THEY EVEN LEFT THEIR BASKETS.
WHAT MADE THEM RUN OFF SO FAST?
YEAH.
I WONDER...
WE WERE FOOLS TO HELP HIM! NOW WE'RE IN TROUBLE WITH THE OUTLAWS!
THAT'S WHAT RESULTS FROM BEING NICE TO PEOPLE!
WE'VE GOT TO GET HIM OUT BEFORE HE'S DISCOVERED!
THOSE BANDITS HAVE EYES AND EARS EVERYWHERE!
THE *SAMURAI* HAS GOT TO LEAVE!
16.

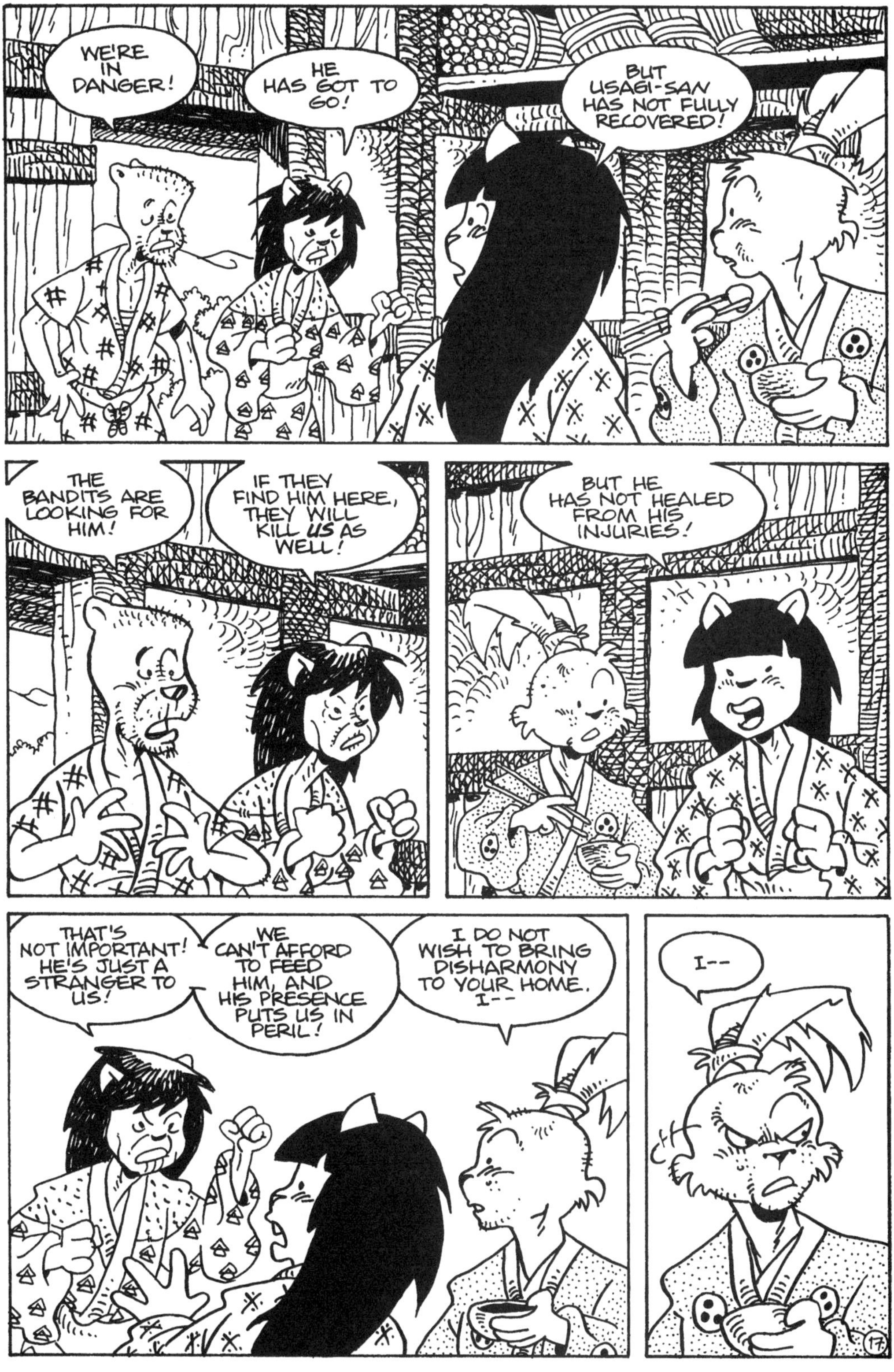
WE'RE IN DANGER!
HE HAS GOT TO GO!
BUT USAGI-SAN HAS NOT FULLY RECOVERED!
THE BANDITS ARE LOOKING FOR HIM!
IF THEY FIND HIM HERE, THEY WILL KILL US AS WELL!
BUT HE HAS NOT HEALED FROM HIS INJURIES!
THAT'S NOT IMPORTANT! HE'S JUST A STRANGER TO US!
WE CAN'T AFFORD TO FEED HIM, AND HIS PRESENCE PUTS US IN PERIL!
I DO NOT WISH TO BRING DISHARMONY TO YOUR HOME. I--
I--
17

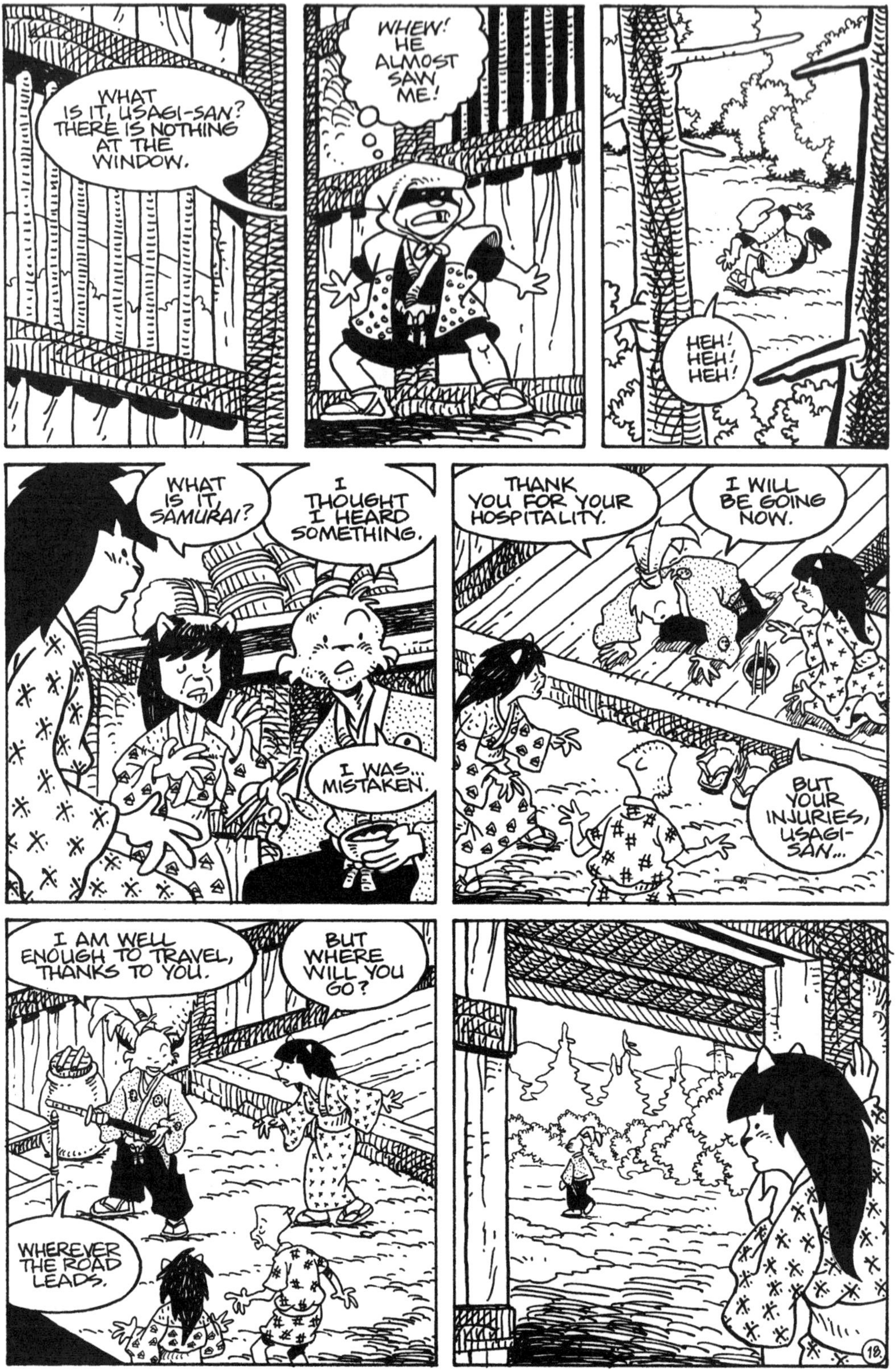

WHAT IS IT, USAGI-SAN? THERE IS NOTHING AT THE WINDOW.
WHEW! HE ALMOST SAW ME!
HEH! HEH! HEH!
WHAT IS IT, SAMURAI?
I THOUGHT I HEARD SOMETHING.
I WAS... MISTAKEN.
THANK YOU FOR YOUR HOSPITALITY.
I WILL BE GOING NOW.
BUT YOUR INJURIES, USAGI-SAN...
I AM WELL ENOUGH TO TRAVEL, THANKS TO YOU.
BUT WHERE WILL YOU GO?
WHEREVER THE ROAD LEADS.
18

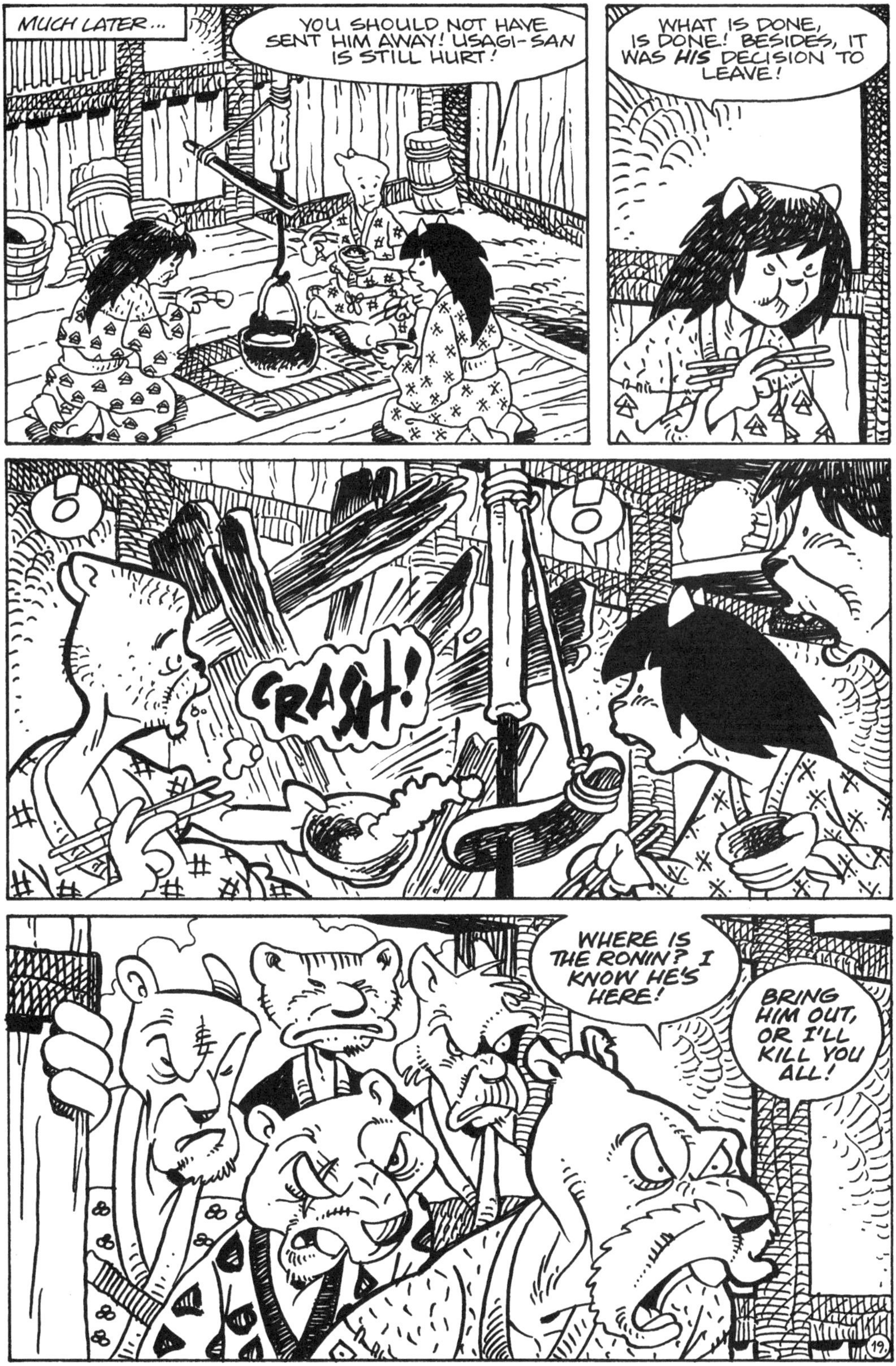
MUCH LATER...
YOU SHOULD NOT HAVE SENT HIM AWAY! USAGI-SAN IS STILL HURT!
WHAT IS DONE, IS DONE! BESIDES, IT WAS HIS DECISION TO LEAVE!
!
!
CRASH!
WHERE IS THE RONIN? I KNOW HE'S HERE!
BRING HIM OUT, OR I'LL KILL YOU ALL!
19.

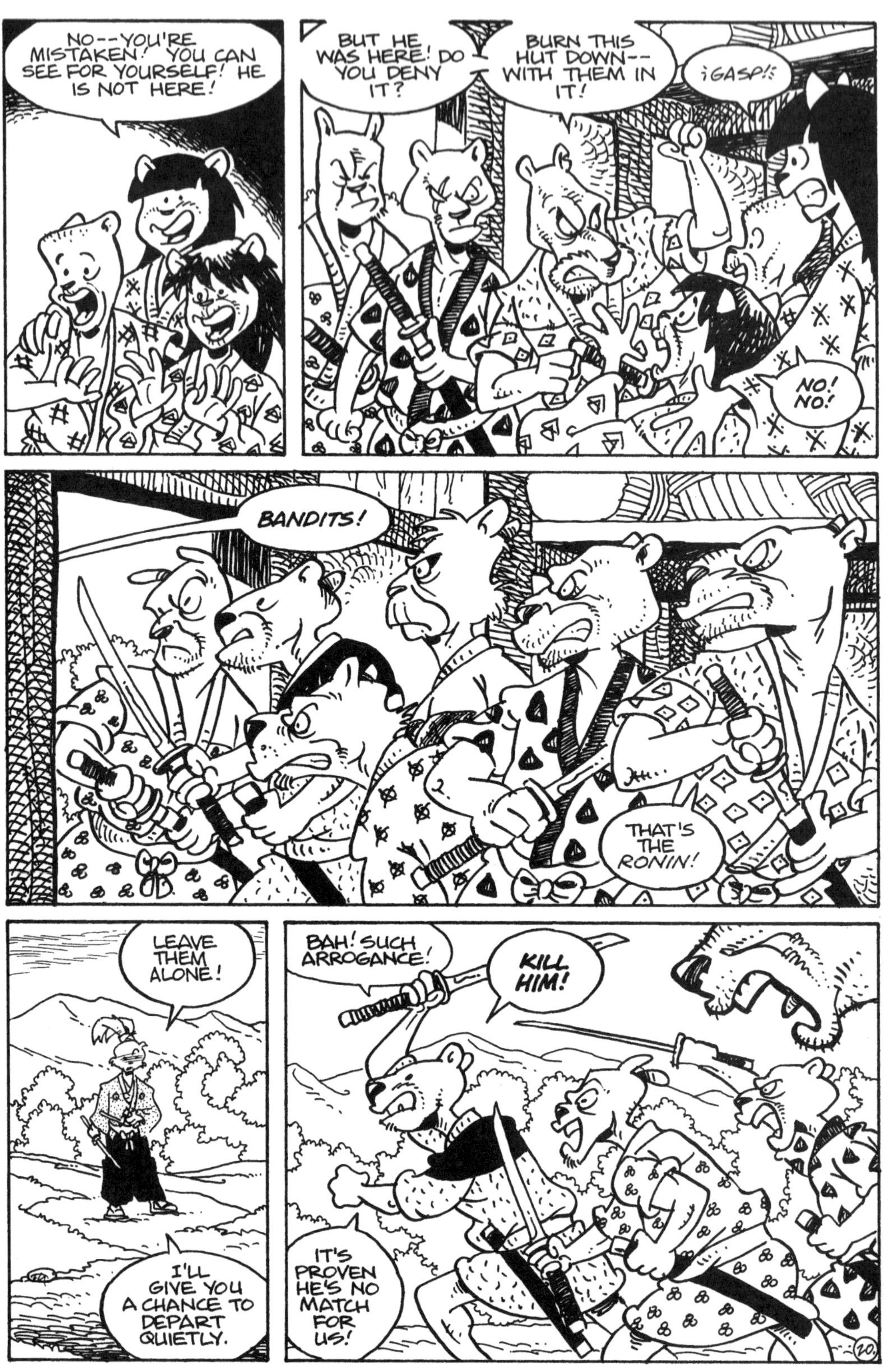
NO--YOU'RE MISTAKEN! YOU CAN SEE FOR YOURSELF! HE IS NOT HERE!
BUT HE WAS HERE! DO YOU DENY IT?
BURN THIS HUT DOWN-- WITH THEM IN IT!
¡GASP!
NO! NO!
BANDITS!
THAT'S THE RONIN!
LEAVE THEM ALONE!
I'LL GIVE YOU A CHANCE TO DEPART QUIETLY.
BAH! SUCH ARROGANCE!
KILL HIM!
IT'S PROVEN HE'S NO MATCH FOR US!
20.

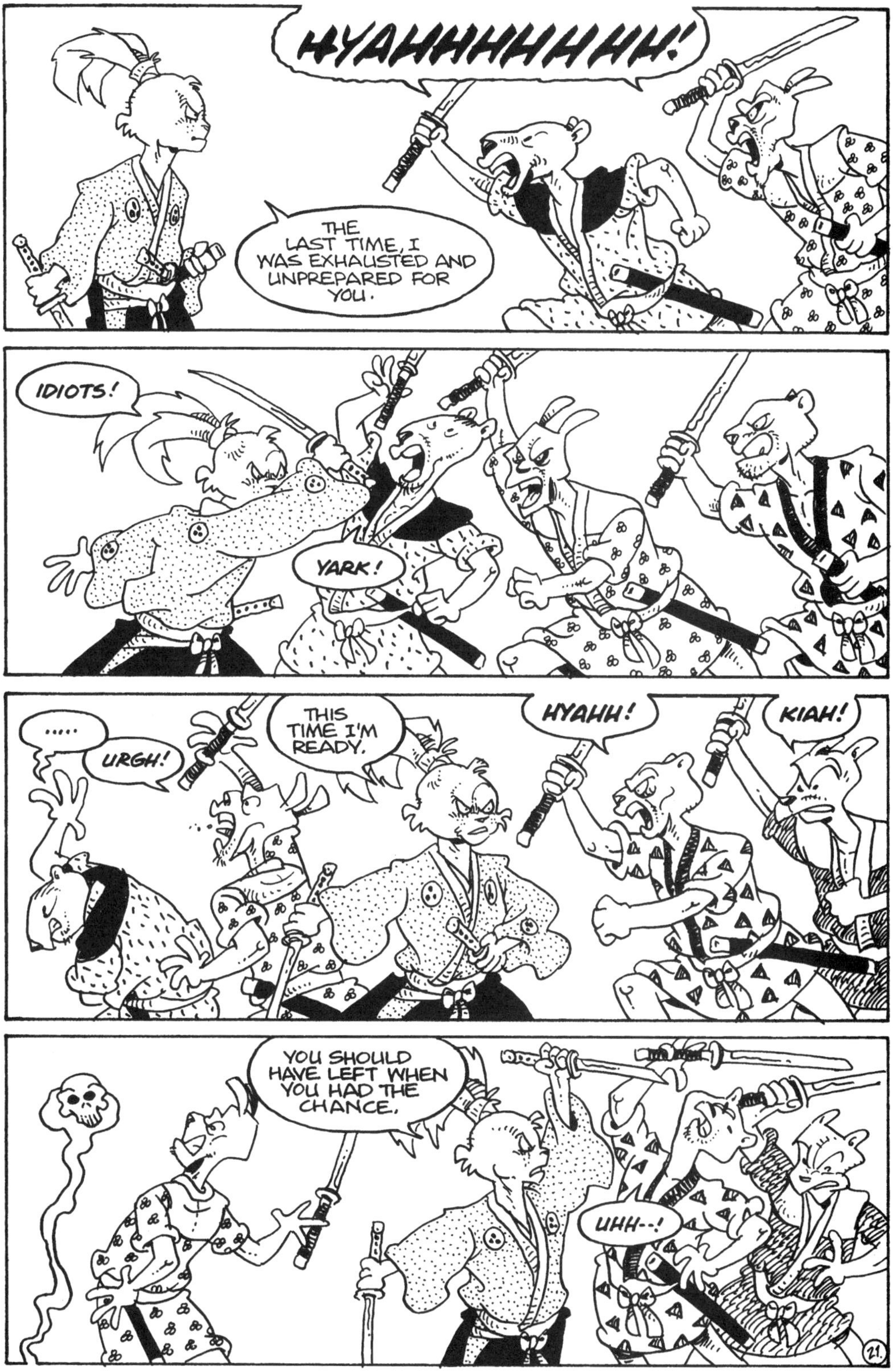
HYAHHHHHHHH!
THE LAST TIME, I WAS EXHAUSTED AND UNPREPARED FOR YOU.
IDIOTS!
YARK!
.....
URGH!
THIS TIME I'M READY.
HYAHH!
KIAH!
YOU SHOULD HAVE LEFT WHEN YOU HAD THE CHANCE.
UHH--!
21.

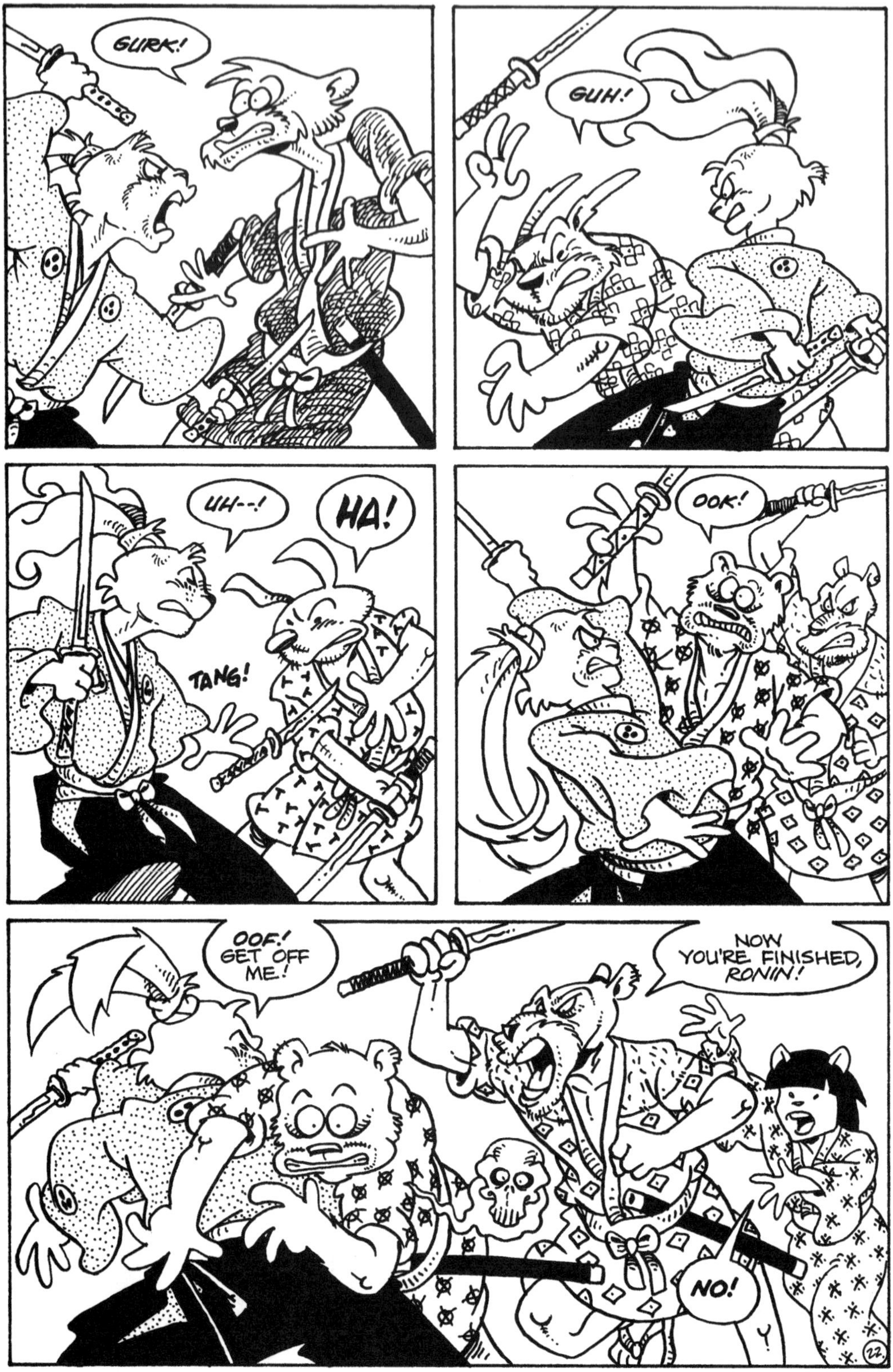
GURK!
GUH!
UH--!
HA!
TANG!
OOK!
OOF! GET OFF ME!
NOW YOU'RE FINISHED, RONIN!
NO!
22.

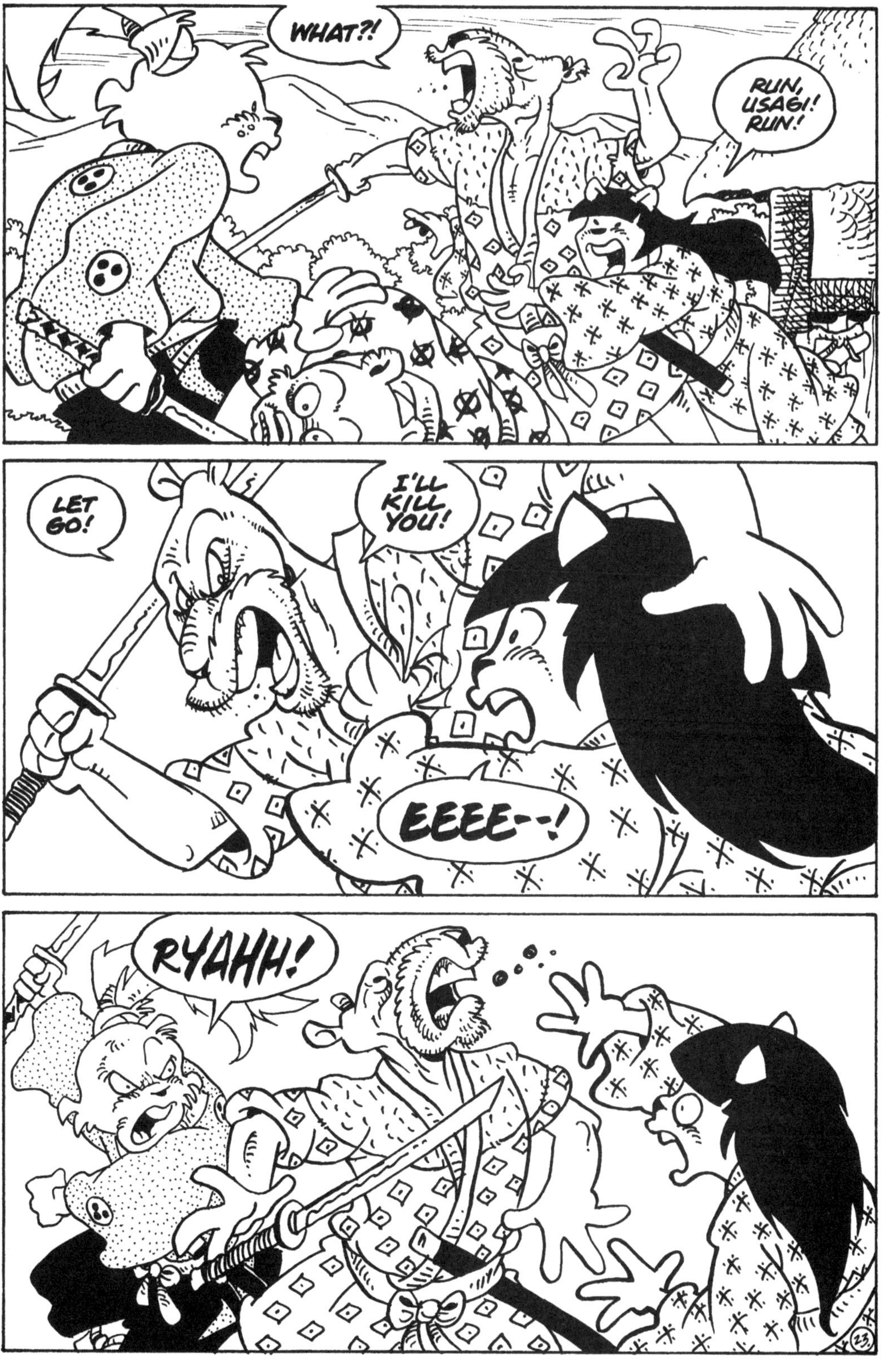
WHAT?!
RUN, USAGI! RUN!
LET GO!
I'LL KILL YOU!
EEEE--!
RYAHH!

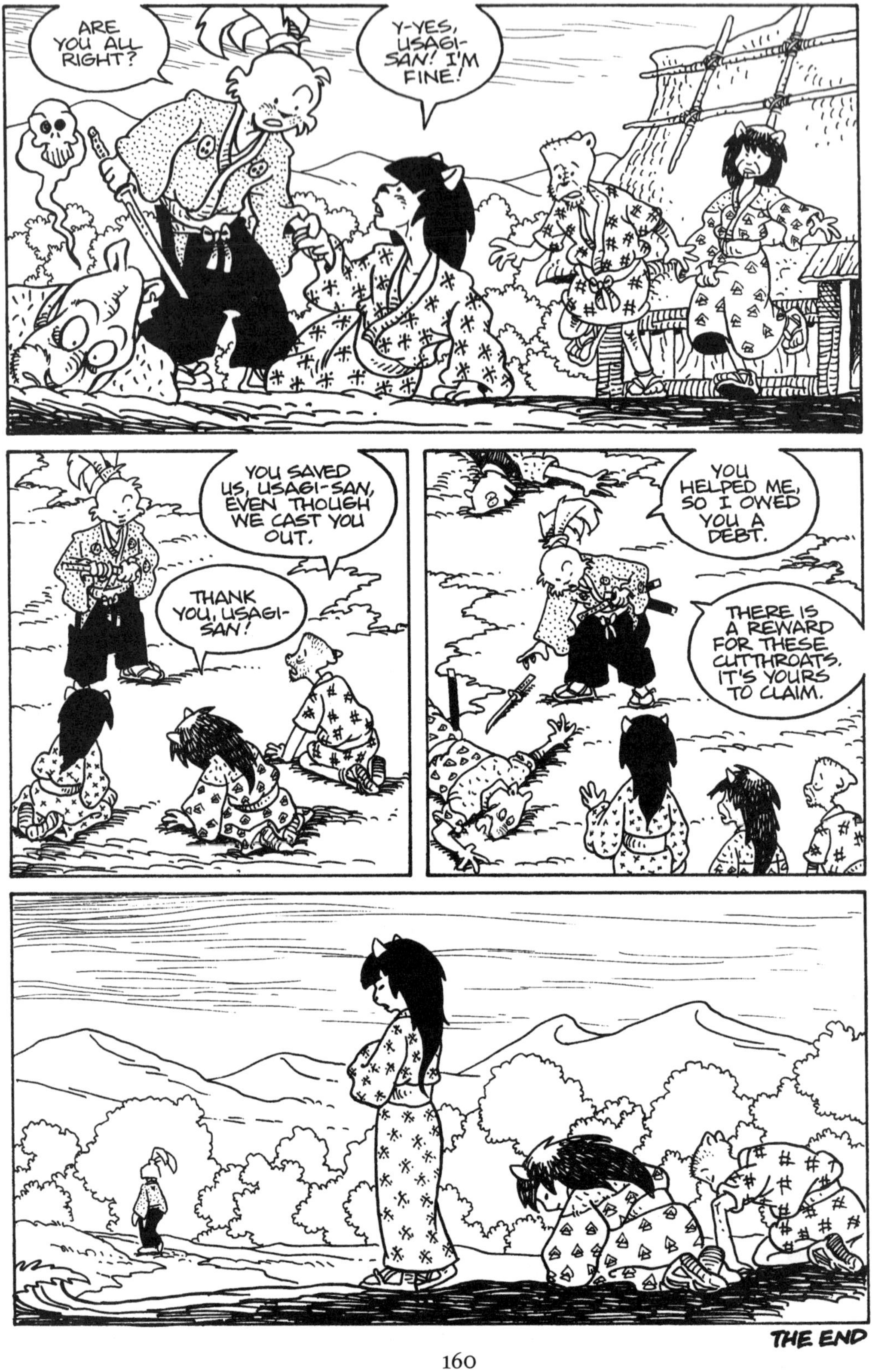
ARE YOU ALL RIGHT?
Y-YES, USAGI-SAN! I'M FINE!
YOU SAVED US, USAGI-SAN, EVEN THOUGH WE CAST YOU OUT.
THANK YOU, USAGI-SAN!
YOU HELPED ME, SO I OWED YOU A DEBT.
THERE IS A REWARD FOR THESE CUTTHROATS. IT'S YOURS TO CLAIM.
THE END

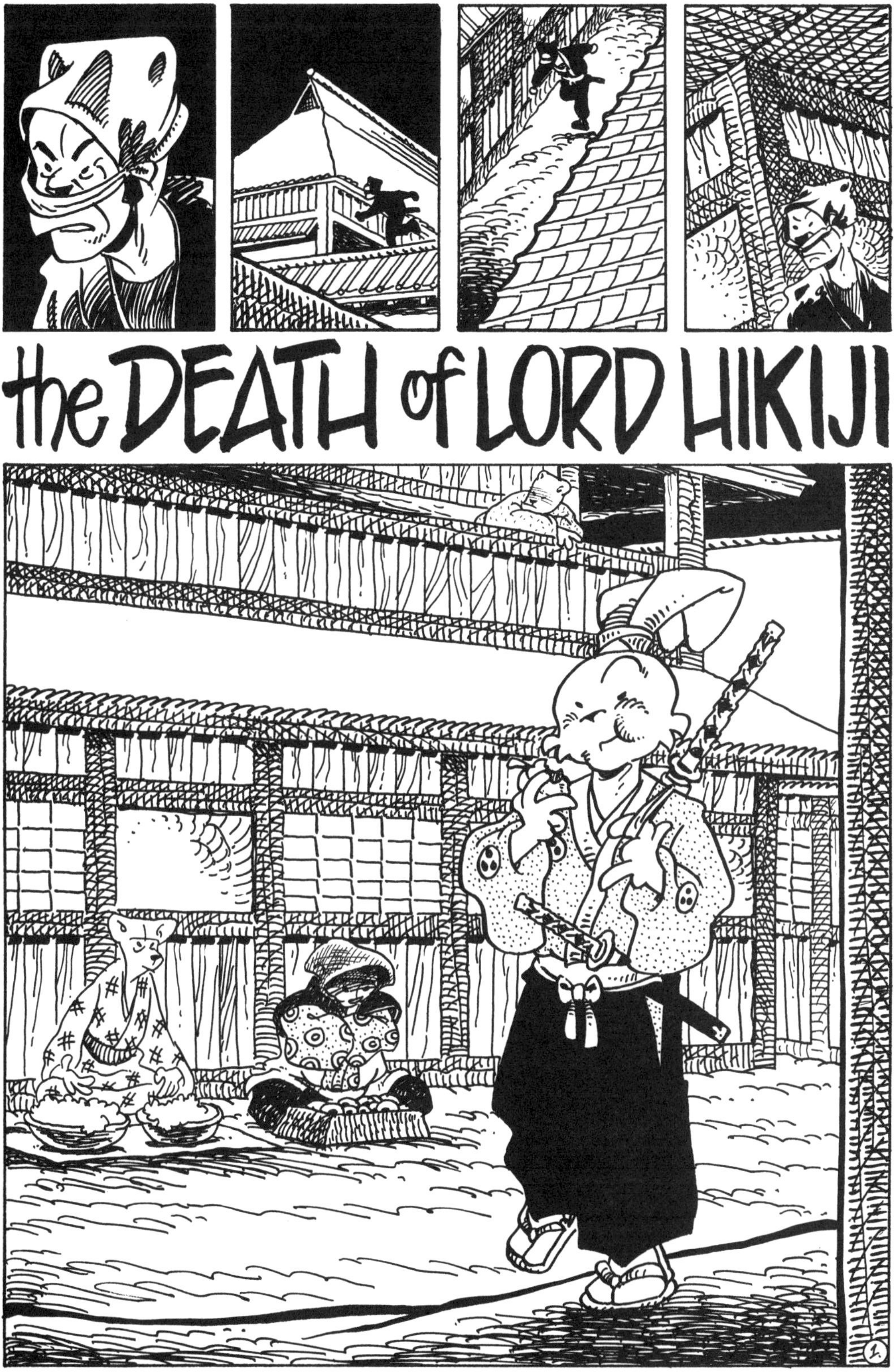
the DEATH of LORD HIKIJI
1.

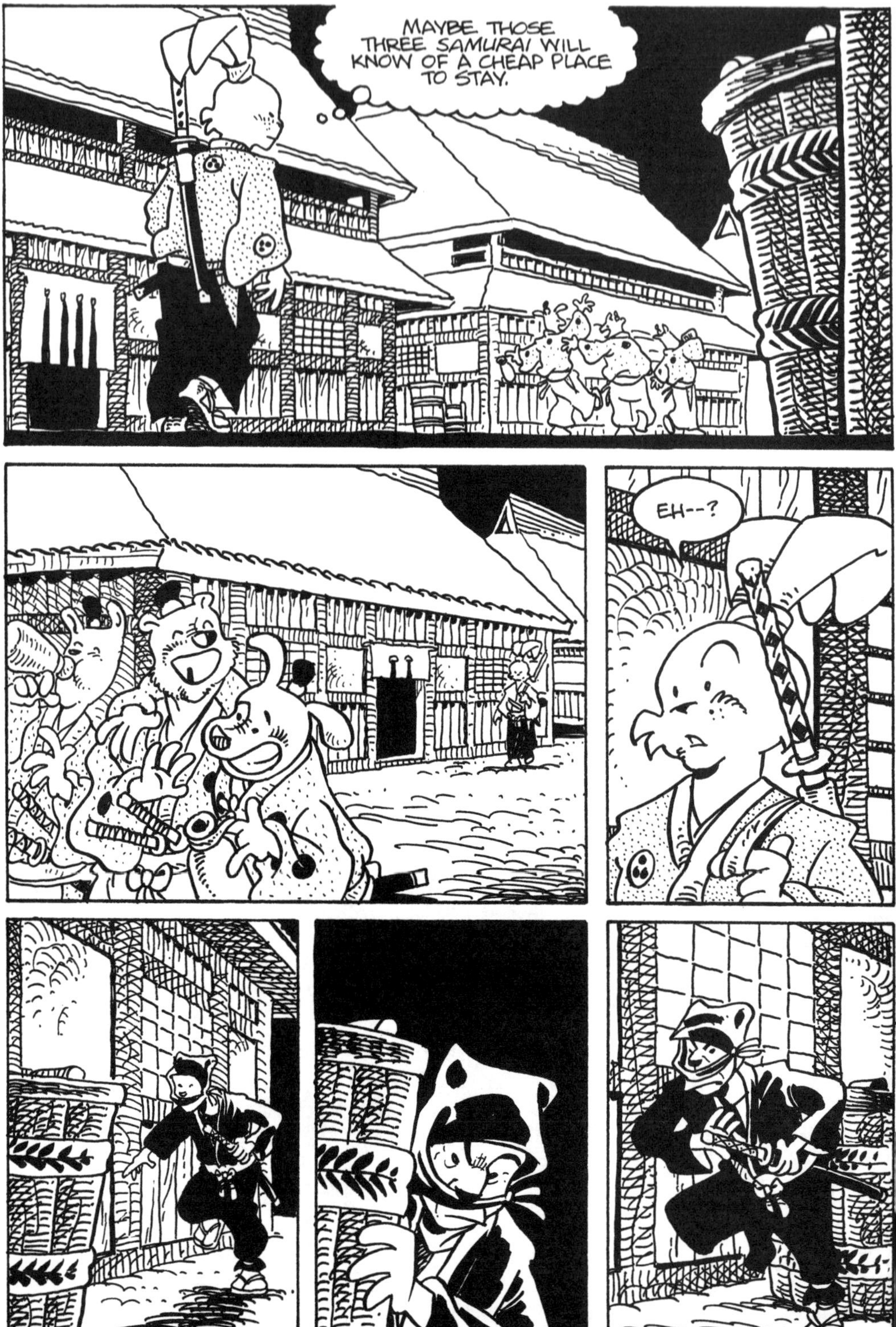
MAYBE THOSE THREE SAMURAI WILL KNOW OF A CHEAP PLACE TO STAY.
EH--?
2.

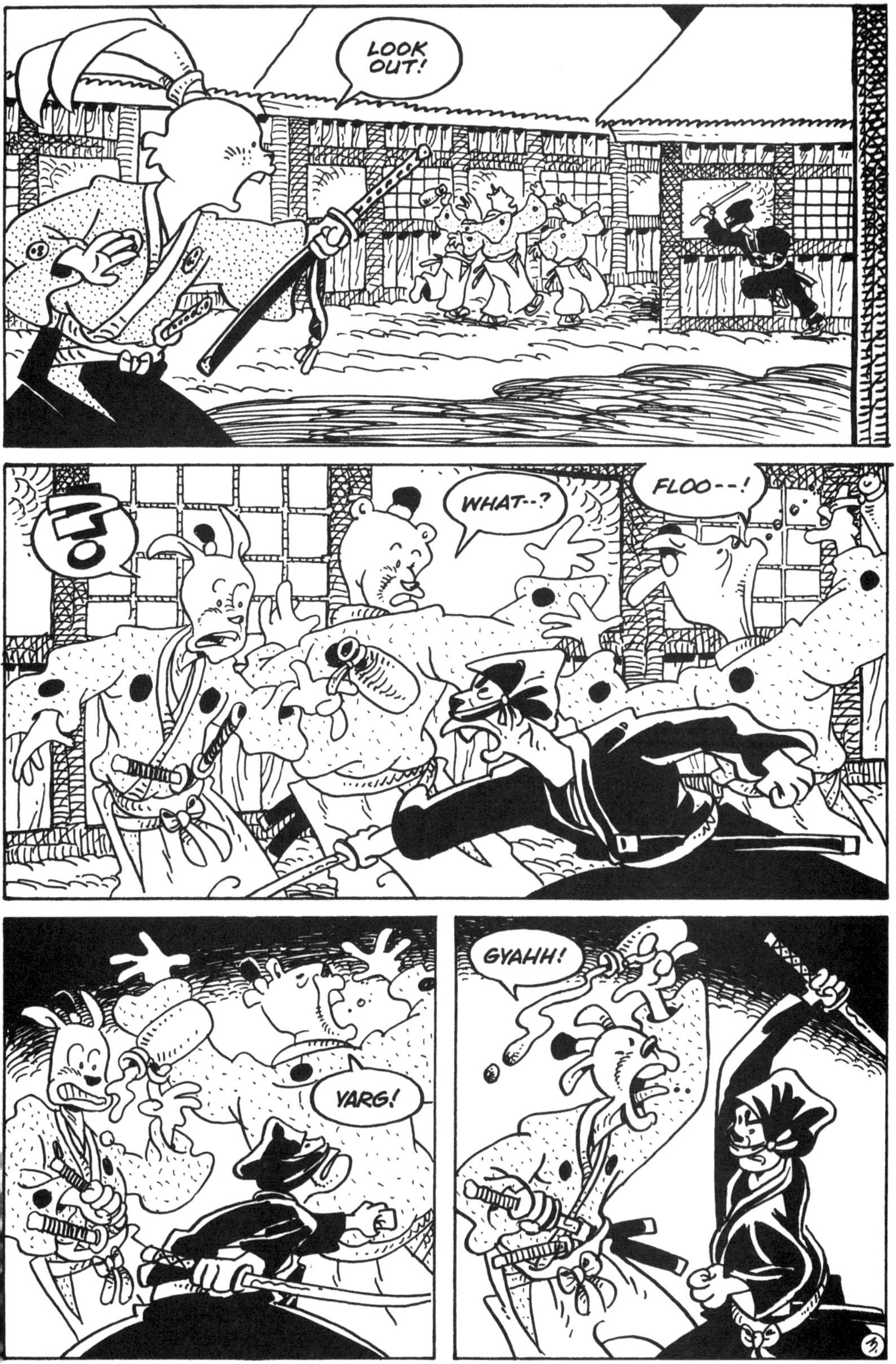

LOOK OUT!
?
WHAT--?
FLOO--!
YARG!
GYAHH!

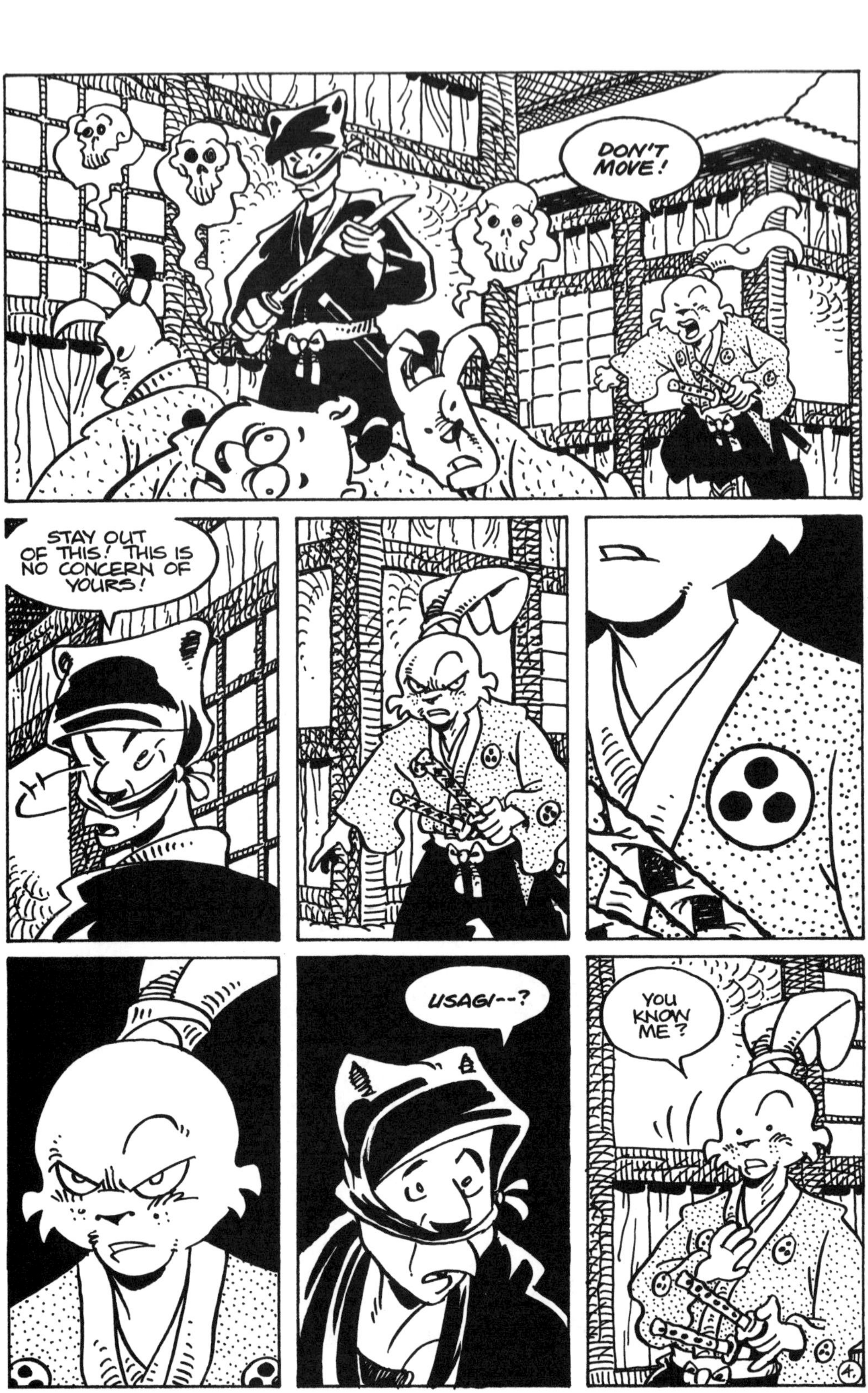

DON'T MOVE!
STAY OUT OF THIS! THIS IS NO CONCERN OF YOURS!
USAGI--?
YOU KNOW ME?

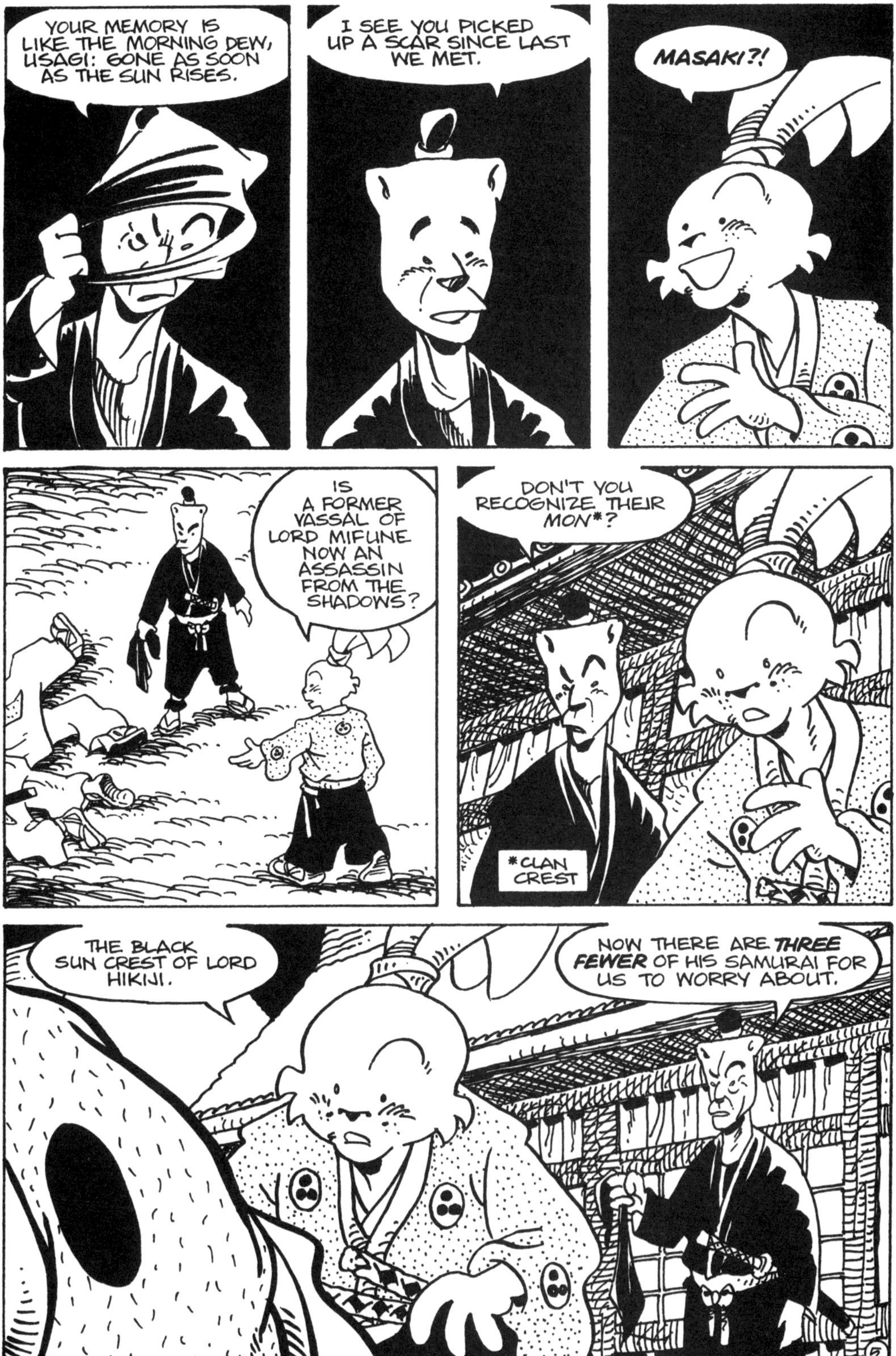
YOUR MEMORY IS LIKE THE MORNING DEW, USAGI: GONE AS SOON AS THE SUN RISES.
I SEE YOU PICKED UP A SCAR SINCE LAST WE MET.
MASAKI?!
IS A FORMER VASSAL OF LORD MIFUNE NOW AN ASSASSIN FROM THE SHADOWS?
DON'T YOU RECOGNIZE THEIR MON*?
*CLAN CREST
THE BLACK SUN CREST OF LORD HIKIJI.
NOW THERE ARE THREE FEWER OF HIS SAMURAI FOR US TO WORRY ABOUT.

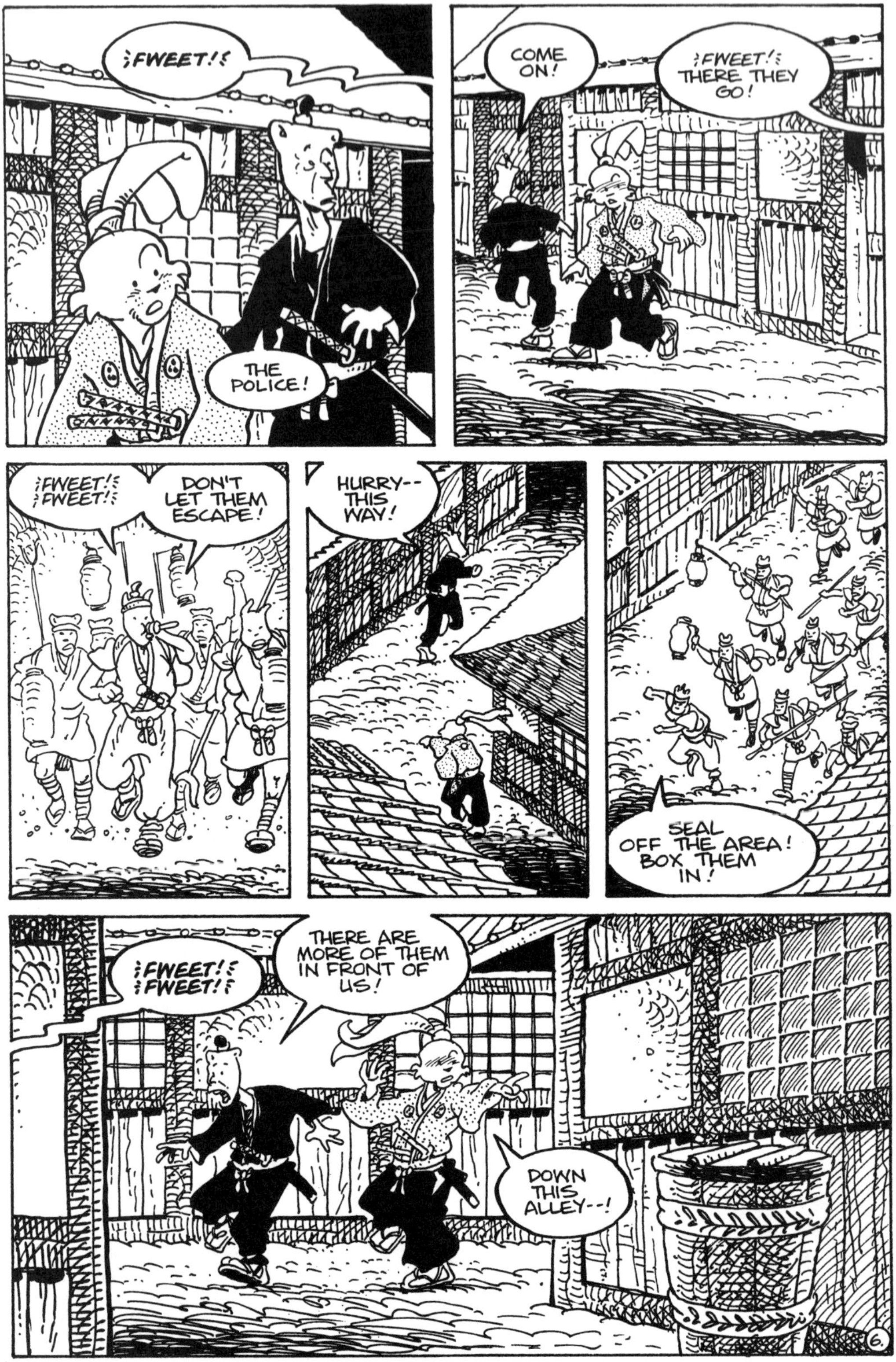
¡FWEET!¡
THE POLICE!
COME ON!
¡FWEET!¡ THERE THEY GO!
¡FWEET!¡ ¡FWEET!¡
DON'T LET THEM ESCAPE!
HURRY-- THIS WAY!
SEAL OFF THE AREA! BOX THEM IN!
¡FWEET!¡ ¡FWEET!¡
THERE ARE MORE OF THEM IN FRONT OF US!
DOWN THIS ALLEY--!
6.

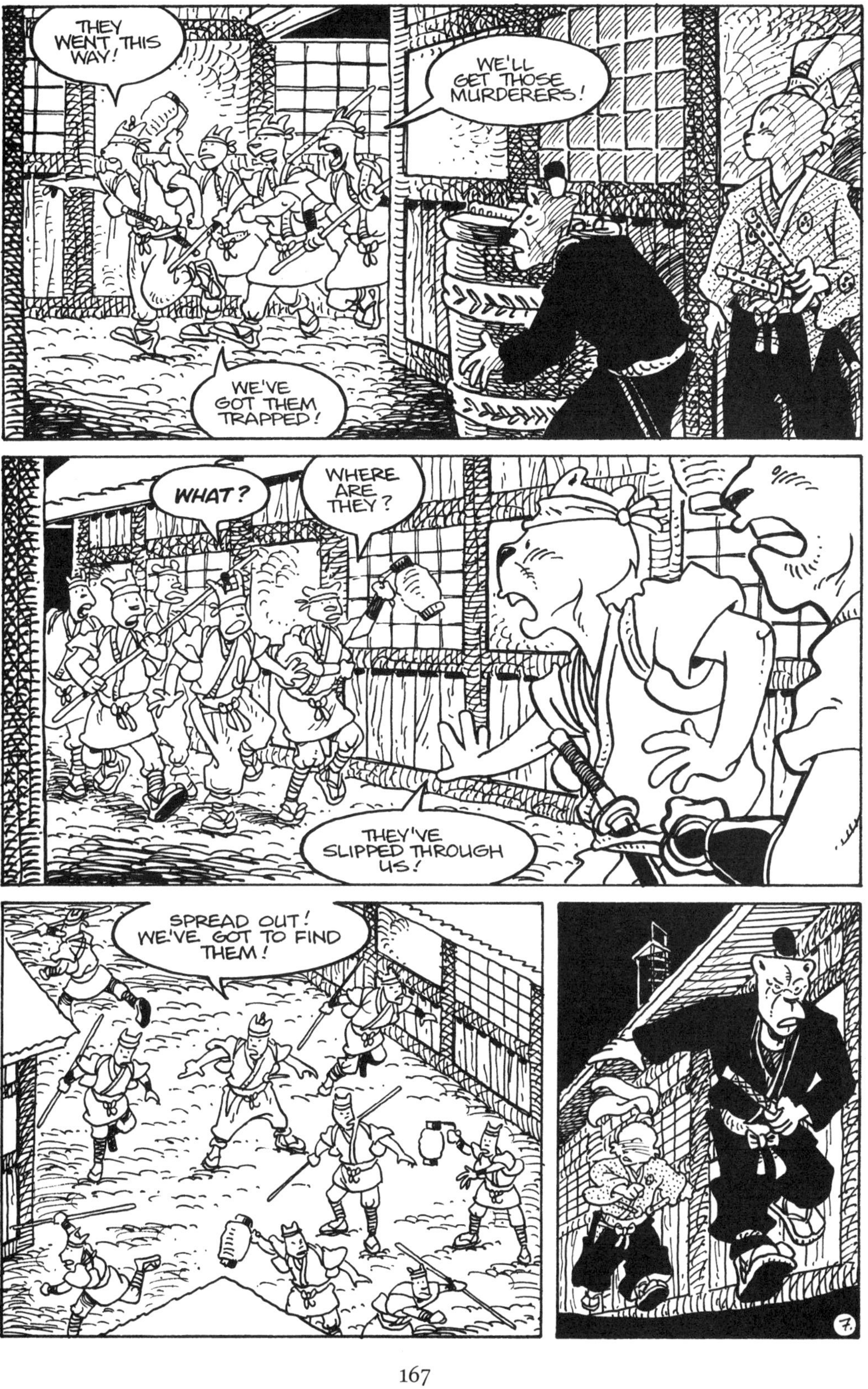
THEY WENT THIS WAY!
WE'LL GET THOSE MURDERERS!
WE'VE GOT THEM TRAPPED!
WHAT?
WHERE ARE THEY?
THEY'VE SLIPPED THROUGH US!
SPREAD OUT! WE'VE GOT TO FIND THEM!
7.

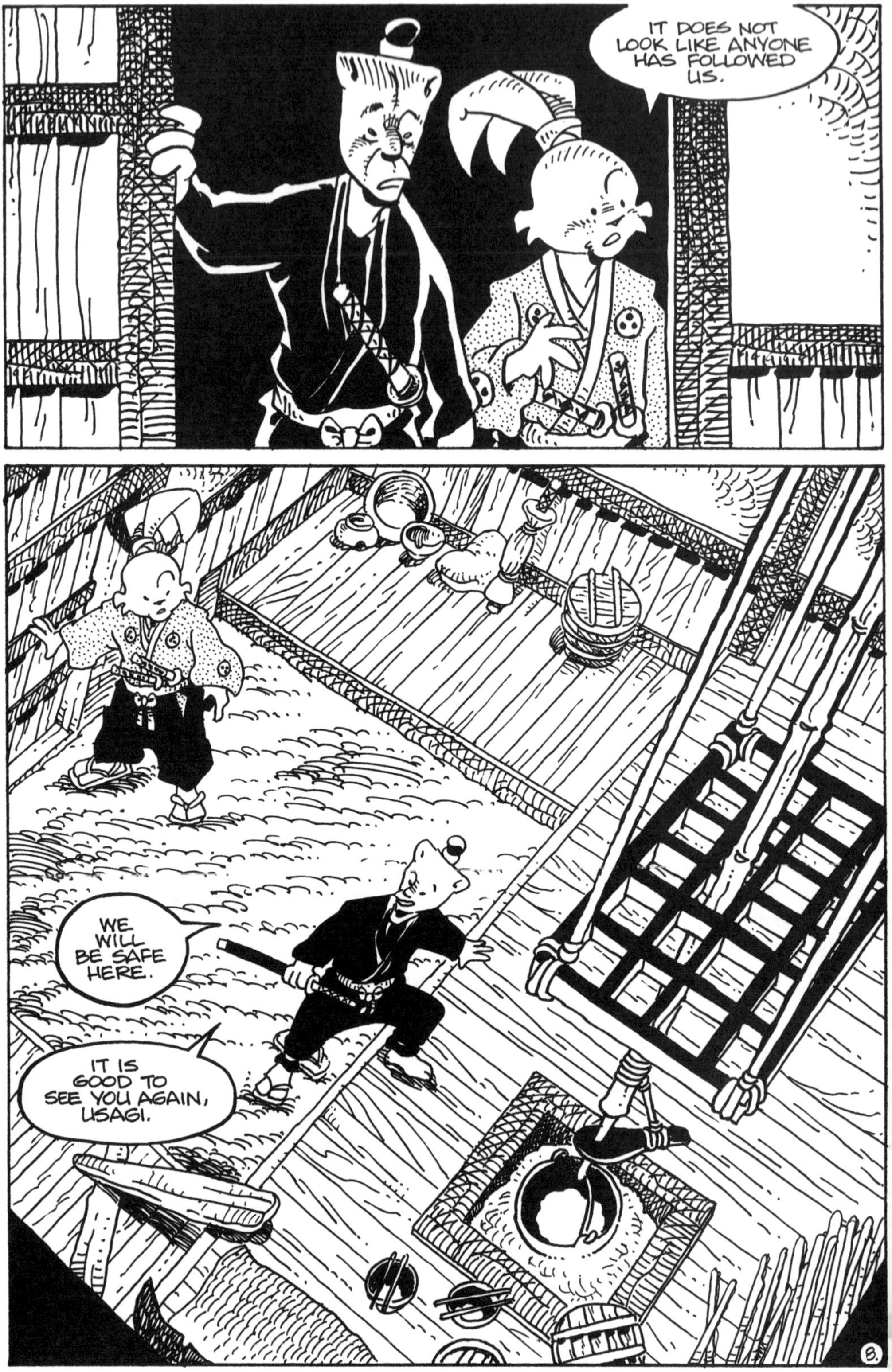
IT DOES NOT LOOK LIKE ANYONE HAS FOLLOWED US.
WE WILL BE SAFE HERE.
IT IS GOOD TO SEE YOU AGAIN, USAGI.
8.

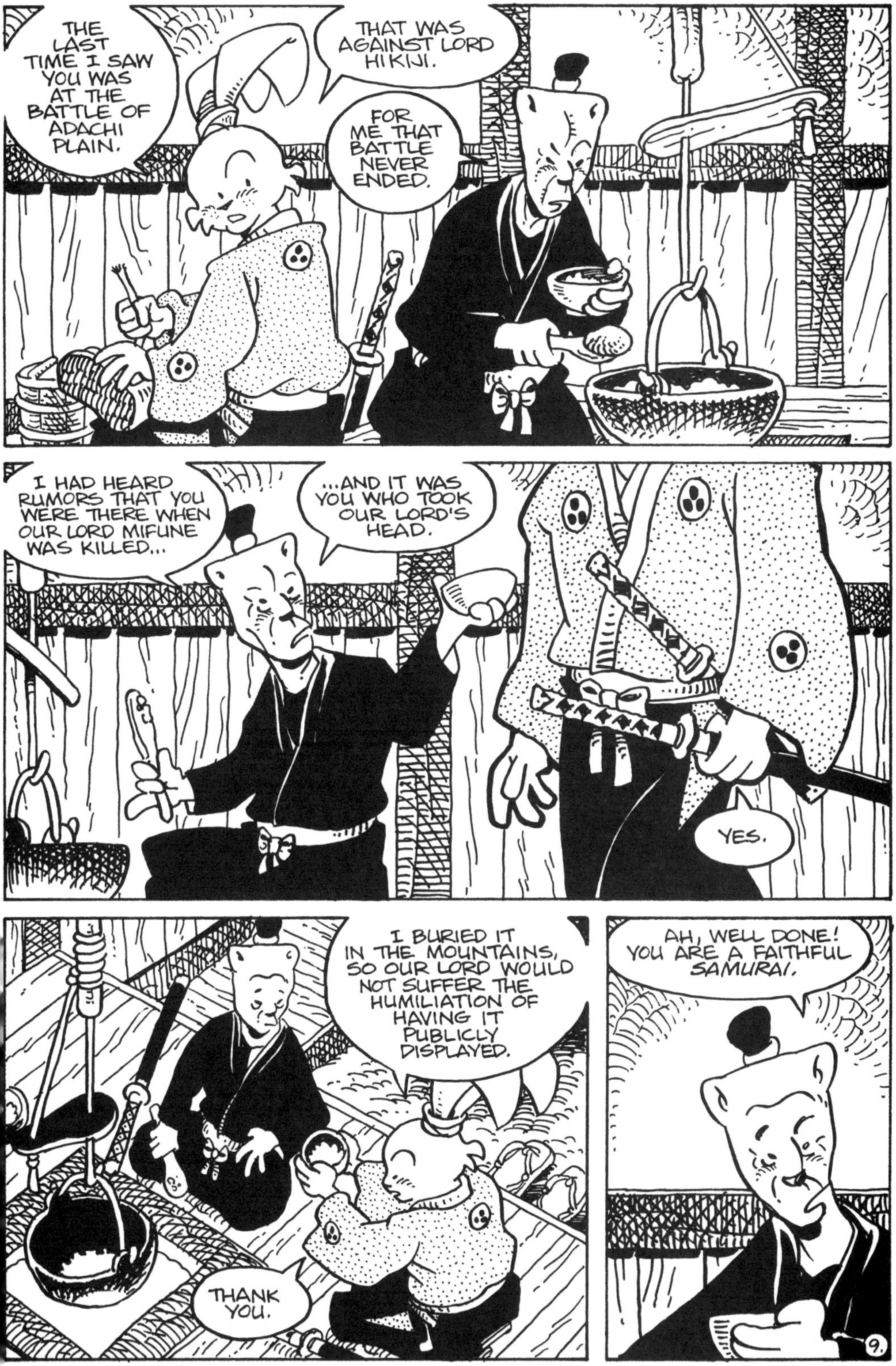
THE LAST TIME I SAW YOU WAS AT THE BATTLE OF ADACHI PLAIN.
THAT WAS AGAINST LORD HIKIJI.
FOR ME THAT BATTLE NEVER ENDED.
I HAD HEARD RUMORS THAT YOU WERE THERE WHEN OUR LORD MIFUNE WAS KILLED...
...AND IT WAS YOU WHO TOOK OUR LORD'S HEAD.
YES.
I BURIED IT IN THE MOUNTAINS, SO OUR LORD WOULD NOT SUFFER THE HUMILIATION OF HAVING IT PUBLICLY DISPLAYED.
THANK YOU.
AH, WELL DONE! YOU ARE A FAITHFUL *SAMURAI*.
9.

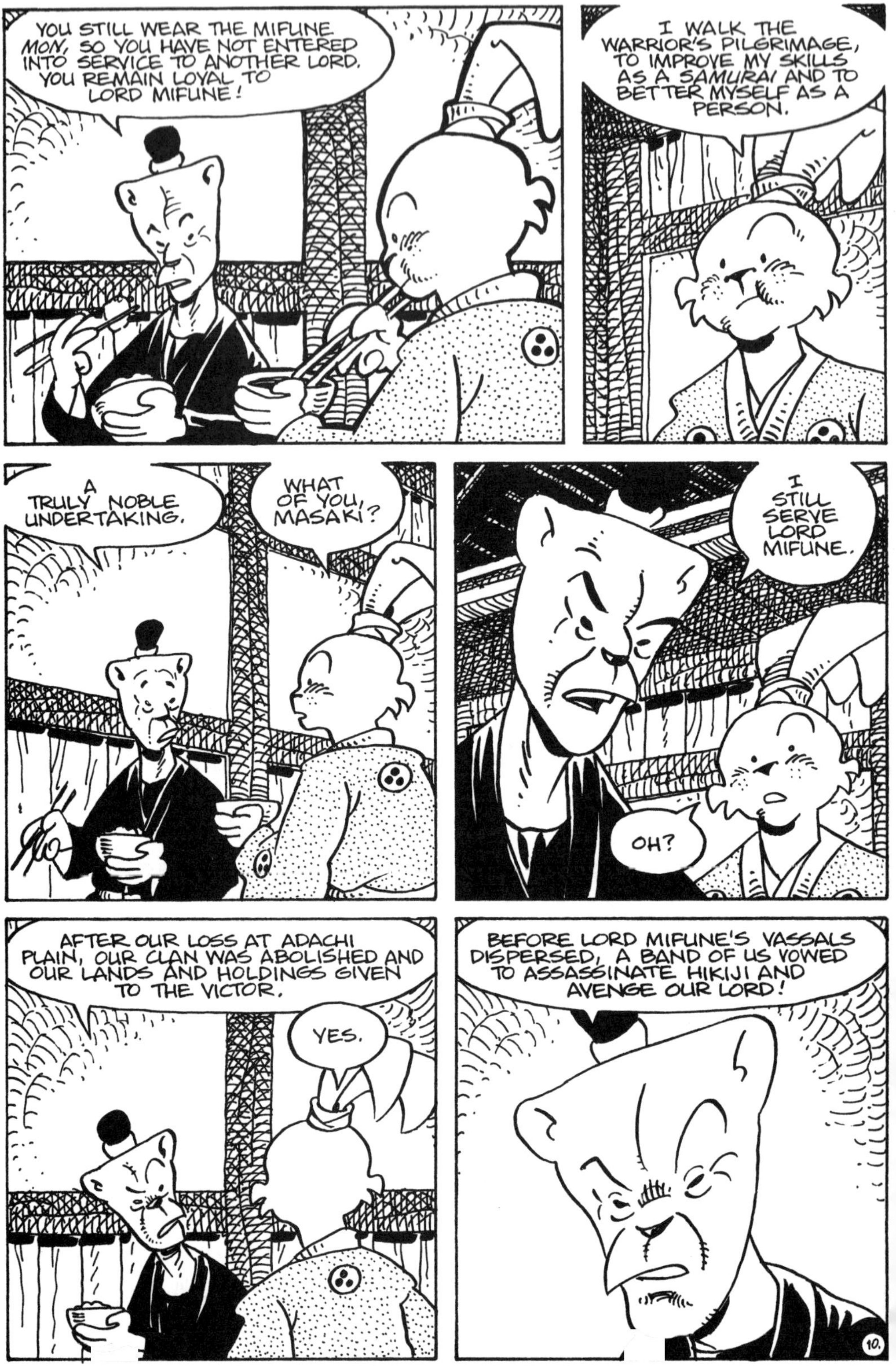
YOU STILL WEAR THE MIFUNE MON, SO YOU HAVE NOT ENTERED INTO SERVICE TO ANOTHER LORD. YOU REMAIN LOYAL TO LORD MIFUNE!
I WALK THE WARRIOR'S PILGRIMAGE, TO IMPROVE MY SKILLS AS A SAMURAI AND TO BETTER MYSELF AS A PERSON.
A TRULY NOBLE UNDERTAKING.
WHAT OF YOU, MASAKI?
I STILL SERVE LORD MIFUNE.
OH?
AFTER OUR LOSS AT ADACHI PLAIN, OUR CLAN WAS ABOLISHED AND OUR LANDS AND HOLDINGS GIVEN TO THE VICTOR.
YES.
BEFORE LORD MIFUNE'S VASSALS DISPERSED, A BAND OF US VOWED TO ASSASSINATE HIKIJI AND AVENGE OUR LORD!
10.

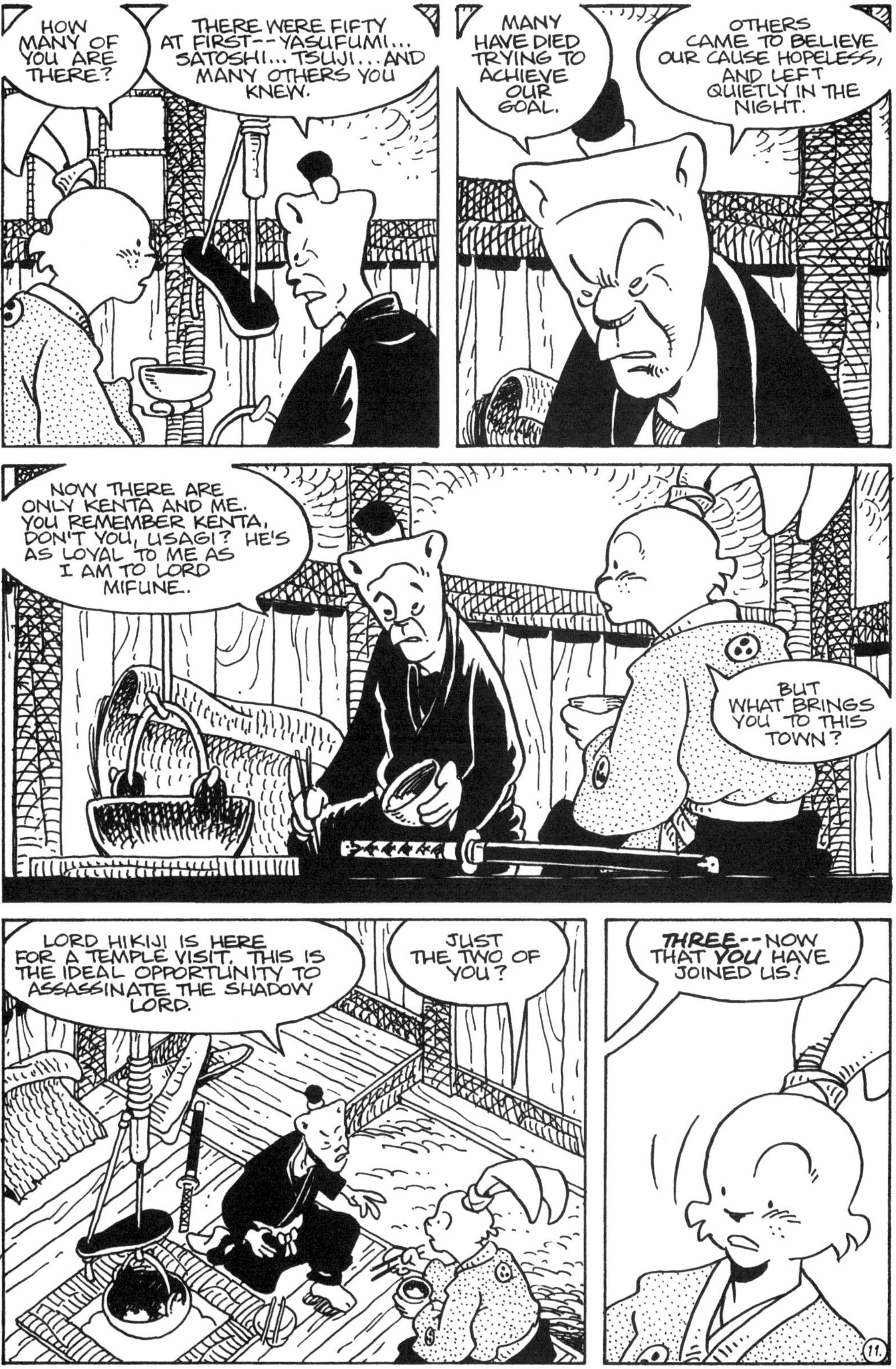
HOW MANY OF YOU ARE THERE?
THERE WERE FIFTY AT FIRST--YASUFUMI... SATOSHI... TSUJI... AND MANY OTHERS YOU KNEW.
MANY HAVE DIED TRYING TO ACHIEVE OUR GOAL.
OTHERS CAME TO BELIEVE OUR CAUSE HOPELESS, AND LEFT QUIETLY IN THE NIGHT.
NOW THERE ARE ONLY KENTA AND ME. YOU REMEMBER KENTA, DON'T YOU, USAGI? HE'S AS LOYAL TO ME AS I AM TO LORD MIFUNE.
BUT WHAT BRINGS YOU TO THIS TOWN?
LORD HIKIJI IS HERE FOR A TEMPLE VISIT. THIS IS THE IDEAL OPPORTUNITY TO ASSASSINATE THE SHADOW LORD.
JUST THE TWO OF YOU?
THREE--NOW THAT ***YOU*** HAVE JOINED US!
11.

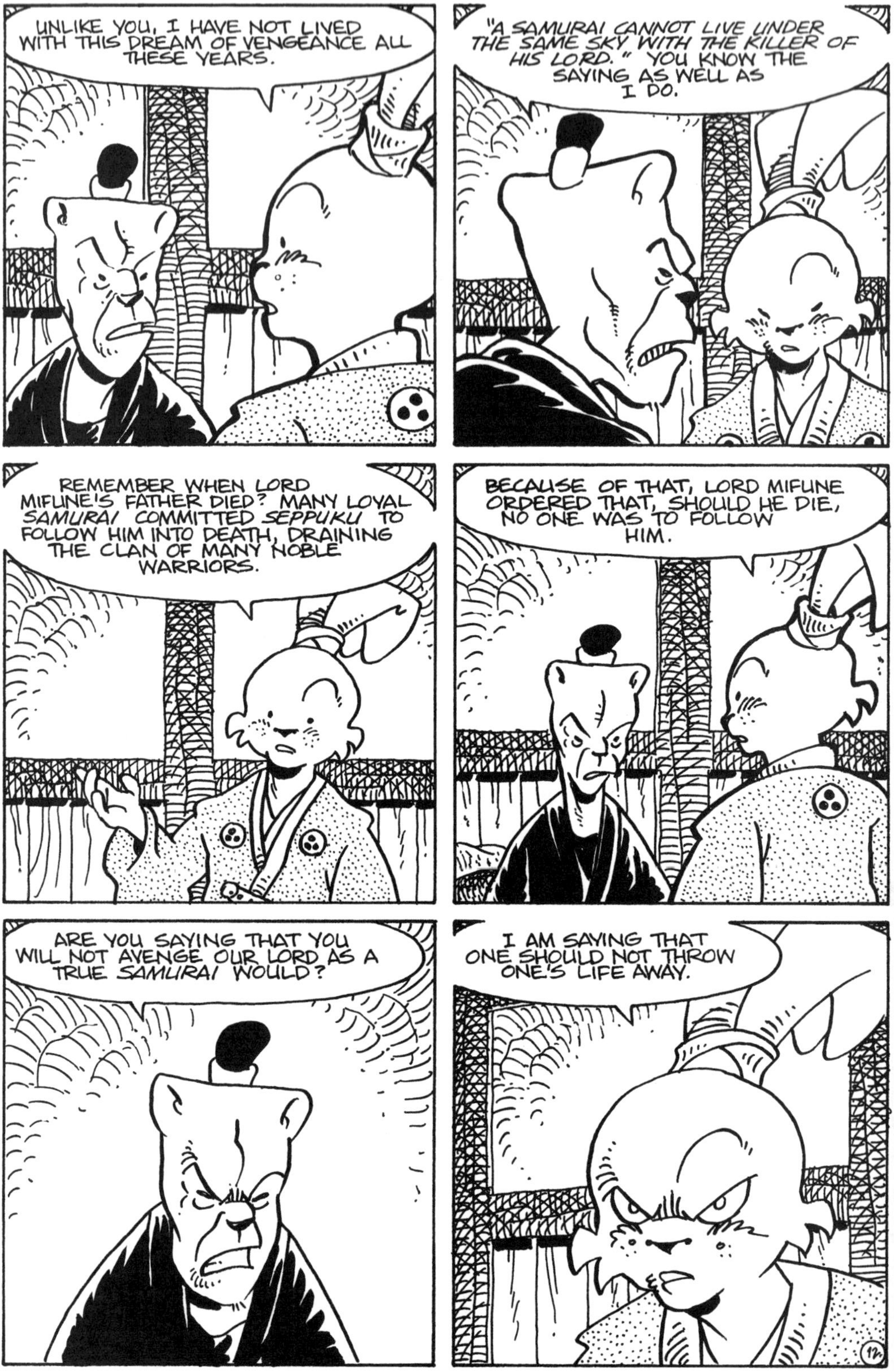
UNLIKE YOU, I HAVE NOT LIVED WITH THIS DREAM OF VENGEANCE ALL THESE YEARS.
"A SAMURAI CANNOT LIVE UNDER THE SAME SKY WITH THE KILLER OF HIS LORD." YOU KNOW THE SAYING AS WELL AS I DO.
REMEMBER WHEN LORD MIFUNE'S FATHER DIED? MANY LOYAL SAMURAI COMMITTED SEPPUKU TO FOLLOW HIM INTO DEATH, DRAINING THE CLAN OF MANY NOBLE WARRIORS.
BECAUSE OF THAT, LORD MIFUNE ORDERED THAT, SHOULD HE DIE, NO ONE WAS TO FOLLOW HIM.
ARE YOU SAYING THAT YOU WILL NOT AVENGE OUR LORD AS A TRUE SAMURAI WOULD?
I AM SAYING THAT ONE SHOULD NOT THROW ONE'S LIFE AWAY.
12

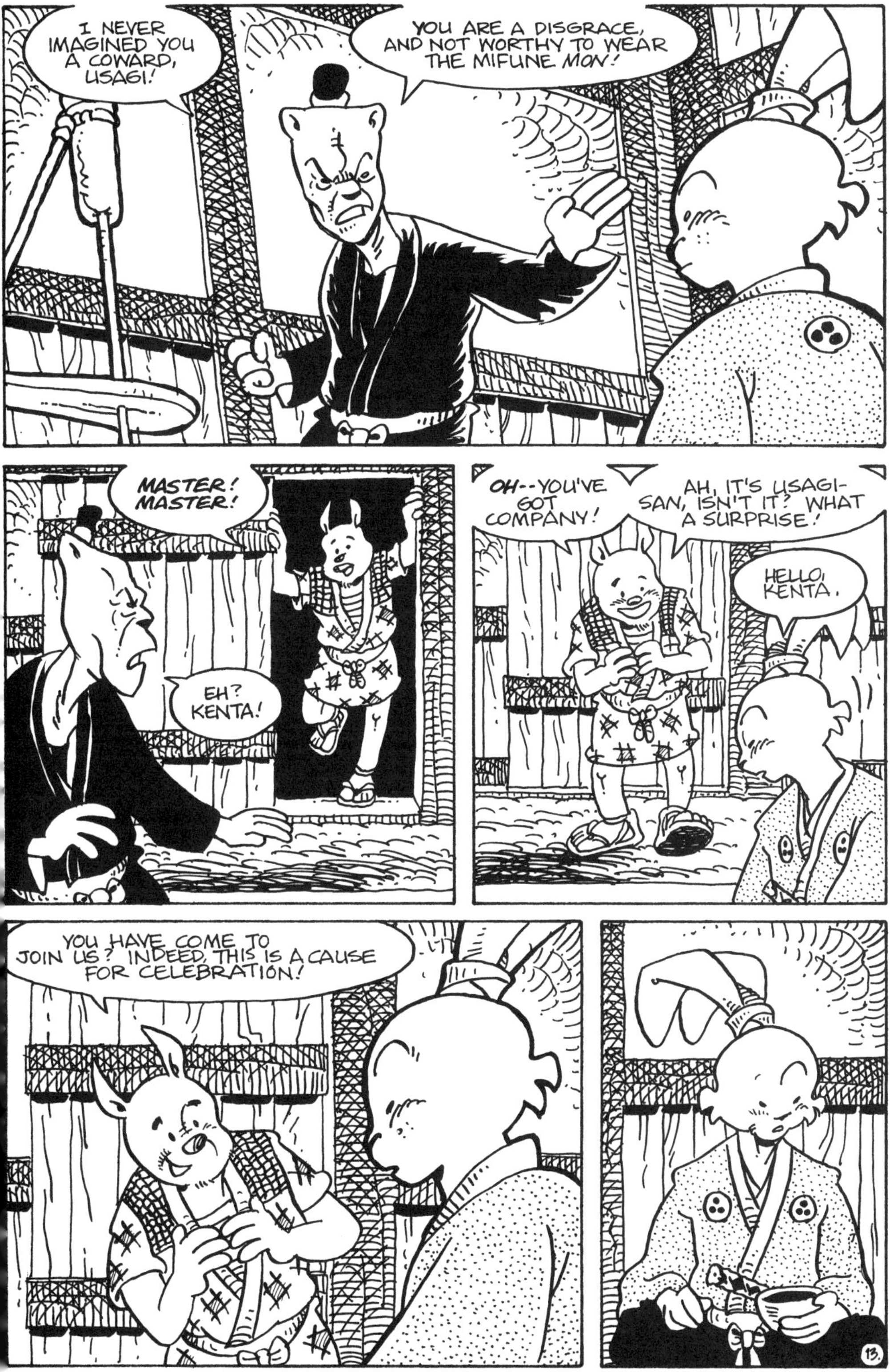
I NEVER IMAGINED YOU A COWARD, USAGI!
YOU ARE A DISGRACE, AND NOT WORTHY TO WEAR THE MIFUNE *MON*!
MASTER! MASTER!
EH? KENTA!
OH--YOU'VE GOT COMPANY!
AH, IT'S USAGI-SAN, ISN'T IT? WHAT A SURPRISE!
HELLO, KENTA.
YOU HAVE COME TO JOIN US? INDEED, THIS IS A CAUSE FOR CELEBRATION!
13.

WHAT DID YOU RUSH IN HERE TO TELL ME?

YES, OF COURSE. I WAS DISGUISED AS A COMMON LABORER, AND HUNG AROUND LORD HIKIJI'S MANSION.

I OVERHEARD THE GUARDS SAY THAT THE SHADOW LORD IS TRAVELING TO THE TEMPLE VERY EARLY TOMORROW MORNING, BEFORE THE PUBLIC ARRIVES.

AT LAST! THIS WILL BE OUR CHANCE-- *TOMORROW!*

YOU DID WELL, KENTA.

WHAT OF YOU, USAGI? ARE YOU WITH US, OR NOT?

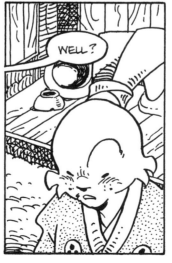

WELL?

I'M WITH YOU!

174

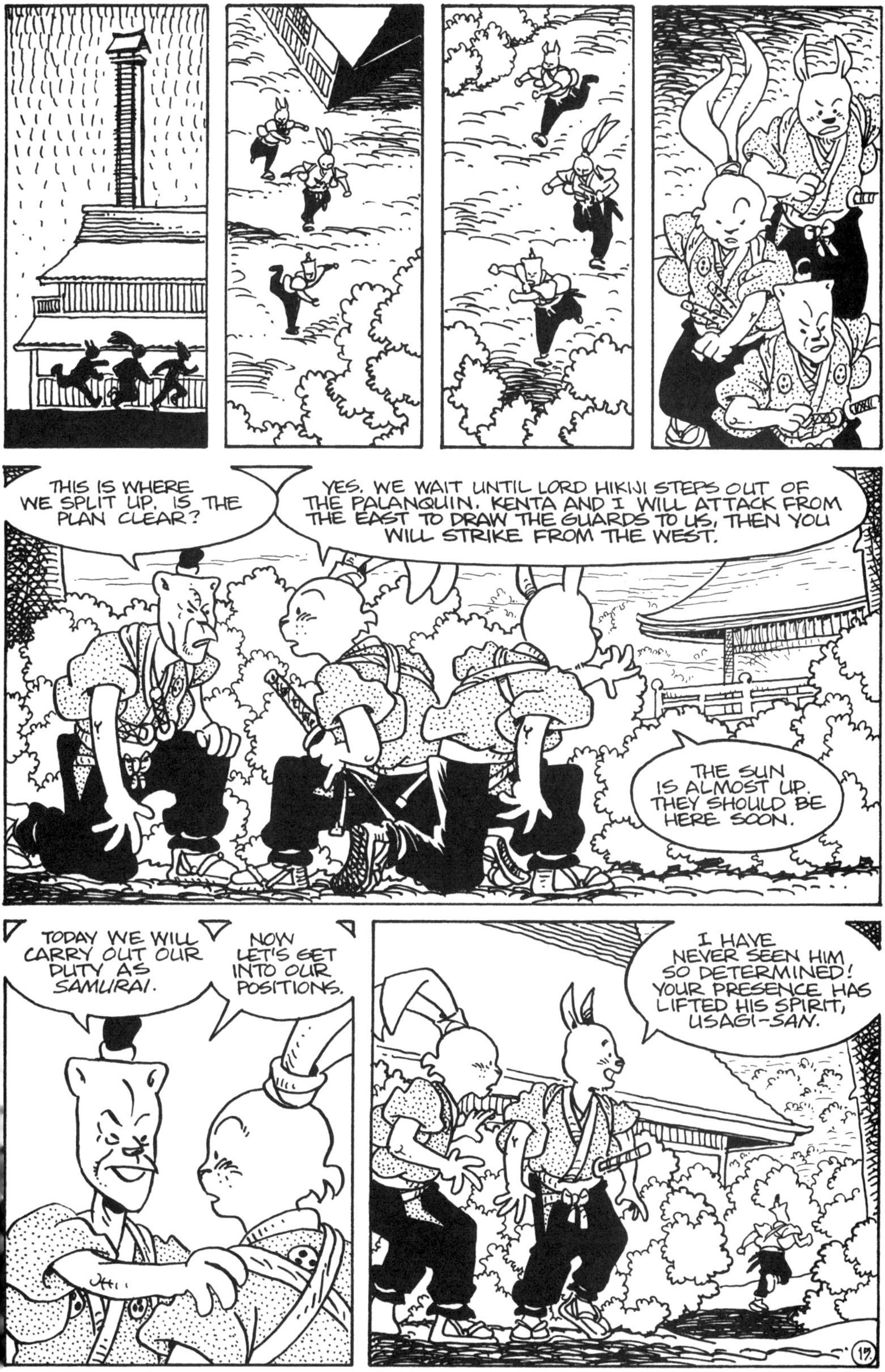
THIS IS WHERE WE SPLIT UP. IS THE PLAN CLEAR?
YES. WE WAIT UNTIL LORD HIKIJI STEPS OUT OF THE PALANQUIN. KENTA AND I WILL ATTACK FROM THE EAST TO DRAW THE GUARDS TO US, THEN YOU WILL STRIKE FROM THE WEST.
THE SUN IS ALMOST UP. THEY SHOULD BE HERE SOON.
TODAY WE WILL CARRY OUT OUR DUTY AS SAMURAI.
NOW LET'S GET INTO OUR POSITIONS.
I HAVE NEVER SEEN HIM SO DETERMINED! YOUR PRESENCE HAS LIFTED HIS SPIRIT, USAGI-SAN.
17

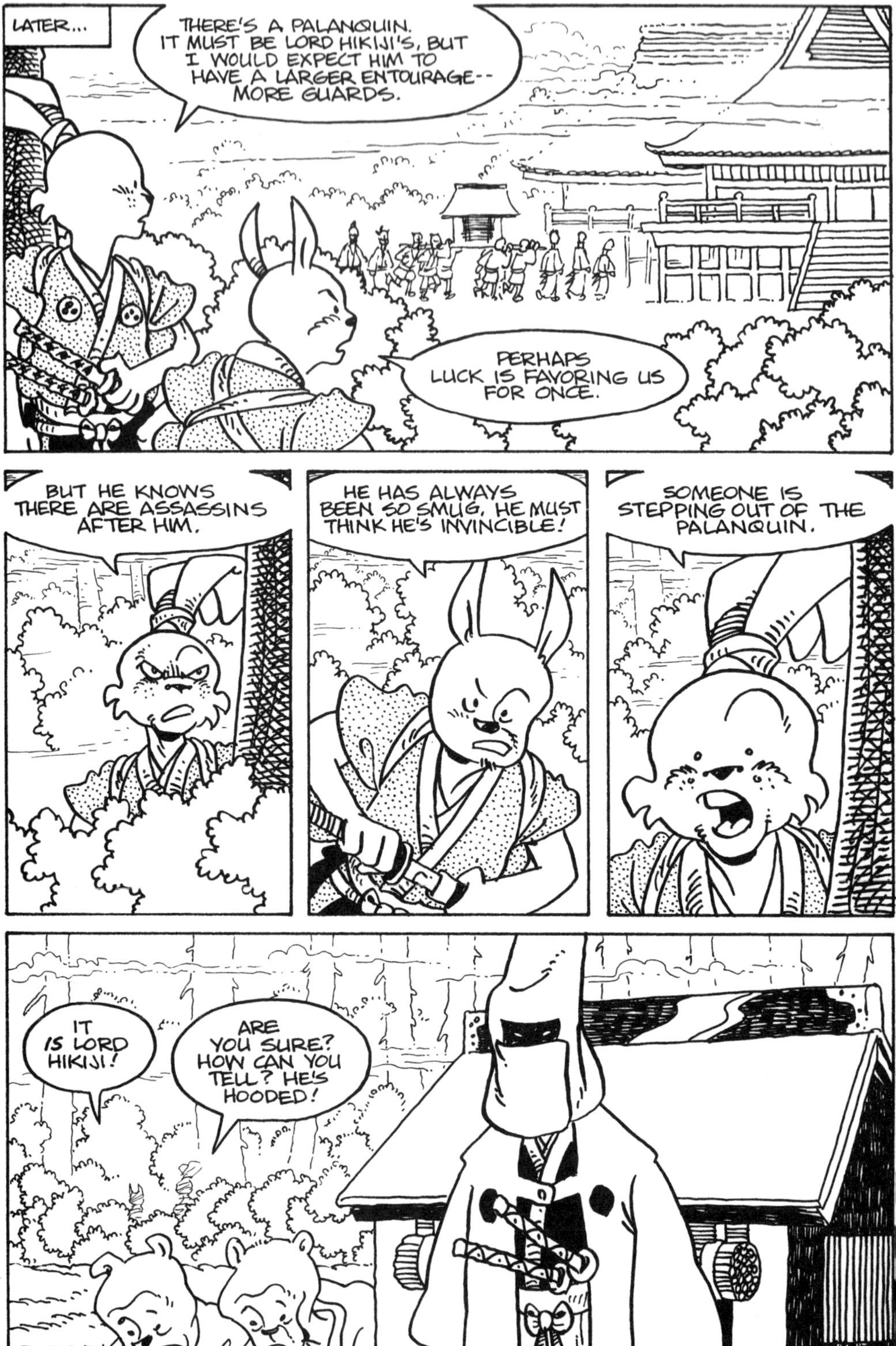
LATER...
THERE'S A PALANQUIN. IT MUST BE LORD HIKIJI'S, BUT I WOULD EXPECT HIM TO HAVE A LARGER ENTOURAGE-- MORE GUARDS.
PERHAPS LUCK IS FAVORING US FOR ONCE.
BUT HE KNOWS THERE ARE ASSASSINS AFTER HIM.
HE HAS ALWAYS BEEN SO SMUG, HE MUST THINK HE'S INVINCIBLE!
SOMEONE IS STEPPING OUT OF THE PALANQUIN.
IT IS LORD HIKIJI!
ARE YOU SURE? HOW CAN YOU TELL? HE'S HOODED!
16.

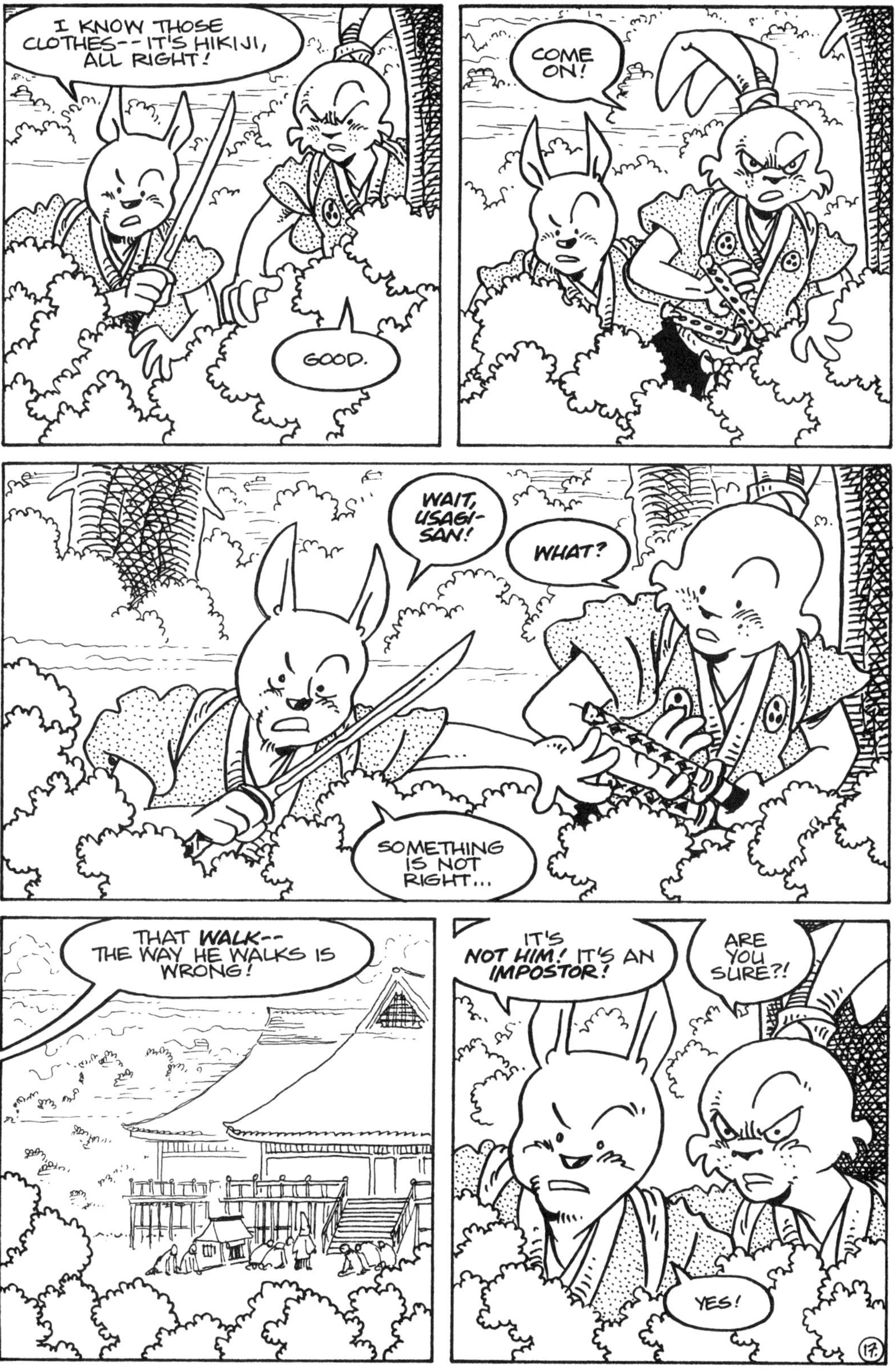
I KNOW THOSE CLOTHES--IT'S HIKIJI, ALL RIGHT!
GOOD.
COME ON!
WAIT, USAGI-SAN!
WHAT?
SOMETHING IS NOT RIGHT...
THAT WALK-- THE WAY HE WALKS IS WRONG!
IT'S NOT HIM! IT'S AN IMPOSTOR!
ARE YOU SURE?!
YES!
17

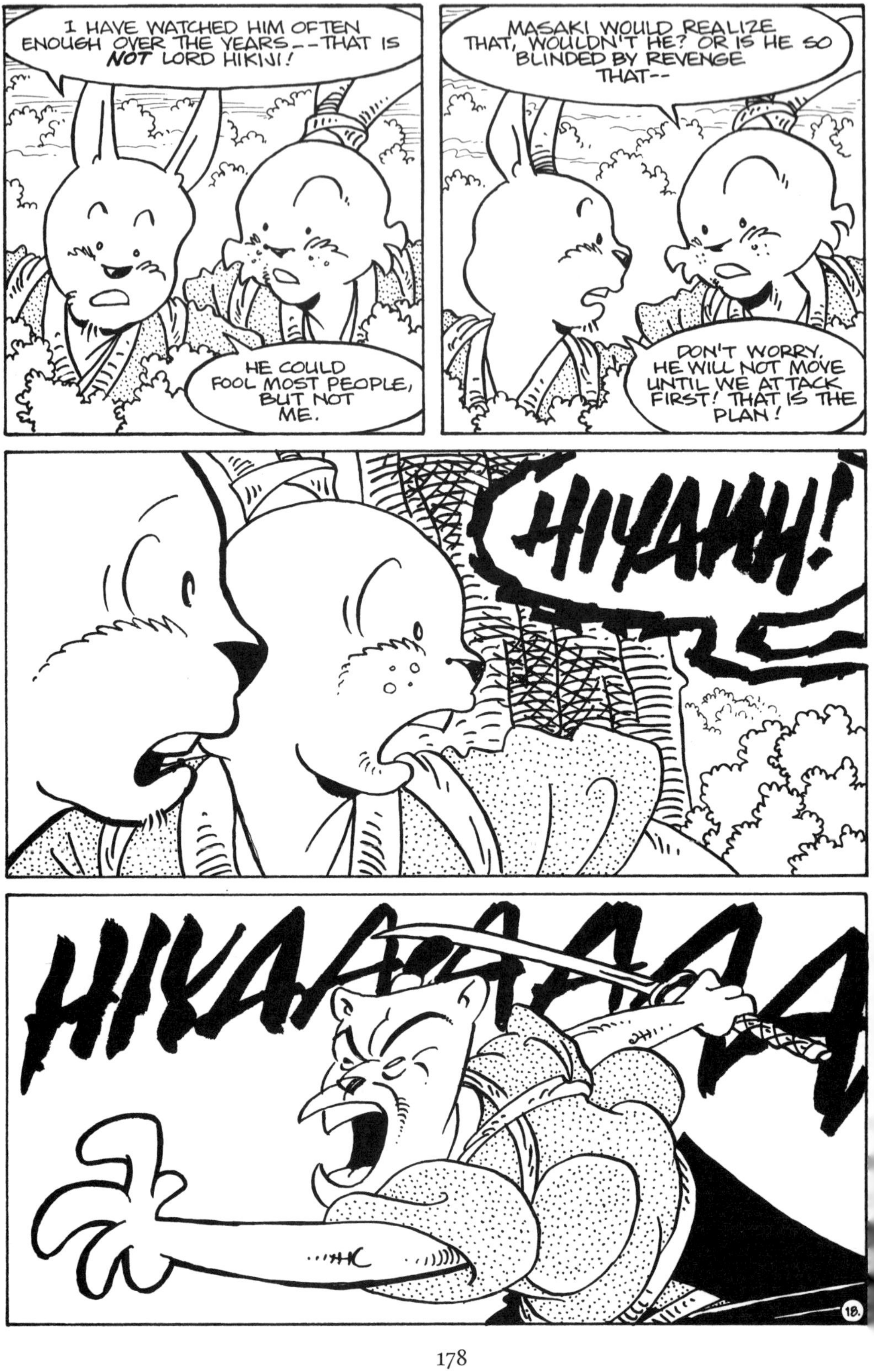
I HAVE WATCHED HIM OFTEN ENOUGH OVER THE YEARS--THAT IS **NOT** LORD HIKIJI!
HE COULD FOOL MOST PEOPLE, BUT NOT ME.
MASAKI WOULD REALIZE THAT, WOULDN'T HE? OR IS HE SO BLINDED BY REVENGE THAT--
DON'T WORRY. HE WILL NOT MOVE UNTIL WE ATTACK FIRST! THAT IS THE PLAN!
HIYAAHH!
HIYAAAAAAAA
18.

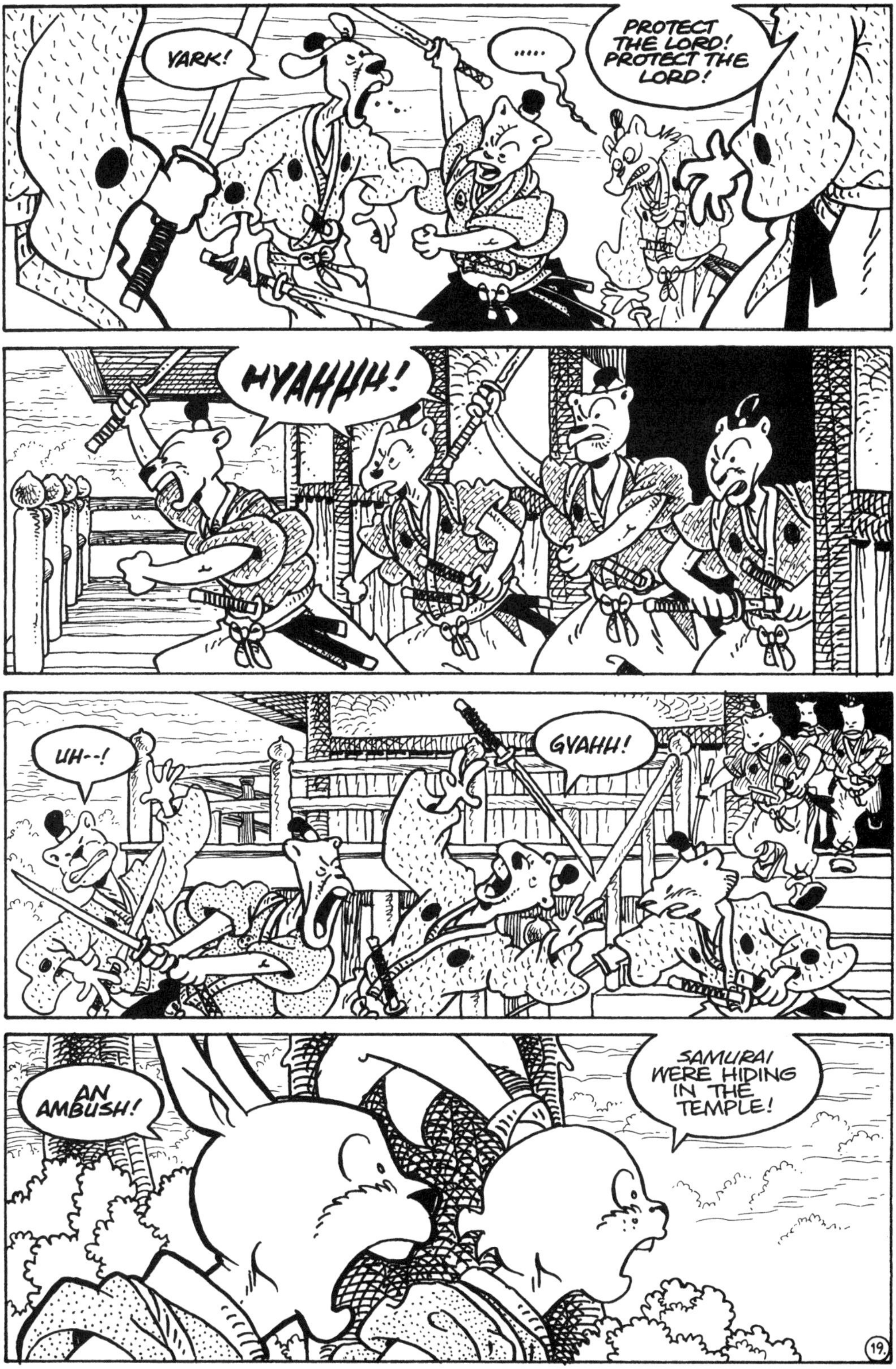
YARK!
.....
PROTECT THE LORD! PROTECT THE LORD!
HYAHHH!
UH--!
GYAHH!
AN AMBUSH!
SAMURAI WERE HIDING IN THE TEMPLE!
19.

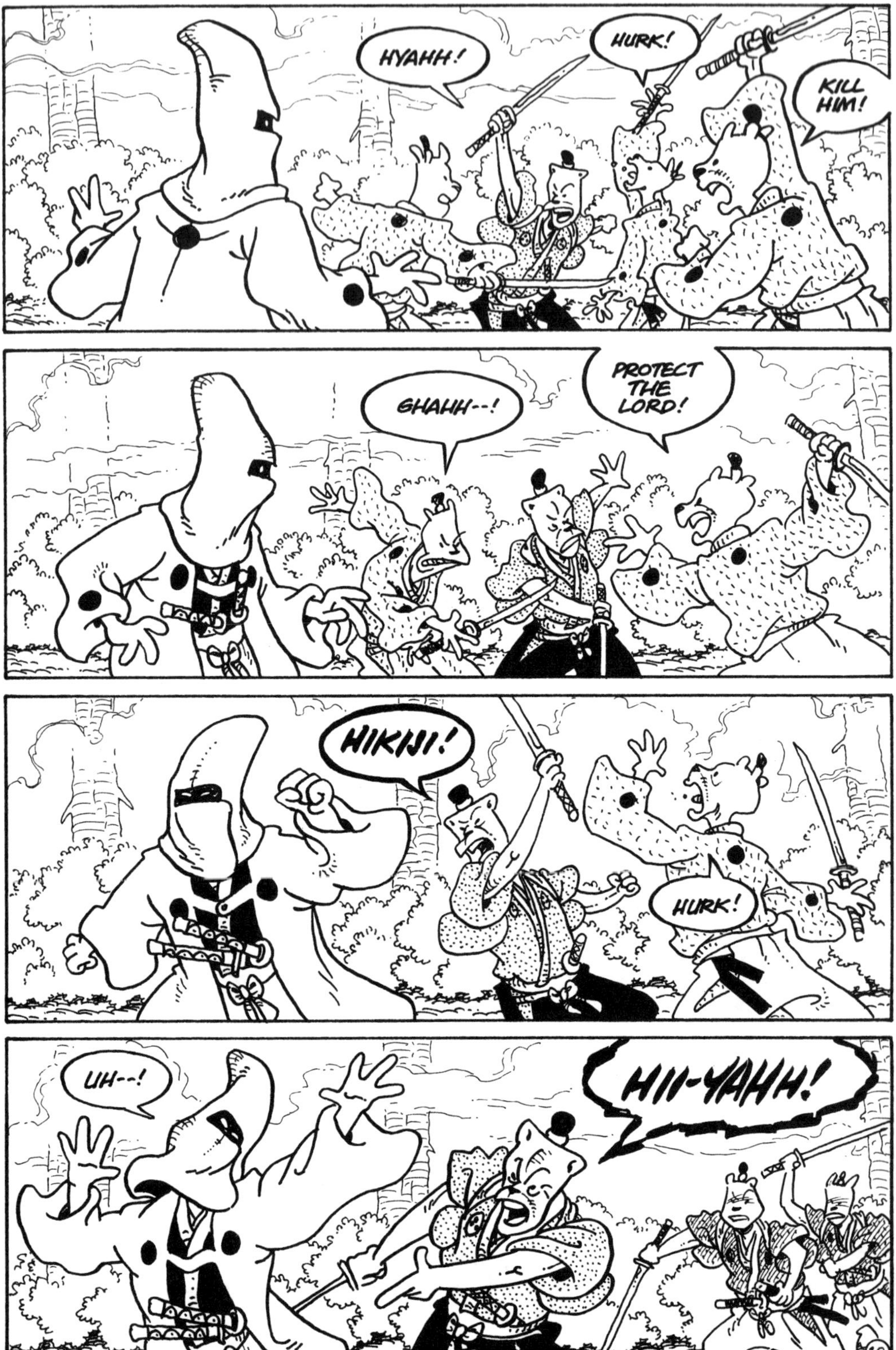
HYAHH!
HURK!
KILL HIM!
GHAHH--!
PROTECT THE LORD!
HIKIJI!
HURK!
UH--!
HII-YAHH!

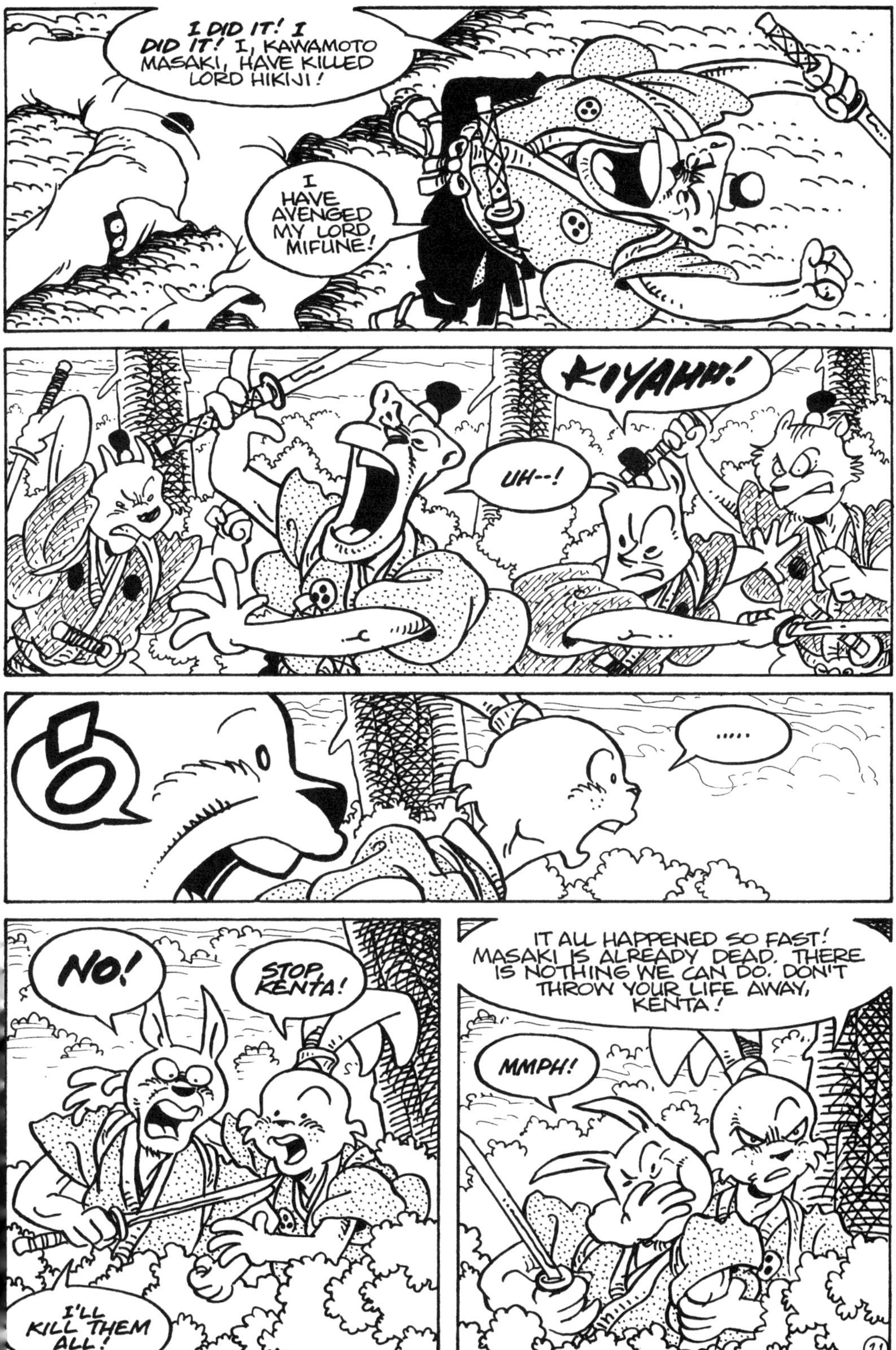
I DID IT! I DID IT! I, KAWAMOTO MASAKI, HAVE KILLED LORD HIKIJI!
I HAVE AVENGED MY LORD MIFUNE!
KIYAHH!
UH--!
.....
NO!
STOP, KENTA!
I'LL KILL THEM ALL!
IT ALL HAPPENED SO FAST! MASAKI IS ALREADY DEAD. THERE IS NOTHING WE CAN DO. DON'T THROW YOUR LIFE AWAY, KENTA!
MMPH!
21

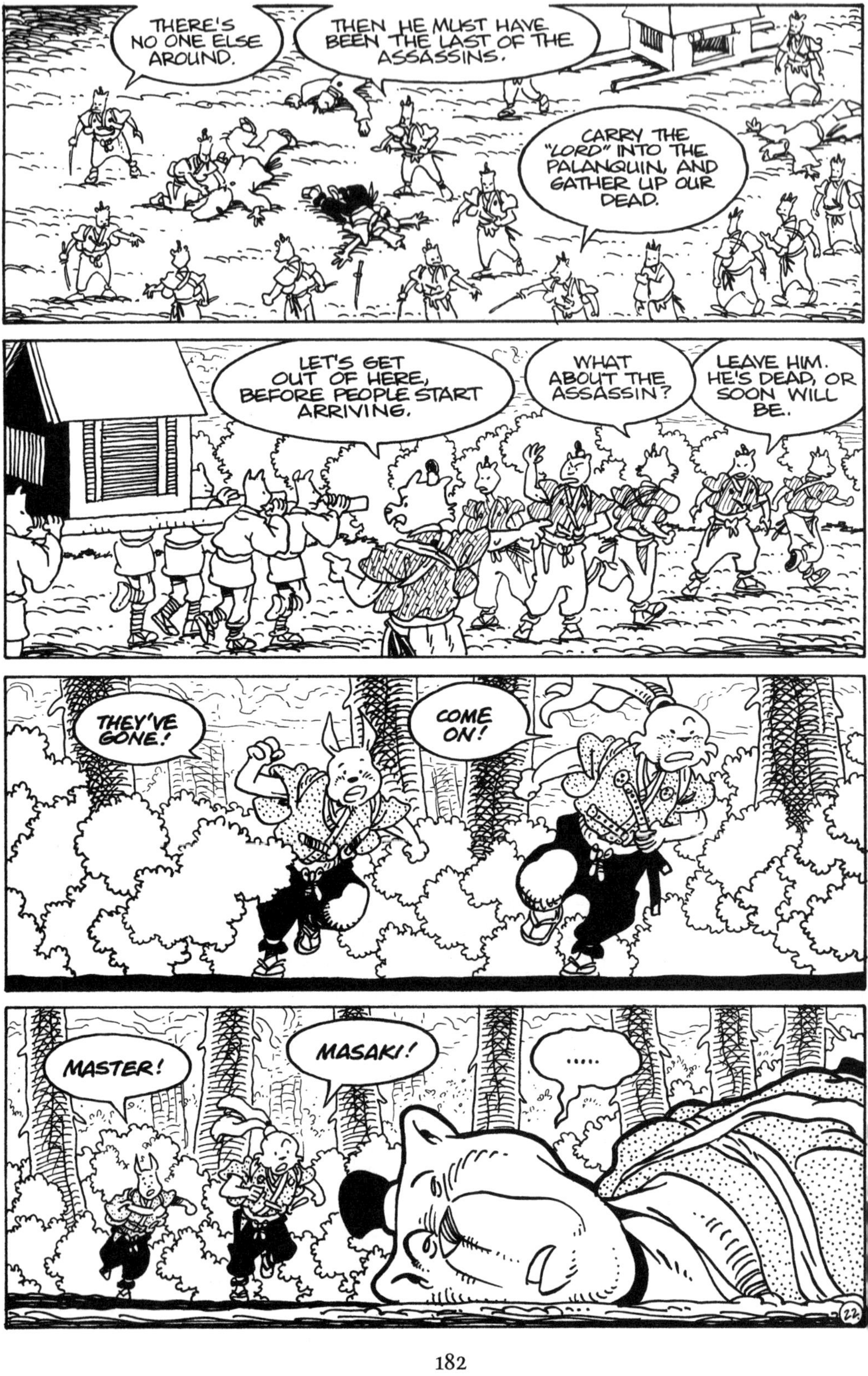
THERE'S NO ONE ELSE AROUND.
THEN HE MUST HAVE BEEN THE LAST OF THE ASSASSINS.
CARRY THE "LORD" INTO THE PALANQUIN, AND GATHER UP OUR DEAD.
LET'S GET OUT OF HERE, BEFORE PEOPLE START ARRIVING.
WHAT ABOUT THE ASSASSIN?
LEAVE HIM. HE'S DEAD, OR SOON WILL BE.
THEY'VE GONE!
COME ON!
MASTER!
MASAKI!
.....
22

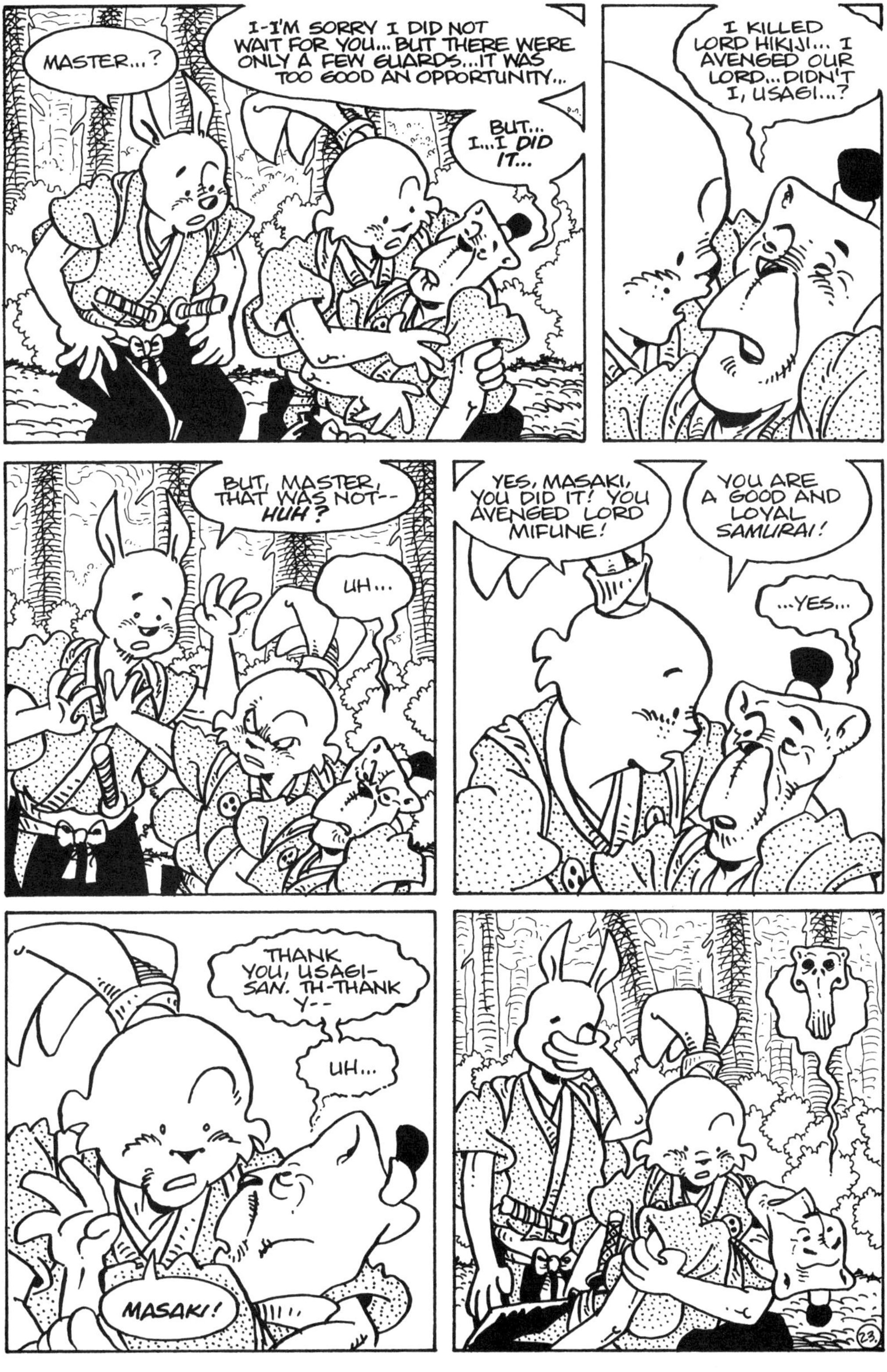
MASTER...?
I-I'M SORRY I DID NOT WAIT FOR YOU... BUT THERE WERE ONLY A FEW GUARDS...IT WAS TOO GOOD AN OPPORTUNITY...
BUT... I...I DID IT...
I KILLED LORD HIKIJI... I AVENGED OUR LORD...DIDN'T I, USAGI...?
BUT, MASTER, THAT WAS NOT-- HUH?
UH...
YES, MASAKI, YOU DID IT! YOU AVENGED LORD MIFUNE!
YOU ARE A GOOD AND LOYAL SAMURAI!
...YES...
THANK YOU, USAGI-SAN. TH-THANK Y--
UH...
MASAKI!
23

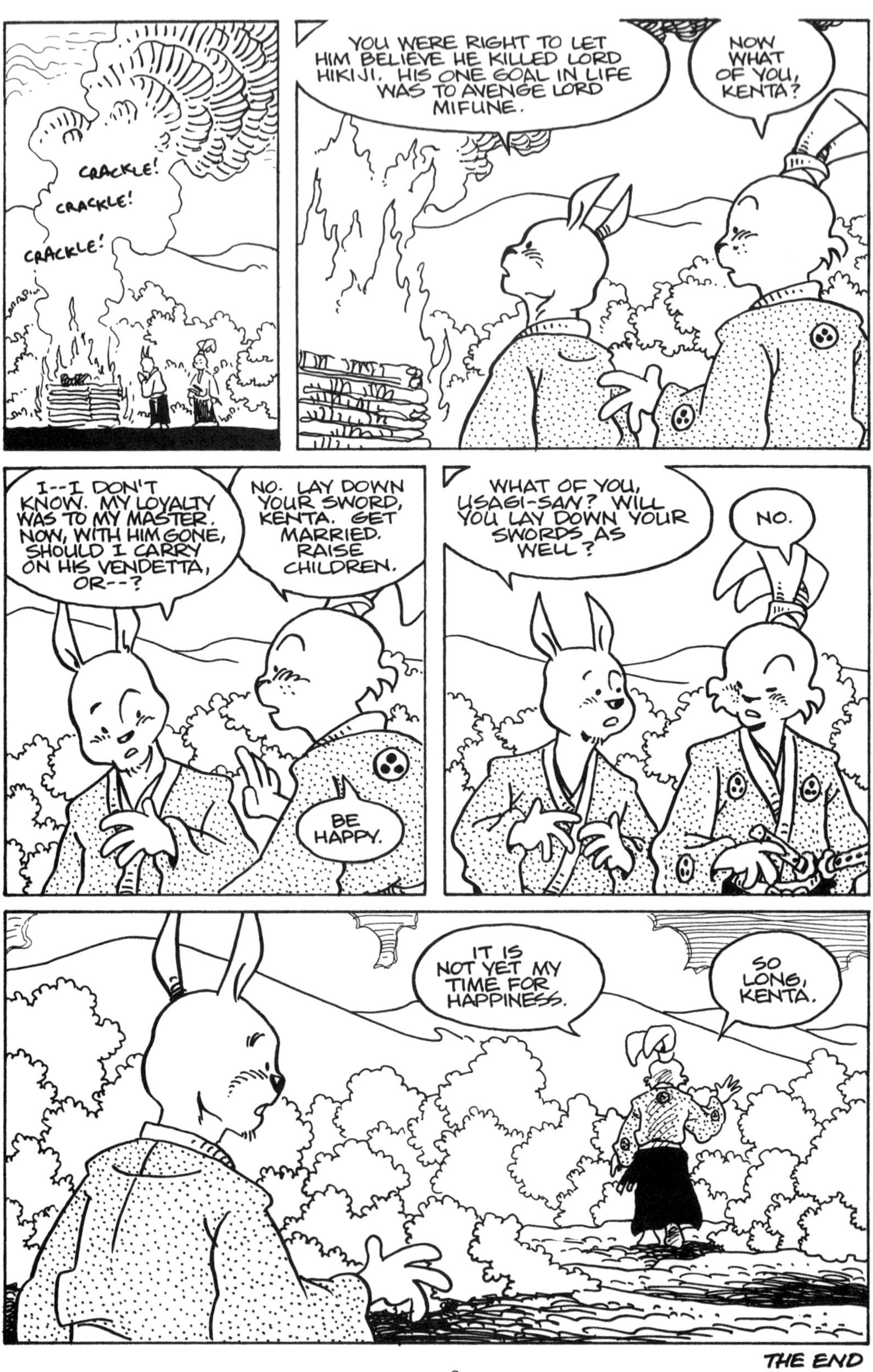
CRACKLE!
CRACKLE!
CRACKLE!
YOU WERE RIGHT TO LET HIM BELIEVE HE KILLED LORD HIKIJI. HIS ONE GOAL IN LIFE WAS TO AVENGE LORD MIFUNE.
NOW WHAT OF YOU, KENTA?
I--I DON'T KNOW. MY LOYALTY WAS TO MY MASTER. NOW, WITH HIM GONE, SHOULD I CARRY ON HIS VENDETTA, OR--?
NO. LAY DOWN YOUR SWORD, KENTA. GET MARRIED. RAISE CHILDREN.
BE HAPPY.
WHAT OF YOU, USAGI-SAN? WILL YOU LAY DOWN YOUR SWORDS AS WELL?
NO.
IT IS NOT YET MY TIME FOR HAPPINESS.
SO LONG, KENTA.
THE END

Usagi Yojimbo

Story Notes

Traitors of the Earth

Netsuke are miniature sculptures, carved as toggles for pouches. (The word's literal meaning is "root for fastening.") They were used as early as the 1400s, but became popular in the seventeenth century. Japanese clothing has no pockets, so possessions were carried in small bags or boxes, which were hung on the *obi* (sash). These hanging containers were called *sagemono*. The *sagemono* were tied to the *obi* with a silken cord and secured with a *netsuke* that prevented the cord from slipping off. A bead, called an *ojime*, between the *netsuke* and *sagemono* could be slid to tighten or loosen the opening of the container.

The most commonly used material was ivory, but *netsuke* could also be made from bone, wood, stone, amber, bamboo, ceramics, or nuts. They could be carved in any variety of subjects: peasants in the field, samurai warriors, gods, animals, plants, and creatures from folklore. *Netsuke* also became status symbols, starting a new art form. The artists were called *netsukeshi*. Some were trained as painters or sculptors, but others were artisans, such as mask- or puppet-makers.

There are four categories of *netsuke*: the *katabori* are small and compact; the *sashi* are long, thin *netsuke*; the *kagamibuta* are shaped like a bowl with a lid; and the *manju* are round, flat, button-shaped *netsuke*.

With the Meiji Restoration in the nineteenth century, the Japanese adopted western-style clothing and *netsuke* became obsolete.

Netsuke have become very collectible, especially in Europe and the US. Neither the materials used nor the existence of a signature has much bearing on the value of a piece. The determining factors are the quality of the carving, its originality, and its charm. A good source of information is the International Netsuke Society (netsuke.org).

My depiction of Shoki is based on a painting by Wu Tao-tzu (720-760), the greatest artist of the T'ang Dynasty. Emperor Ming-huang had a nightmare in which he was being tormented by a demon. Before he could summon his guards, a huge bearded giant appeared and seized the demon, gouged out its eyes,

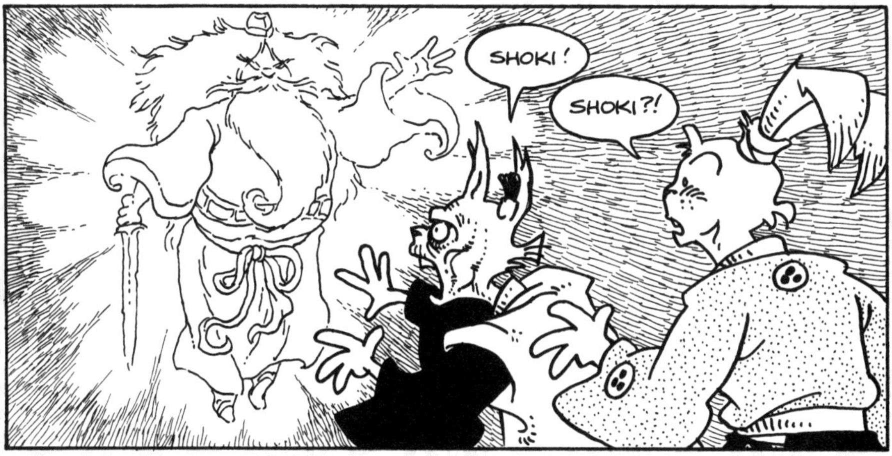
SHOKI!
SHOKI?!

and ate it. The giant identified himself as Chung K'uei, a scholar who had failed the imperial examinations and killed himself in despair. The emperor at the time had nonetheless allowed him an official burial, and, in gratitude, Chung K'uei vowed to rid the world of demons. Emperor Ming-huang commissioned Wu Tao-tzu to paint the image he had dreamed. The likeness was so striking that the emperor rewarded the artist with one hundred *taels* (an early Chinese currency) of gold. Stories of Chung K'uei became widespread, and Wu Tao-tzu's painting became the basis for his likeness. Eventually, the stories made their way to Japan and its folklore, and "Shoki" is the Japanese reading of the kanji characters that make up "Chung K'uei."

The *Komainu* are a pair of stone dogs that face each other either at the entrance to a Shinto shrine or at the approach to the oratory on the shrine grounds. They are usually carved from stone but are sometimes made of wood or metal. One dog, named A, breathes in with an open mouth, while his companion, Un, breathes out with his mouth closed, suggesting the inhalation and exhalation of heavenly forces and the balance of yin and yang. The phrase, *a-un-no-kokyu*, or "A-Un breathing," describes the relationship of people so close that they can communicate without speech. The two dogs protect the shrine against evil spirits with their fierce appearance.

The *Komainu* can be traced to India and that culture's stylized representation of the lion. The Chinese adopted the lion and added attributes of their native tiger as well as the Pekinese dogs that were the pride of the Chinese Imperial family. That passed over to the Korean peninsula and on to Japan, where the lions were transformed into dogs. They are sometimes called *Karashishi* (Chinese lions). Okinawa has a similar creature called *Shissa*.

WHAT THE LITTLE THIEF HEARD

Pickled plums, or *umeboshi*, are reputed to have amazing medicinal properties, such as neutralizing fatigue, flushing out toxins, helping digestion, and providing an overall remedy for hangovers. Instead of an apple a day, the Japanese regard daily *umeboshi* as great preventative medicine.

The origin of the *umeboshi* in Japan is not really known. They probably came by way of China, where dried, smoked plums, or *ubai*, are still used for a variety of medical purposes, including reducing nausea and fever. The oldest record of *umeboshi* as medicine dates from about a thousand years ago, when they were used to prevent fatigue as well as to cure food poisoning and other diseases.

Umeboshi were the samurai's most important field rations, and were used to flavor foods, cure fatigue, and increase endurance. Because of their high acid content, *umeboshi* were also used to purify water.

Plums (*ume*) are picked in late May or early June, when they are still green. They are layered in salt and weighed down with a heavy rock until late August, sun-dried on bamboo mats, then put in brine. Their red color comes from purplish *shiso* (perilla) leaves, which are pickled with the plums.

Fuku-ume (*ume* of good fortune) are dropped in cups of tea, and drunk on New Year's Day to ensure good health for the year ahead.

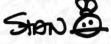

GROO VS. USAGI: WHO WOULD WIN?

This page was originally drawn for the International Comic-Con: San Diego souvenir book, in celebration of the twenty-fifth anniversary of Sergio Aragonés's Groo.

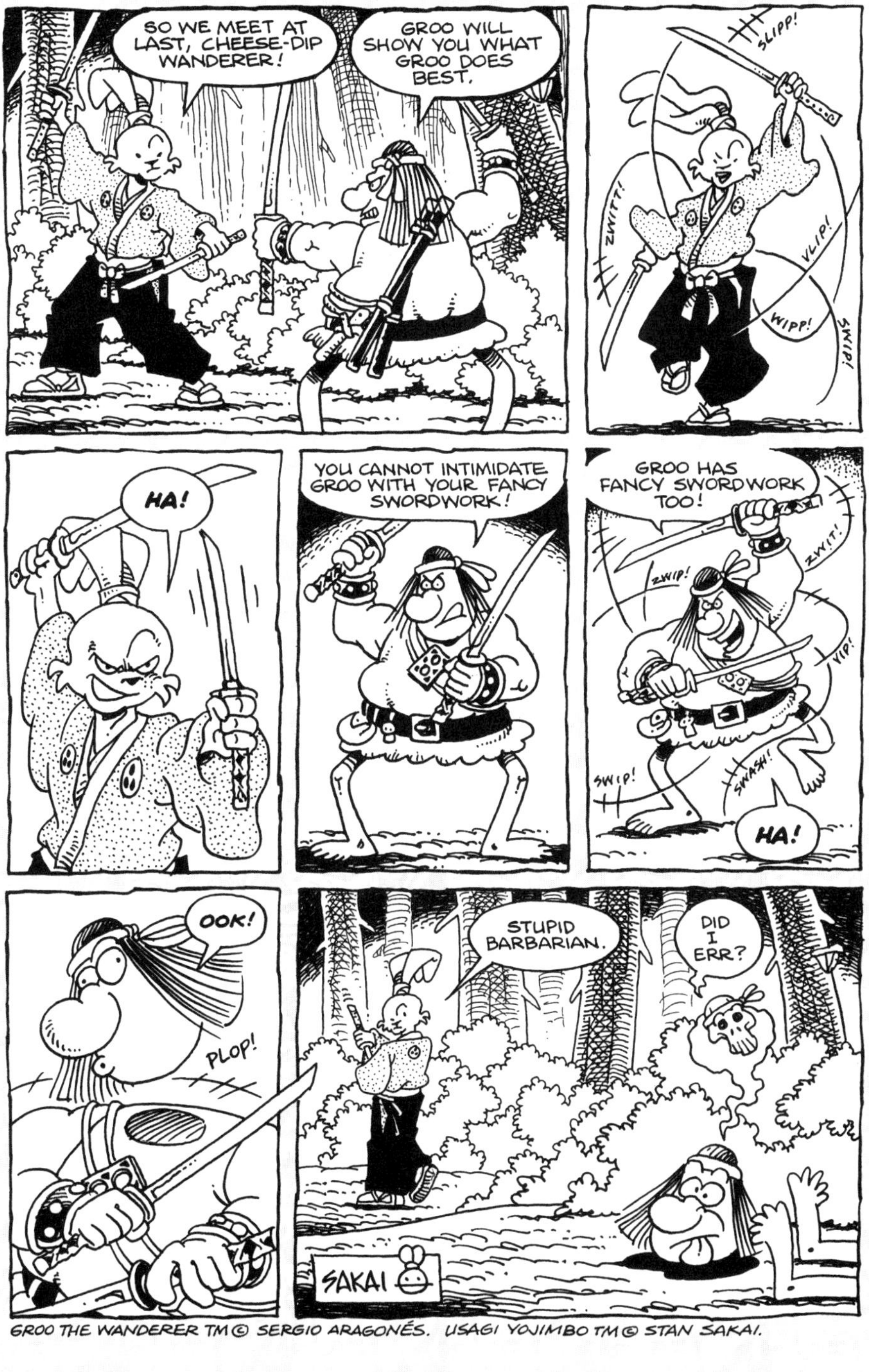
SO WE MEET AT LAST, CHEESE-DIP WANDERER!
GROO WILL SHOW YOU WHAT GROO DOES BEST.
SLIPP!
ZWITT!
VLIP!
WIPP!
SWIP!
HA!
YOU CANNOT INTIMIDATE GROO WITH YOUR FANCY SWORDWORK!
GROO HAS FANCY SWORDWORK TOO!
ZWIP!
ZWIT!
VIP!
SWIP!
SWASH!
HA!
OOK!
PLOP!
STUPID BARBARIAN.
DID I ERR?
SAKAI

GROO THE WANDERER TM© SERGIO ARAGONÉS. USAGI YOJIMBO TM© STAN SAKAI.

Gallery

The following pages feature Stan Sakai's cover art from issues 117 through 123 of Dark Horse's Usagi Yojimbo Volume Three *series*.

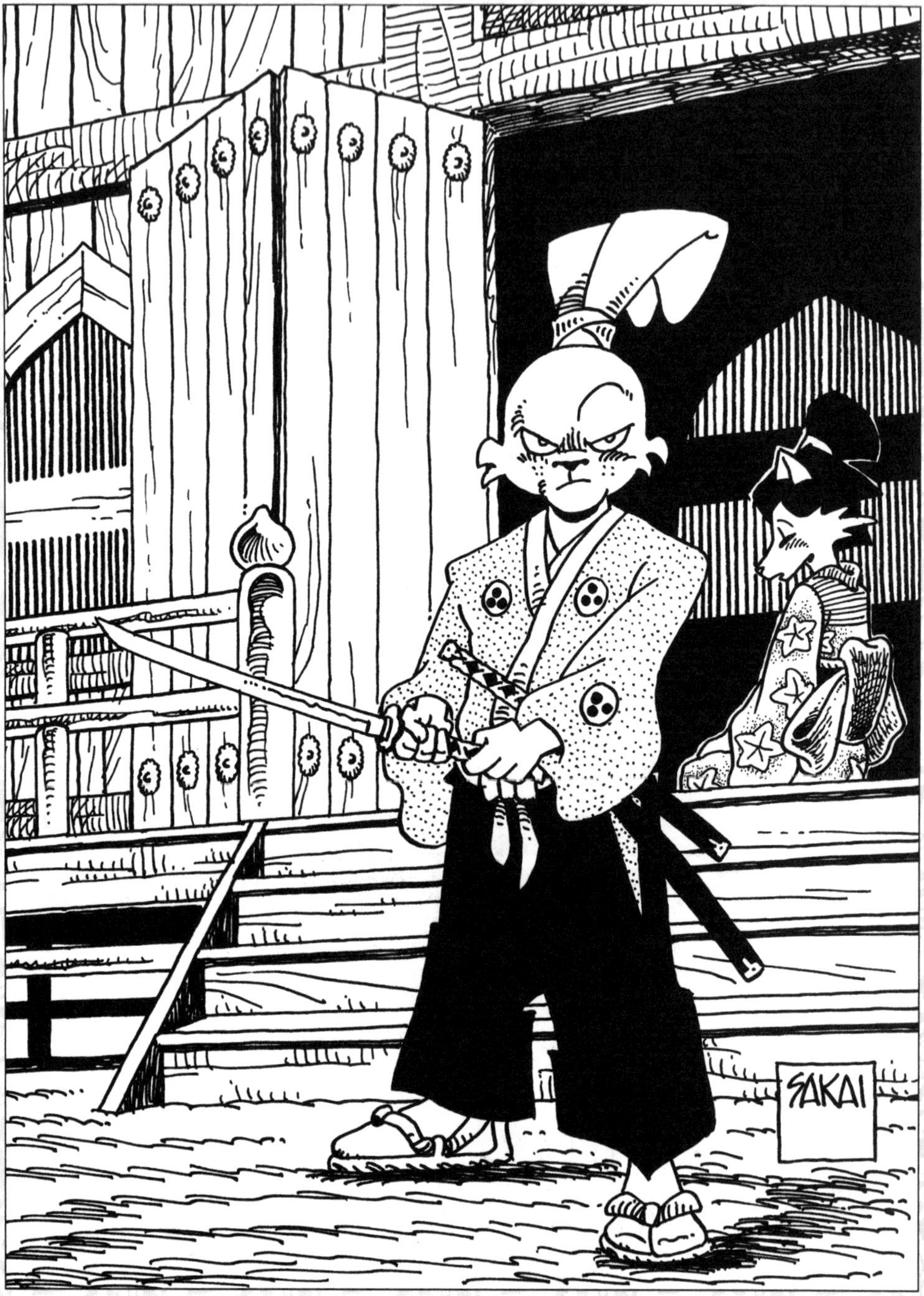
SAKAI

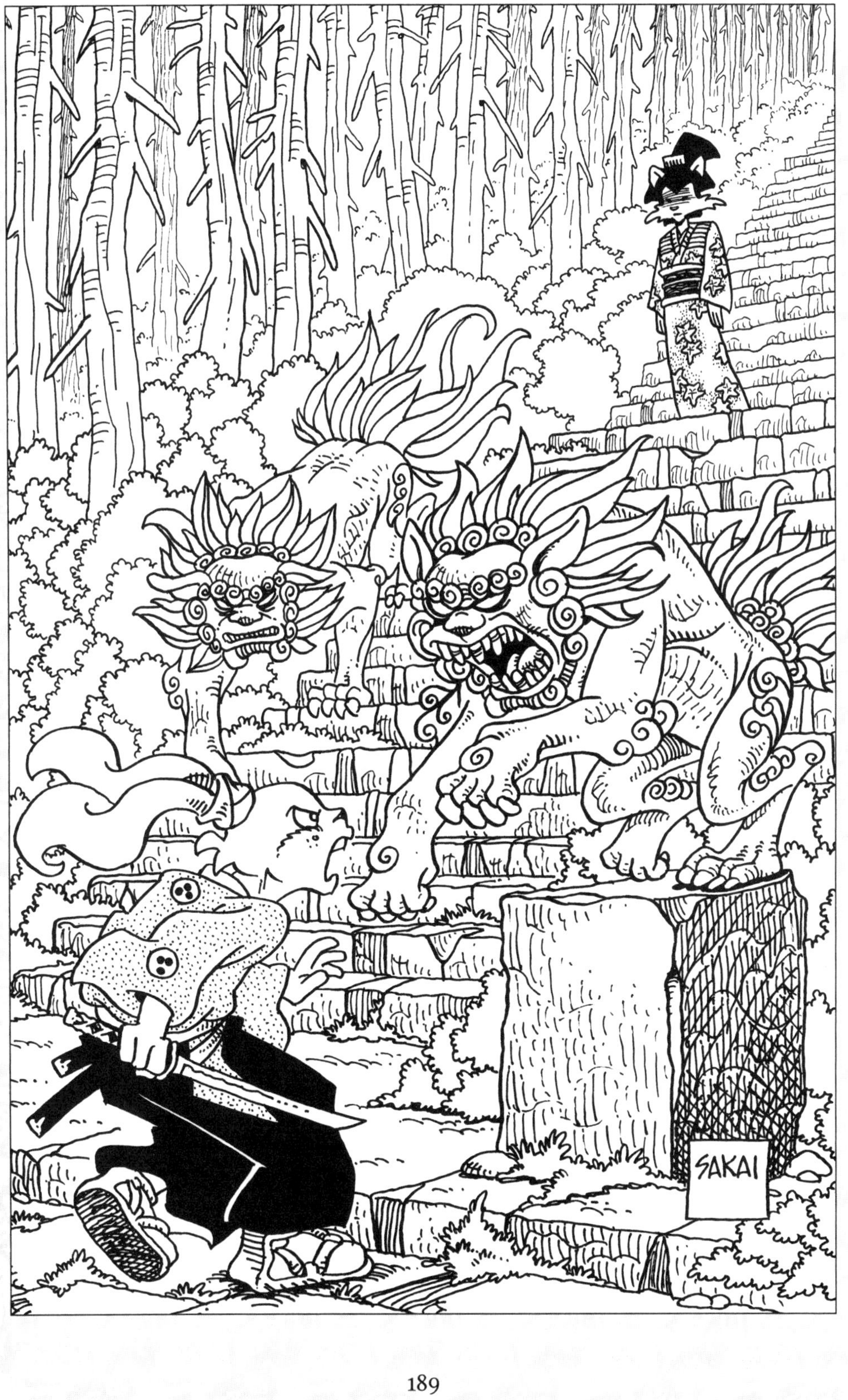
SAKAI

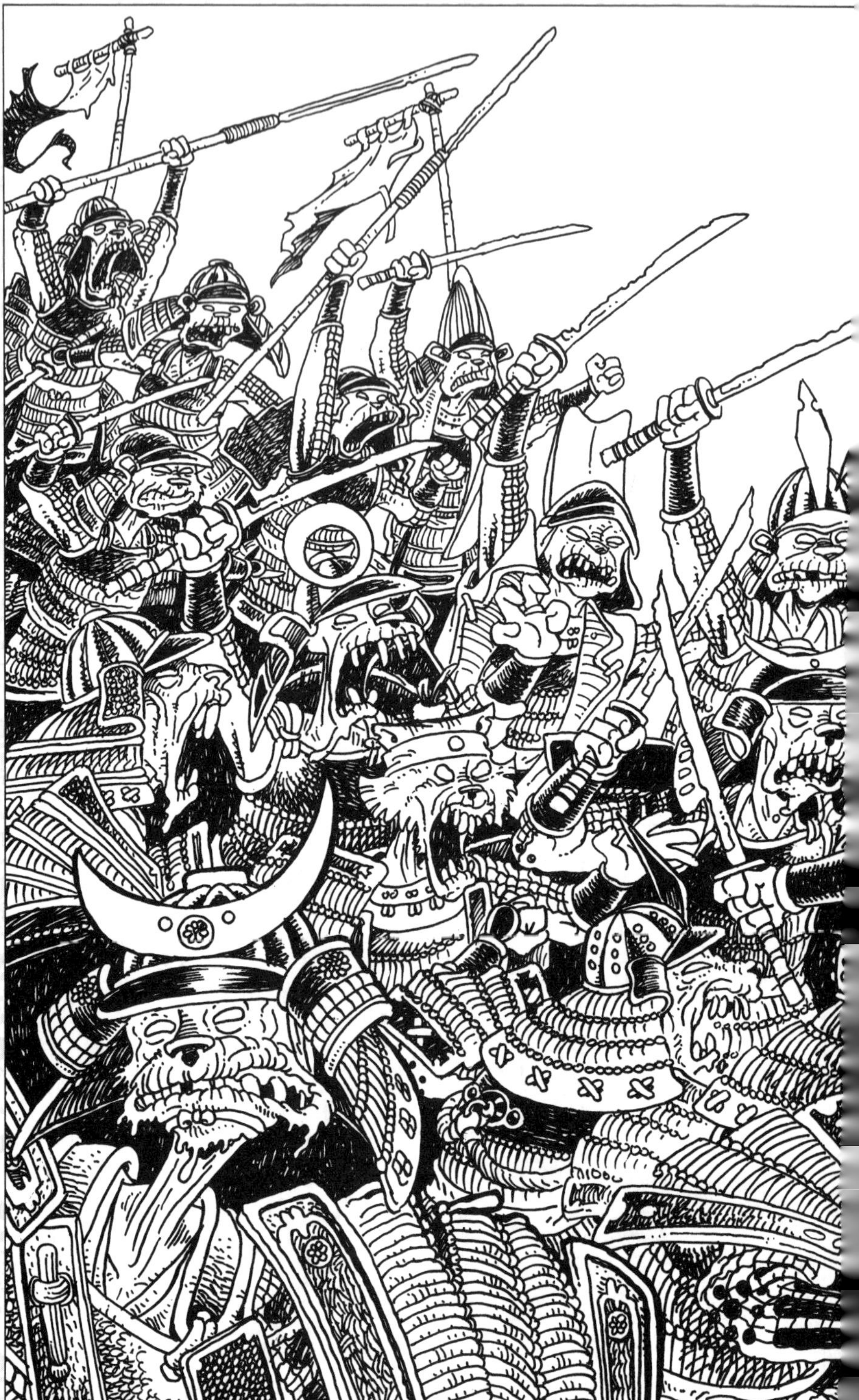

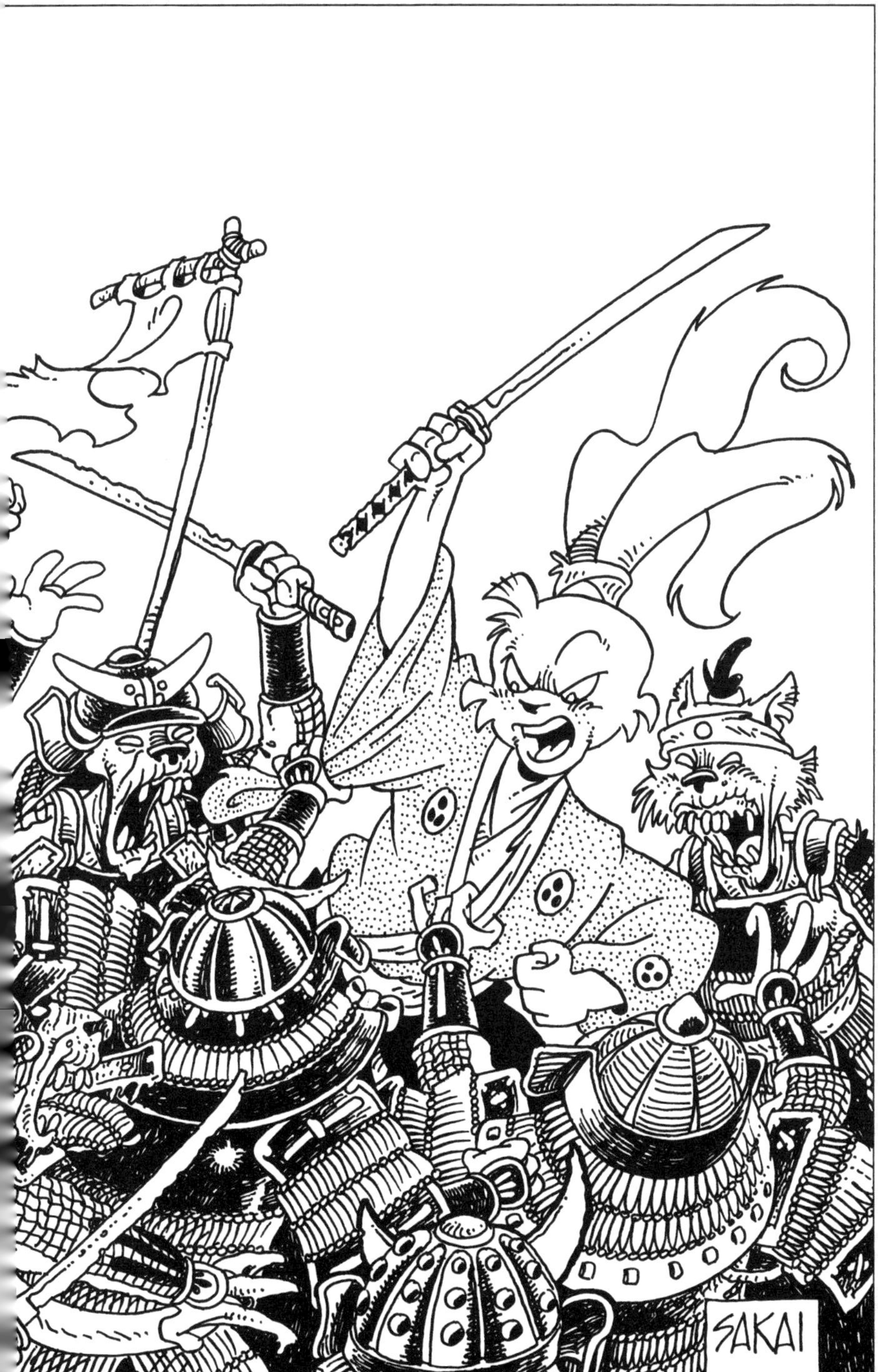
SAKAI

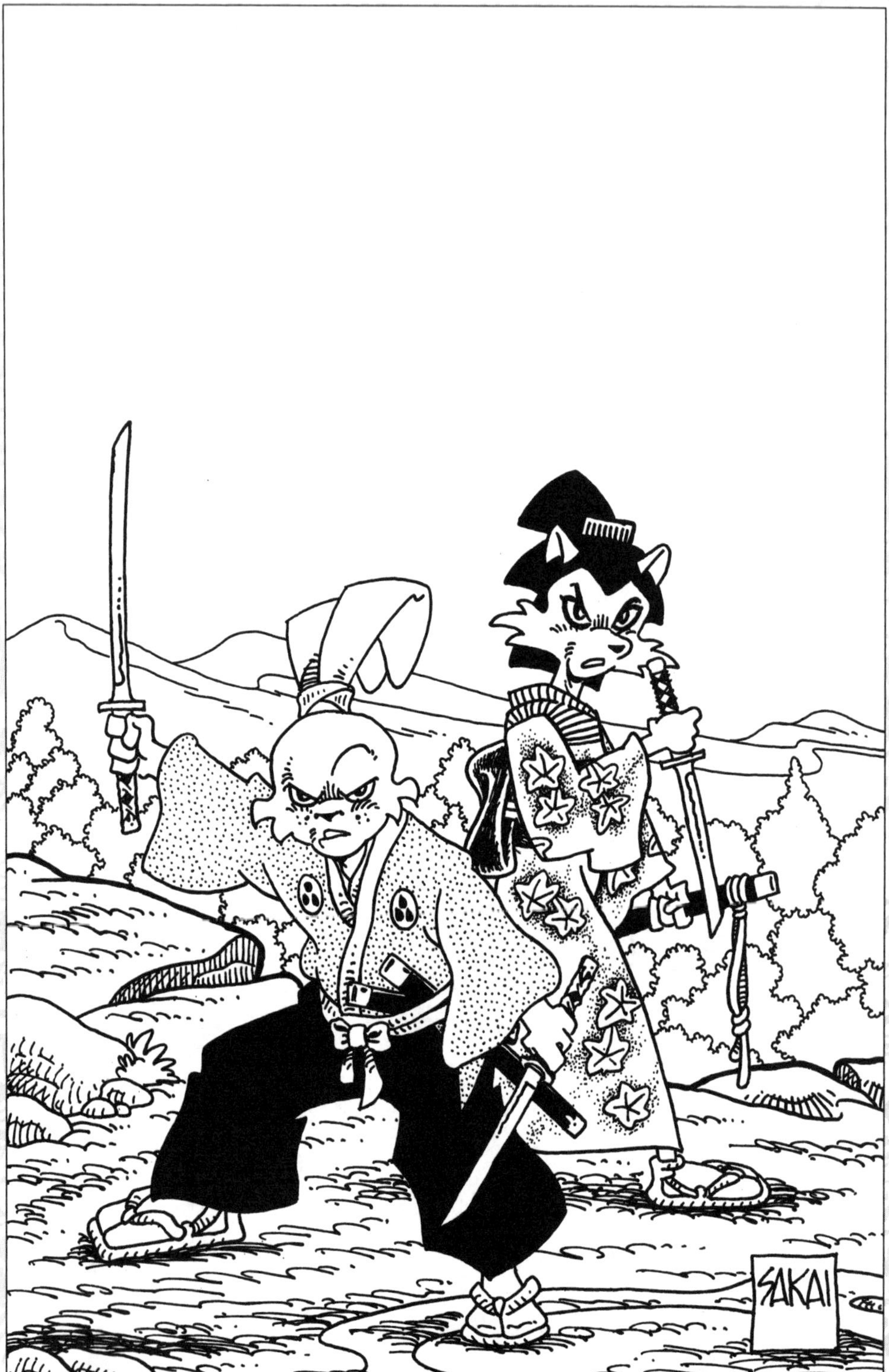
SAKAI

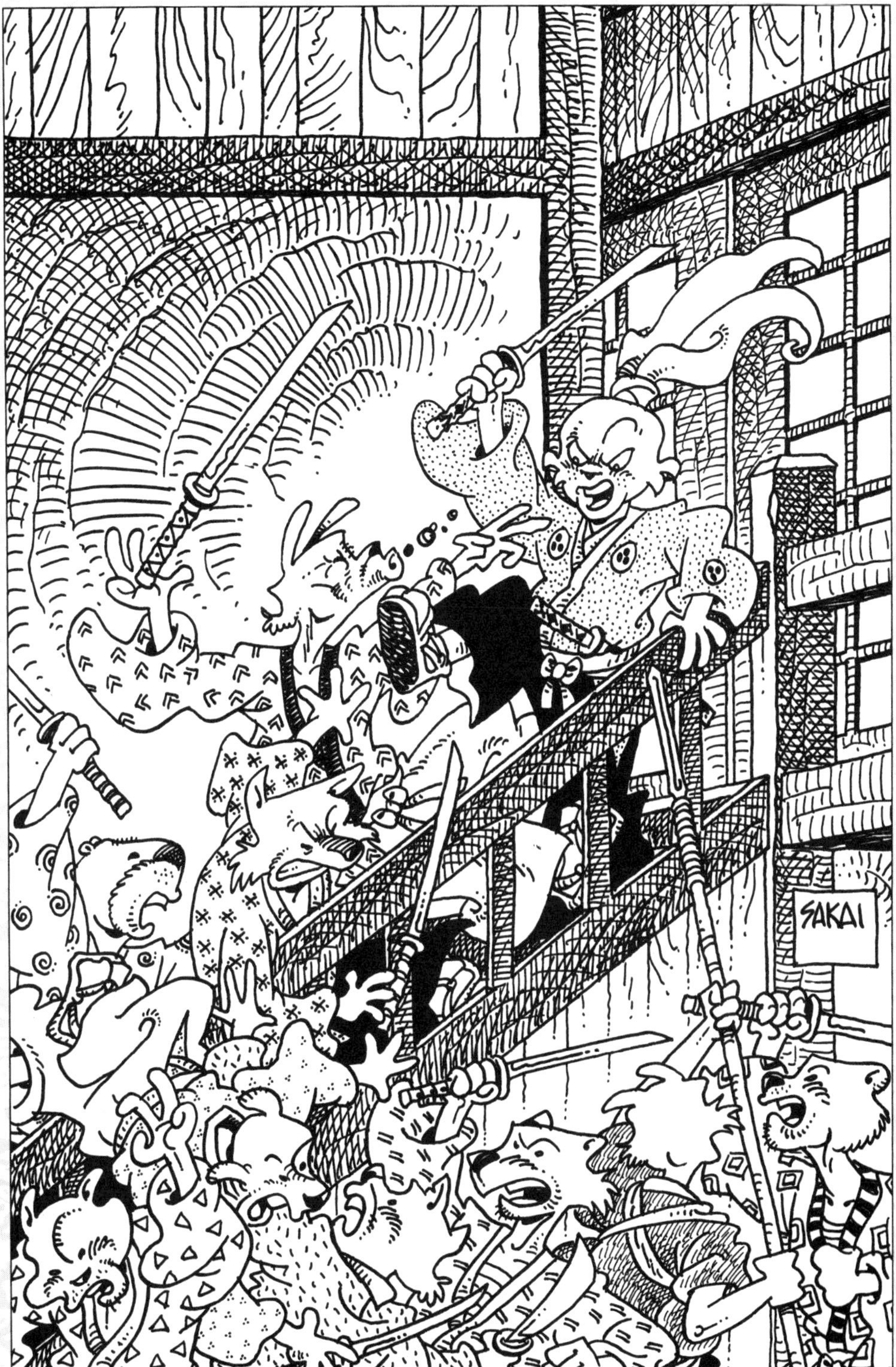
SAKAI

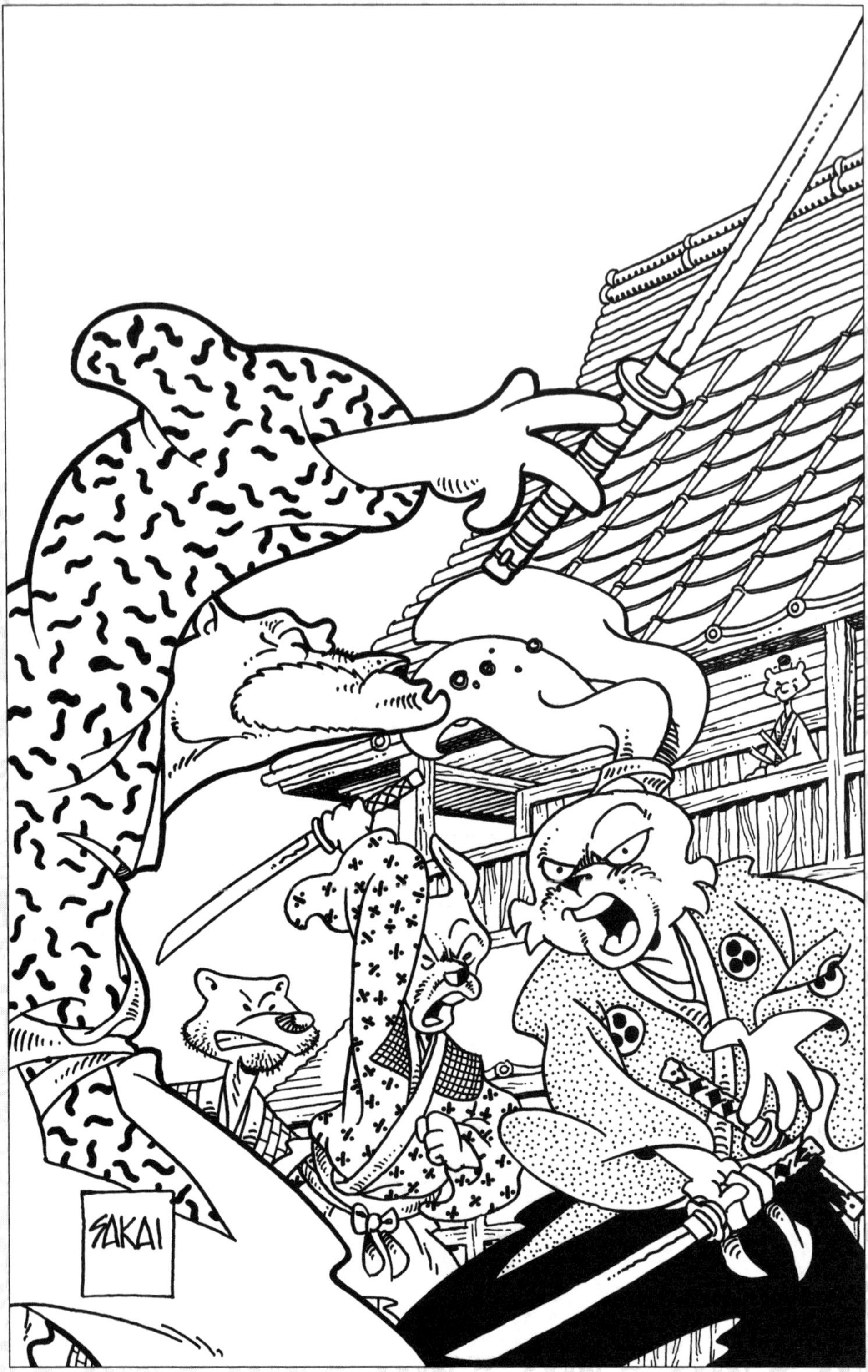
SAKAI

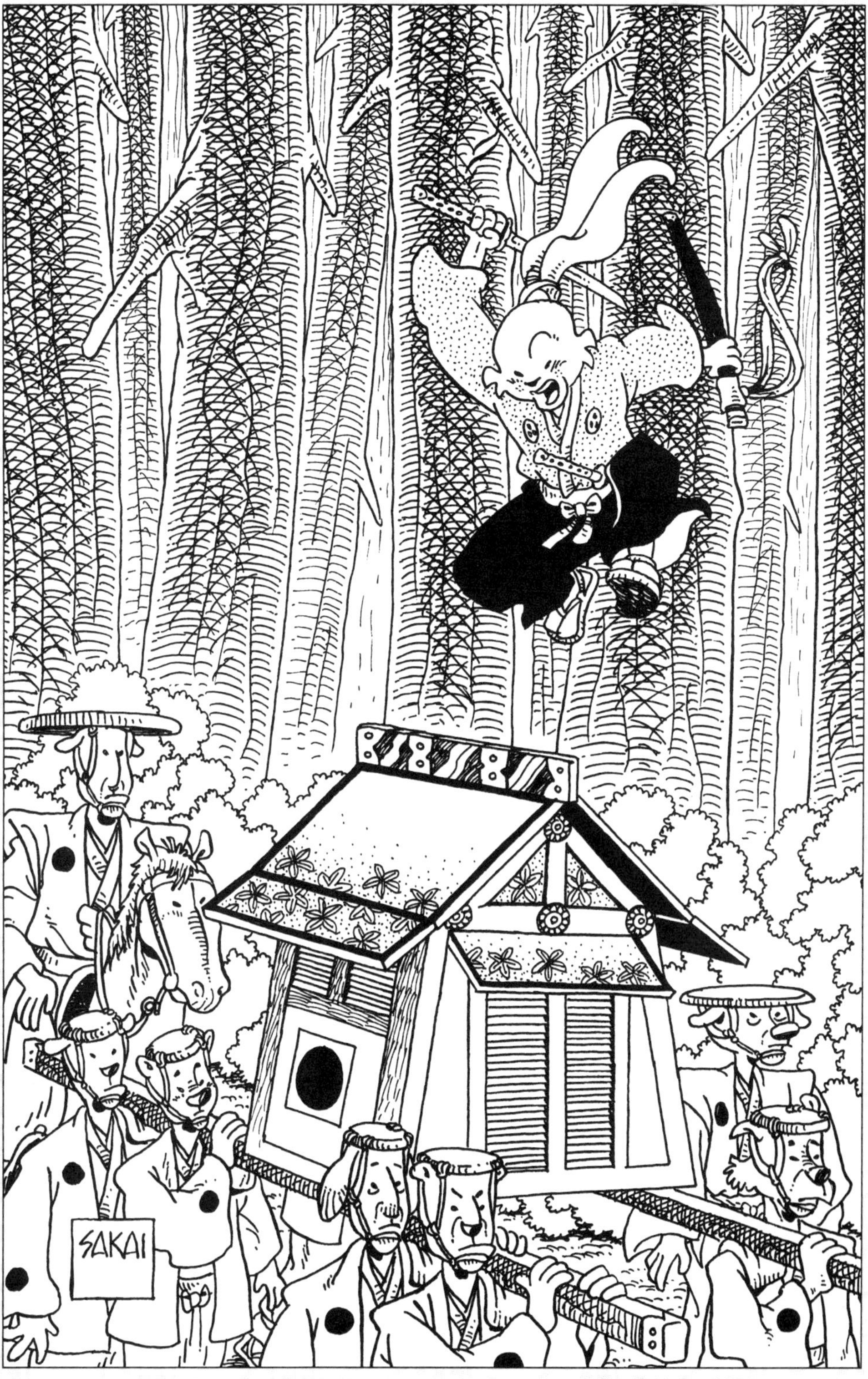
SAKAI

This special alternate cover was created for Usagi Yojimbo *#123 as part of the Dark Horse 100 retailer program.*

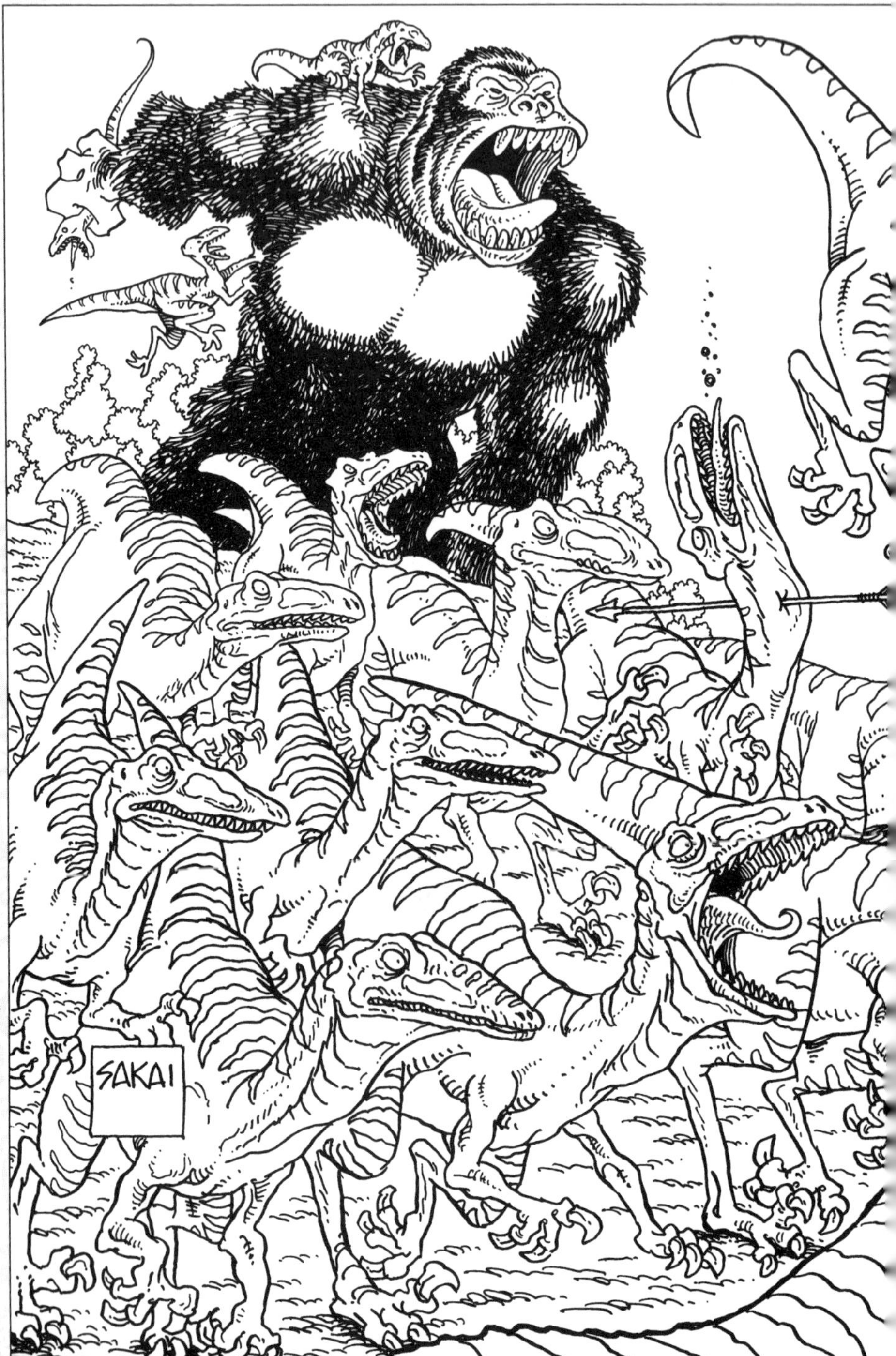
SAKAI

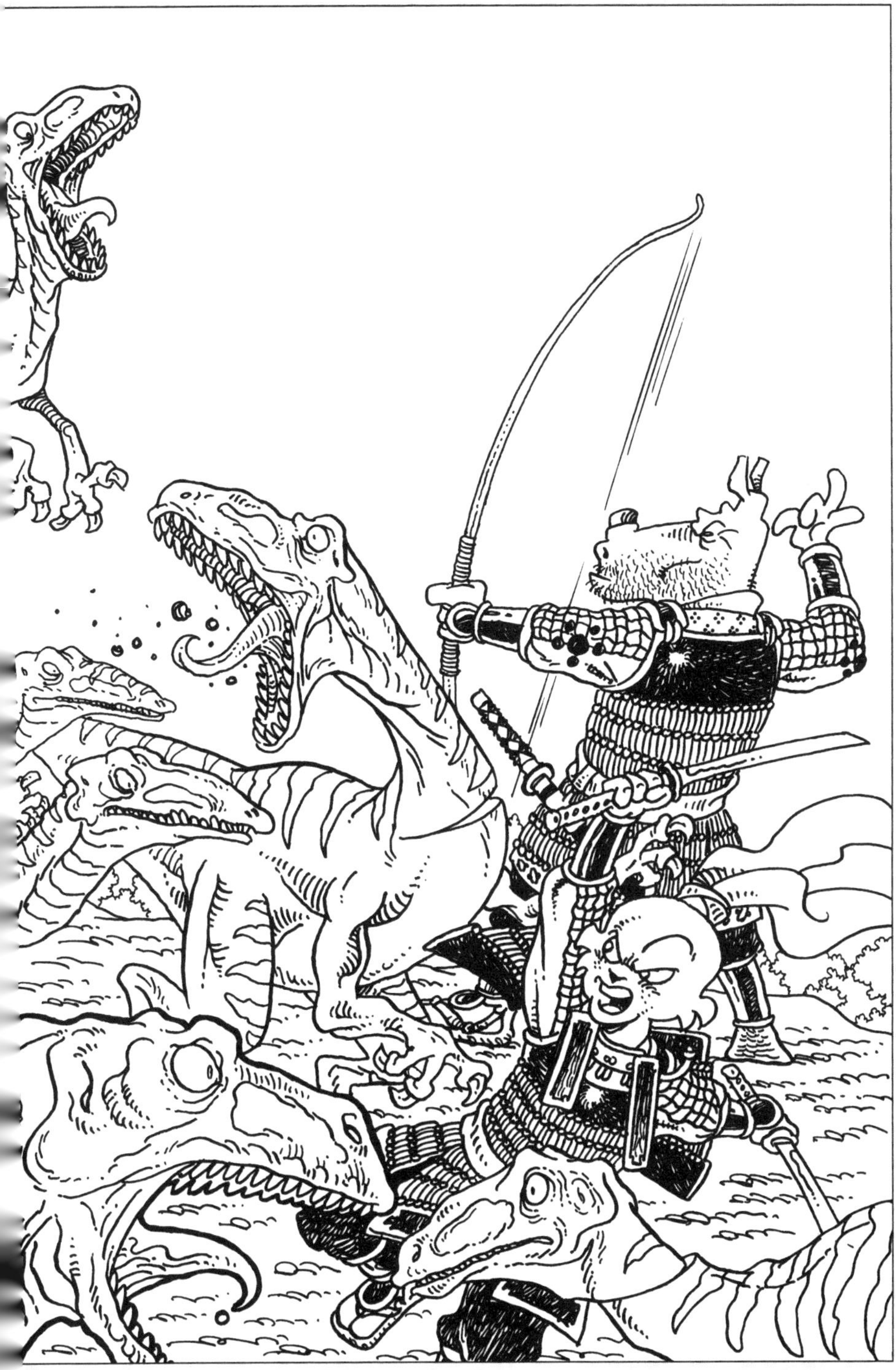

BIOGRAPHY
Stan Sakai

Photo by Sergio Aragonés

Stan Sakai with Stan Lee at the Montreal Comic-Con in September 2011.

Stan Sakai was born in Kyoto, Japan, grew up in Hawaii, and now lives in California with his wife, Sharon, and two children, Hannah and Matthew. He received a Fine Arts degree from the University of Hawaii and furthered his studies at Art Center College of Design in Pasadena, California.

His creation, Usagi Yojimbo, first appeared in comics in 1984. Since then, Usagi has been on television as a guest of the Teenage Mutant Ninja Turtles and has been made into toys, seen on clothing, and featured in a series of graphic novel collections.

In 1991, Stan created *Space Usagi*, a series dealing with samurai in a futuristic setting, featuring the adventures of a descendant of the original Usagi.

Stan is also an award-winning letterer for his work on Sergio Aragonés's *Groo*, the "Spider-Man" Sunday newspaper strips, and *Usagi Yojimbo*.

Stan is the recipient of a Parents' Choice Award, an Inkpot Award, an American Library Association Award, a Harvey Award, four Spanish Haxtur Awards, and several Eisner Awards. In 2003 he won the prestigious National Cartoonists Society Award in the Comic Book Division, and in 2011 Stan received the Cultural Ambassador Award from the Japanese American National Museum.

Usagi Yojimbo

Books by Stan Sakai

From Dark Horse Comics
DarkHorse.com

BOOK 8: SHADES OF DEATH

BOOK 9: DAISHO

BOOK 10: THE BRINK OF LIFE AND DEATH

BOOK 11: SEASONS

BOOK 12: GRASSCUTTER

BOOK 13: GREY SHADOWS

BOOK 14: DEMON MASK

BOOK 15: GRASSCUTTER II — JOURNEY TO ATSUTA SHRINE

BOOK 16: THE SHROUDED MOON

BOOK 17: DUEL AT KITANOJI

BOOK 18: TRAVELS WITH JOTARO

BOOK 19: FATHERS AND SONS

BOOK 20: GLIMPSES OF DEATH

BOOK 21: THE MOTHER OF MOUNTAINS

BOOK 22: TOMOE'S STORY

BOOK 23: BRIDGE OF TEARS

BOOK 24: RETURN OF THE BLACK SOUL

BOOK 25: FOX HUNT

BOOK 26: TRAITORS OF THE EARTH

SPACE USAGI

USAGI YOJIMBO: YOKAI

From Fantagraphics Books
fantagraphics.com

BOOK 1: THE RONIN

BOOK 2: SAMURAI

BOOK 3: THE WANDERER'S ROAD

BOOK 4: THE DRAGON BELLOW CONSPIRACY

BOOK 5: LONE GOAT AND KID

BOOK 6: CIRCLES

BOOK 7: GEN'S STORY

Dark Horse Comics, Inc.

President and Publisher
MIKE RICHARDSON

Executive Vice President
NEIL HANKERSON

Chief Financial Officer
TOM WEDDLE

Vice President of Publishing
RANDY STRADLEY

Vice President of Book Trade Sales
MICHAEL MARTENS

Vice President of Business Affairs
ANITA NELSON

Vice President of Product Development
DAVID SCROGGY

Vice President of Information Technology
DALE LaFOUNTAIN

Senior Director of Print, Design, and Production
DARLENE VOGEL

General Counsel
KEN LIZZI

Senior Director of Marketing
MATT PARKINSON

Editorial Director
DAVEY ESTRADA

Senior Managing Editor
SCOTT ALLIE

Senior Books Editor
CHRIS WARNER

Executive Editor
DIANA SCHUTZ

Director of Print and Development
CARY GRAZZINI

Art Director
LIA RIBACCHI

Director of Scheduling
CARA NIECE